DAVID BUSCH'S SONY® α DSLR-A390/A290

GUIDE TO DIGITAL PHOTOGRAPHY

David D. Busch

Course Technology PTR
A part of Cengage Learning

COURSE TECHNOLOGY
CENGAGE Learning™

Australia, Brazil, Japan, Korea, Mexico, Singapore, Spain, United Kingdom, United States

COURSE TECHNOLOGY
CENGAGE Learning™

David Busch's Sony® α DSLR-A390/A290 Guide to Digital Photography
David D. Busch

Publisher and General Manager, Course Technology PTR:
Stacy L. Hiquet

Associate Director of Marketing:
Sarah Panella

Manager of Editorial Services:
Heather Talbot

Marketing Manager:
Jordan Castellani

Executive Editor:
Kevin Harreld

Project Editor:
Jenny Davidson

Technical Reviewer:
Michael D. Sullivan

Interior Layout Tech:
Bill Hartman

Cover Designer:
Mike Tanamachi

Indexer:
Katherine Stimson

Proofreader:
Sara Gullion

Library of Congress Control Number: 2010936612

ISBN-13: 978-1-4354-5916-8

ISBN-10: 1-4354-5916-4

Course Technology, a part of Cengage Learning
20 Channel Center Street
Boston, MA 02210
USA

Cengage Learning is a leading provider of customized learning solutions with office locations around the globe, including Singapore, the United Kingdom, Australia, Mexico, Brazil, and Japan. Locate your local office at: **international.cengage.com/region**.

Cengage Learning products are represented in Canada by Nelson Education, Ltd.

For your lifelong learning solutions, visit **courseptr.com**.

Visit our corporate Web site at **cengage.com**.

Printed in the United States of America
1 2 3 4 5 6 7 12 11 10

For Cathy

Acknowledgments

Once again thanks to the folks at Course Technology PTR, who have pioneered publishing digital imaging books in full color at a price anyone can afford. Special thanks to executive editor Kevin Harreld, who always gives me the freedom to let my imagination run free with a topic, as well as my veteran production team, including project editor, Jenny Davidson and technical editor, Mike Sullivan. Also thanks to Bill Hartman, layout; Katherine Stimson, indexing; Sara Gullion, proofreading; Mike Tanamachi, cover design; and my agent, Carole Jelen, who has the amazing ability to keep both publishers and authors happy.

About the Author

With more than a million books in print, **David D. Busch** is one of the best-selling authors of books on digital photography and imaging technology, and the originator of popular series like *David Busch's Pro Secrets* and *David Busch's Quick Snap Guides.* He has written several dozen hugely successful guidebooks for Sony and other digital SLR models, including the all-time #1 bestsellers for several different cameras, additional user guides for other camera models, as well as many popular books devoted to dSLRs, including *Mastering Digital SLR Photography, Second Edition* and *Digital SLR Pro Secrets.* As a roving photojournalist for more than 20 years, he illustrated his books, magazine articles, and newspaper reports with award-winning images. He's operated his own commercial studio, suffocated in formal dress while shooting weddings-for-hire, and shot sports for a daily newspaper and upstate New York college. His photos and articles have been published in *Popular Photography & Imaging, The Rangefinder, The Professional Photographer*, and hundreds of other publications. He's also reviewed dozens of digital cameras for CNet and *Computer Shopper.*

When About.com named its top five books on Beginning Digital Photography, debuting at the #1 and #2 slots were Busch's *Digital Photography All-In-One Desk Reference for Dummies* and *Mastering Digital Photography.* During the past year, he's had as many as five of his books listed in the Top 20 of Amazon.com's Digital Photography Bestseller list—simultaneously! Busch's 100-plus other books published since 1983 include bestsellers like *David Busch's Quick Snap Guide to Using Digital SLR Lenses.*

Busch is a member of the Cleveland Photographic Society (www.clevelandphoto.org), which has operated continuously since 1887. Visit his website at:

http://www.dslrguides.com/blog.

Contents

Chapter 3
Setting Up Your Sony Alpha DSLR-A390/A290 51

Chapter 7 Making Light Work for You 173

Chapter 8 Downloading and Editing Your Images 207

Preface

You don't want good pictures from your new Sony Alpha DSLR-A390 or A290—you demand *outstanding* photos. After all, these two Alpha models are the most advanced entry-level cameras that Sony has ever introduced. They both boast 14.2 megapixels of resolution, blazing-fast automatic focus, and the A390 offers cool new features like the real-time preview system called Live View. But your gateway to pixel proficiency is dragged down by the slim little book included in the box as a manual. You know everything you need to know is in there, somewhere, but you don't know where to start. In addition, the camera manual doesn't offer much information on photography or digital photography. Nor are you interested in spending hours or days studying a comprehensive book on digital SLR photography that doesn't necessarily apply directly to your Alpha.

What you need is a guide that explains the purpose and function of the Alpha's basic controls, how you should use them, and *why*. Ideally, there should be information about file formats, resolution, aperture/priority exposure, and special autofocus modes available, but you'd prefer to read about those topics only after you've had the chance to go out and take a few hundred great pictures with your new camera. Why isn't there a book that summarizes the most important information in its first two or three chapters, with lots of full-color illustrations showing what your results will look like when you use this setting or that?

Now there is such a book. If you want a quick introduction to the Alpha's focus controls, flash synchronization options, how to choose lenses, or which exposure modes are best, this book is for you. If you can't decide on what basic settings to use with your camera because you can't figure out how changing ISO or white balance or focus defaults will affect your pictures, you need this guide.

Introduction

Sony has done it again! They've revised and compacted their popular entry-level dSLRs into two fresh versions in smaller highly affordable bodies that retain the best features of the earlier models. No matter which of these models you buy, you'll find your new camera is loaded with capabilities that few would have expected to find in an "entry-level" dSLR. Indeed, the Alpha retains the ease of use that smoothes the transition for those new to digital photography. For those just dipping their toes into the digital pond, the experience is warm and inviting. These Alpha models aren't snapshot cameras—they are point-and-shoots (if you want to use them in that mode) for the thinking photographer.

Nor will you easily outgrow these cameras. Both have 14.2 megapixels of resolution, autofocus that's improved over their predecessors, and many customization options. Sony must love fledgling photographers, because it seems to work extra hard to give them incredible value for their money in entry-level cameras.

But once you've confirmed that you made a wise purchase decision, the question comes up, *how do I use this thing?* All those cool features can be mind numbing to learn, if all you have as a guide is the manual furnished with the camera. Help is on the way. I sincerely believe that this book is your best bet for learning how to use your new camera, and for learning how to use it well.

If you're a Sony Alpha dSLR owner who's looking to learn more about how to use your camera, you've probably already explored your options. There are DVDs and online tutorials—but who can learn how to use a camera by sitting in front of a television or computer screen? Do you want to watch a movie or click on HTML links, or do you want to go out and take photos with your camera? Videos are fun, but not the best answer.

There's always the manual furnished with the Alpha. It's compact and filled with information, but there's really very little about *why* you should use particular settings or features, and its organization may make it difficult to find what you need. Multiple cross-references may send you flipping back and forth between two or three sections of the book to find what you want to know. The basic manual is also hobbled by black-and-white line drawings and tiny monochrome pictures that aren't very good examples of what you can do.

Also available are third-party guides to the Alpha, like this one. I haven't been happy with some of these guidebooks, which is why I wrote this one. The existing books range from skimpy and illustrated with black-and-white photos to lushly illustrated in full color but too generic to do much good. Photography instruction is useful, but it needs to be related directly to the Sony Alpha dSLR as much as possible.

I've tried to make *David Busch's Sony Alpha DSLR-A390/A290 Guide to Digital Photography* different from your other Alpha learn-up options. The roadmap sections use larger, color pictures to show you where all the buttons and dials are, and the explanations of what they do are longer and more comprehensive. I've tried to avoid overly general advice, including the two-page checklists on how to take a "sports picture" or a "portrait picture" or a "travel picture." Instead, you'll find tips and techniques for using all the features of your Sony Alpha dSLR to take *any kind of picture* you want. If you want to know where you should stand to take a picture of a quarterback dropping back to unleash a pass, there are plenty of books that will tell you that. This one concentrates on teaching you how to select the best autofocus mode, shutter speed, f/stop, or flash capability to take, say, a great sports picture under any conditions.

This book is not a lame rewriting of the manual that came with the camera. Some folks spend five minutes with a book like this one, spot some information that also appears in the original manual, and decide "Rehash!" without really understanding the differences. Yes, you'll find information here that is also in the owner's manual, such as the parameters you can enter when changing your Alpha's operation in the various menus. Basic descriptions—before I dig in and start providing in-depth tips and information—may also be vaguely similar. There are only so many ways you can say, for example, "Hold the shutter release down halfway to lock in exposure." But not *everything* in the manual is included in this book. If you need advice on when and how to use the most important functions, you'll find the information here.

David Busch's Sony Alpha DSLR-A390/A290 Guide to Digital Photography is aimed at both Sony dSLR veterans as well as newcomers to digital photography and digital SLRs. Both groups can be overwhelmed by the options the Alpha offers, while underwhelmed by the explanations they receive in their user's manual. The manuals are great if you already know what you don't know, and you can find an answer somewhere in a booklet arranged by menu listings and written by a camera vendor employee who last threw together instructions on how to operate a camcorder.

Once you've read this book and are ready to learn more, I hope you pick up one of my other guides to digital SLR photography. Four of them are offered by Course Technology PTR, each approaching the topic from a different perspective. They include:

Quick Snap Guide to Digital SLR Photography
Consider this a prequel to the book you're holding in your hands. It might make a good gift for a spouse or friend who may be using your Alpha, but who lacks even basic knowledge about digital photography, digital SLR photography, and Sony Alpha photography. It serves as an introduction that summarizes the basic features of digital SLR cameras in general (not just the Alpha), and what settings to use and when, such as continuous autofocus/single autofocus, aperture/shutter priority, EV settings, and so forth. The guide also includes recipes for shooting the most common kinds of pictures, with step-by-step instructions for capturing effective sports photos, portraits, landscapes, and other types of images.

David Busch's Quick Snap Guide to Using Digital SLR Lenses
A bit overwhelmed by the features and controls of digital SLR lenses, and not quite sure when to use each type? This book explains lenses, their use, and lens technology in easy-to-access two- and four-page spreads, each devoted to a different topic, such as depth-of-field, lens aberrations, or using zoom lenses. If you have a friend or significant other who is less versed in photography, but who wants to borrow and use your Sony Alpha dSLR from time to time, this book can save you a ton of explanation.

Mastering Digital SLR Photography, Second Edition
This book is an introduction to digital SLR photography, with nuts-and-bolts explanations of the technology, more in-depth coverage of settings, and whole chapters on the most common types of photography. While not specific to the Alpha, this book can show you how to get more from its capabilities.

Digital SLR Pro Secrets
This is my more advanced guide to dSLR photography with greater depth and detail about the topics you're most interested in. If you've already mastered the basics in *Mastering Digital SLR Photography*, this book will take you to the next level.

Why the Sony Alpha dSLR Needs Special Coverage

There are many general digital photography books on the market. Why do I concentrate on books about specific digital SLRs like the Alpha? The two Alpha models covered in this book are virtually identical, so I've been able to provide information and tips that apply to both in a single volume. The chief difference between the A390 and A290 is that the latter lacks a tilting LCD, and does not offer Live View mode. So, no matter which of these Alpha models you own, this book applies directly to your camera.

When I started writing digital photography books in 1995, digital SLRs cost $30,000 and few people other than certain professionals could justify them. Most of my readers a dozen years ago were stuck using the point-and-shoot low-resolution digital cameras of the time—even if they were advanced photographers. I took thousands of digital pictures with an Epson digital camera with 1024 × 768 (less than 1 megapixel!) resolution, and which cost $500.

As recently as 2003 (years before the original Alpha was introduced), the lowest-cost dSLRs were priced at $3,000 or more. Today, around $600 buys you a sophisticated model like the Sony Alpha DSLR-A390 (with lens). The digital SLR is no longer the exclusive bailiwick of the professional, the wealthy, or the serious photography addict willing to scrimp and save to acquire a dream camera. Digital SLRs have become the favored camera for anyone who wants to go beyond point-and-shoot capabilities. And Sony cameras (and the Minolta models that preceded them) have enjoyed a favored position among digital SLRs because of Sony's innovation in introducing affordable cameras with interesting features, such as SteadyShot image stabilization, and outstanding performance. It doesn't hurt that Sony also provides both full-frame cameras (like the amazing sub-$2,000 Sony Alpha DSLR-A850) and smaller format digital cameras and a clear migration path between them (if you stick to the Sony lenses that are compatible with both).

Who Are You?

When preparing a guidebook for a specific camera, it's always wise to consider exactly who will be reading the book. Indeed, thinking about the potential audience for *David Busch's Sony Alpha DSLR-A390/A290 Guide to Digital Photography* is what led me to taking the approach and format I use for this book. I realized that the needs of readers like you had to be addressed both from a functional level (what you will use the Sony Alpha DSLR-A390/A290 for) as well as from a skill level (how much experience you may have with digital photography, dSLRs, or Sony cameras specifically).

From a functional level, you probably fall into one of these categories:

- Professional photographers who understand photography and digital SLRs, and simply want to learn how to use the Sony Alpha DSLR-A390/A290 as a backup camera, or as a camera for personal "off-duty" use.
- Individuals who want to get better pictures, or perhaps transform their growing interest in photography into a full-fledged hobby or artistic outlet with a Sony Alpha and advanced techniques.
- Those who want to produce more professional-looking images for their personal or business website, and feel that the Sony Alpha will give them more control and capabilities.

- Small business owners with more advanced graphics capabilities who want to use the Sony Alpha DSLR-A390/A290 to document or promote their business.
- Corporate workers who may or may not have photographic skills in their job descriptions, but who work regularly with graphics and need to learn how to use digital images taken with a Sony Alpha for reports, presentations, or other applications.
- Professional webmasters with strong skills in programming (including Java, JavaScript, HTML, Perl, etc.) but little background in photography, but who realize that the Sony Alpha can be used for sophisticated photography.
- Graphic artists and others who already may be adept in image editing with Photoshop or another program, and who may already be using a film SLR, but who need to learn more about digital photography and the special capabilities of the Sony dSLR.

Addressing your needs from a skills level can be a little trickier, because the Sony Alpha is such a great camera that a full spectrum of photographers will be buying it, from absolute beginners who have never owned a digital camera before up to the occasional professional with years of shooting experience who will be using the Sony Alpha as a backup body.

Before tackling this book, it would be helpful for you to understand the following:

- **What a digital SLR is:** It's a camera that generally shows an optical (not LCD) view of the picture that's being taken through the (interchangeable) lens that actually takes the photo, thanks to a mirror that reflects an image to a viewfinder, but flips up out of the way to allow the sensor to be exposed.
- **How digital photography differs from film:** The image is stored not on film (which I call the *first* write-once optical media), but on a memory card as pixels that can be transferred to your computer, and then edited, corrected, and printed without the need for chemical processing.
- **What the basic tools of correct exposure are:** Don't worry if you don't understand these; I'll explain them later in this book. But if you already know something about shutter speed, aperture, and ISO sensitivity, you'll be ahead of the game. If not, you'll soon learn that shutter speed determines the amount of time the sensor is exposed to incoming light; the f/stop or aperture is like a valve that governs the quantity of light that can flow through the lens; the sensor's sensitivity (ISO setting) controls how easily the sensor responds to light. All three factors can be varied individually and proportionately to produce a picture that is properly exposed (neither too light nor too dark).

It's tough to provide something for everybody, but I am going to try to address the needs of each of the following groups and skill levels:

- **Digital photography newbies:** If you've used only point-and-shoot digital cameras, or have worked only with non-SLR film cameras, you're to be congratulated for selecting one of the very best entry-level digital SLRs available as your first dSLR camera. This book can help you understand the controls and features of your Sony Alpha, and lead you down the path to better photography with your camera. I'll provide all the information you need, but if you want to do some additional reading for extra credit, you can also try one of the other books I mentioned earlier. They complement this book well.
- **Advanced point-and-shooters moving on up:** There are some quite sophisticated pocket-sized digital cameras available, including those with many user-definable options and settings, so it's possible you are already a knowledgeable photographer, even though you're new to the world of the digital SLR. You've recognized the limitations of the point-and-shoot camera: even the best of them have more noise at higher sensitivity (ISO) settings than a camera like the Sony Alpha; the speediest still have an unacceptable delay between the time you press the shutter and when the photo is actually taken; even a non-interchangeable super-zoom camera with 12X to 20X magnification often won't focus close enough, include an aperture suitable for low-light photography, or take in the really wide view you must have. Interchangeable lenses and other accessories available for the Sony Alpha are another one of the reasons you moved up. Because you're an avid photographer already, you should pick up the finer points of using the Sony Alpha from this book with no trouble.
- **Film SLR veterans new to the digital world:** You understand photography, you know about f/stops and shutter speeds, and thrive on interchangeable lenses. If you have used a newer film SLR, it probably has lots of electronic features already, including autofocus and sophisticated exposure metering. Perhaps you've even been using a Minolta film SLR (a distant predecessor of the current Alphas, which used the same lens system) and understand many of the available accessories that work with both film and digital cameras. All you need is information on using digital-specific features, working with the Sony Alpha itself, and how to match—and exceed—the capabilities of your film camera with your new Sony Alpha DSLR-A390/A290.
- **Experienced dSLR users broadening their experience to include the Sony Alpha DSLR-A390/A290:** Perhaps you started out with another Sony or Konica Minolta digital SLR. You may have used a digital SLR from another vendor and are making the switch. You understand basic photography, and want to learn more. And,

most of all, you want to transfer the skills you already have to the Sony Alpha, as quickly and seamlessly as possible.

- **Pro photographers and other advanced shooters:** I expect my most discerning readers will be those who already have extensive experience with other advanced dSLR cameras. I may not be able to teach you folks much about photography. But, even so, an amazing number of Sony Alpha DSLR-A390/A290 cameras have been purchased by those who feel it is a good complement to their favorite advanced Sony dSLR.

Who Am I?

After spending years as the world's most successful unknown author, I've become slightly less obscure in the past few years, thanks to a horde of camera guidebooks and other photographically oriented tomes. You may have seen my photography articles in *Popular Photography & Imaging* magazine. I've also written about 2,000 articles for magazines like *Petersen's PhotoGraphic* (which is now defunct through no fault of my own), plus *The Rangefinder*, *Professional Photographer*, and dozens of other photographic publications. But, first, and foremost, I'm a photojournalist and made my living in the field until I began devoting most of my time to writing books. Although I love writing, I'm happiest when I'm out taking pictures, which is why during the past 12 months I've taken off chunks of time to travel to Ireland and Barcelona, Spain. The past 18 months also took me to Zion National Park in Utah, the Sedona "red rocks" area and Grand Canyon in Arizona, Major League Baseball Spring training, and, for a few days, Las Vegas (I did a lot more shooting than gambling in Sin City). You'll find photos of some of these visual treats within the pages of this book.

Like all my digital photography books, this one was written by someone with an incurable photography bug. One of my first SLRs was a Minolta SRT-101, from the company whose technology was eventually absorbed by Sony in 2006. I've used a variety of newer models since then. I've worked as a sports photographer for an Ohio newspaper and for an upstate New York college. I've operated my own commercial studio and photo lab, cranking out product shots on demand and then printing a few hundred glossy 8 × 10s on a tight deadline for a press kit. I've served as a photo-posing instructor for a modeling agency. People have actually paid me to shoot their weddings and immortalize them with portraits. I even prepared press kits and articles on photography as a PR consultant for a large Rochester, N.Y., company, which shall remain nameless. My trials and travails with imaging and computer technology have made their way into print in book form an alarming number of times, including a few dozen on scanners and photography.

Like you, I love photography for its own merits, and I view technology as just another tool to help me get the images I see in my mind's eye. But, also like you, I had to master this technology before I could apply it to my work. This book is the result of what I've learned, and I hope it will help you master your Alpha digital SLR, too.

As I write this, I'm currently in the throes of upgrading my website, which you can find at www.dslrguides.com/blog. I hope you'll stop by for a visit. Send your comments to questions@dslrguides.com.

1

Getting Started with Your Sony Alpha DSLR-A390/A290

I once read a camera guide that began with the author advising the Gentle Reader to resist the temptation to go out and take pictures until the proper amount of time had been spent Setting Up The Camera, apparently to avoid wasting electrons on shots that were doomed to failure if the arcane operational knowledge that was forthcoming wasn't first absorbed. What universe was he from?

Relax! I fully expect that you took several hundred or a thousand (or two) photos before you ever cracked the cover of this book—for several reasons. First, and foremost, the Sony Alpha DSLR-A390 and A290 cameras are incredibly easy to use, especially for the absolute beginner. Even the newest digital camera owner can rotate the mode dial to the green Auto position and go out and begin taking great pictures. Getting to that point by charging the battery, mounting a lens, and inserting a Secure Digital or Memory Stick memory card isn't exactly rocket science, either. Sony has cleverly marked the power switch (located concentrically with the shutter release button) with large ON and OFF labels, and the Scene icons will provide a major clue for anyone interested in photographing something resembling a human profile, a mountain, a flower, a person leaning forward in racing stride, or a starlit scene.

So, budding photographers are likely to muddle their way through getting the camera revved up and working well enough to take a bunch of pictures without the universe collapsing. Eventually, though, many may turn to this book when they realize that they can do an even better job with a little guidance.

Second, I know that many of you will be previous owners of the predecessors of these cameras, such as the Alpha DSLR-A100, the more recent DSLR-A380/A330/A230-series cameras, or one of the earlier Minolta Maxxum models. Most of the basic operations of this new camera are quite similar to that of the older models. So, veteran Sony/Minolta dSLR owners can venture out, shoot first, and ask questions later.

Finally, I realize that most of you didn't buy this book at the same time you purchased your Sony Alpha. As much as I'd like to picture thousands of avid photographers marching out of their camera stores with an Alpha box under one arm, and my book in hand, I know that's not going to happen *all* the time. A large number of you had your camera for a week, or two, or a month, became comfortable with it, and sought out this book in order to learn more. So, a chapter on "setup" seems like too little, too late, doesn't it?

In practice, though, it's not a bad idea, once you've taken a few orientation pictures with your camera, to go back and review the basic operations of the camera from the beginning, if only to see if you've missed something. This chapter is my opportunity to review the setup procedures for the camera for those among you who are already veteran users, and to help ease the more timid (and those who have never worked with a digital SLR before) into the basic preflight checklist that needs to be completed before you really spread your wings and take off. For the uninitiated, as easy as it is to use initially, the Sony Alpha *does* have lots of dials, buttons, and settings that might not make sense at first, but will surely become second nature after you've had a chance to review the instructions in this chapter.

But don't fret about wading through a manual to find out what you must know to take those first few tentative snaps. I'm going to help you hit the ground running with this chapter (or keep on running if you've already jumped right in). If you *haven't* had the opportunity to use your Alpha yet, I'll help you set up your camera and begin shooting in minutes. You won't find a lot of detail in this chapter. Indeed, I'm going to tell you just what you absolutely *must* understand, accompanied by some interesting tidbits that will help you become acclimated. I'll go into more depth and even repeat some of what I explain here in later chapters, so you don't have to memorize everything you see. Just relax, follow a few easy steps, and then go out and begin taking your best shots—ever.

Differences Between the A390 and A290 Models

Everybody knows that one size does *not* always fit all. With this latest pair of cameras, Sony has continued the clever step of offering two *very* similar models, priced only $100 or so apart, which share many of the same features and capabilities. So, you can choose the Alpha model that best fits your needs and budget, secure in the knowledge that all the basic stuff that makes the latest Sony cameras so good is included. Each of these cameras has SteadyShot to provide anti-shake resistance to camera vibration. Both have an advanced 9-point autofocus system with an extra-sensitive cross-type sensor in the center. Each gives you a bright 2.7-inch LCD. The menus, user interface, camera body controls, and most other operational features of the two cameras are identical. If you know how to use one, you can work with the other.

The Vulcan philosopher Spock once said, "A difference that makes no difference is no difference," and most of the differences between these two cameras have little significance. But here are a few that you *should* be aware of.

- **The DSLR-A390 has Live View.** This feature allows you to preview your image on the back-panel LCD in living color, and with full brightness, thanks to a novel pivoting mirror in the viewing system that directs virtually all the incoming light to either the optical viewfinder or the Live View LCD prior to taking the picture. The A290 does not have Live View.
- **The DSLR-A390 has an articulated LCD.** You can angle the LCD up or down, which makes both Live View and picture review a great deal more useful. The camera can be placed high overhead, or down low, and you can still see the display. The A290 does not have a pivoting LCD.
- **Optical viewfinder differences.** The A290 offers 0.83X magnification, which presents a view that is 83 percent of life size when using a 50mm focal length. The A390 has a less magnified 0.74X view with that 50mm lens.

Because so many of the actual differences between these two models are of the Spockian "no difference" variety, I'm going to treat them as a single camera for the purposes of this book. When I refer to the "Sony Alpha" throughout, I am talking about the A390 and A290. In the few cases where the variations do make a difference, I'll mention the camera model by name. Most of the illustrations in this book use the DSLR-A390. The exterior and menus of the cameras are the same and the A290 is virtually identical visually, save for the lack of a Live View/OVF switch and tilting LCD.

Your Out-of-Box Experience

Your Sony Alpha comes in an impressive box filled with stuff, including connecting cords, booklets, a CD, and lots of paperwork. The most important components are the camera and lens, battery, battery charger, and, if you're the nervous type, the neck strap. You'll also need a Secure Digital or Memory Stick card, as one is not included. If you purchased your Alpha from a camera shop, as I did, the store personnel probably attached the neck strap for you, ran through some basic operational advice that you've already forgotten, tried to sell you a Secure Digital card, and then, after they'd given you all the help you could absorb, sent you on your way with a handshake.

Perhaps you purchased your Sony Alpha from one of those mass merchandisers that also sell a washing machines and vacuum cleaners. In that case, you might have been sent on your way with only the handshake, or, maybe, not even that if you resisted the efforts to sell you an extended warranty. You save a few bucks at the big-box stores, but you don't get the personal service a professional photo retailer provides. It's your choice. There's a third alternative, of course. You might have purchased your camera from a mail order or Internet source, and your camera arrived in a big brown (or purple/red) truck. Your only interaction when you took possession of your camera was to scrawl your signature on an electronic clipboard.

In all three cases, the first thing to do is to carefully unpack the camera and double-check the contents with the checklist on one end of the box. While this level of setup detail may seem as superfluous as the instructions on a bottle of shampoo, checking the contents *first* is always a good idea. No matter who sells a camera, it's common to open boxes, use a particular camera for a demonstration, and then repack the box without replacing all the pieces and parts afterwards. Someone might actually have helpfully checked out your camera on your behalf—and then mispacked the box. It's better to know *now* that something is missing so you can seek redress immediately, rather than discover two months from now that the video cable you thought you'd never use (but now *must* have) was never in the box.

So, check the box at your earliest convenience, and make sure you have (at least) the following:

- **Sony Alpha dSLR camera.** This is hard to miss. The camera is the main reason you laid out the big bucks, and it is tucked away inside a nifty bubble-wrap envelope you should save for protection in case the Alpha needs to be sent in for repair. It almost goes without saying that you should check out the camera immediately, making sure the color LCD on the back isn't scratched or cracked, the memory card and battery doors open properly, and, when a charged battery is inserted and lens mounted, the camera powers up and reports for duty. Out-of-the-box defects like these are rare, but they can happen. It's probably more common that your dealer played with the camera or, perhaps, it was a customer return. That's why it's best to buy your Alpha from a retailer you trust to supply a factory-fresh camera.
- **Rubber eyecup.** This slide-on soft-rubber eyecup should be attached to the viewfinder when you receive the camera. It helps you squeeze your eye tightly against the window, excluding extraneous light, and also protects your eyeglasses (if you wear them) from scratching.
- **Eyepiece cover.** Use this to keep light from entering the camera and affecting exposure when the camera is used on a tripod or other non-Live View situations where pictures are taken without having the camera up to your eye.

- **ALC-B55 body cap.** The twist-off body cap keeps dust from entering the camera when no lens is mounted. Even with automatic sensor cleaning built into the Alpha, you'll want to keep the amount of dust to a minimum. The body cap belongs in your camera bag if you contemplate the need to travel with the lens removed.
- **Lens (if purchased).** The Sony Alpha may come in a kit with the SAL-1855 DT 18-55mm f/3.5-5.6 zoom lens. Or, you may purchase it with another lens. The lens will come with a lens cap on the front, and a rear lens cap aft.
- **Battery pack NP-FH50.** The power source for your Sony Alpha is packaged separately. It should be charged as soon as possible (as described next) and inserted in the camera. Save the protective cover. If you transport a battery outside the camera, it's a good idea to re-attach the cover to prevent the electrical contacts from shorting out. It's smart to have more than one battery pack (they usually cost less than $40, although the Sony list price is $59), so you can continue shooting when your battery is discharged or, after many uses, peters out entirely. This battery also fits many Sony camcorders, so you may be able to use a single pack as a backup for both your still and video cameras.
- **Battery charger BC-VH1.** This battery charger and power cord will be included.
- **Shoulder strap.** Sony provides you with a suitable neck strap, emblazoned with Sony advertising. While I am justifiably proud of owning a fine Sony camera, I never attach the factory strap to my cameras, and instead opt for a more serviceable strap from UPstrap (www.upstrap-pro.com) or Op-Tech (www.optechusa.com). If you carry your camera over one shoulder, as many do, I particularly recommend UPstrap (shown in Figure 1.1). It has a patented non-slip pad that offers reassuring traction and eliminates the contortions we sometimes go through to keep the camera from slipping off. I know several photographers who refuse to use anything else. If you do purchase an UPstrap, be sure to tell photographer-inventor Al Stegmeyer that I sent you hence.
- **USB cable.** This is a USB cable that can be used to link your Sony Alpha to a computer, and it is especially useful when you need to transfer pictures but don't have a card reader handy.
- **Application software CD.** The disk contains useful software that will be discussed in more detail in Chapter 9.
- **Printed instruction manuals.** These include the Instruction Manual, the Quick Start Guide, and an Accessories brochure.

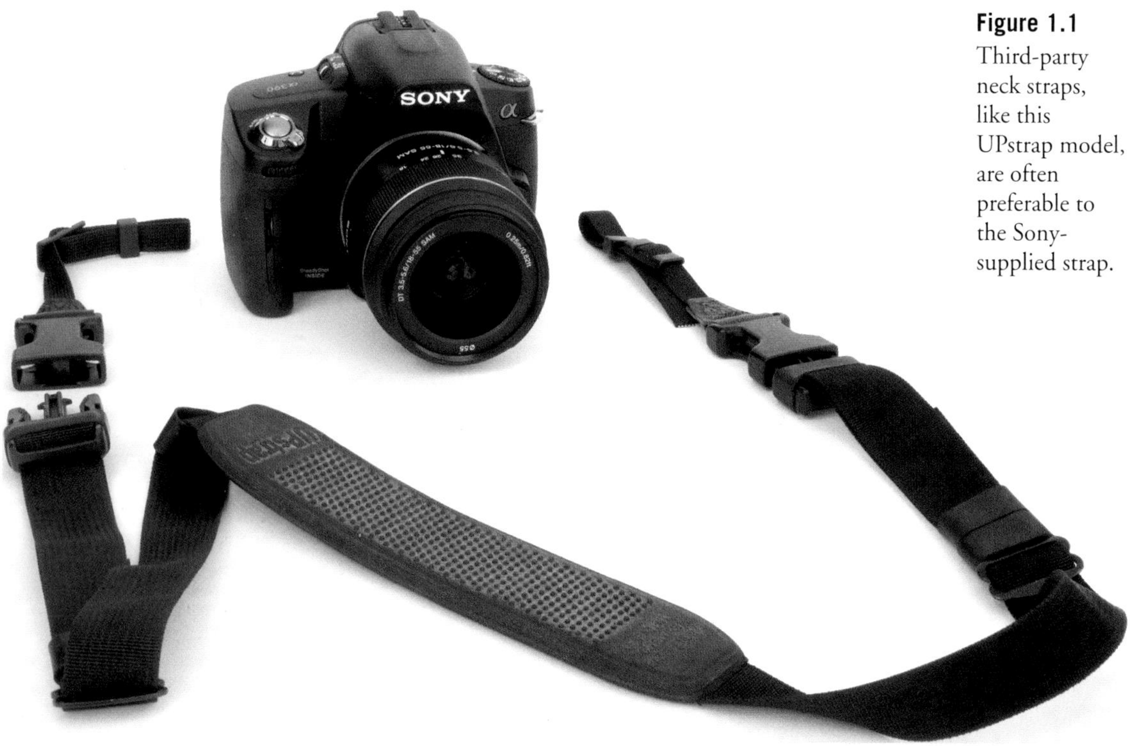

Figure 1.1
Third-party neck straps, like this UPstrap model, are often preferable to the Sony-supplied strap.

Initial Setup

The initial setup of your Sony Alpha dSLR is fast and easy. Basically, you just need to charge the battery, attach a lens, and insert a memory card. I'll address each of these steps separately, but if you already feel you can manage these setup tasks without further instructions, feel free to skip this section entirely. You should at least skim its contents, however, because I'm going to list a few options that you might not be aware of.

Battery Included

Your Sony Alpha dSLR is a sophisticated hunk of machinery and electronics, but it needs a charged battery to function, so rejuvenating the NP-FH50 lithium-ion battery pack furnished with the camera should be your first step. A fully charged power source should be good for approximately 500 shots under normal temperature conditions, based on standard tests defined by the Camera & Imaging Products Association (CIPA) document DC-002. If most of your pictures use the built-in flash or you are using Live View mode with the A390, you can expect about half as many shots before it's time for a recharge. While those figures sound like a lot of shooting, things like picture review can use up more power than you might expect. If your pictures are important to you, always take along one spare, fully charged battery.

And remember that all rechargeable batteries undergo some degree of self-discharge just sitting idle in the camera or in the original packaging. Lithium-ion power packs of this type typically lose a small amount of their charge every day, even when the camera isn't turned on. Li-ion cells lose their power through a chemical reaction that continues when the camera is switched off. So, it's very likely that the battery purchased with your camera, even if charged at the factory, has begun to poop out after the long sea voyage on a banana boat (or, more likely, a trip by jet plane followed by a sojourn in a warehouse), so you'll want to revive it before going out for some serious shooting.

Charging the Battery

When the battery is inserted into the charger properly (it's impossible to insert it incorrectly), a Charge light begins glowing yellow-orange, without flashing (see Figure 1.2). It continues to glow until the battery completes the charge and the lamp turns off. Charging times vary from about 205 minutes for a normal charge, to 265 minutes to completely rejuvenate a fully discharged battery. The full charge is complete about one hour after the charging lamp turns off, so if your battery was really dead, don't remove it from the charger until the additional time has elapsed.

If the charging lamp flashes when you insert the battery, that indicates an error condition. There are two flash error "modes:"

- **Fast flash.** If the lamp blinks repeatedly at a rate of several times per second (Sony indicates a frequency of 0.15 seconds per flash), you should remove the battery pack and reinsert it. Should the flashing recur, there may be something wrong with your battery. Try your backup battery; if it charges okay, you'll know that the problem is with your other battery pack, and not the charger itself.

Figure 1.2 The yellow-orange status light indicates that the battery is being charged.

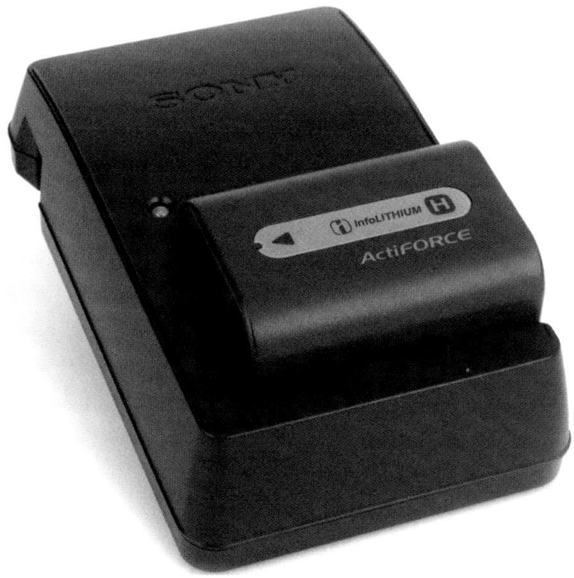

- **Slow flash.** A more leisurely flashing rate (about once every 1.5 seconds) indicates that the battery charger has shifted into standby mode because the ambient temperature is outside the recommended 50-86 degree F range. You can try removing and re-inserting the battery, checking the ambient temperature, and, if necessary, moving to a more favorable location to try charging again.

When the battery is charged, slide the lever on the bottom of the camera and ease the battery in (see Figure 1.3). To remove the battery, you must press a blue lever in the battery compartment (not shown in the figure) that prevents the pack from slipping out when the door is opened.

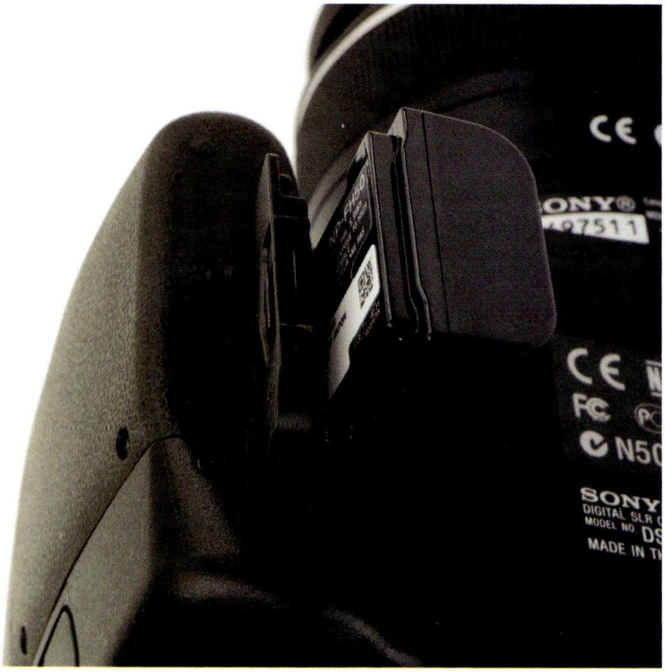

Figure 1.3
Insert the battery in the camera; it only fits one way.

Final Steps

Your Sony Alpha dSLR is almost ready to fire up and shoot. You'll need to select and mount a lens, adjust the viewfinder for your vision, and insert a memory card. Each of these steps is easy, and if you've used any Sony camera in the past, you already know exactly what to do. I'm going to provide a little extra detail for those of you who are new to the Sony or digital SLR worlds.

Mounting the Lens

As you'll see, my recommended lens mounting procedure emphasizes protecting your equipment from accidental damage, and minimizing the intrusion of dust. If your Alpha has no lens attached, select the lens you want to use and loosen (but do not remove) the rear lens cap. I generally place the lens I am planning to mount vertically in a slot in my camera bag, where it's protected from mishaps but ready to pick up quickly. By loosening the rear lens cap, you'll be able to lift it off the back of the lens at the last instant, so the rear element of the lens is covered until then.

After that, remove the body cap by rotating the cap towards the shutter release button. You should always mount the body cap when there is no lens on the camera, because it helps keep dust out of the interior of the camera, where it can settle on the mirror, focusing screen, the interior mirror box, and potentially find its way past the shutter onto the sensor. (While the Alpha's sensor cleaning mechanism works fine, the less dust it has to contend with, the better.) The body cap also protects the vulnerable mirror from damage caused by intruding objects (including your fingers, if you're not cautious).

Once the body cap has been removed, remove the rear lens cap from the lens, set it aside, and then mount the lens on the camera by matching the red-orange alignment indicator on the lens barrel with the red-orange dot on the camera's lens mount (see Figure 1.4). Rotate the lens toward the mode dial until it seats securely. (Don't press the lens release button during mounting.) If the lens hood is bayoneted on the lens in the reversed position (which makes the lens/hood combination more compact for transport), twist it off and remount with the rim facing outward (see Figure 1.5). A lens hood protects the front of the lens from accidental bumps, and reduces flare caused by extraneous light arriving at the front element of the lens from outside the picture area.

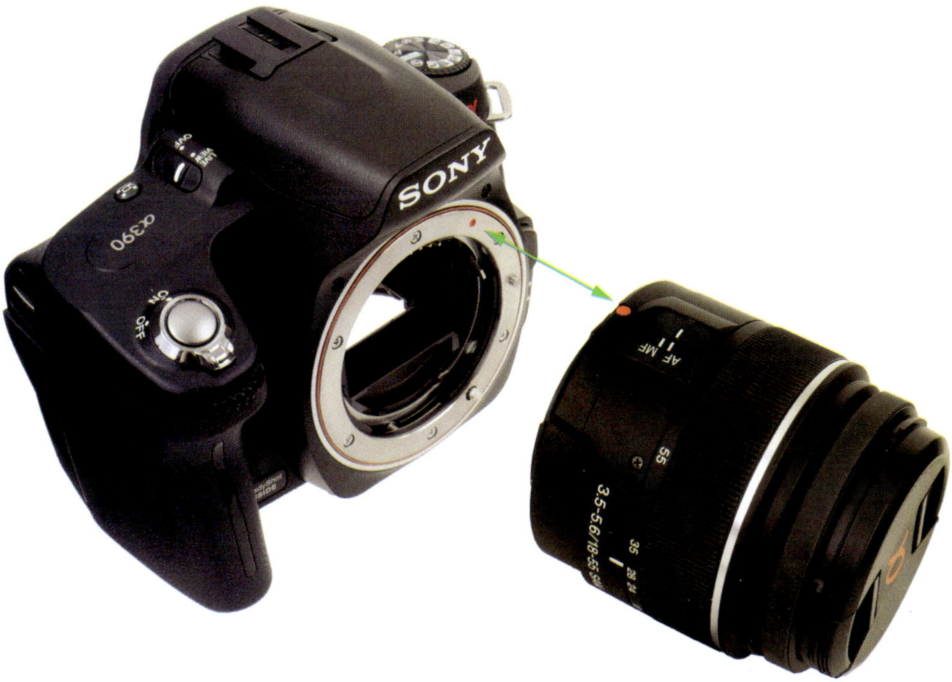

Figure 1.4
Match the red-orange dot on the lens with the red-orange dot on the camera mount to properly align the lens with the bayonet mount.

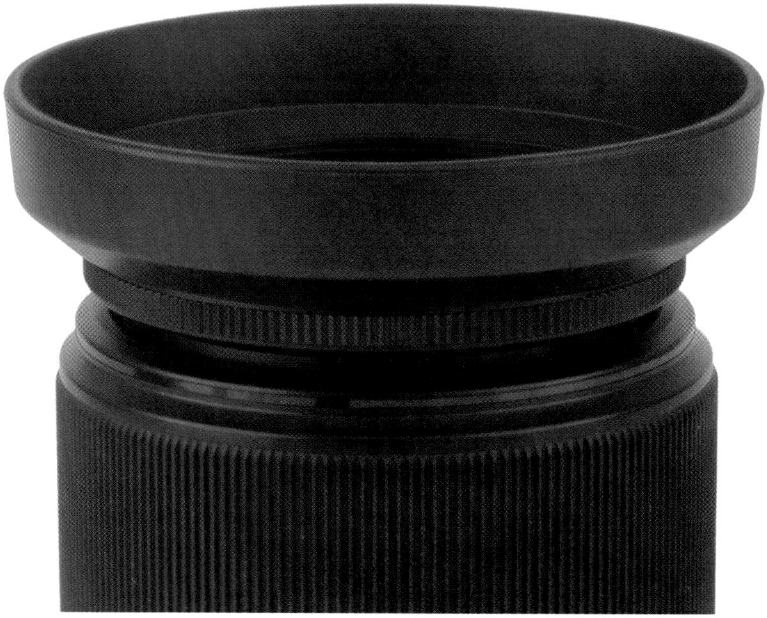

Figure 1.5
A lens hood protects the lens from extraneous light and accidental bumps.

Adjusting Diopter Correction

Those of us with less than perfect eyesight can often benefit from a little optical correction in the viewfinder. Your contact lenses or glasses may provide all the correction you need, but if you are a glasses wearer and want to use the Sony Alpha without your glasses, you can take advantage of the camera's built-in diopter adjustment correction to match that of your glasses or your eyesight with your glasses on. Press the shutter release halfway to illuminate the indicators in the viewfinder, then rotate the diopter correction wheel (see Figure 1.6) while looking through the viewfinder until the indicators appear sharp.

If the available correction is insufficient, Sony offers nine different Eyepiece Correctors for the viewfinder window, from +3 to –4 diopters. If more than one person uses your Alpha, and each requires a different diopter setting, you can save a little time by noting the number of clicks and direction (clockwise to increase the diopter power; counterclockwise to decrease the diopter value) required to change from one user to the other. There are 14 detents in all.

Inserting a Memory Card

You can't take actual photos without a memory card inserted in your Sony Alpha, but the camera will snap off "pictures" that are all dressed up, with no place to go. They can be displayed on the LCD, with a No Card warning shown at bottom right, and a flashing 0 indicator appearing in the viewfinder. So, your final step will be to insert a memory card.

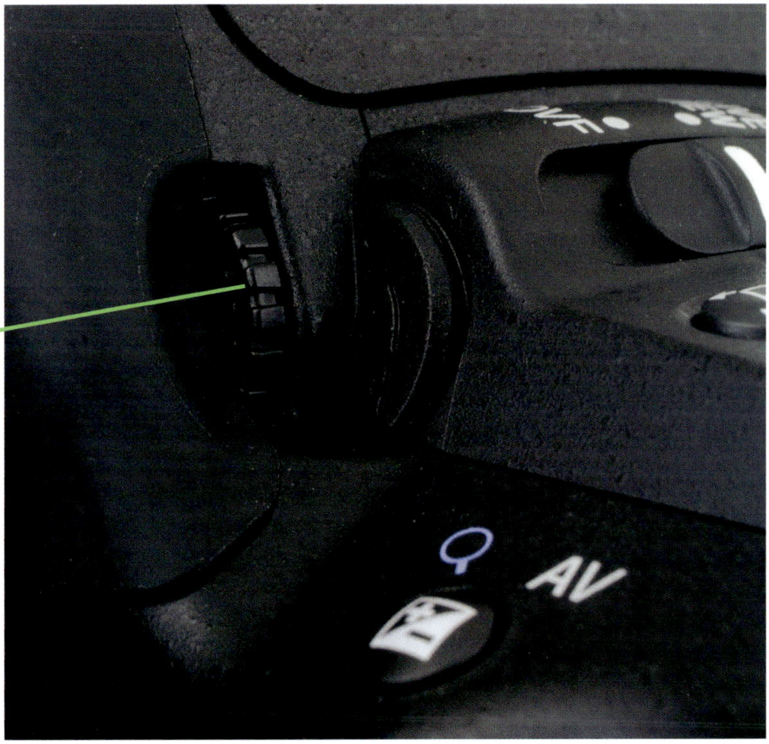

Figure 1.6 Viewfinder diopter correction can be dialed in.

Diopter correction wheel

The Alpha accepts both Secure Digital and Sony Memory Stick Pro Duo (or Memory Stick Pro-HG Duo) cards. (It doesn't matter which type you use, and the camera will accept both cards at once, although it will only use one or the other at any given time.) The cards fit in slots underneath a door on the left side of the camera (when viewed as you hold it). You should only remove the memory card when the camera is switched off, but the Alpha will remind you if the door is opened while the camera is still writing photos to the card.

Insert the memory card with the label facing the back of the camera (for a Memory Stick Pro Duo), or towards the front of the camera if inserting a Secure Digital card (as shown in Figure 1.7). In either case, the card should be oriented so the edge with the metal contacts goes into the slot first. Then, slide a switch located just above the card slots to either the SD (top-most) or Memory Stick (bottom-most) positions. If you turn on the Alpha and see a No Card message on the screen even though you have, in fact, inserted a card, you've failed to set this switch to the correct position. (See Figure 1.8.)

Close the door, and your preflight checklist is done! (I'm going to assume you remember to remove the lens cap when you're ready to take a picture!) When you want to remove the memory card later, just press down on the card edge that protrudes from the slot, and it will pop right out.

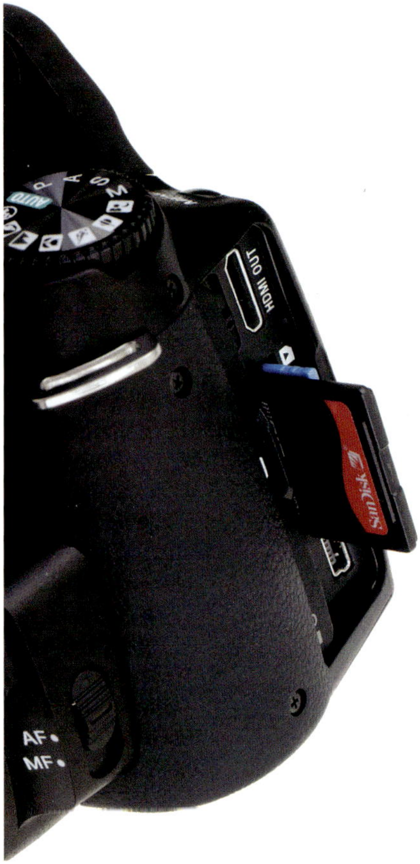

Figure 1.7
The memory card is inserted in the slot on the side of the camera.

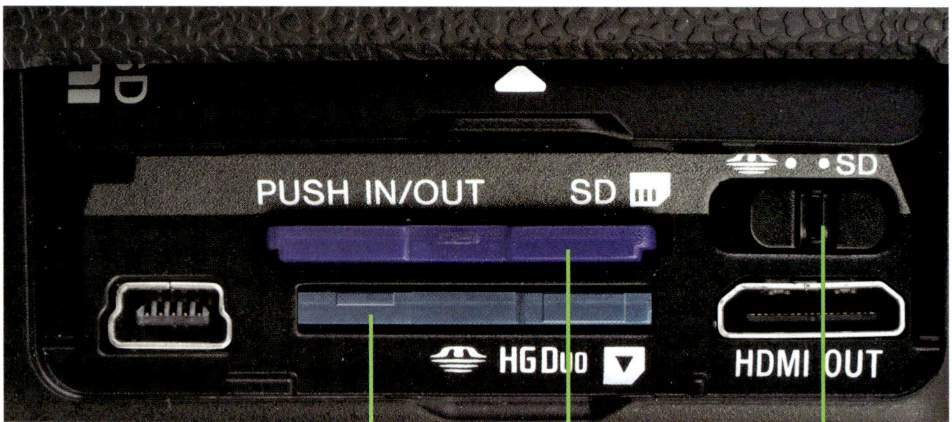

Figure 1.8
Set the sliding switch for the type of memory card you want to use.

Turn on the Power

Slide the ON/OFF switch that surrounds the shutter release button clockwise, to the ON position. The camera will remain on or in a standby mode until you manually turn it off. After 30 seconds of idling, the Alpha goes into the standby mode to save battery power. Just tap the shutter release button to bring it back to life.

When the camera first powers up, you may be asked to set the date and time. The procedure is fairly self-explanatory (although I'll explain it in detail in Chapter 3). Press the MENU button, use the controller keys to move to the Setup 2 menu, and choose Date and Time. You can then use the left/right controller keys to navigate among the date, year, and date format and the up/down keys to enter the correct settings. When finished, press the center controller button, choose OK in the screen that pops up, and press the center button again to confirm the date.

TAKING CONTROL

Sony's nomenclature for the Alpha's controls can be confusing. The large pad on the back of the camera is officially called the control button, and the directional/function keys at the north, south, east, west positions of this pad are referred to only by triangle icons pointing in the requisite directions. The button in the center of the pad that activates your choices is called the control (Enter) button. For this book, I've elected to refer to the thumbpad as the controller; the "Enter" button will be called the center controller button, and the directional keys will be the left/right/up/down buttons, or given the names of their additional functions, such as DISP, Drive, Flash, and ISO. Oh, and that wheel on the front of the camera is the control dial.

Once the Sony Alpha is satisfied that it knows what time it is, the recording information display should appear on the LCD. Press the DISP button (the controller up key) to activate this display when it is not active. There are two versions, a Standard display (see Figure 1.9), and a Graphic display (Figure 1.10). When you rotate the camera to shoot vertical pictures, the text and icons on the recording information display reorient themselves, too, for easy viewing.

The recording information display shows the basic settings of the camera, including current shutter speed and lens opening, shooting mode, ISO sensitivity, and other parameters. I'll explain these features in later chapters of this book, too (especially in Chapter 4, which deals with exposure).

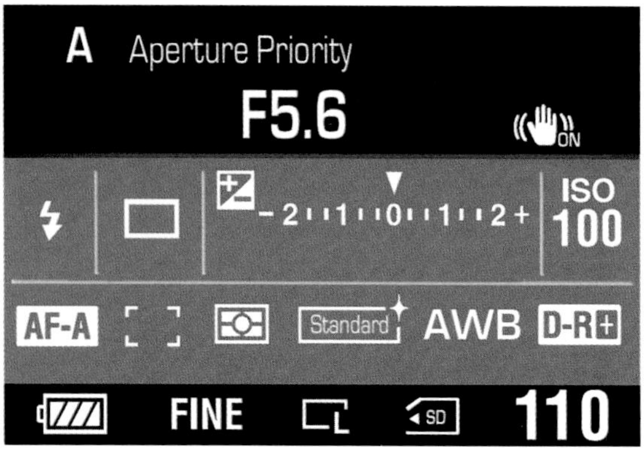

Figure 1.9

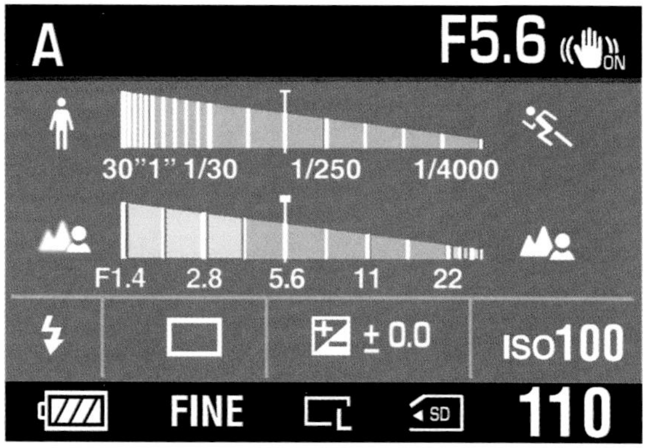

Figure 1.10

> **Tip**
>
> When using Live View (with the A390 model only; the A290 does not have this feature), the back-panel LCD switches to a preview of the image you're about to take. The standard recording information display is not shown. Instead, the Live View image is overlaid with the normal viewfinder-style display, plus indicators for battery power remaining, image size and quality, number of pictures remaining, and Dynamic Range Optimizing status. In this mode, pressing the DISP key cycles through full display (viewfinder plus indicator overlay), histogram only (viewfinder plus a display of a brightness histogram), and indicators off (only the viewfinder display is shown, with no additional indicators). Later in this book you can read about Live View (Chapter 5), as well as Histograms (in Chapter 4).

Formatting a Memory Card

There are three ways to create a blank Secure Digital or Memory Stick Pro Duo card for your Sony Alpha, and two of them are at least partially wrong. Here are your options, both correct and incorrect:

- **Transfer (move) files to your computer.** When you transfer (rather than copy) all the image files to your computer from the memory card (either using a direct cable transfer or with a card reader and appropriate software, as described later in this chapter), the old image files can, at your option, be erased from the card, leaving the card blank. Theoretically. Unfortunately, this method does *not* remove files that you've labeled as Protected (by choosing Protect from the Function menu during playback), nor does it identify and lock out parts of your card that have become corrupted or unusable since the last time you formatted the card. Therefore, I recommend always formatting the card, rather than simply moving the image files, each time you want to make a blank card. The only exception is when you *want* to leave the protected/unerased images on the card for awhile longer, say, to share with friends, family, and colleagues.

- **(Don't) Format in your computer.** With the memory card inserted in a card reader or card slot in your computer, you can use Windows or Mac OS to reformat the memory card. Don't! The operating system won't necessarily arrange the structure of the card the way the Alpha likes to see it (in computer terms, an incorrect *file system* may be installed). The only way to ensure that the card has been properly formatted for your camera is to perform the format in the camera itself. The only exception to this rule is when you have a seriously corrupted memory card that your camera refuses to format. Sometimes it is possible to revive such a corrupted card by allowing the operating system to reformat it first, then trying again in the camera.
- **Playback menu format.** To use the recommended method to format a memory card, press the MENU button, use the left/right buttons of the controller pad to choose the Playback menu (which is represented by the right-pointing triangle), and then press the down key to navigate to the Format entry. Press the center controller button, and select OK using the up key from the screen that appears. Press the center button once more to begin the format process.

HOW MANY SHOTS?

The Sony Alpha provides a fairly accurate estimate of the number of shots remaining on the LCD. It is only an estimate, because the actual number will vary, depending on the capacity of your memory card, the file format(s) you've selected (more on those later), the aspect ratio (proportions) of the image (the Alpha can use both traditional 3:2 proportions and 16:9—HDTV—aspect ratios), and the content of the image itself. (Some photos may contain large areas that can be more efficiently squeezed down to a smaller size.)

Table 1.1 shows the typical number of shots you can expect using a moderately sized 8GB SD memory card (which I expect will be a popular size card among Alpha users as prices continue to plummet during the life of this book). All figures are by actual count with my own 8GB SD card. Take those numbers and cut them in half if you're using a 4GB SD card; multiply by 25 percent if you're using a 2GB card, or by 12.5 percent if you're working with a 1GB SD card.

Table 1.1 Typical Shots with an 8GB Memory Card

	Large	Medium	Small
3:2 Aspect Ratio			
JPEG Fine	1,600	2,132	3,712
JPEG Standard	2,228	2,912	4,724
RAW	364	N/A	N/A
RAW+JPEG	292	N/A	N/A
16:9 Aspect Ratio			
JPEG Fine	1,844	2,820	4,132
JPEG Standard	2,544	3,736	5,164
RAW	364	N/A	N/A
RAW+JPEG	300	N/A	N/A

Selecting a Shooting Mode

You can choose a shooting method from the mode dial located on the top left of the Sony Alpha dSLR (see Figure 1.11). There are eight Scene shooting modes (counting Auto), in which the camera makes virtually all the decisions for you (except when to press the shutter), and four Semi-automatic and Manual modes, which allow you to provide input over the exposure and settings the camera uses. You'll find a complete description of both Scene and Semi-automatic and Manual modes in Chapter 4.

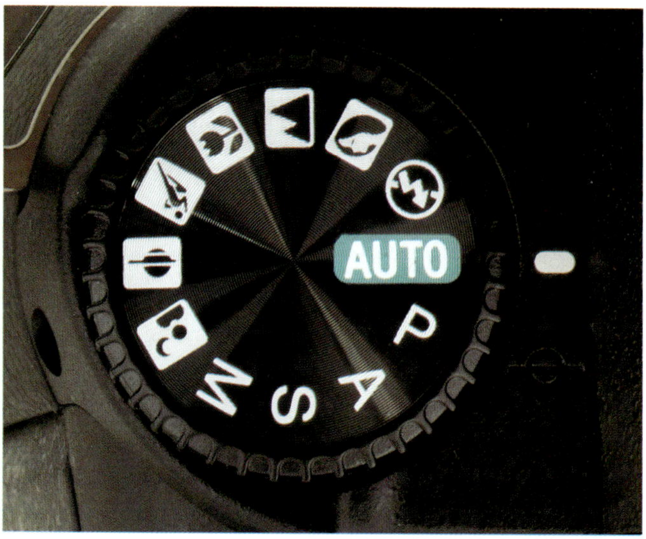

Figure 1.11
The mode dial includes Scene, Semi-automatic, and Manual exposure settings.

Turn your camera on by flipping the power switch to ON. Next, you need to select which shooting mode to use. If you're very new to digital photography, you might want to set the camera to Auto (the green AUTO setting on the mode dial) or P (Program mode) and start snapping away. Either mode will make all the appropriate settings for you for many shooting situations. If you have a specific type of picture you want to shoot, you can try out one of the Scene modes indicated on the mode dial, shown in Figure 1.12. When you first switch to a shooting mode, a help screen like the one shown in Figure 1.13 appears for a few seconds to provide a "briefing" about that mode. Then, it disappears when you press the control button or touch the shutter release and is replaced by either the Standard or Graphic recording information display shown in Figures 1.9 and 1.10 earlier.

- **Auto.** In this mode, the Alpha makes all the exposure decisions for you, and will pop up the flash if necessary under low-light conditions.
- **Flash Off.** This is the mode to use in museums and other locations where flash is forbidden or inappropriate. It otherwise operates exactly like the Auto setting but disables the pop-up internal flash unit.

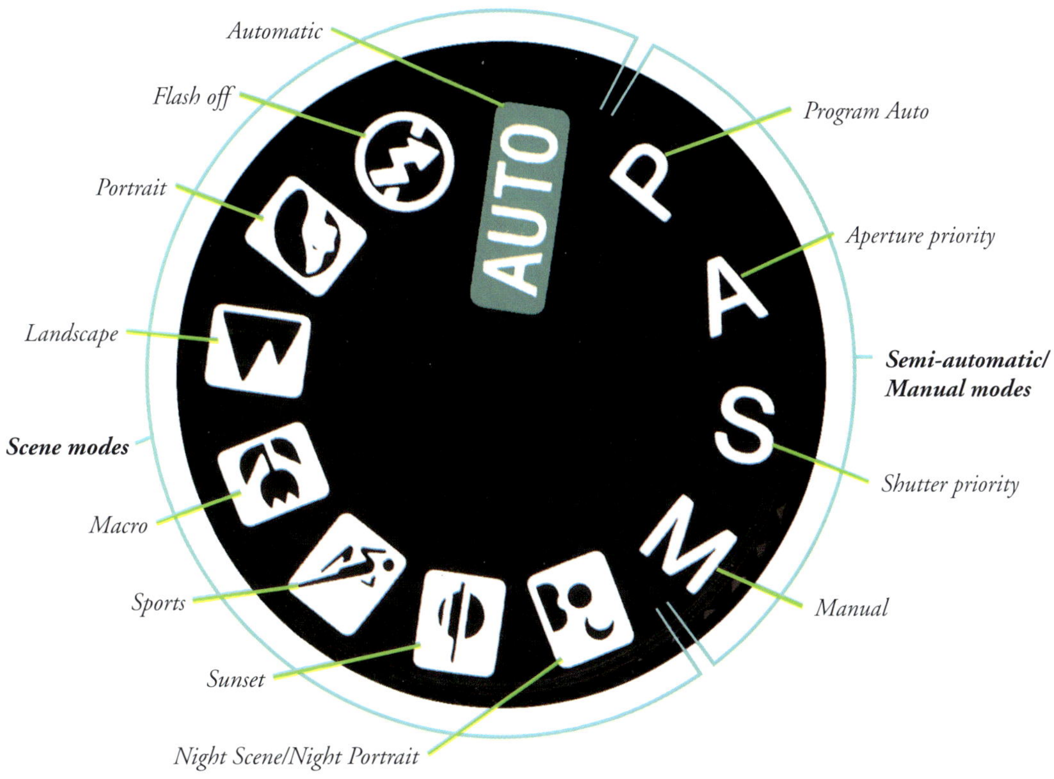

Figure 1.12 The Semi-automatic and Manual modes (right side of dial as shown) let the photographer control how exposures are made, to increase creative options. The Scene settings (left side of the dial) make all the exposure decisions for you.

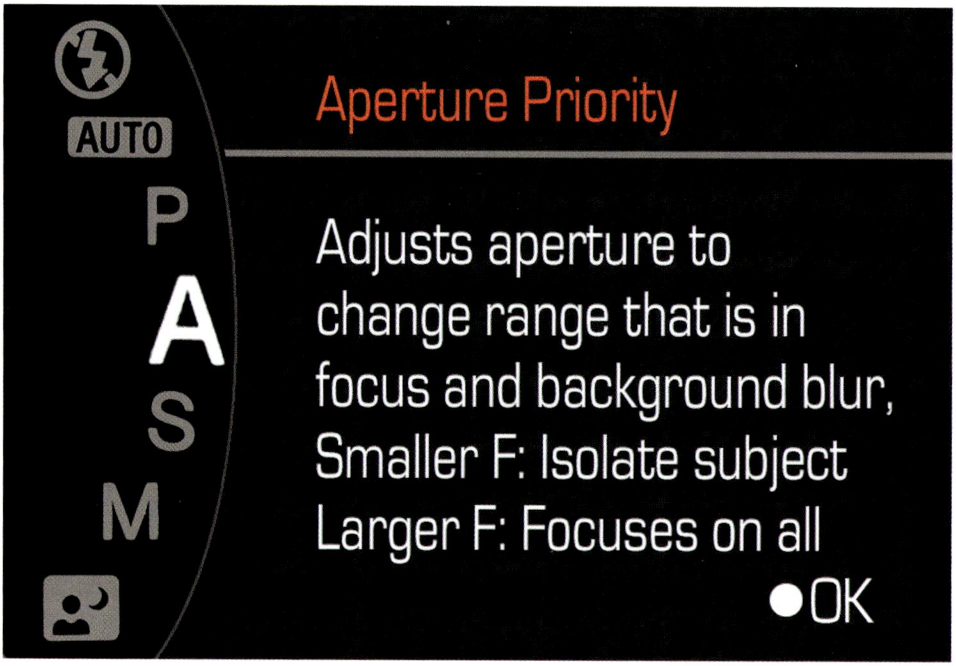

Figure 1.13 This Help Guide screen appears when you first select a shooting mode.

- **Landscape.** Select this mode when you want extra sharpness and rich colors of distant scenes.
- **Portrait.** Use this mode when you're taking a portrait of a subject standing relatively close to the camera and want to de-emphasize the background, maximize sharpness, and produce flattering skin tones.
- **Macro.** This mode is helpful when you are shooting close-up pictures of a subject from about one foot away or less.
- **Sports.** Use this mode to freeze fast-moving subjects.
- **Sunset.** This is a great mode to accentuate the colors of a sunrise or sunset.
- **Night Portrait/Night Scene.** Choose this mode when you want to illuminate a subject in the foreground with flash, but still allow the background to be exposed properly by the available light. Be prepared to use a tripod or make sure SteadyShot is activated to reduce the effects of camera shake. (You'll find more about IS and camera shake in Chapter 6.)

If you have more photographic experience, you might want to opt for one of the Semiautomatic or Manual modes, also shown in Figure 1.12. These, too, are described in more detail in Chapter 4. These modes let you apply a little more creativity to your camera's settings.

These modes are indicated on the mode dial by letters P, A, S, and M:

- **P (Program Auto).** This mode allows the Alpha to select the basic exposure settings, but you can still override the camera's choices to fine-tune your image.
- **A (Aperture priority).** Choose when you want to use a particular lens opening, especially to control sharpness or how much of your image is in focus. The Alpha will select the appropriate shutter speed for you.
- **S (Shutter priority).** This mode is useful when you want to use a particular shutter speed to stop action or produce creative blur effects. The Alpha will select the appropriate f/stop for you.
- **M (Manual).** Select when you want full control over the shutter speed and lens opening, either for creative effects or because you are using a studio flash or other flash unit not compatible with the Alpha's automatic flash metering.

Choosing a Metering Mode

You might want to select a particular metering mode for your first shots, although the default Multi segment metering (which is set automatically when you choose a Scene mode) is probably the best choice as you get to know your camera. To change metering modes (you must not be using one of the Scene modes), press the Fn button (located on the back of the camera to the right of the LCD) and select Metering mode from the Function menu. Then, use the up/down controller keys (the buttons on the control pad to the right of the LCD), and select one of the three modes described below. Press the center controller button to confirm your choice. The options are shown in Figure 1.14:

- **Multi segment metering.** The standard metering mode; the Alpha attempts to intelligently classify your image and choose the best exposure based on readings from 40 different zones in the frame. You can read about these zones in Chapter 4.
- **Center weighted metering.** The Alpha meters the entire scene, but gives the most emphasis to the central area of the frame.
- **Spot metering.** Exposure is calculated from a smaller central spot.

You'll find a detailed description of each of these modes in Chapter 4.

Choosing a Focus Mode

You can easily switch between automatic and manual focus by moving the AF/MF switch on the lens mounted on your camera. However, you'll still need to choose an appropriate focus mode. (You can read more on selecting focus parameters in Chapter 5.) If you're using a Scene mode, the focus method is set for you automatically.

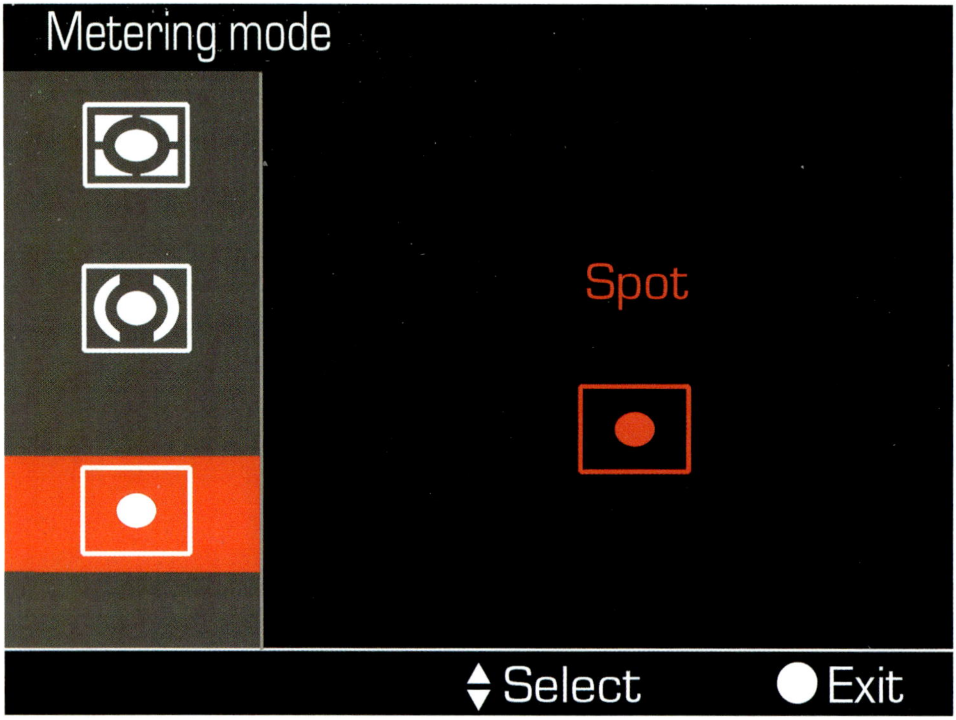

Figure 1.14 Metering modes (top to bottom) Multi segment, Center weighted, and Spot.

To set the focus mode, press the Fn button and choose Autofocus mode from the Function menu. Then select the mode you want from the screen that pops up (see Figure 1.15) using the up/down controller keys. Press the center controller button to confirm your selection. The three choices are as follows:

- **Single-shot (AF-S).** This mode, sometimes called *single autofocus*, locks in a focus point when the shutter button is pressed down halfway, and the focus confirmation light glows in the viewfinder. The focus will remain locked until you release the button or take the picture. If the camera is unable to achieve sharp focus, the focus confirmation light will blink. This mode is best when your subject is relatively motionless.
- **Continuous AF (AF-C).** This mode, sometimes called *continuous servo*, sets focus when you partially depress the shutter button, but continues to monitor the frame and refocuses if the camera or subject is moved. This is a useful mode for photographing sports and moving subjects.
- **Automatic AF (AF-A).** In this mode, the Alpha switches between Single-shot and Continuous AF as appropriate. That is, it locks in a focus point when you partially depress the shutter button (Single-shot mode), but switches automatically to Continuous AF if the subject begins to move. This mode is handy when photographing a subject, such as a child at quiet play, who might move unexpectedly.

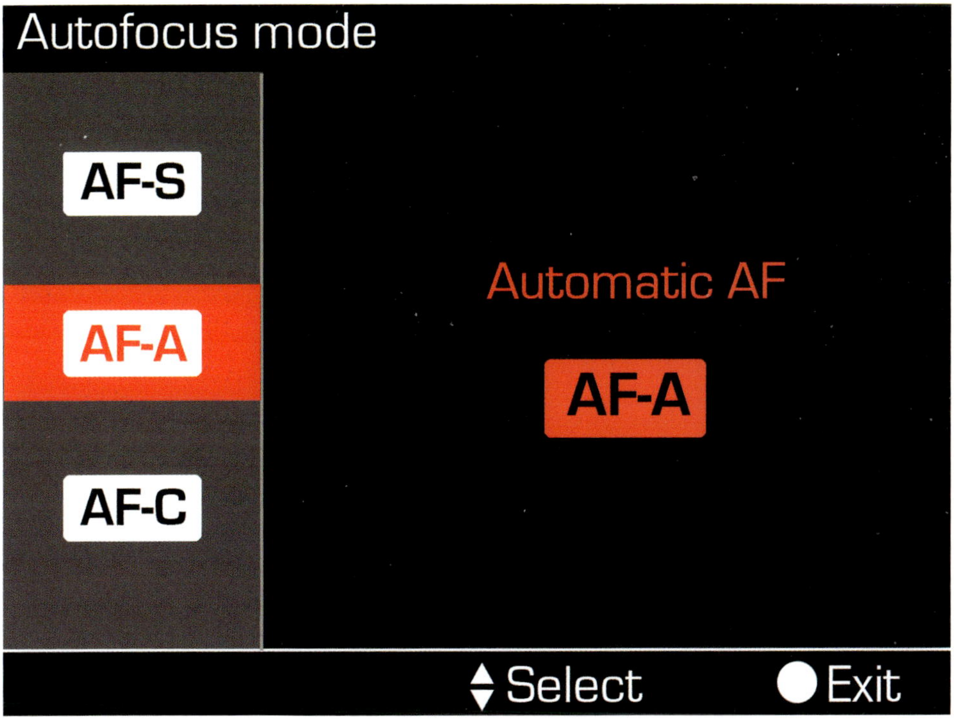

Figure 1.15 Set Autofocus mode.

Selecting a Focus Point

The Sony Alpha dSLR uses nine different focus points to calculate correct focus. In Scene modes, the focus point is selected automatically by the camera. In the other Semi-automatic and Manual modes, you can allow the camera to select the focus point automatically, or you can specify which focus point should be used.

You can specify which of the nine focus points the Sony dSLR uses to calculate correct focus, or allow the camera to select the point for you. There are three AF area options, shown in Figure 1.16, and also described in Chapter 5. Press the Fn button (just to the upper right of the LCD), navigate to the AF area selection, press the controller button, and select one of these three choices. Press the controller button again to confirm.

- **Wide.** The Alpha chooses the appropriate focus zone from the nine AF areas on the screen. However, you can switch to the center (Spot) focus zone while shooting by pressing the center controller button.
- **Spot.** The Alpha always uses the center, cross-type focus zone to calculate correct focus.
- **Local.** Use the left/right/up/down controller buttons to move the focus zone among the nine available zones. Press the center controller button to switch to the center, cross-type focus sensor quickly.

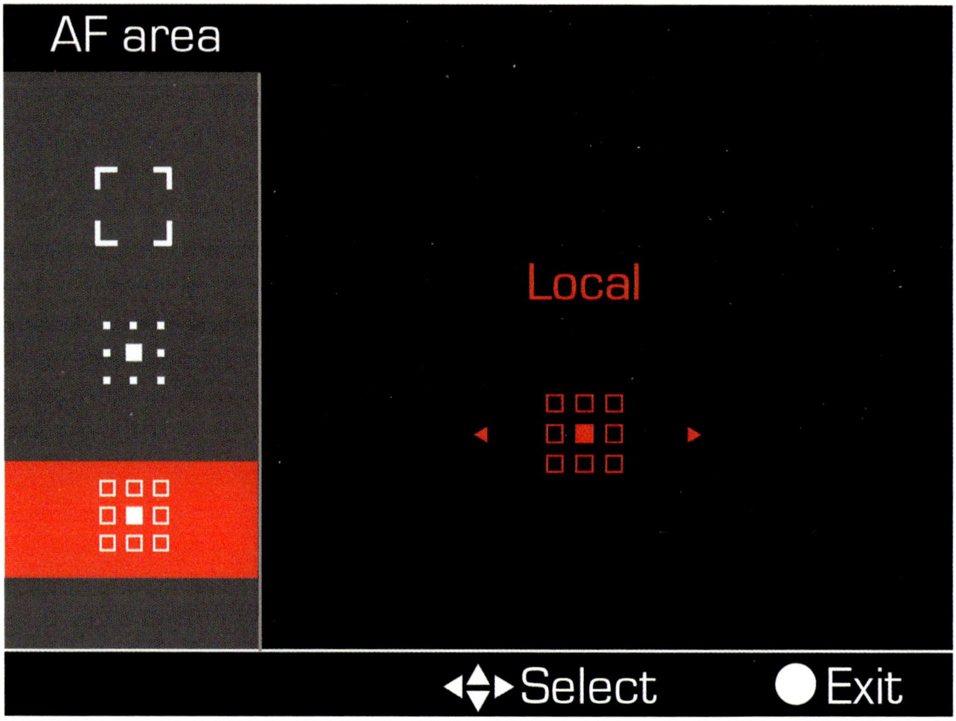

Figure 1.16 Select from Wide (the Alpha selects one of the nine AF areas), Spot (only the center focus spot is used), or Local (you can choose which area to use).

Other Settings

There are a few other settings you can make if you're feeling ambitious, but don't feel ashamed if you postpone using these features until you've racked up a little more experience with your Sony Alpha.

Adjusting White Balance and ISO

If you like, you can custom-tailor your white balance (color balance) and ISO sensitivity settings. To start out, it's best to set white balance (WB) to Auto, and ISO to ISO 100 or ISO 200 for daylight photos, and ISO 400 for pictures in dimmer light. You'll find complete recommendations for both settings in Chapters 3 and 4. You can adjust white balance by pressing the Fn key and navigating to the White Balance menu. The ISO setting menu can be invoked by pressing the controller down button.

Using the Self-Timer

If you want to set a short delay before your picture is taken, you can use the self-timer. Press the Drive button (the left controller key), and use the up/down controller buttons to highlight the self-timer icon, and press the left/right controller buttons to select from either the 10-second self-timer (which also can be used with the optional RM-S1AM or RM-L1AM Remote Commanders) or 2-second self-timer. Press the center controller button to confirm your choice (see Figure 1.17) and a self-timer icon will appear on the recording information display on the back of the Sony Alpha. Press the shutter release to lock focus and start the timer. The self-timer lamp will blink and the beeper will sound (unless you've silenced it in the menus) until the final two seconds (in 10-second mode), when the lamp remains on and the beeper beeps more rapidly.

Sony recommends slipping off the eyepiece cup and replacing it with the viewfinder cap, in order to keep extraneous light from reaching the exposure meter through the viewfinder "back door." I usually just shade the viewfinder window with my hand (if I'm using the self-timer to reduce camera shake for a long exposure) or drape something over the back of the camera (if I'm scurrying to get into the picture myself).

In addition to the Self-timer, Continuous shooting, and Single-shot choices in the Drive menu, there are also bracketing and infrared remote control options (not shown in the figure). I'll explain these in Chapter 2, too.

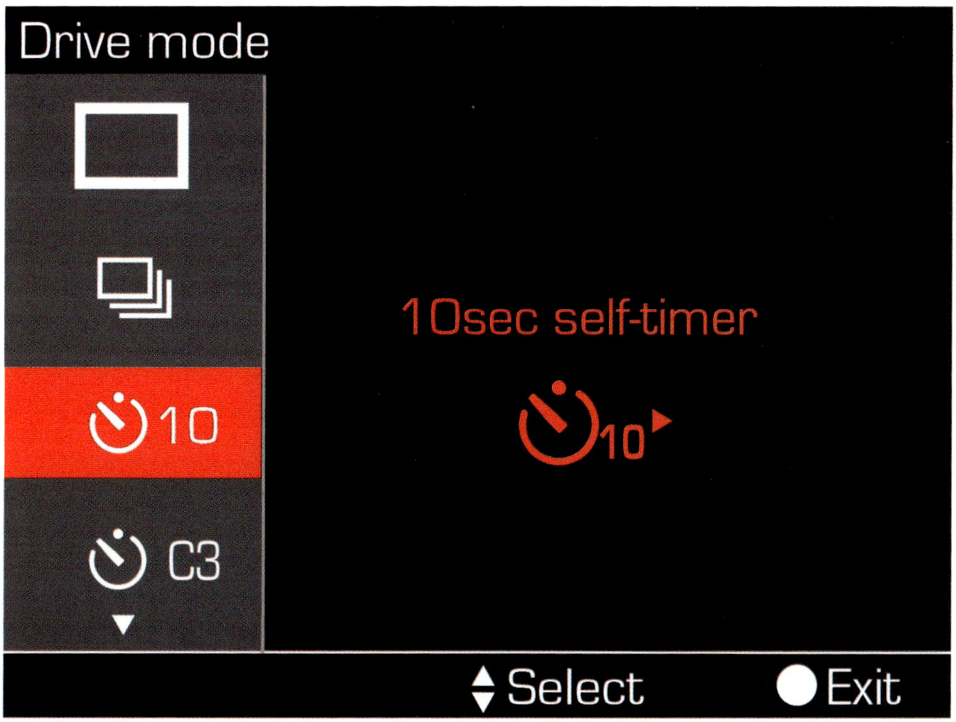

Figure 1.17 The Drive modes include (top to bottom) Single-shot, Continuous, 10-second delay/2-second delay, and Self-timer with three continuous shots after the delay.

Reviewing the Images You've Taken

The Sony Alpha dSLR has a broad range of playback and image review options. I'll cover them in more detail in Chapters 2 and 3. For now, you'll want to learn just the basics. Here is all you really need to know at this time, as shown in Figure 1.18. There are other playback options that I'll cover in Chapter 3:

- **Display last image shot.** Press the Playback button (the bottom button to the lower right of the LCD, marked with a hard-to-see dark blue right-pointing triangle) to display the most recent image on the LCD.
- **Reverse.** Press the left controller key to view a previous image.
- **Forward.** Press the right controller key to view the next image.
- **Delete.** Press the Trash button to delete the currently displayed image.
- **Rotate.** Press the Fn button and choose Rotate from the menu that pops up, followed by the center controller button to rotate the image 90 degrees. (I'll explain how to activate/deactivate automatic rotation in Chapter 3.)
- **Zoom/Full-screen.** Press the Zoom/AV button on the top surface of the camera to alternate between zoomed and full-screen views.

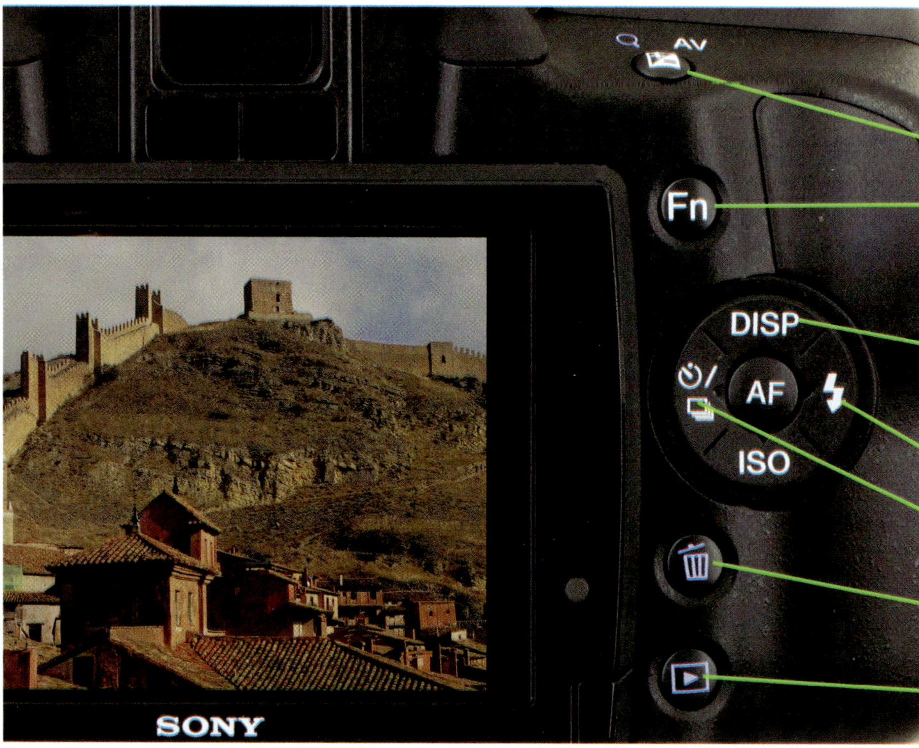

Figure 1.18
Review your images.

- **Zoom in/out.** Rotate the control dial located on the front of the camera to zoom in and out.
- **Move zoom area.** Use the controller left/right/up/down keys to scroll around within a magnified image. An inset box shows the relationship of the magnified image to the entire frame.
- **Change info display.** Press the DISP button repeatedly to cycle among views that have no recording data, full recording data (f/stop, shutter speed, image quality/size, etc.), or a thumbnail image with histogram display. (I'll explain all these in Chapter 2.)
- **View thumbnails.** Press the Fn button and choose Image Index from the menu that pops up, and set the display to 4, 9, or 25 thumbnail images that can be scrolled among using the controller keys.

You'll find more information on viewing thumbnail indexes of images and other image review functions in Chapter 2.

Transferring Photos to Your Computer

The final step in your picture taking session will be to transfer the photos you've taken to your computer for printing, further review, or image editing. (You can also take your memory card to a retailer for printing if you don't want to go the do-it-yourself route.) Your Alpha allows you to print directly to PictBridge-compatible printers and to create print orders right in the camera, plus you can select which images to transfer to your computer. I'll outline those options in Chapter 3.

For now, you'll probably want to transfer your images by either using a cable transfer from the camera to the computer or removing the memory card from the Alpha and transferring the images with a card reader (shown in Figure 1.19). The latter option is usually the best, because it's usually much faster and doesn't deplete the battery of your camera. However, you can use a cable transfer when you have the cable and a computer but no card reader (perhaps you're using the computer of a friend or colleague, or at an Internet café).

To transfer images from a memory card to the computer using a card reader:

1. Turn off the camera.
2. Slide open the memory card door, and press on the card, which causes it to pop up so it can be removed from the slot. (You can see a memory card being removed in Figure 1.7.)
3. Insert the memory card into your memory card reader. Your installed software detects the files on the card and offers to transfer them. (You'll find descriptions of your transfer software options in Chapter 8.) The card can also appear as a mass storage device on your desktop, which you can open and then drag and drop the files to your computer.

To transfer images from the camera to a Mac or PC computer using the USB cable:

1. Turn off the camera.
2. Open the memory card door and plug the USB cable furnished with the camera into the USB/Video port. Make sure the memory card is pushed all the way into the slot. (See Figure 1.20.)
3. Connect the other end of the USB cable to a USB port on your computer.
4. Turn on the camera. Your installed software usually detects the camera and offers to transfer the pictures, or the camera appears on your desktop as a mass storage device, enabling you to drag and drop the files to your computer. I'll cover using the Sony Alpha's bundled software to transfer images in Chapter 8.

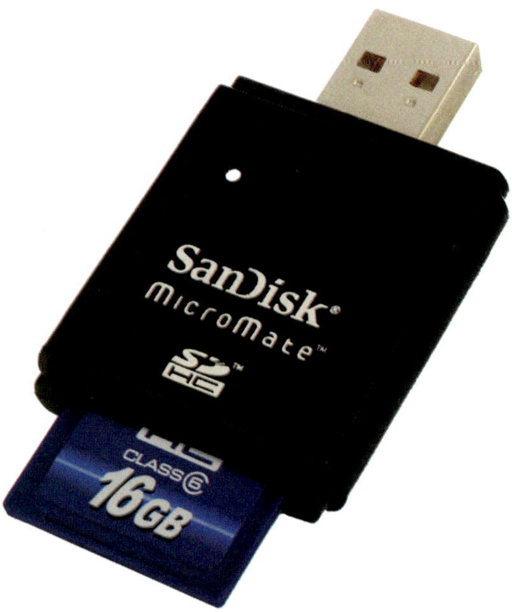

Figure 1.19 A card reader is the fastest way to transfer photos.

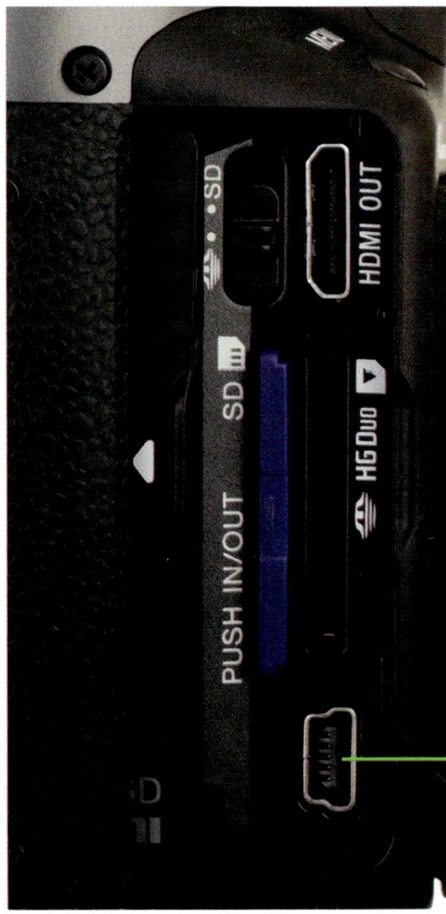

Figure 1.20 Images can be transferred to your computer using a USB cable plugged into the USB/Video port.

2

Sony Alpha DSLR-A390/A290 Roadmap

One thing that always surprises new owners of the Sony Alpha DSLR-A390/A290 is that the cameras have a total of 397 buttons, dials, switches, levers, latches, and knobs bristling from its surface. Okay, I lied. Actually, the real number is closer to two dozen controls and adjustments, but that's still a lot of components to master, especially when you consider that many of these controls serve double-duty to give you access to multiple functions.

Traditionally, there have been two ways of providing a roadmap to guide you through this maze of features. One approach uses two or three tiny 2-inch black-and-white line drawings or photos impaled with dozens of callouts labeled with cross-references to the actual pages in the book that tell you what these components do. You'll find this tactic used in the pocket-sized manual Sony provides with the Sony Alpha A390 and A290, and most of the other third-party guidebooks as well. Deciphering one of these miniature camera layouts is a lot like being presented with a world globe when what you really want to know is how to find the capital of Belgium.

I originated a more useful approach in my field guides, providing you, instead of a satellite view, a street-level map that includes close-up full-color photos of the camera from several angles (see Figure 2.1), with a smaller number of labels clearly pointing to each individual feature. And, I don't force you to flip back and forth among dozens of pages to find out what a particular component does. Each photo is accompanied by a brief description that summarizes the control, so you can begin using it right away. Only when a particular feature deserves a lengthy explanation do I direct you to a more detailed write-up later in the book.

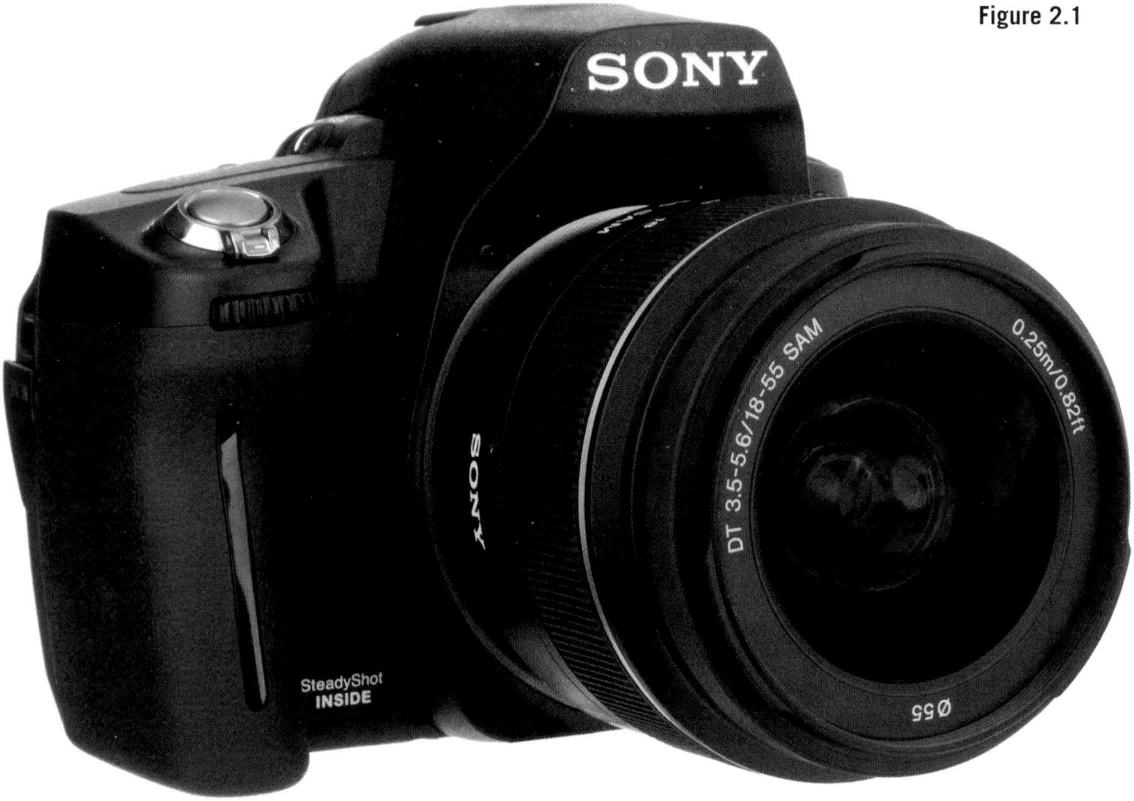

Figure 2.1

So, if you're wondering what the Fn button does, I'll tell you the basics up front, rather than have you flip to page 1,581. This book is not a scavenger hunt. But after I explain how to use the ISO button to change the sensitivity of the Alpha, I *will* provide a cross-reference to a longer explanation later in the book that clarifies noise reduction, ISO, and its effects on exposure. I've had some readers write me and complain about even my minimized cross-reference approach; they'd like to open the book to one page and read everything there is to know about bracketing, for example. Unfortunately, it's impossible to understand some features without having a background in what related features do. So, I'll provide you with introductions in the introductory chapters, covering simple features completely, and relegating some of the really in-depth explanations to later chapters. I think this kind of organization works best for a camera as sophisticated as the Sony Alpha.

By the time you finish this chapter, you'll have a basic understanding of every control and what it does. I'm not going to delve into menu functions here—you'll find a discussion of your Recording, Setup, Playback, and Custom menu options in Chapter 3. Everything here is devoted to the button pusher and dial twirler in you.

WHICH CAMERA?

The illustrations in this book show the Sony Alpha DSLR-A390 camera. If you own the A290 model, your camera looks and operates almost exactly the same. The chief differences are that you're missing the Live View/OVF (optical viewfinder) switch. The LCD on the back of your camera stubbornly refuses to tilt. But you still get the same, sharp, sparkling 14.2-megapixel images that the A390 does.

Front View

When we picture a given camera, we always imagine the front view. That's the view that your subjects see as you snap away, and the aspect that's shown in product publicity and on the box. The frontal angle is, essentially, the "face" of a camera like the Sony Alpha. But, not surprisingly, most of the "business" of operating the camera happens *behind* it, where the photographer resides. The front of the Alpha actually has very few controls and features to worry about. Five of them are most obvious in Figure 2.2:

- **Shutter release button.** Angled on top of the hand grip is the shutter release button. Press this button down halfway to lock exposure and focus (in Single-shot mode and Continuous AF with non-moving subjects). The Alpha assumes that when you tap or depress the shutter release, you are ready to take a picture, so the release can be tapped to activate the exposure meter or to exit from menus.
- **Control dial.** This dial is used to change shooting settings. When settings are available in pairs (such as shutter speed/aperture), this dial will be used to make one type of setting, such as shutter speed. The other setting, say, the aperture, is made using an alternate control, such as spinning the control dial while holding down an additional button like the Exposure Compensation button (which resides conveniently under the thumb next to the viewfinder window on the back of the camera).
- **Power switch.** Turns the camera on and off.
- **Self-timer lamp.** This LED flashes red while your camera counts down the 2-second or 10-second self-timer, flashing slowly at first, then switching to rapid blinking followed by a constant glow in the final moments of the countdown.
- **Hand grip.** This provides a comfortable handhold, and also contains the Alpha's battery.

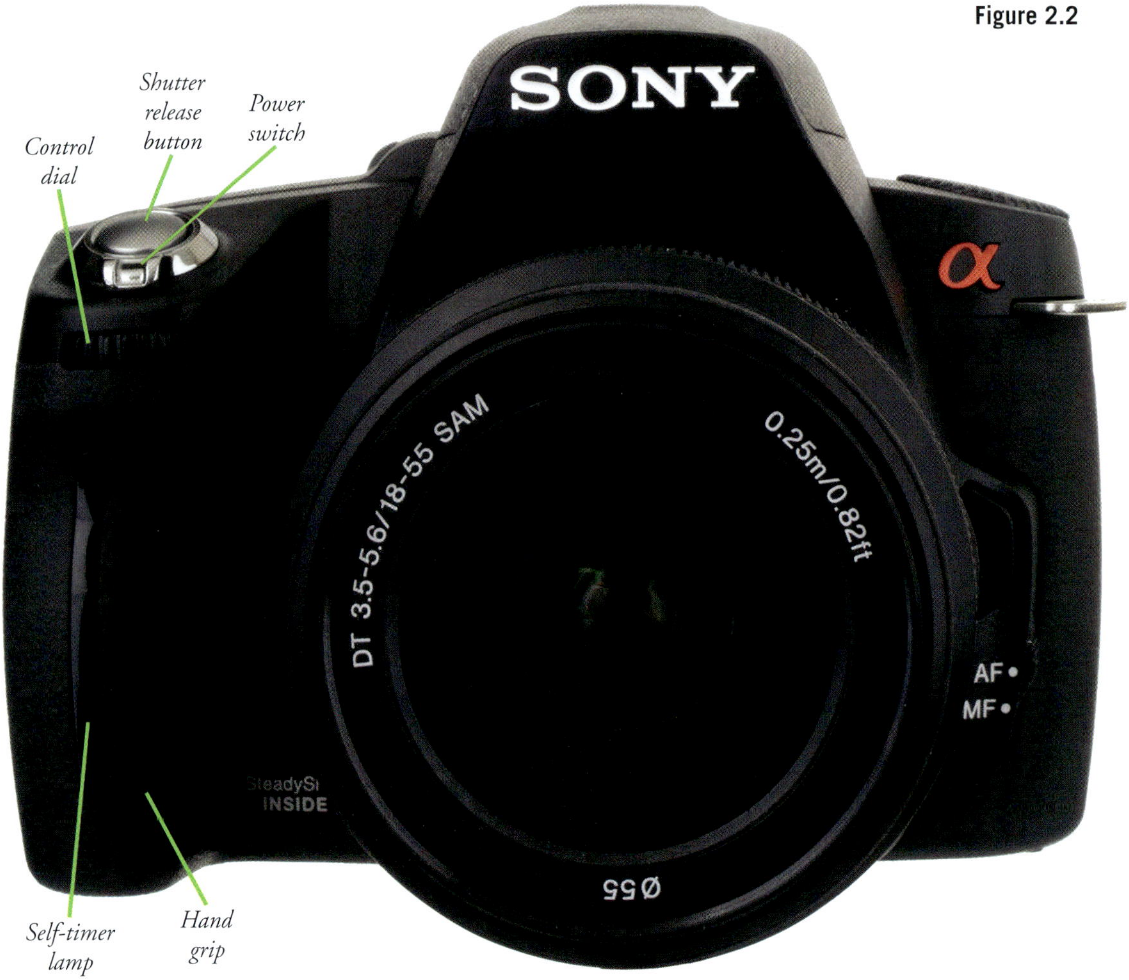

Figure 2.2

You'll find more controls on the other side of the Alpha, shown in Figure 2.3.

- **Pop-up flash.** This is your Alpha's internal flash. It pops up automatically when needed while using Auto, Portrait, Close-Up, and Night Scene modes, and may be manually flipped up when you're using Program, Aperture priority, Shutter priority, and Manual exposure modes. (It can be manually elevated when using other Scene modes as well, but will not fire.) Use a fingernail to grab the flash—Sony has deleted the flash pop-up button found on some earlier Alpha models.
- **Lens release button.** Press and hold this button to unlock the lens so you can rotate the lens to remove it from the camera.
- **Lens mounting index.** Match this raised, red-orange index button with a red-orange indicator on the camera's lens mount to line the two up for attaching the lens to the Alpha.

- **Autofocus/Manual focus switch.** There are two switches shown in the figure; one on the lens and one on the camera body. (Not all lenses will have an autofocus/manual focus switch.) Slide the switch to the AF position or set the Alpha for automatic focus; slide it to the MF position if you want to focus manually. If two switches are present, they must agree. If either is set to MF, then manual focus is used by default.
- **Neck strap mounting ring.** Attach the strap that comes with your Alpha to this ring, or use a third-party strap of your choice.

Figure 2.3

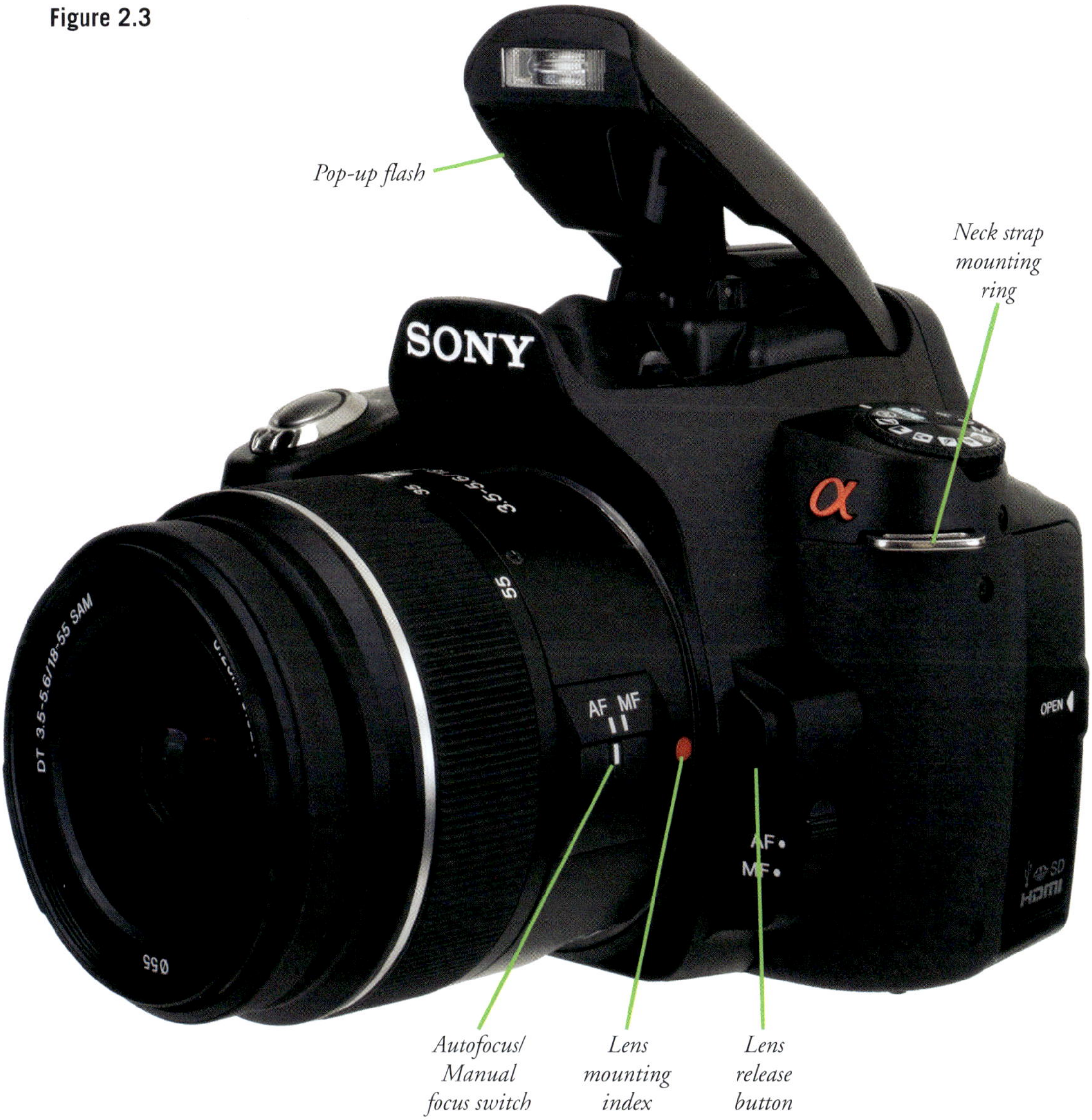

The main feature on the side of the Sony Alpha is a sliding door (see Figure 2.4) that provides a modicum of protection for the ports and memory card slots underneath from dust and moisture. The connectors, shown in Figure 2.5, are as follows:

- **HDMI terminal.** If you'd like to see the images from your camera on a television screen, you'll need to buy an HDMI cable (not included with the camera) to connect this port to an HDTV set or monitor. The Alpha no longer supports video output to an old-style TV to a yellow composite video jack. The good news is that if you own a TV that supports Sony's Bravia sync protocol, you can use your Bravia remote control to control image display, mark images for printing, switch to index view, or perform other functions.
- **SD card slot.** Slide a Secure Digital card into this slot, with the label facing the front of the camera and the metal contact "fingers" inward. To remove the card, press inward, release, and it will pop out.
- **Memory Stick Pro Duo slot.** You might own some of the less-common Memory Stick Pro Duo cards (because you own other Sony products that use them). You can put them to work in your Sony Alpha, too. Insert with the metal contacts facing inwards and towards the front of the camera; the label will face the back of the camera. Press and release to pop out your memory card.
- **USB port.** Connect your camera to your computer using this port.

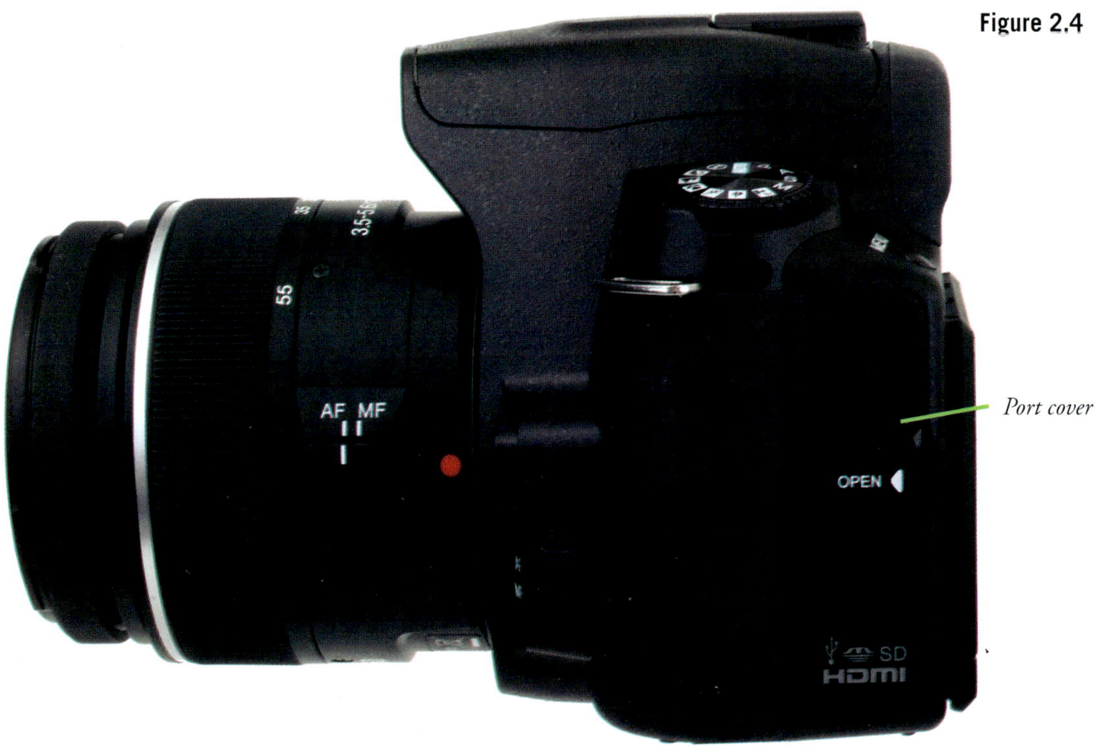

Figure 2.4

Figure 2.5

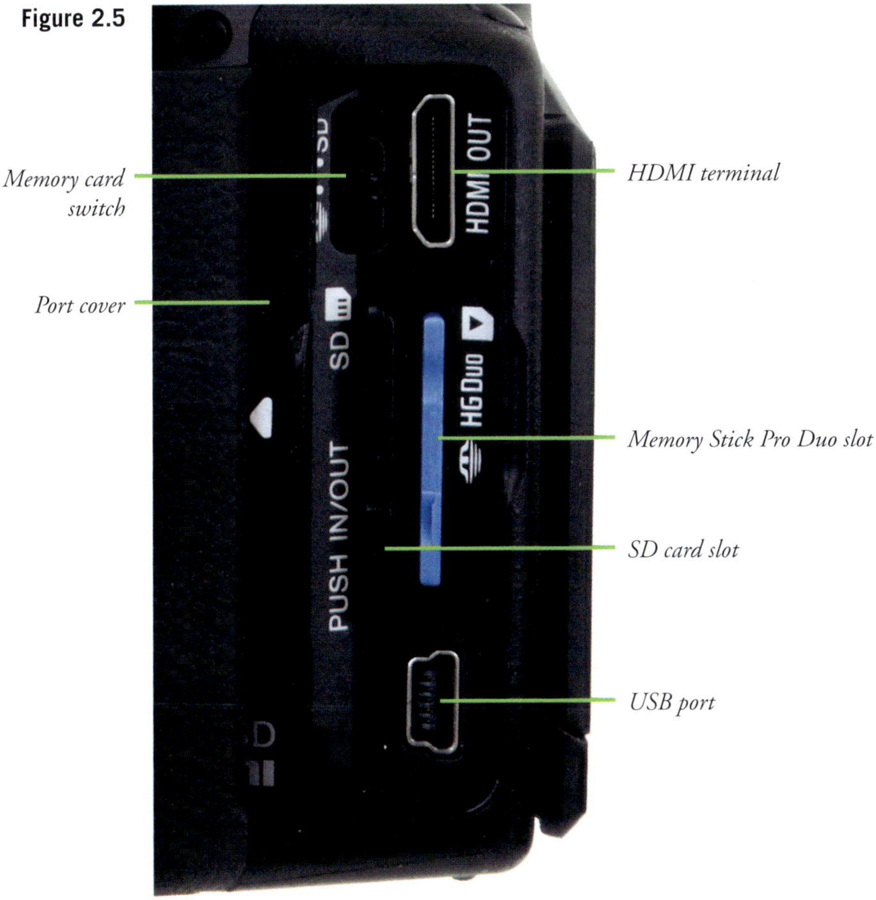

- **Memory card switch.** Your Alpha needs to be told which memory card to use. If you have only one of the two types of cards installed and the switch is set incorrectly, the camera will report that no card is inserted. If you see the flashing orange No Card message at the bottom right of the LCD, slide this switch to the correct orientation.
- **Port cover.** This sliding panel protects your slots and ports from dust and dirt when they're not in use. Keep it closed at other times.

The Sony Alpha's Business End

The back panel of the Sony Alpha bristles with more than a dozen different controls, buttons, and knobs. That might seem like a lot of controls to learn, but you'll find, as I noted earlier, that it's a lot easier to press a dedicated button and spin a dial than to jump to a menu every time you want to change a setting. The two models in this class, the A390 and A290 look identical, except that the A290's LCD does not tilt.

Most of the controls on the back panel of the Alpha are clustered on the right side of the body, with the exception of the MENU button perched on the back slope, just northeast of the LCD. The key components labeled in Figure 2.6 include

- **MENU button.** Summons/exits the menu displayed on the rear LCD of the Alpha. When you're working with submenus, this button also serves to exit a submenu and return to the main menu.
- **Memory card access lamp.** When lit or blinking, this lamp indicates that the memory card is being read from or written to.
- **DC power port (on side).** Plug in an optional DC power supply to this port. The optional Sony AC-PW10AM includes a cable that can be plugged directly into the Alpha to provide power.

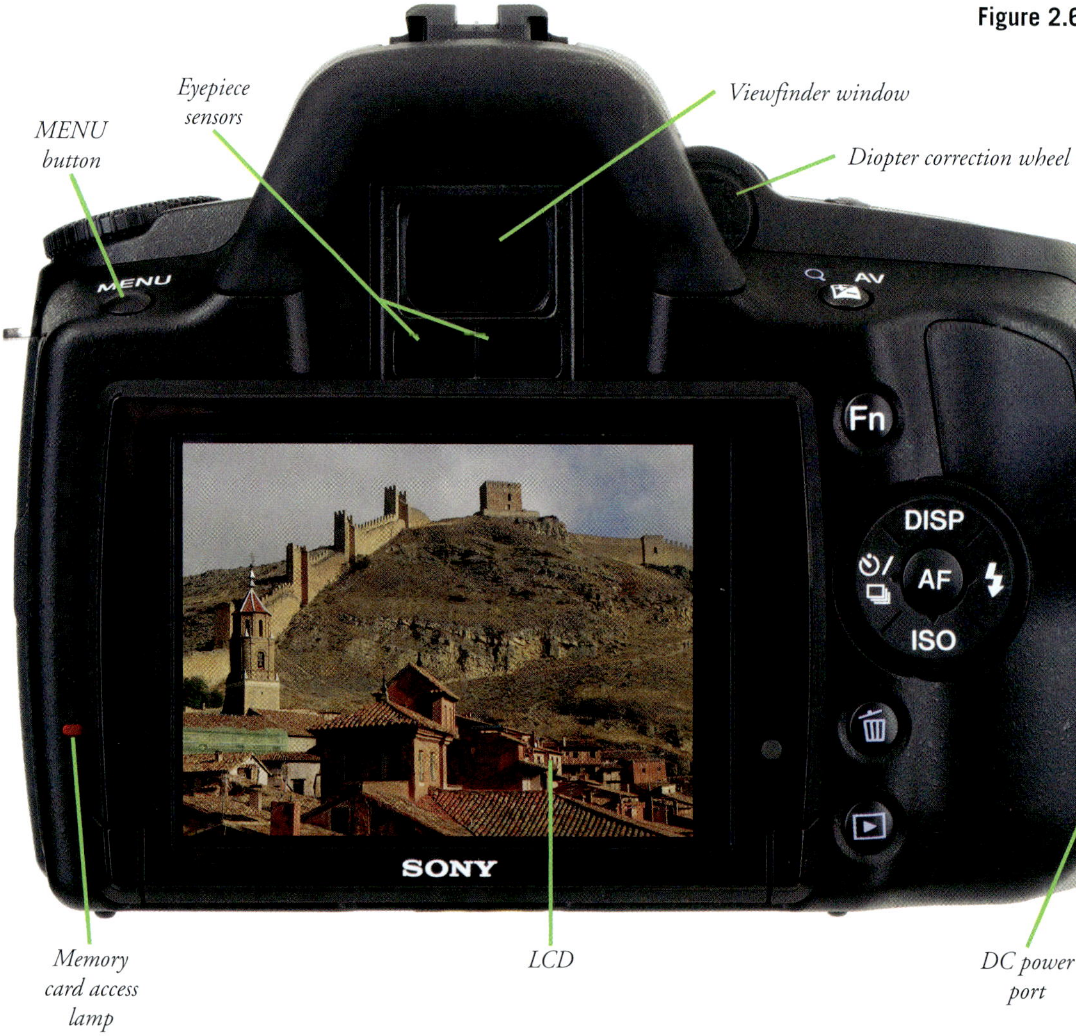

Figure 2.6

- **Viewfinder eyepiece.** You can frame your composition by peering into the viewfinder. It's surrounded by a removable soft rubber frame that seals out extraneous light when pressing your eye tightly up to the viewfinder, and it also protects your eyeglass lenses (if worn) from scratching. It can be removed and replaced by the viewfinder cap attached when you use the camera on a tripod, to ensure that light coming from the back of the camera doesn't venture inside and possibly affect the exposure reading. (I just cover the viewfinder with my hand, most of the time.)
- **Eye-Start sensors.** These sensors detect when your face or some other object approaches the viewfinder, and activates automatic focusing while turning off the LCD display. Some find this feature annoying, because it can be triggered by other objects (such as your body when carrying the camera, switched on, over your shoulder). In Chapter 3, I'll show you how to disable this function. You might also want to turn it off when using the optional FDA-M1AM magnifying eyepiece or FDA-A1AM right-angle finder, because your viewing position with these accessories attached may not allow the Eye-Start sensor to be activated.
- **Diopter correction wheel.** Rotate this to adjust eyesight correction applied when looking through the Alpha's viewfinder.
- **LCD.** This is the 2.7-inch display that shows your Live View preview (on the A390); image review after the picture is taken; recording information display before the photo is snapped; and all the menus used by the Sony Alpha.

The control cluster on the right side of the back of the camera includes these buttons, shown in Figure 2.7:

- **Zoom in/Exposure compensation button.** This button has several functions, which differ depending on the camera's active mode.

  In Shooting mode, with Program, Aperture priority, or Shutter priority modes, press this button to produce the Exposure Compensation display. Then, press the left/right controller keys to dial in more or less exposure. In Manual exposure mode, press this button while spinning the control dial to change the aperture. Release the button and spin the control dial to change the shutter speed.

  In Playback mode, press this button to zoom in, and press again to return to full screen view. When zoomed in, rotate the control dial to change from 1.1X to 14X magnification, with 27 intermediate steps.
- **Fn (Function) button.** In Shooting mode, pressing this button pops up a screen with options for selecting Autofocus mode, AF area, Metering mode, the Dynamic Range Optimizer (to improve highlight/shadow detail), White Balance (color bias) settings, or a Creative Style (such as Vivid, Portrait, or Sunset). (See Figure 2.8.)

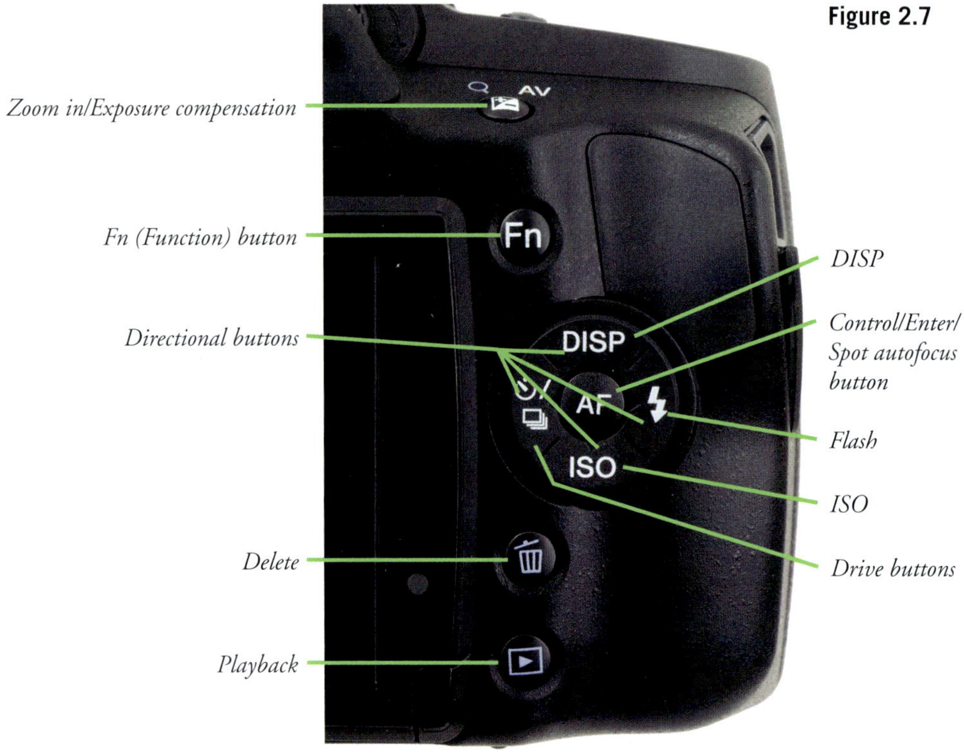

Figure 2.7

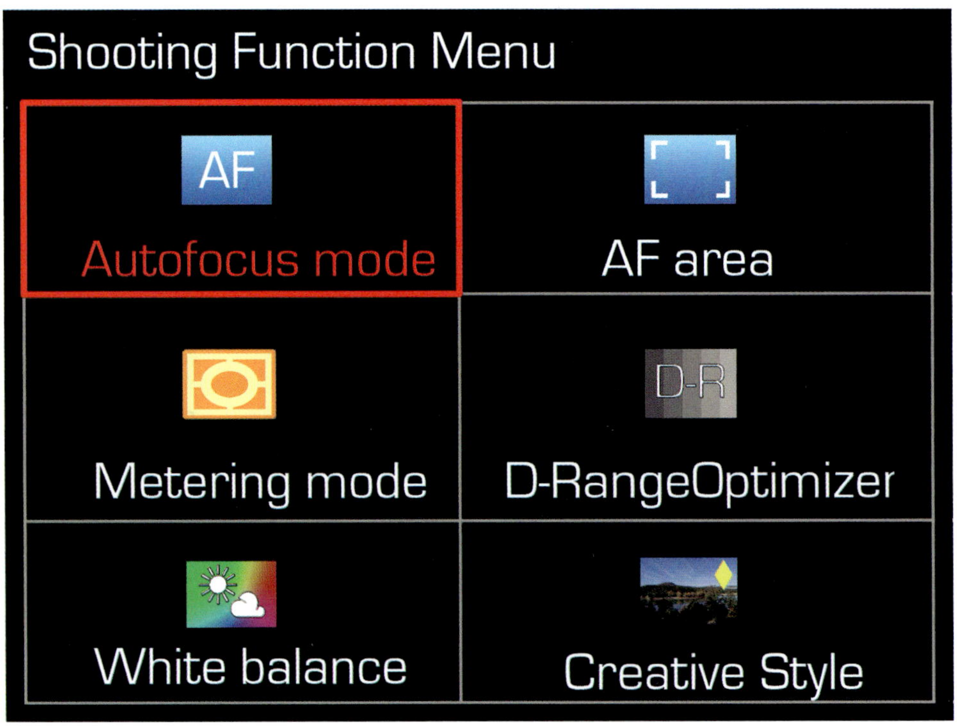

Figure 2.8

In Playback mode, press this button to pop up a screen that allows you to delete selected images, display a slide show, view image thumbnails, protect images from deletion, specify images for printing, or rotate the image 90 degrees. (See Figure 2.9.) All these menu choices will be explained in Chapter 3.

- **Controller/Enter/Spot button.** The center controller button can be used as an Enter key to confirm menu choices when a menu is shown on the screen. In Shooting mode, pressing this button switches to Spot autofocus. (I'll discuss autofocus options in Chapter 5.)
- **Directional buttons.** Press the left/right/up/down keys to navigate menus and to move the viewing area around within images. The left/right keys move to the previous/next image on your memory card in Playback mode, and allow you to navigate within displays of image thumbnails. Each of the four directional buttons also has a second function that is available when a menu or image is not displayed on the screen.
- **DISP button.** When in Shooting mode, press the DISP (up) button repeatedly to cycle between the two recording information displays available while you are taking photos. They are the Standard display (Figure 2.10) and Graphic display (Figure 2.11). I'll describe the data shown in the displays later in this chapter.

Figure 2.9

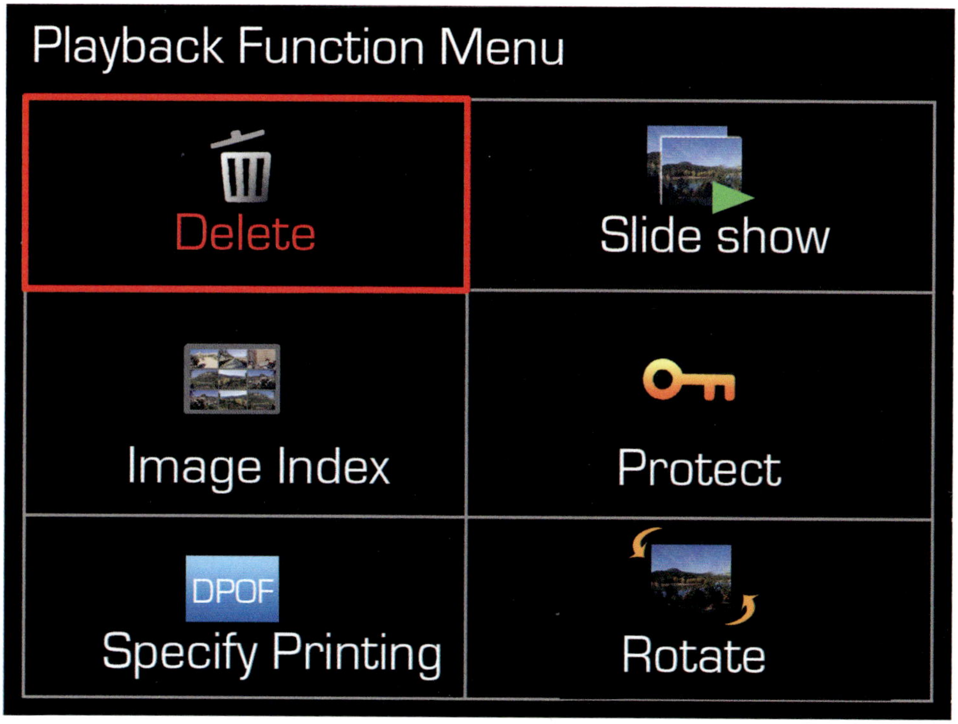

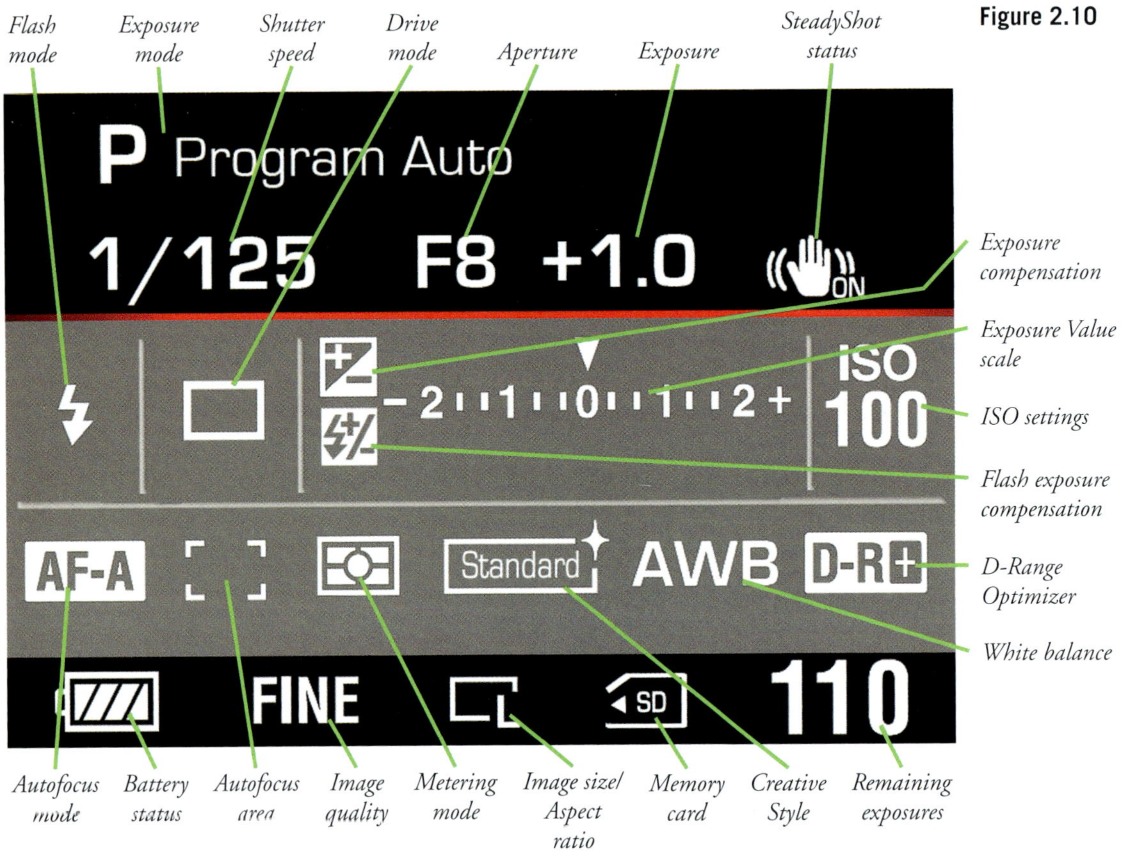

Figure 2.10

- **Drive button.** Press this button to produce a screen that allows choosing a Drive mode. Then press the up/down controller keys to select from either Single-shot advance; Continuous advance; Self-timer (with 10- and 2-second options available by pressing the left/right keys), Self-timer (cont.), which causes the Alpha to shoot either three or five images in a burst after a 10-second pause; Single-shot Bracketing, Continuous-shot Bracketing (three shots taken in a row with your choice of 0.3 or 0.7 increments selected with the left/right keys); and Remote Commander shooting (either immediately or after a two-second delay) when using the optional RMT-DSLR1 Wireless Remote Commander. You'll find more about these Drive modes in Chapter 4.
- **Flash button.** Press to access a menu of choices for flash mode, including Flash Off, Auto Flash, Fill-flash, Slow sync, Rear sync, and Wireless. I'll explain all the flash options in detail in Chapter 7.

Figure 2.11

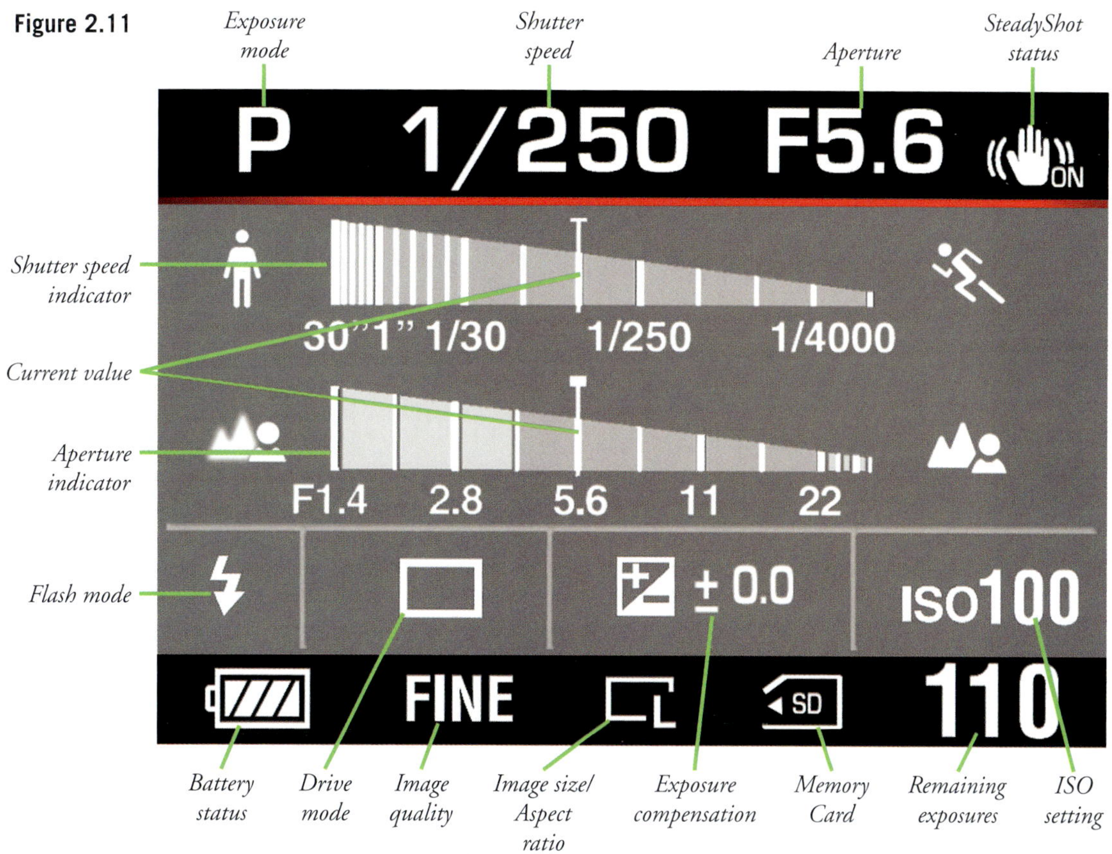

- **ISO button.** This button gives you access to a menu for specifying ISO sensor sensitivity settings, from ISO 100 to ISO 3200, plus Auto.
- **Delete button.** Press once if you want to delete the image displayed on the LCD. Then press the up/down controller keys to choose Delete (to confirm your action) or Cancel (if you change your mind). Press the center controller button (Enter) to confirm your choice.
- **Playback button.** Displays the last picture taken. Thereafter, you can move back and forth among the available images by pressing the left/right controller keys or spinning the control dial to advance or reverse one image at a time. To quit playback, press this button again. The Alpha also exits Playback mode automatically when you press the shutter button (so you'll never be prevented from taking a picture on the spur of the moment because you happened to be viewing an image).

With the DSLR-A390, the LCD monitor can be pulled away from the camera body and tilted up or down to provide a variety of views from different viewing positions (see Figure 2.12).

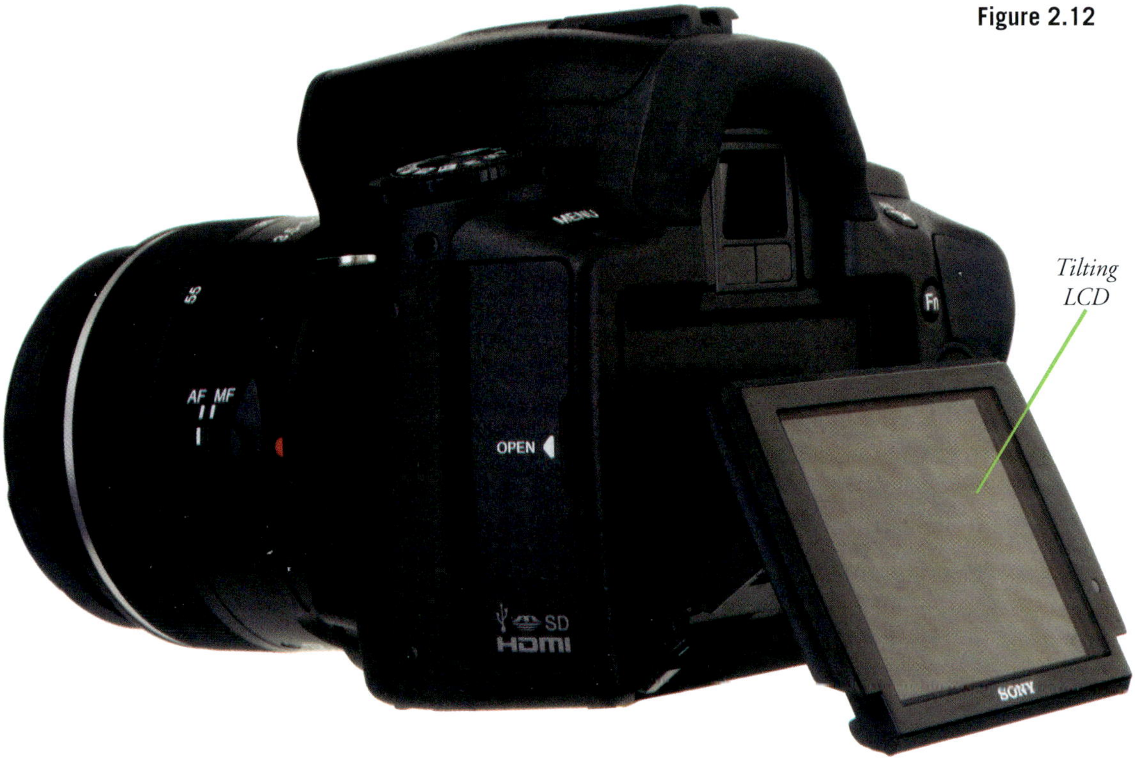

Figure 2.12

Going Topside

The top surface of the Sony Alpha DSLR-A390/A290 has a few frequently accessed controls of its own. Only a few are located on the left side of the camera. They are labeled in Figure 2.13:

- **Mode dial.** Rotate this dial to switch among Scene modes and Semi-automatic and Manual exposure modes. You'll find these exposure modes and options described in more detail in Chapter 4.
- **Accessory/Flash hot shoe.** Slide an electronic flash into this mount when you need a more powerful Speedlight. A dedicated flash unit, like those from Sony, can use the multiple contact points shown to communicate exposure, zoom setting, white balance information, and other data between the flash and the camera. There's more on using electronic flash in Chapter 7. Unfortunately, Sony, like its Minolta predecessors (since 1988), uses a non-standard accessory/flash shoe mount, rather than

Figure 2.13

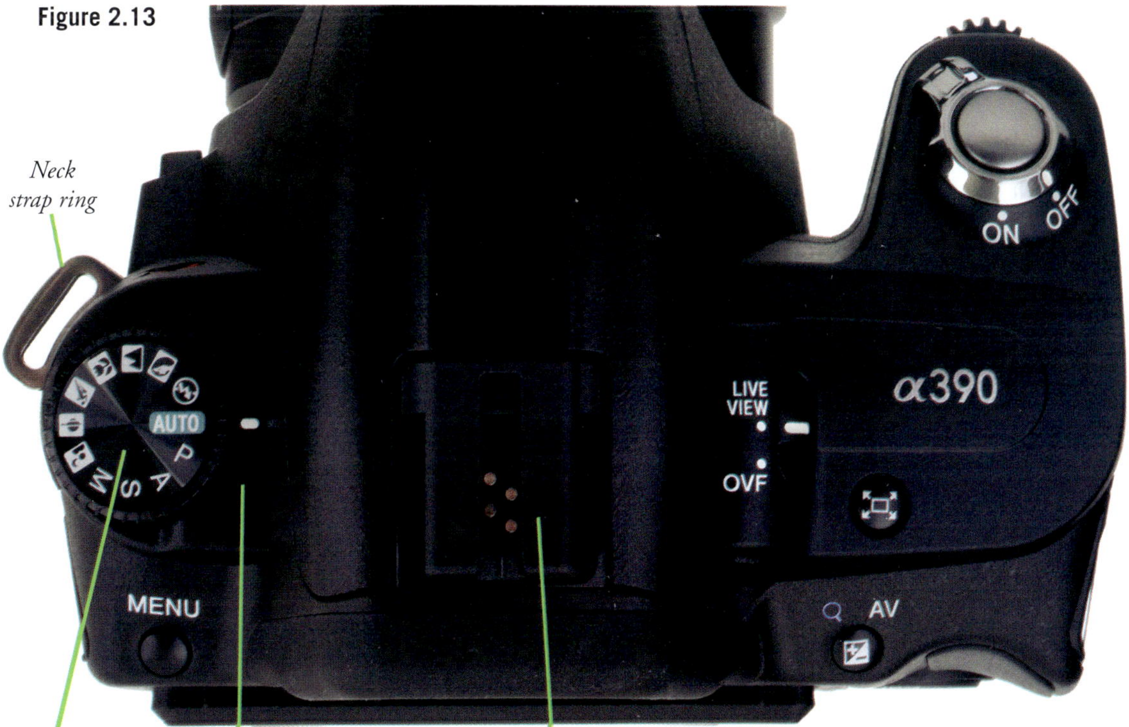

the industry standard ISO 518 configuration. This keeps you from attaching electronic flash units, radio triggers, and other accessories built for the standard shoe, unless you use one of the available adapters.

- **Neck strap rings.** Attach your strap to these two anchor points.
- **Sensor focal plane.** Precision macro and scientific photography sometimes requires knowing exactly where the focal plane of the sensor is. The symbol etched on the side of the pentaprism marks that plane.

On the right side of the camera, you can see a cluster of controls, labeled in Figure 2.14.

- **Power switch.** Rotate all the way clockwise to turn the Alpha on; in the opposite direction to switch it off.
- **Smart teleconverter (A390 only).** This is an oddball feature that you won't see a lot outside of the Sony product line. Available only in Live View, press the button once or twice, and it activates a digital "zoom" feature that crops a center portion of your image and stores it as a Medium resolution or Small resolution file. This "zoom" provides the illusion of a 1.4X (one press) or 2X (two press) magnification. But what you end up with is a cropped, lower resolution image. For example, with the A390, the 1.4X crop results in a 3264 × 2176-pixel, 7 MP (Medium resolution) image

carved out of the center of your original 14.2 MP picture. The 2X crop gives you a 2416 × 1600-pixel, 3.8 MP (Small resolution) image. I'm not crazy about digital zooms, but the 1.4X crop and the A390's 14.2 MP original resolution can give you decent results.

- **Control dial.** This dial on the front of the camera is used to make many shooting settings. In Manual exposure mode, the control dial is used to set shutter speed; press the Exposure Compensation button while spinning the control dial to set aperture.
- **Shutter release button.** Partially depress this button to lock in exposure and focus. Press all the way to take the picture. Tapping the shutter release when the camera has turned off the autoexposure and autofocus mechanisms reactivates both. When a review image is displayed on the back-panel color LCD, tapping this button removes the image from the display and reactivates the autoexposure and autofocus mechanisms.
- **Live View/Optical Viewfinder switch (A390 only).** Slide this switch forward to turn on Live View, discussed in much more detail in Chapter 5. In the aft position, Live View is disabled, and viewing is done through the optical viewfinder (OVF).

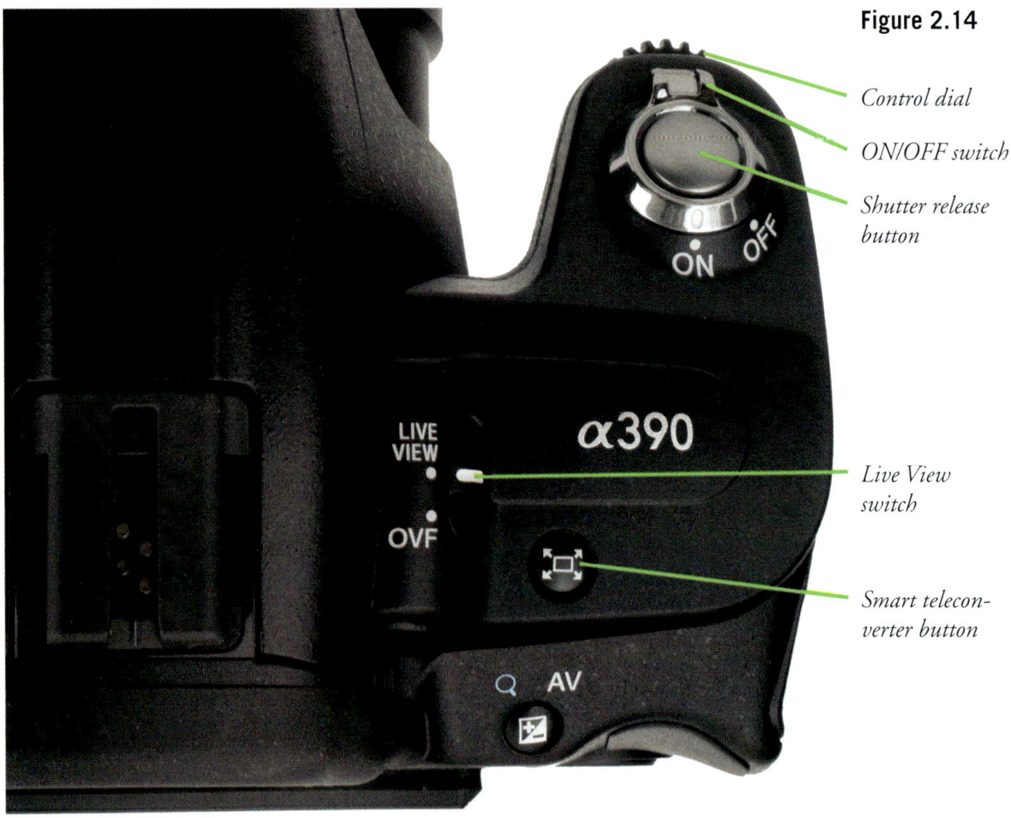

Figure 2.14

Underneath Your Sony Alpha

The bottom panel of your Sony Alpha is pretty bare. You'll find a tripod socket, which secures the camera to a tripod, and the battery cover. Figure 2.15 shows the underside view of the camera.

Figure 2.15

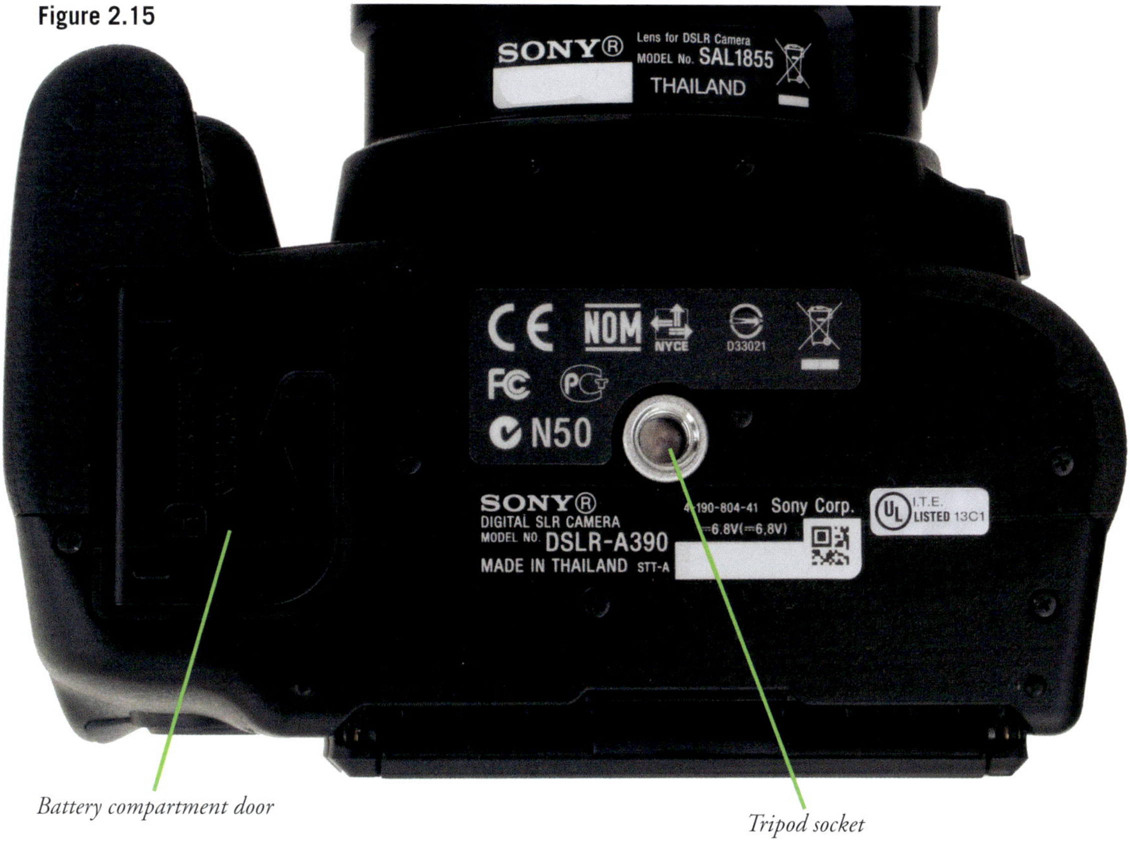

Lens Components

There's not a lot going on with most Sony lenses in terms of controls because, in the modern electronic age, most of the functions previously found in lenses in the ancient film era, such as autofocus options, are taken care of by the camera itself. Nor do Sony lenses require an on/off switch for image stabilization, because SteadyShot is built into the sensor components. Figure 2.16 shows a Sony 18-70mm lens and its components. I'm also going to mention some other features not found in this particular lens.

- **Lens hood bayonet.** This is used to mount the lens hood for lenses that don't use screw-mount hoods (the majority).
- **Zoom ring.** Turn this ring to change the zoom setting.

- **Zoom scale.** These markings on the lens show the current focal length selected.
- **Focus ring.** This is the ring you turn when you manually focus the lens.
- **Electrical contacts.** On the back of the lens (see Figure 2.16) are electrical contacts that the camera uses to communicate focus, aperture setting, and other information.
- **Lens bayonet.** This mount is used to attach the lens to a matching bayonet on the camera body.
- **Filter thread (not shown).** Lenses (including those with a bayonet lens hood mount) have a thread on the front for attaching filters and other add-ons. Some also use this thread for attaching a lens hood (you screw on the filter first, and then attach the hood to the screw thread on the front of the filter). Both the 18-70 and 18-55mm lenses have a 55mm filter thread, not shown in this figure.
- **Distance scale (not shown).** Some upscale lenses, including the Zeiss optics designed for Sony cameras, have this readout that rotates in unison with the lens's focus mechanism to show the distance at which the lens has been focused. (The illustrated lens does not have a distance scale.) It's a useful indicator for double-checking autofocus, roughly evaluating depth-of-field, and for setting manual focus guesstimates.

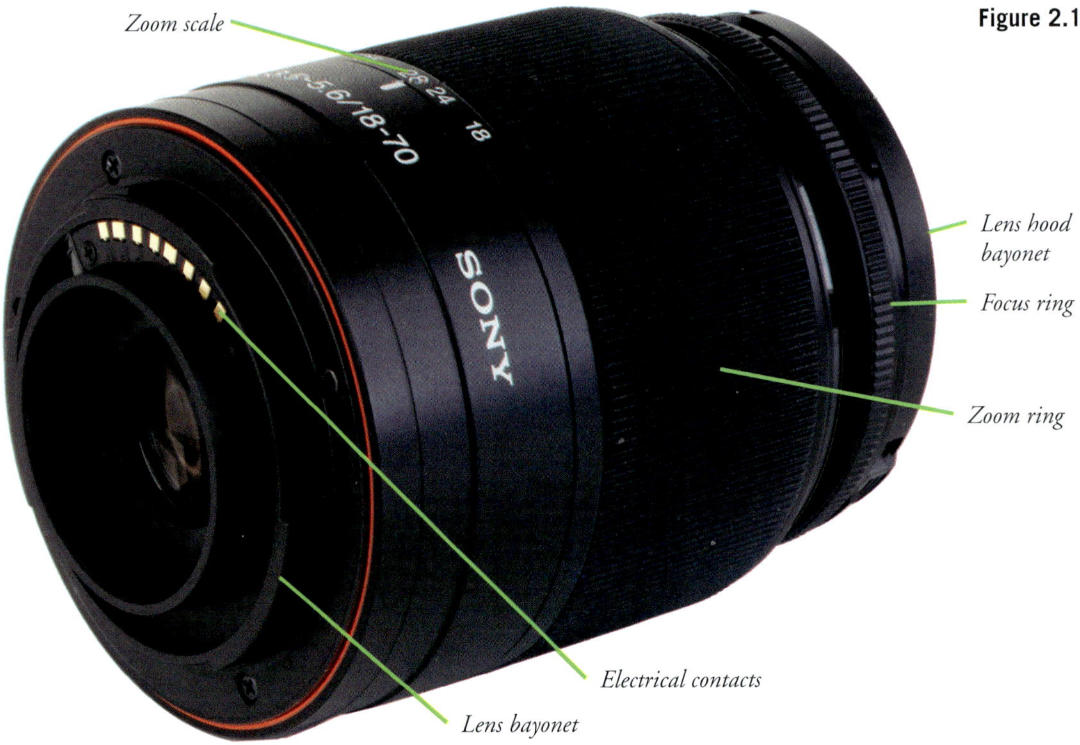

Figure 2.16

LCD Panel Readouts

The Sony Alpha's generously expansive 2.7-inch color LCD shows you everything you need to see, from images to a collection of informational data displays. Here's an overview of these displays. The recording information displays, shown earlier in Figures 2.10 and 2.11, should appear on the LCD when you're shooting photos. If you have the Eye-Start autofocus feature activated, the camera will begin to autofocus and the recording information display will vanish when you bring the Alpha up to your face, or the viewfinder is near any other object. (Press the DISP button to produce it if you want to activate this display when it is not active.) When you rotate the camera to shoot vertical pictures, the text and icons on the recording information displays re-orient themselves, too, for easy viewing.

The information shown in the Standard and Graphic recording information displays includes the following information, with not all of the data available all the time, and the two types of screens showing slightly different types of data. I've indicated which information is available in only one of the two display modes.

- **Exposure mode.** Shows whether you're using Program auto, Aperture priority, Shutter priority, Manual, or one of the Scene modes.
- **Shutter speed.** Shows the current shutter speed.
- **Aperture.** Displays the current f/stop.
- **SteadyShot status.** Shows whether the Alpha's anti-shake features are on or off.
- **Flash mode.** Provides flash mode information.
- **Drive mode.** Shows whether camera is set for Single-shot, Continuous shooting, or Self-timer.
- **Exposure compensation.** Displays whether exposure compensation is in effect. In Graphic mode, the amount of EV correction is shown next to the icon; in Standard mode, it's shown on the top line of the display.
- **Battery status.** Remaining battery life is indicated by this icon.
- **Image quality.** Your image quality setting (JPEG Fine, JPEG Standard, RAW, or RAW+JPEG).
- **Image size/Aspect Ratio.** Shows whether you are shooting Large, Medium, or Small resolution images, and whether the Alpha is set for the 3:2 aspect ratio or wide-screen 16:9 aspect ratio (the icon changes to a "stretched" version).
- **Memory card.** Indicates whether a Secure Digital or Memory Stick Pro Duo card is being used.
- **Remaining Exposures.** Shows the number of shots remaining on the memory card.

- **ISO settings.** Indicates the sensor ISO sensitivity setting.
- **Exposure value scale (Standard only).** This scale shows the relative exposure.
- **Exposure (Standard only).** The amount of exposure compensation is shown here in Standard display mode.
- **Flash exposure compensation (Standard only).** This icon is shown when flash exposure compensation is being applied.
- **Autofocus mode (Standard only).** Tells whether AF-S, AF-C, or AF-A autofocus mode is active, as described in Chapter 1.
- **Autofocus area (Standard only).** Shows the autofocus area mode in use: Wide (the camera chooses one of the nine AF areas to use; or the center area when the control button is pressed); Spot (the camera uses the center AF area exclusively); or Local (you choose which of the nine areas to use, except when the control button is held down and the center spot is used instead). I'll explain autofocus options in more detail in Chapter 5.
- **Metering mode (Standard only).** The icons represent Multi segment, Center weighted, or Spot metering. (See Chapter 4 for more detail.)
- **Creative Style (Standard only).** Indicates which of the Creative Style settings are being applied.
- **White balance (Standard only).** Shows current white balance setting.
- **D-Range Optimizer (Standard only).** Indicates the type of D-Range optimization (highlight/shadow enhancement) in use, either Standard, Advanced, or Off, as described in Chapter 3.
- **Shutter speed indicator (Graphics only).** Graphically illustrates that faster shutter speeds are better for action/slower for scenes with less movement.
- **Aperture indicator (Graphics only).** Icons indicate that wider apertures produce less depth-of-field (represented by a "blurry" background icon).

When reviewing images you've taken (press the Playback button to summon the last shot exposed to the LCD), the Alpha shows you a picture for review; you can select from among three different information overlays. To switch among them, press the DISP button while the image is on the screen. The LCD will cycle among the Single image display with no extra data at all (Figure 2.17); Single image display with recording data (Figure 2.18); and a Histogram display, which shows basic shooting information as well as a brightness histogram at bottom right, with individual histograms for the red, green, and blue channels (Figure 2.19). I'll explain how to work with histograms in Chapter 4.

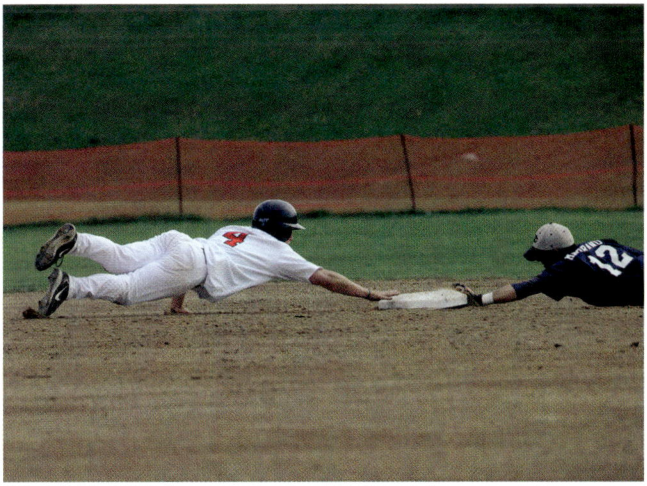

Figure 2.17
Image playback display: Single image.

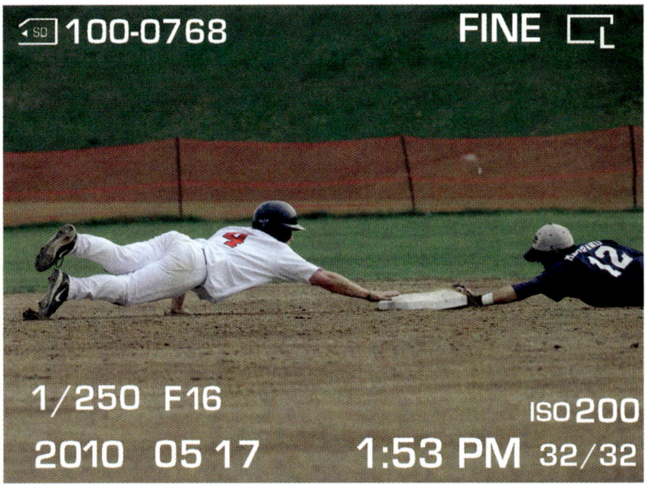

Figure 2.18
Image playback display: Single image with recording information.

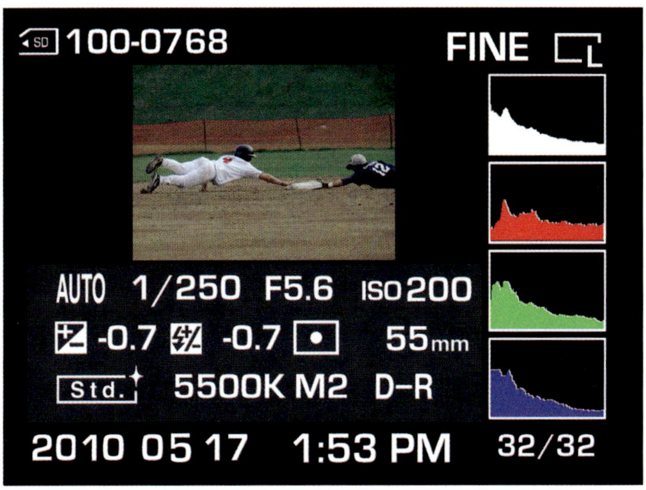

Figure 2.19
Image playback display: Histogram view.

Looking Inside the Viewfinder

Much of the important shooting status information is shown inside the viewfinder of the Sony Alpha. As with the displays shown on the color LCD, not all of this information will be shown at any one time. Figure 2.20 shows what you can expect to see. I'll explain all of these readouts later in this book, with those pertaining to exposure in Chapter 4, and those relating to flash in Chapter 7. These readouts include

- **Image area for 16:9 aspect ratio.** These four lines, arranged in pairs at the top and bottom of the viewfinder, can be used as your guideline for framing images when the Alpha is set to shoot using a 16:9 (HDTV) aspect ratio, as described in Chapter 3.
- **Autofocus area.** The four brackets show the area in which the Alpha's nine autofocus sensors operate.

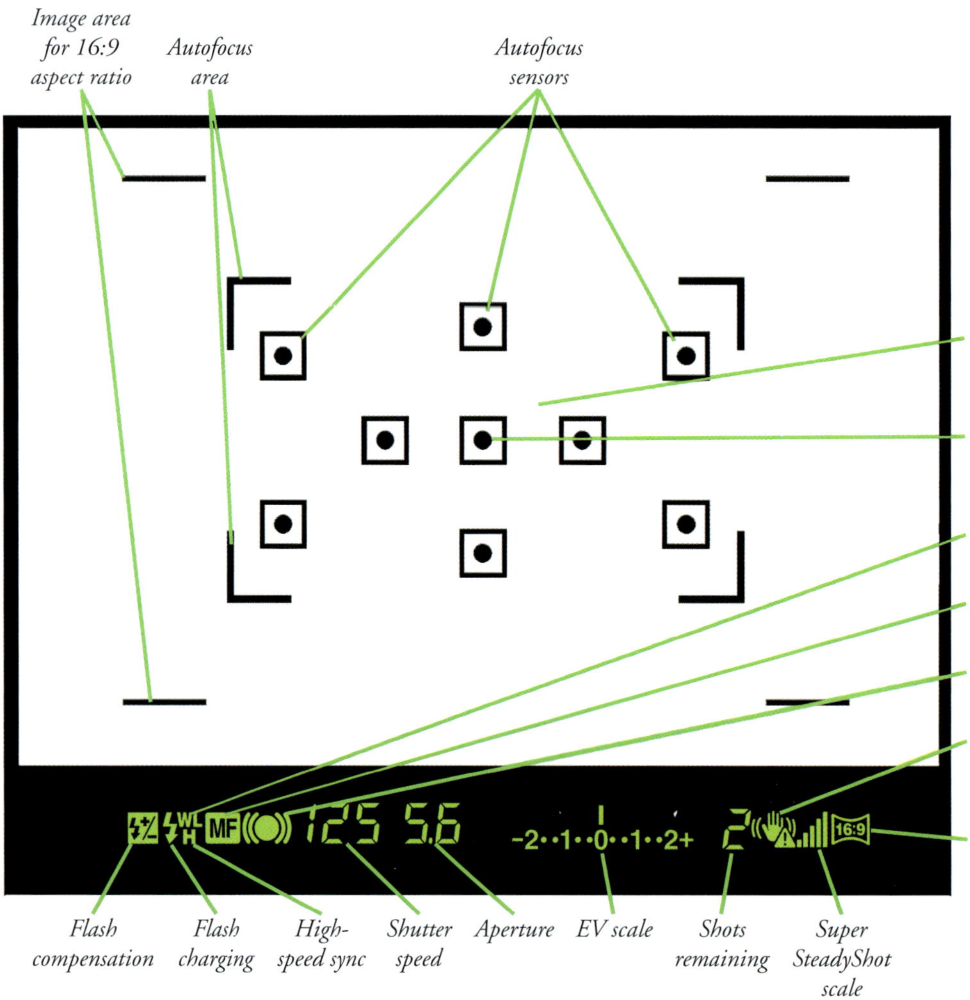

Figure 2.20

- **Autofocus sensors.** The nine boxes in the center of the viewfinder area show the position of the sensors used by the Alpha to focus. The camera can select the appropriate focus zone for you, or you can manually select one or all of the zones.
- **Autofocus center spot.** This marks the ninth autofocus sensor, which is a cross-type sensor that operates in both horizontal and vertical directions.
- **Flash charging indicator.** This icon appears when the flash is fully charged. It also shows when the flash exposure lock has been applied for an inappropriate exposure value.
- **Flash exposure compensation.** Appears when flash EV changes have been made.
- **Wireless flash.** This icon appears when you are using an external flash that is not attached to the camera but linked through wireless mode. You can read about this capability in Chapter 7.
- **High-speed sync.** You can synchronize Sony's external flash units with any shutter speed using high-speed sync mode. This icon appears when you are using that mode. Read about it in Chapter 7.
- **Manual focus.** The MF indicator appears when you have set the camera for manual focus, using the switch on the side of the camera, or when you are using a manual focus lens.
- **Focus status.** Shows current focus status: an illuminated circle when focus is locked; a circle flanked by round brackets when focus is confirmed, but the Alpha is still following the movement of a non-stationary object; a set of circular brackets when the camera is still focusing; or a flashing disk when the Alpha is unable to focus and has locked the shutter release.
- **Shutter speed/aperture readouts.** These readouts show the current shutter speed and aperture.
- **EV scale.** This scale shows the current exposure level, with the bottom indicator centered when the exposure is correct as metered. The indicator may also move to the left or right to indicate under- or overexposure (respectively). When bracketing, three indicators appear on the scale, showing the relative exposure of each bracketed image.
- **Camera shake warning.** If the Alpha is setting the shutter speed (for example, in Scene modes, or Aperture priority mode), this alert appears when the shutter speed is so slow that camera shake is likely to cause blurring. That's your signal to use SteadyShot, take control of the shutter speed yourself (switching to Manual, Shutter priority, or Program auto modes), or to mount your camera on a tripod (which can be necessary for very long exposures, even when using SteadyShot).

- **SteadyShot scale.** When SteadyShot is active, this scale shows the relative amount of camera shake that SteadyShot is dealing with. High levels of shake show more "bars" on the scale. You should wait until the number of bars decreases before shooting, as that indicates that camera shake is under control.
- **16:9 aspect ratio.** This indicator shows that you have set the Alpha to capture images using the cropped 16:9 (HDTV) aspect ratio, rather than the normal 3:2 ratio.
- **Shots remaining.** Changes to a number to indicate the number of frames that can be taken consecutively using the current settings.

3

Setting Up Your Sony Alpha DSLR-A390/A290

The Sony Alpha DSLR-A390 and A290 have a remarkable number of options and settings you can use to customize the way your camera operates. Not only can you change shooting settings used at the time the picture is taken, but you can adjust the way your camera behaves. This chapter will help you sort out the settings for all the Alpha's menus. These include the Recording and Playback menus, which determine how the Alpha uses many of its shooting features to take a photo and how it displays images on review. I'll also show you how to use the Setup menu to adjust power-saving timers, specify Live View options (with the A390), control your built-in flash, and work with the Sony Alpha's useful Custom menu functions.

This book isn't intended to replace the manual you received with your Alpha, nor have I any interest in rehashing its contents. You'll still find the original manual useful as a standby reference that lists every possible option in exhaustive (if mind-numbing) detail—without really telling you how to use those options to take better pictures. There is, however, some unavoidable duplication between the Sony manual and this chapter, because I'm going to explain all the key menu choices and the options you may have in using them. You should find, though, that I will give you the information you need in a much more helpful format, with plenty of detail on why you should make some settings that are particularly cryptic.

I'm not going to waste a lot of space on some of the more obvious menu choices in these chapters. For example, you can probably figure out, even without my help, that the Audio Signals option deals with the solid-state beeper in your camera that sounds off during various activities (such as the self-timer countdown). You can certainly decipher the import of the two options available for the Audio Signals (On and Off). In this chapter, I'll devote no more than a sentence or two to the blatantly obvious settings and concentrate on the more confusing aspects of Alpha setup, such as autofocus. I'll start with an overview of using the Alpha's menus themselves.

Anatomy of the Sony Alpha's Menus

The Alpha has one of the best designed menu systems of any digital SLR in its price class, with a remarkable amount of consistency with other cameras in the Sony current product line. The menu system is significantly revamped from the original Sony Alpha DSLR-A100, but the changes have been for the better.

The Sony Alpha has a series of seven separate tabbed menus, each with a single screen of entries, arranged in rows. You'll never need to scroll within a menu to see all the entries; however, if you scroll down to the bottom of any given menu, and then past the last entry, you'll be taken automatically to the first entry in the next tab. The menus are much cleaner, too. Just press the MENU button, located in the upper-left corner of the back of the camera, and use the left/right controller keys to highlight the menu tab you want to access, and then use the up/down controller keys or spin the control dial to highlight the menu entry you want. What could be easier?

Pressing the MENU button brings up a typical menu. (If the camera goes to "sleep" while you're reviewing a menu, you may need to wake it up again by tapping the shutter release button.) There are seven menu tabs: Recording 1, Recording 2, Custom, Playback, Setup 1, Setup 2, and Setup 3.

Of course, not everything is set using these menus. The Alpha also has direct setting controls, such as the AV/zoom button and Smart Teleconverter buttons that bypass the multilayered menu system to provide quick access to some features. The DISP, Drive, Flash, and ISO menus can be accessed by pressing the directional buttons on the control pad that are assigned to them. And even more direct access adjustment screens are available when you press the Fn (Function) button, which produces the Shooting Functions and Playback Function menus and submenus, introduced in Chapters 1 and 2 and discussed in more detail in this chapter.

When working with any of these different menus, after you've moved the menu highlighting with the up/down controller keys to the menu item you want to work with, press the center controller button to select it. A submenu with a list of options for the selected menu item will appear. Within the submenu options, you can scroll up or down with the up/down controller keys to choose a setting, and then press the center controller button to confirm the choice you've made. Press the MENU button again to exit.

Recording 1/2 Menu

The various direct setting buttons on the Alpha for Drive mode, ISO, or Exposure Compensation are likely to be the most frequent settings modifications you make, with changes during a particular session fairly common. You'll find that the Recording menu options are those that you access second-most frequently when you're using your Sony Alpha. You might make such adjustments as you begin a shooting session, or when you move from one type of subject to another. Sony makes accessing these changes very easy.

Figure 3.1 shows Recording 1 menu.

This section explains the options of the two Recording menus and how to use them. The options you'll find in these menus include the following:

- Image size
- Aspect ratio
- Quality
- Flash compensation
- AF illuminator
- SteadyShot
- Color Space
- Long exp. NR
- High ISO NR

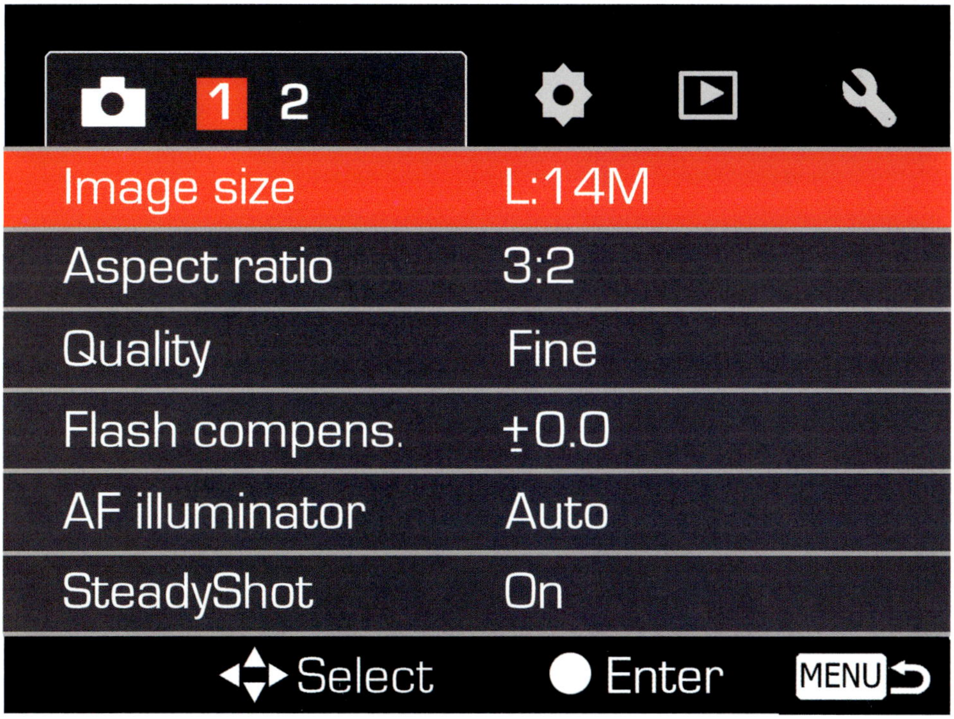

Figure 3.1 The Sony Alpha's Recording 1 menu.

Image Size

Options: Large, Medium, and Small

Default: L (Large)

Here you can choose the A390/A290's Large, Medium, and Small image settings. Select the menu option, and use the up/down controller keys to choose L, M, or S. Then press the center controller button to confirm your choice. Of course, the resolution of each of these options depends on whether you're using the standard 3:2 aspect ratio or the optional 16:9 HDTV aspect ratio (described next). Table 3.1 provides a comparison.

There are few reasons to use anything other than the Large setting with either camera, even if reduced resolution is sufficient for your application, such as photo ID cards or web display. Starting with a full-size image gives you greater freedom for cropping and fixing problems with your image editor. An 800 × 600-pixel web image created from a full-resolution original often ends up better than one that started out at 1920 × 1280 pixels.

Of course, the Medium and Small settings make it possible to squeeze more pictures onto your memory card, and if you're working with an A390, a 7.7 MP image is nothing to sneeze at—it's a resolution that approaches the maximum of some very fine cameras of the last few years. Smaller image sizes might come in handy in situations where your storage is limited and/or you don't have the opportunity to offload the pictures you've taken to your computer. For example, if you're on vacation and plan to make only 4 × 6-inch snapshot prints, a lower resolution can let you stretch your memory card's capacity. The A390 can fit 1,108 of those 7.7 MP Medium shots in JPEG Fine quality mode onto a 4GB memory card. Most of the time, however, it makes more sense to simply buy more memory cards and use your camera at its maximum resolution.

Table 3.1 Image Sizes Available

DSLR-A390	Megapixels 3:2 Aspect Ratio	Resolution 3:2 Aspect Ratio	Megapixels 16:9 Aspect Ratio	Resolution 16:9 Aspect Ratio
Large (L)	14 MP	4,592 × 3,056	12 MP	4,592 × 2,576
Medium (M)	7.7 MP	3,408 × 2,272	6.5 MP	3,408 × 1,920
Small (S)	3.5 MP	2,288 × 1,520	2.5 MP	2,288 × 1,280
DSLR-A290				
Large (L)	10 MP	3,872 × 2,592	8.4 MP	3,872 × 2,176
Medium (M)	5.6 MP	2,896 × 1,936	4.7 MP	2,896 × 1,632
Small (S)	3.5MP	1,920 × 1,280	2.1 MP	1,920 × 1,088

Aspect Ratio

Options: 3:2, 16:9 aspect ratios

Default: 3:2

The aspect ratio is simply the proportions of your image as stored in your image file. The standard aspect ratio for digital photography is approximately 3:2; the image is two-thirds as tall as it is wide. These proportions conform to that of the most common snapshot size in the USA, 4 × 6 inches. Of course, if you want to make a standard 8 × 10-inch enlargement, you'll need to trim some image area from either end, or use larger paper and end up with an 8 × 12-inch print. Aspect ratios are nothing new for 35mm film photographers (or those lucky enough to own a "full-frame" digital SLR). The 36 × 24mm frame (or 24 × 36mm) also has a 3:2 (2:3) aspect ratio.

If you're looking for images that will "fit" a wide-screen computer display, or a high-definition television, the Alpha models can be switched to a 16:9 aspect ratio that is much wider than it is tall. The camera performs this magic by cutting off the top and bottom of the frame, and storing a reduced resolution image. Your 14 MP image becomes a 12 MP shot. If you need the wide-screen look, the 16:9 aspect ratio will save you some time in image editing, but you can also achieve the same proportions (or any other aspect ratio) by trimming a full resolution image in your editor. As with the other basic menu choices in this chapter, just navigate to the entry, press the center controller button, choose the option you want, and press the center controller button again to confirm your choice.

Quality

Options: RAW, RAW & JPEG, Fine, Standard

Default: Fine

You can choose the image quality settings used by the Alpha to store its files. You have choices to make within this menu entry: RAW, RAW & JPEG, Fine, and Standard. (The two latter options are JPEG formats.) Here's what you need to know to choose intelligently:

- **JPEG compression.** To reduce the size of your image files and allow more photos to be stored on a given memory card, the Alpha uses JPEG compression to squeeze the images down to a smaller size. This compacting reduces the image quality a little, so you're offered your choice of Fine compression and Standard compression. Fine should really be your *standard,* because if offers the best image quality of the two JPEG options.

- **JPEG, RAW, or both.** You can elect to store only JPEG versions of the images you shoot (Fine and Standard), or you can save your photos as "unprocessed" RAW files, which consume several times as much space on your memory card. Or, you can store both at once as you shoot. Many photographers elect to save *both* JPEG and a RAW file (RAW & JPEG), so they'll have a JPEG version that might be usable as-is, as well as the original "digital negative" RAW file in case they want to do some processing of the image later. You'll end up with two different versions of the same file: one with a .jpg extension, and one with the .arw extension that signifies a Sony RAW.

As I noted under Image Size, there are some limited advantages to using the Medium and Small resolution settings, and similar space-saving benefits accrue to the Standard JPEG compression setting. They all allow stretching the capacity of your memory card so you can shoehorn quite a few more pictures onto a single memory card. That can come in useful when on vacation and you're running out of storage, or when you're shooting non-critical work that doesn't require full resolution (such as photos taken for real estate listings, web page display, photo ID cards, or similar applications). Some photographers like to record RAW+JPEG Fine so they'll have a JPEG file for review, while retaining access to the original RAW file for serious editing.

But for most work, using lower resolution and extra compression is false economy. You never know when you might actually need that extra bit of picture detail. Your best bet is to have enough memory cards to handle all the shooting you want to do until you have the chance to transfer your photos to your computer or a personal storage device.

JPEG vs. RAW

You'll sometimes be told that RAW files are the "unprocessed" image information your camera produces, before it's been modified. That's nonsense. RAW files are no more unprocessed than your camera film is after it's been through the chemicals to produce a negative or transparency. A lot can happen in the developer that can affect the quality of a film image—positively and negatively—and, similarly, your digital image undergoes a significant amount of processing before it is saved as a RAW file. Sony even applies a name (BIONZ) to the digital image processing (DIP) chip used to perform this magic in the Sony Alpha.

A RAW file is more similar to a film camera's processed negative. It contains all the information, with no compression, no sharpening, no application of any special filters or other settings you might have specified when you took the picture. Those settings are *stored* with the RAW file so they can be applied when the image is converted to a form compatible with your favorite image editor. However, using RAW conversion software such as Adobe Camera Raw or Sony's Image Data Converter SR, you can override those settings and apply settings of your own. You can select essentially the same changes there that you might have specified in your camera's picture-taking options.

RAW exists because sometimes we want to have access to all the information captured by the camera, before the camera's internal logic has processed it and converted the image to a standard file format. RAW doesn't save as much space as JPEG. What it does do is preserve all the information captured by your camera after it's been converted from analog to digital form.

So, why don't we always use RAW? Although some photographers do save only in RAW format, it's more common to use either RAW plus the JPEG option, or just shoot JPEG and eschew RAW altogether. While RAW is overwhelmingly helpful when an image needs to be fine-tuned, in other situations working with a RAW file can slow you down significantly. RAW images take longer to store on the memory card, and require more post-processing effort, whether you elect to go with the default settings in force when the picture was taken, or make minor adjustments.

As a result, those who depend on speedy access to images or who shoot large numbers of photos at once may prefer JPEG over RAW. Wedding photographers, for example, might expose several thousand photos during a bridal affair and offer hundreds to clients as electronic proofs for inclusion in an album. Wedding shooters take the time to make sure that their in-camera settings are correct, minimizing the need to post process photos after the event. Given that their JPEGs are so good, there is little need to get bogged down shooting RAW. Sports photographers also avoid RAW files for similar reasons.

JPEG was invented as a more compact file format that can store most of the information in a digital image, but in a much smaller size. JPEG predates most digital SLRs, and was initially used to squeeze down files for transmission over slow dialup connections. Even if you were using an early dSLR with 1.3-megapixel files for news photography, you didn't want to send them back to the office over a modem at 1,200 bps.

But, as I noted, JPEG provides smaller files by compressing the information in a way that loses some image data. JPEG remains a viable alternative because it offers several different quality levels. At the highest quality Fine level, you might not be able to tell the difference between the original RAW file and the JPEG version. With Standard compression, you'll usually notice a quality loss when making big enlargements or cropping your image tightly.

In my case, I shoot virtually everything at RAW & JPEG. Most of the time, I'm not concerned about filling up my memory cards, as I usually have a minimum of three 32GB memory cards with me. If I know I may fill up all those cards, I have a tiny battery-operated personal storage device that can copy a typical card in about 15 minutes. As I mentioned earlier, when shooting sports I'll shift to JPEG FINE (with no RAW file) to squeeze a little extra speed out of my Alpha's continuous shooting mode, and to reduce the need to wade through long series of photos taken in RAW format. On the other hand, on my last trip to Europe, I took only RAW photos and transferred more images onto my netbook as I planned on doing at least some post-processing on many of the images for a travel book I was working on.

MANAGING LOTS OF FILES

The only long-term drawback to shooting everything in RAW & JPEG is that it's easy to fill up your computer's hard drive if you are a prolific photographer. Here's what I do. My most recent photos are stored on my working hard drive in a numbered folder, say Alpha-01, with subfolders named after the shooting session, such as 100202Groundhog, for pictures of groundhogs taken on February 2, 2010. An automatic utility called Allway Sync copies new and modified photos to a different hard drive for backup as soon as they appear.

When the top-level folder accumulates about 30GB of images, I back it up to multiple DVDs and then move the folder to a drive dedicated solely for storage of folders that have already been backed up onto DVD. Then I start a new folder, such as Alpha-02, on the working hard drive and repeat the process. I always have at least one backup of every image taken, either on another hard drive or on a DVD.

Flash Compensation

Options: Flash compensation from –2 to +2 f/stops

Default: 0

This works like exposure compensation (discussed in Chapter 4), and allows you to dial in more or less exposure when using the flash. If your photo (such as a test shot) is too dark or too light, access this menu entry. Press the left/right controller keys to reduce or increase flash exposure; then press the center controller button to confirm your choice. If you've made a flash compensation adjustment, the amount of your compensation will be indicated by a pointer in the lower half of the exposure scale in the Detailed recording information display, and the Flash Compensation icon will be illuminated in the viewfinder whenever the flash is flipped up.

To nullify your flash compensation, return to this menu entry and return the pointer to the center of the scale.

AF Illuminator

Options: Auto, Off

Default: Auto

The AF illuminator is a pre-flash that fires when the flash is elevated and there is insufficient light for the Alpha's autofocus mechanism to zero in. The extra blast from the AF illuminator (either the built-in flash, or the equivalent function on an external flash) helps the camera focus sharply. The default setting, Auto, allows the AF illuminator to work any time the camera judges that it is necessary. Turn it off when you want to use flash, but would prefer not to use this feature. For example, the AF illuminator doesn't work when using AF-C focus mode, or when AF-A autofocus is used with a moving subject (which means it has shifted into AF-C mode). Nor will it work with lenses with focal lengths and zoom settings of 300mm or longer, or in manual focus mode.

SteadyShot

Options: On/Off

Default: On

This entry can be used to switch off the SteadyShot feature. You might want to do that when the camera is mounted on a tripod, as the additional anti-shake feature is not needed, and slight movements of the tripod can sometimes "confuse" the system. However, it's so rarely necessary to turn SteadyShot off that Sony removed the control switch for this option from the back of the camera (in the previous A350/A300/A200 models) to this simpler location in the menu system.

Color Space

Options: sRGB/Adobe RGB

Default: sRGB

The Alpha's Color Space option, the first entry on the second page of the Shooting menu (see Figure 3.2), gives you three variations of two different color spaces (also called *color gamuts*), named Adobe RGB (because it was developed by Adobe Systems in 1998), and sRGB (supposedly because it is the *standard* RGB color space). These two color gamuts define a specific set of colors that can be applied to the images your Alpha captures.

You're probably surprised that the Alpha doesn't automatically capture *all* the colors we see. Unfortunately, that's impossible because of the limitations of the sensor and the filters used to capture the fundamental red, green, and blue colors, as well as that of the phosphors used to display those colors on your camera and computer monitors. Nor is it possible to *print* every color our eyes detect, because the inks or pigments used don't absorb and reflect colors perfectly.

Instead, the colors that can be reproduced by a given device are represented as a color space that exists within the full range of colors we can see. That full range is represented by the odd-shaped splotch of color shown in Figure 3.3, as defined by scientists at an international organization back in 1931. The colors possible with Adobe RGB are represented by the larger, black triangle in the figure, while the sRGB gamut is represented by the smaller white triangle.

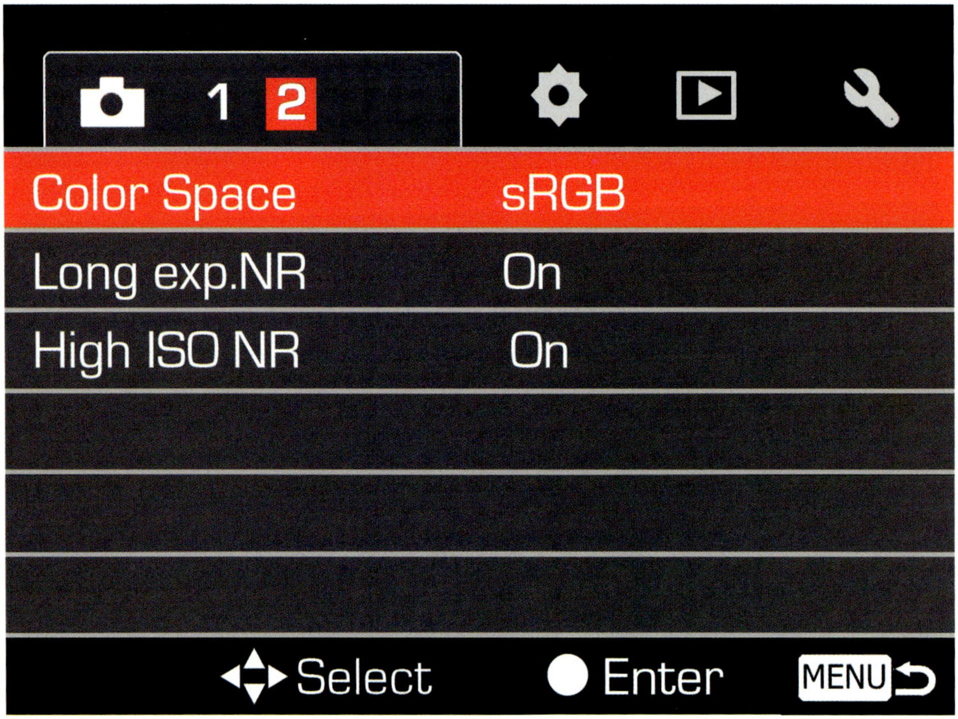

Figure 3.2
The Sony Alpha's Recording 2 menu.

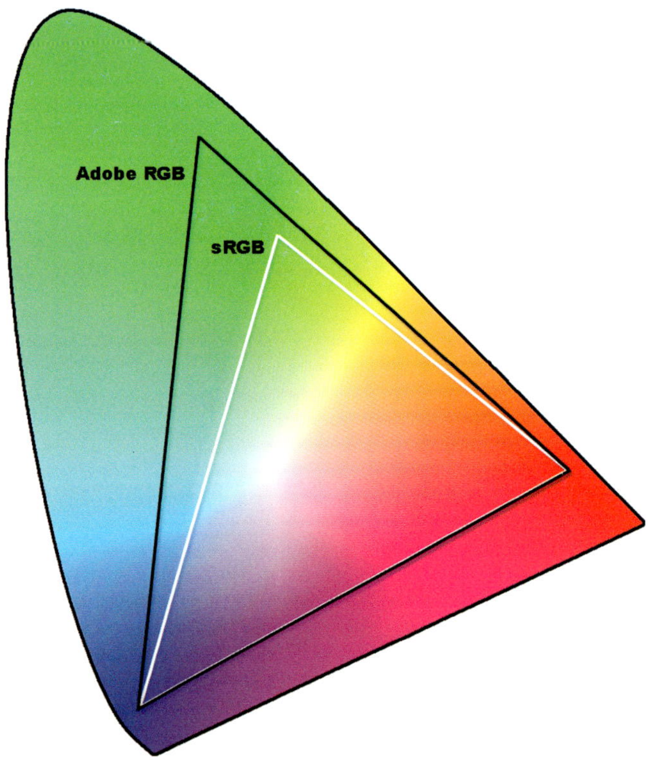

Figure 3.3
The outer figure shows all the colors we can see; the two inner outlines show the boundaries of Adobe RGB (black triangle) and sRGB (white triangle).

Regardless of which triangle—or color space—is used by the Alpha, you end up with 16.8 million different colors that can be used in your photograph. (No one image will contain all 16.8 million!) But, as you can see from the figure, the colors available will be *different*.

Adobe RGB is what is often called an *expanded* color space, because it can reproduce a range of colors that is spread over a wider range of the visual spectrum. Adobe RGB is useful for commercial and professional printing.

ADOBE RGB vs. sRGB

You might prefer sRGB, which is the default for the Sony Alpha cameras, as it is well suited for the colors displayed on a computer screen and viewed over the Internet. The sRGB setting is recommended for images that will be output locally on the user's own printer, or at a retailer's automated kiosk.

Adobe RGB is an expanded color space useful for commercial and professional printing, and it can reproduce a wider range of colors. It can also come in useful if an image is going to be extensively retouched within an image editor. You don't need to automatically "upgrade" your camera to Adobe RGB, because images tend to look less saturated on your monitor and, it is likely, significantly different from what you will get if you output the photo to your personal inkjet.

Strictly speaking, both sRGB and Adobe RGB can reproduce the exact same absolute *number* of colors (16.8 million when reduced to 8 bits per channel from the original capture). Adobe RGB spreads those colors over a larger space, much like a giant box of crayons in which some of the basic colors have been removed and replaced with new hues not in the original box. The "new" gamut contains a larger proportion of "crayons" in the cyan-green portion of the box, a better choice for reproduction with cyan, magenta, and yellow inks at commercial printers, rather than the red, green, and blue pixels of your computer display.

Long Exp. NR/High ISO NR

Options: On/Off

Default: On

I've grouped these two menu options together, because they work together, each under slightly different circumstances. Moreover, the causes and cures for noise involve some overlapping processes.

Your Alpha can reduce the amount of grainy visual noise in your photo, but, at the same time eliminate some of the detail along with the noise. These two menu choices let you choose whether to apply noise reduction to exposures of longer than one second and/or to apply noise reduction to exposures made at high ISO settings (ISO 1600 and ISO 3200), or to turn it off when you want to preserve detail even if it means a little extra noise.

Visual noise is that awful graininess that shows up as multicolored specks in images, and this setting helps you manage it. In some ways, noise is like the excessive grain found in some high-speed photographic films. However, while photographic grain is sometimes used as a special effect, it's rarely desirable in a digital photograph.

The visual noise-producing process is something like listening to a CD in your car, and then rolling down all the windows. You're adding sonic noise to the audio signal, and while increasing the CD player's volume may help a bit, you're still contending with an unfavorable signal to noise ratio that probably mutes tones (especially higher treble notes) that you really want to hear.

The same thing happens when the analog signal is amplified: You're increasing the image information in the signal, but boosting the background fuzziness at the same time. Tune in a very faint or distant AM radio station on your car stereo. Then turn up the volume. After a certain point, turning up the volume further no longer helps you hear better. There's a similar point of diminishing returns for digital sensor ISO increases and signal amplification as well.

These processes create several different kinds of noise. As I noted, noise can be produced from high ISO settings. As the captured information is amplified to produce higher ISO sensitivities, some random noise in the signal is amplified along with the photon information. Increasing the ISO setting of your camera raises the threshold of sensitivity so that fewer and fewer photons are needed to register as an exposed pixel. Yet, that also increases the chances of one of those phantom photons being counted among the real-life light particles, too.

A second way noise is created is through longer exposures. Extended exposure times allow more photons to reach the sensor, but increase the likelihood that some photosites will react randomly even though not struck by a particle of light. Moreover, as the sensor remains switched on for the longer exposure, it heats, and this heat can be mistakenly recorded as if it were a barrage of photons.

While noise reduction is often a good thing, you might want to turn it off for both long exposures and high ISOs to preserve image detail, and when the delay caused by the noise reduction process (it can take roughly the same amount of time as the exposure itself) interferes with your shooting. Or, you simply may not need NR. For example, you might be shooting waves crashing into the shore at ISO 100 with the camera mounted on a tripod, using a neutral-density filter and long exposure to cause the pounding water to blur slightly. To maximize detail in the non-moving portions of your photos, you can switch off long exposure noise reduction.

Custom Menu

The single Custom menu (see Figure 3.4) allows you to specify how your Alpha operates. If you find the Eye-Start autofocus feature distracting, you can change it here. If you'd like the control dial to adjust the aperture, rather than shutter speed by default in Manual mode, you can choose that behavior. There are five menu entries overall in the Custom menu.

- Eye-Start AF
- Ctrl dial setup
- Red-eye reduction
- Auto review
- Auto off /w VF

Eye-Start AF

Options: On, Off

Default: On

It's great how the Sony Alpha is able to read your mind and start autofocusing the instant you move the viewfinder to your eye. The image on the LCD vanishes, the camera adjusts autofocus, and, if you've selected an automatic exposure mode, it sets shutter

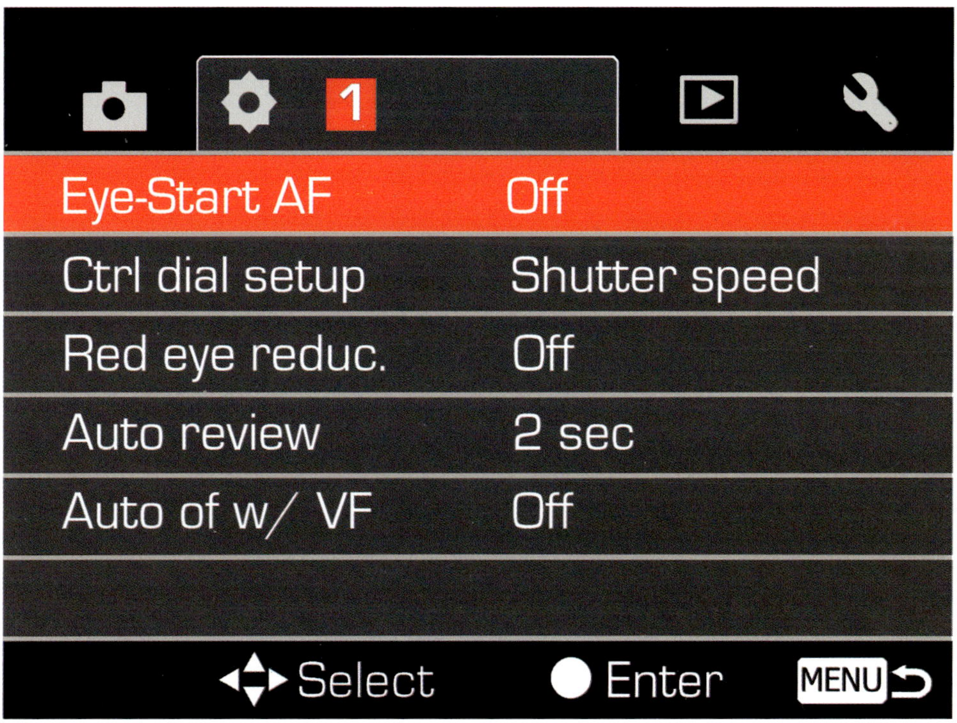

Figure 3.4 The Sony Alpha's Custom menu.

speed and/or aperture for you. You don't even have to partially depress the shutter release. Of course, it's not magic. There are a pair of sensors just below the viewfinder window that detect when your face (or anything else) approaches the finder.

On the one hand, Eye-Start AF can be convenient, especially when you're shooting fast-moving subjects and want to take pictures quickly. Indeed, you discover that focus is frequently achieved more rapidly than when Eye-Start AF is switched off and the Alpha defaults to the boring old behavior of not initiating focus until you partially depress the shutter button. On the other hand, some people find this feature annoying. The camera may turn off the LCD and switch on autofocus when a stray hand or other object passes near the viewfinder, and the feature does use significantly more battery power. If you choose to, you can turn off Eye-Start AF using this menu setting.

Ctrl Dial Setup

Options: Shutter speed, Aperture

Default: Shutter speed

Normally, spinning the control dial in Manual exposure mode changes the shutter speed; the aperture must be changed by holding down the Exposure Compensation/AV button while rotating the control dial. Use this setting to specify that the aperture is changed, instead, and that the shutter speed must be changed by pressing the AV button first.

In Program auto mode, the camera selects both shutter speed and aperture for you.

Use this menu option so that the exposure control (shutter speed or aperture) that you prefer to use is the default for both Manual and Program auto exposure modes.

Red-Eye Reduction

Options: On, Off

Default: Off

Unfortunately, your camera is unable, on its own, to *eliminate* the red-eye effects that occur when an electronic flash (or, rarely, illumination from other sources) bounces off the retinas of the eye and into the camera lens. Animals seem to suffer from yellow or green glowing pupils, instead; the effect is equally undesirable. The effect is worst under low-light conditions (exactly when you might be using a flash) as the pupils expand to allow more light to reach the retinas. The best you can hope for is to *reduce* or minimize the red-eye effect.

It's fairly easy to remove red-eye effects in an image editor (some image importing programs will do it for you automatically as the pictures are transferred from your camera or memory card to your computer). But, it's better not to have glowing red eyes in your photos in the first place.

When this feature is activated, the Alpha's flip-up flash issues a few brief bursts prior to taking the photo, theoretically causing your subjects' pupils to contract, reducing the effect. This option works only with the built-in flash, and doesn't produce any prebursts if you have an external flash attached. In most cases, the higher elevation of the external flash effectively prevents red-eye anyway.

Auto Review

Options: Off, 2 seconds, 5 seconds, 10 seconds

Default: 2 seconds

The Sony Alpha can display an image on the LCD for your review after the photo is taken. (When you shoot a continuous or bracketed series of images, only the last picture exposed is shown.) During this display, you can delete a disappointing shot by pressing the Delete key, or cancel picture review by tapping the shutter release, or performing another function. (You'll never be prevented from taking another picture because you were reviewing images on your LCD.) This option can be used to specify whether the review image appears on the LCD for 2, 5, or 10 seconds, or not at all. Of course, if Eye-Start is activated and the camera is near your eye, image review is cancelled, unless you use the Auto Off w/ VF function, described next.

Depending on how you're working, you might want a quick display (especially if you don't plan to glance at each picture as it's taken), or might prefer a more leisurely examination (when you're carefully checking compositions). Other times, you might not want to have the review image displayed at all, such as when you're taking photos in a darkened theater or concert venue, and the constant flashing of images might be distracting to others. Turning off picture review or keeping the duration short also saves power. You can always review the last picture you took at any time by pressing the Playback button.

Auto Off w/ VF

Options: On, Off

Default: On

The Sony Alpha's Eye-Start sensors automatically turn off the LCD display when you bring the camera to your eye (assuming you're not using Live View when working with the A390). If you'd rather have the LCD on all the time, you could always disable Eye-Start AF (as described earlier in this section), but that might be throwing the baby out with the bathwater. Instead, just set this menu item to Off, and your LCD display will remain even when you're looking through the viewfinder, and Eye-Start AF will function as normal.

Playback Menu

The Playback menu controls functions for deleting, protecting, displaying, and printing images. The Playback menu is shown in Figure 3.5.

- Delete
- Format
- Slide show
- Protect
- Specify Printing
- Playback Display

Delete

Options: Marked images, All images

Default: None

All of us sometimes take pictures that we know should never see the light of day. Maybe you were looking into the lens and accidentally tripped the shutter. Perhaps you really goofed up your settings. You want to erase that photo *now,* before it does permanent damage. While you can delete a photo immediately after you take it by pressing the Delete key, sometimes you need to wait for an idle moment to erase pictures. This menu choice makes it easy to remove selected photos (Marked images), or to erase all the photos on a memory card (All images). Note that neither function removes images marked Protected (described in the section "Protect").

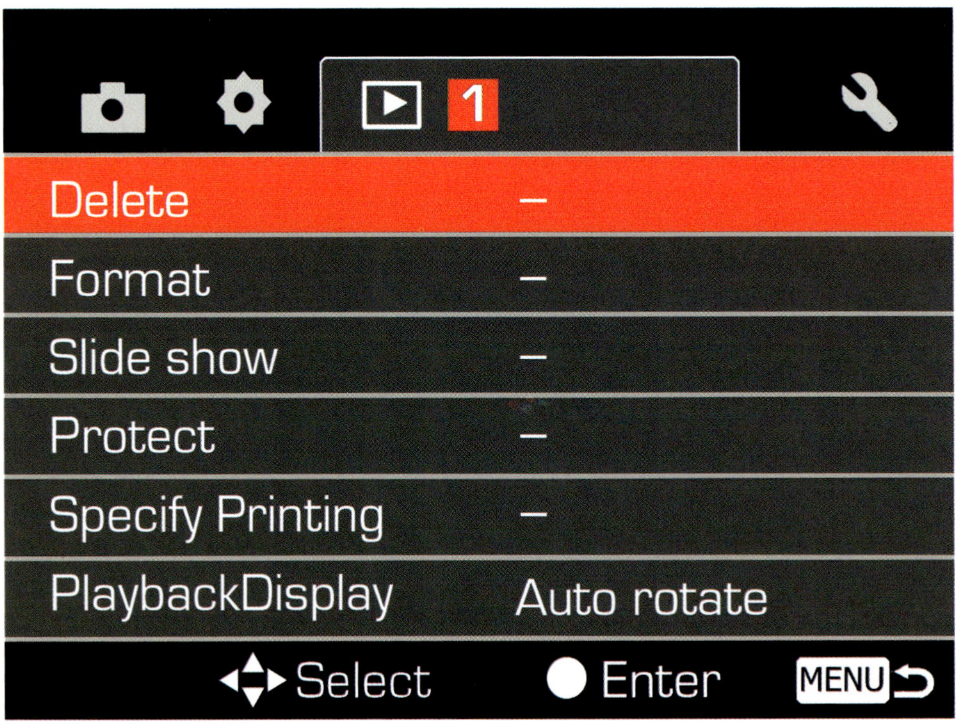

Figure 3.5 The Sony Alpha's Playback menu.

To remove selected images, select the Delete menu item, and use the up/down keys to choose Marked images. Press the center controller button, and the most recent image appears on the LCD. Press the center controller button again, and a green trash can icon is superimposed over your image, and the number of images marked for deletion is incremented in the indicator at lower left. Press the left/right controller keys to move forward and backward among the images to mark or unmark additional shots. When you're satisfied (or have expressed your dissatisfaction with the really bad ones), press the MENU button to go back, where you can choose Marked images to erase the ones you've selected.

While you can use this menu choice to delete All images, the process can take some time. You're better off using the Format command, described next.

Format

Options: Format, Cancel format

Default: Cancel format

To reformat your memory card, choose the Format menu entry and press the center controller button. Choose OK when the "All data will be deleted. Format?" message appears.

Use this item to erase everything on your memory card and set up a fresh file system ready for use. It removes all the images on the memory card, and reinitializes the card's file system by defining anew the areas of the card available for image storage, locking out defective areas, and creating a new folder in which to deposit your images. It's usually a good idea to reformat your memory card in the camera (not in your camera's card reader using your computer's operating system) before each use. Formatting is generally much quicker than deleting images one by one.

Slide Show Interval

Options: Activate show

Options: 1 second, 3 seconds, 5 seconds, 10 seconds, 30 seconds

Default: 3 seconds

This option allows you to display all the images on your memory card using a three-second delay between images, or another delay period you select by choosing the Interval suboption. Choose 1, 3, 5, 10, or 30 seconds for your interval. During the show you can:

- Press the center controller button to pause the show. Press again to resume the show.
- Move forward or reverse in the show by pressing the controller left/right keys.

- Stop the show at any time by pressing the MENU button.
- Press the DISP button to toggle between full screen images and the same images with recording information overlaid. The latter option is useful when you want to view a group of images automatically (and hands free), while monitoring the exposure settings.
- Choose the Repeat option to have your slide show run continuously.

Protect

Options: Marked images, All images, Cancel all (unmark all images)

Default: None

You might want to protect images on your memory card from accidental erasure, either by you or by others who may use your camera from time to time. This menu choice enables you to protect only Marked images (using a procedure similar to the Delete Marked images process described earlier), protect All images on the memory card, or Cancel All, which unmarks and unprotects any photos you have previously marked for protection.

To protect only selected images, select the Protect menu item, and choose Marked images. Press the center controller button, and the images appear one by one on your LCD as you browse through them with the left/right controller keys. When an image you want to protect is highlighted, press the center controller button to mark it for protection (or to unmark an image that has already been marked). A key icon appears over marked images. When you've marked all the images you want to protect, press the center controller button to return to the menu screen.

Specify Printing

Options (DPOF Setup): Marked images, All images, Cancel all (unmark all images)

Options (Number of Copies): 1-9

Options (Date Imprint): On, Off

Defaults: None

Most digital cameras are compatible with the DPOF (Digital Print Order Format) protocol, which enables you to mark in your camera which of the JPEG images on the memory card (but not RAW files) that you'd like to print, and specify the number of copies of each that you want. You can then transport your memory card to your retailer's digital photo lab or do-it-yourself kiosk, or use your own compatible printer to print out the marked images and quantities you've specified.

You can access the Specify printing options from this menu choice, or by pressing the Fn button when an image is displayed on the screen, and then choosing Specify printing from the Playback Function menu discussed later in this chapter.

- **DPOF Setup.** You can choose to print All images, Marked images, or Cancel. Selecting images is similar to the method you use to mark images for deletion or protection. To print selected images, select the DPOF Setup menu item, and press the right key to choose Marked images. Press the center controller button, and browse through the images you want to print. For each image, press the controller button to increment the number of prints to be made of that image, from 2 to 11. A printer icon in the lower-left corner shows the number selected for the image on display. If you continue pressing the controller button past 11 copies, the count wraps around to 2 copies again.

  When finished, press the MENU button to exit picture selection. Cancel all removes all DPOF print selection and quantity marks. This entry is useful if you print photos from a memory card, but then leave the images on the card while you shoot additional pictures. Removing the DPOF markings clears the card of print requests so you can later select additional or different images for printing from the same collection.

- **Number of copies.** You can set the number of copies to be printed when All images have been marked. From 2 to 11 copies can be requested.
- **Date imprint.** Choose this menu item to superimpose the current date onto images when they are printed. Select On to add the date; Off (the default value) skips date imprinting. The date is added during printing by the output device, which controls its location on the final print.

Playback Display

Options: Auto rotate, Manual rotate

Default: Auto rotate

When activated, the Sony Alpha rotates pictures taken in vertical orientation on the LCD screen so you don't have to turn the camera to view them comfortably. However, this orientation also means that the longest dimension of the image is shown using the shortest dimension of the LCD, so the picture is reduced in size. Choose Manual rotate instead, and you can rotate only those photos you want to re-orient, using the Fn/Rotate menu option.

Setup 1/2/3 Menus

Use the three Setup menus to change infrequently changed settings, such as language, date/time, and power saving settings. Setup 1 menu is shown in Figure 3.6.

- LCD brightness
- Power Save (Live View)
- Power Save (Optical Viewfinder)
- CTRL for HDMI
- Display Color
- Help Guide display
- Date/Time setup
- Language
- File number
- Folder name
- Select folder
- New folder
- USB Connection
- Audio signals
- Pixel mapping
- Cleaning mode
- Version
- Reset default

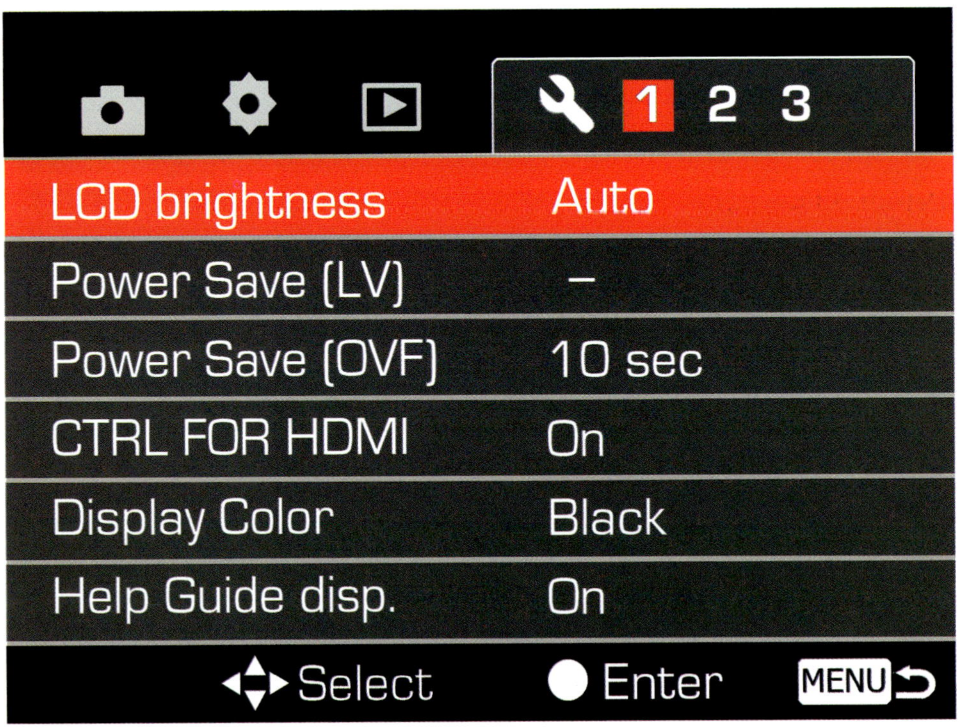

Figure 3.6 The Sony Alpha's Setup 1 menu.

LCD Brightness

Options: Auto/Manual: Plus or minus 2

Default: 0

When you access this menu choice, a pair of grayscale steps and a color chart appear on the screen, allowing you to see the effect of your brightness changes on the dark, light, and middle tones as well as colors. Select Auto to have the Alpha choose screen brightness for you. Choose Manual instead and a scale appears. Use the left/right controller buttons to adjust the brightness by plus or minus two (arbitrary) increments.

Power Save (Live View) (Alpha A390 Only)

Options: 10 seconds, 20 seconds, 1 minute, 5 minutes, 30 minutes

Default: 20 seconds

This setting determines how long the Live View display remains active before the Alpha switches to Power Save mode. Then, the display vanishes but can be restored by tapping the shutter release button. If you want to set the time period for display of the info screen, choose 10 or 20 seconds, or 1, 5, or 30 minutes here.

Power Save (Optical Viewfinder)

Options: 10 seconds, 20 seconds, 1 minute, 5 minutes, 30 minutes

Default: 10 seconds

This setting allows you to determine how long the Sony Alpha remains active before going into Power Save mode when you are using the optical viewfinder instead of Live View. (I find Sony's choice of nomenclature for this menu item confusing on the A390,

SAVING POWER WITH THE Sony Alpha

There are several settings and techniques you can use to help you stretch the longevity of your Alpha's battery. These include setting the Auto Review, Auto Off w/VF, LCD Brightness, Power Save, and Info. Disp Time options to turn the LCD and/or camera off as quickly as possible when not needed. That big 2.7-inch LCD uses a lot of juice, so reducing the amount of time it is used (either for automatic review or for manually playing back your images) can boost the effectiveness of your battery. If you're willing to shade the LCD with your hand, you can often get away with lower LCD brightness settings outdoors, which will further increase the useful life of your battery. The techniques? Use the internal flash as little as possible; no flash at all or fill flash use less power than a full blast. Turn off SteadyShot if you feel you don't need it. When transferring pictures from your Alpha to your computer, use a card reader instead of the USB cable. Linking your camera to your computer and transferring images using the cable takes longer and uses a lot more power.

as it almost implies that using the optical viewfinder itself calls for some power saving measures. With the A290, which does not have Live View, the option is just called Power Save.) You can select 1, 3, 5, 10, or 30 minutes. (If the camera is connected to a video display through the video cable, it will shut off after 30 minutes regardless of the time period this option is set for.) However, even if the camera has shut itself off, if the power switch remains in the On position, you can bring the camera back to life by performing a function, such as pressing the shutter button halfway.

CTRL for HDMI

Options: On/Off

Default: On

You can view the display output of your Alpha on a high-definition television (HDTV) if you make the investment in an HDMI cable with a mini-HDMI connector on the camera end (which Sony does not supply) and you own an HDTV (which Sony does not supply with the camera, either). When connecting HDMI to HDMI, the camera automatically selects the correct image settings, including color broadcast system, for viewing. (Earlier Alpha models, which used a composite video connection instead of HDMI, had to be set to either NTSC or PAL broadcast cameras.)

If you're lucky enough to own a TV that supports the Sony Bravia synchronization protocol, you can operate the camera using that TV's remote control. Just press the Link Menu button on the remote, and then use the device's controls to delete images, display an image index of photos in the camera, display a slide show, protect/unprotect images in the camera, specify printing options, and play back single images on the TV screen.

Help Guide Display

Options: On/Off

Default: On

The Alpha's Help Guide display provides quick snippets of information about various functions as you select them, and then removes the information from the screen when you press the center button or shutter release. Once you've learned how to use the camera you may find that these factoids slow down operation of the Alpha. You can turn them off with this menu option.

Display Color

Options: Black, white, brown, pink

Default: White

You can change the background color of the display to black, white, brown, or pink. I used black for the illustrations in this book because the color combination seems to be the most legible on the printed page. But you may prefer one of the other color schemes.

Date/Time Setup

Options: Year, Day, Month, Time, Date Format

Default: None

Use this option, the first on the Setup 2 menu page (see Figure 3.7), to specify the date and time that will be embedded in the image file along with exposure information and other data. You can select year, day, month, hour, and date format, but cannot choose AM/PM specifically. To set, say 2:32 AM rather than 2:32 PM, you'll have to pretend you're using a digital clock and cycle past midnight or noon to get to the AM/PM hours, respectively.

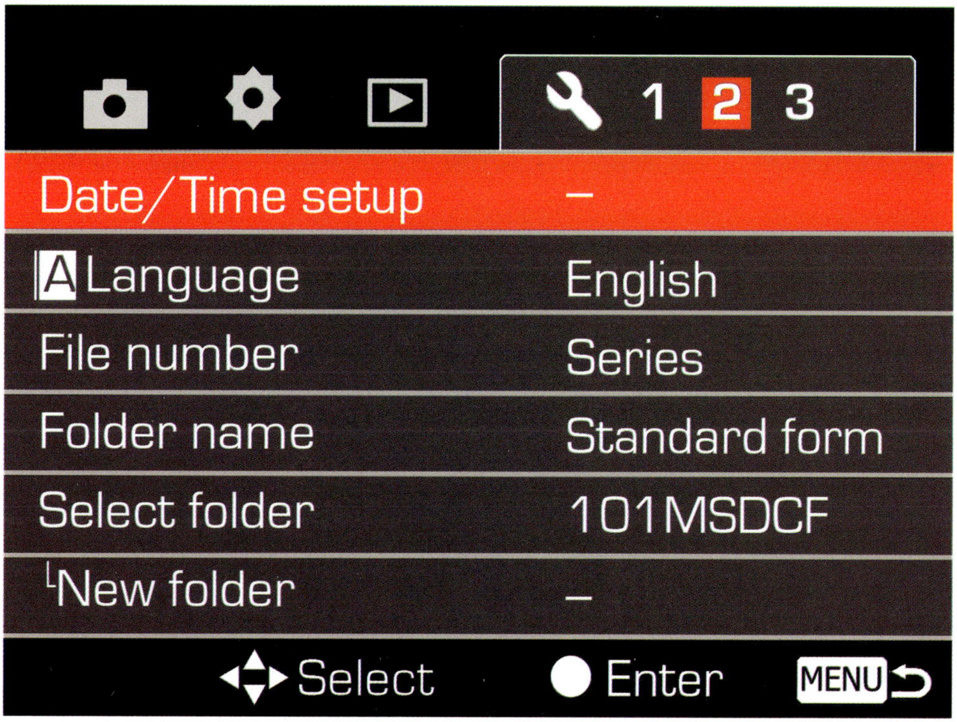

Figure 3.7 The Sony Alpha's Setup 2 menu.

Language

Options: English, French, Spanish, Italian, Japanese, Chinese languages

Default: Language of country where camera is sold

If you accidentally set a language you don't read and find yourself with incomprehensible menus, don't panic. Just choose the second option from the top of the Setup 2 menu, and select the idioma, lingua, or langue of your choice.

File Number

Options: Series, Reset

Default: Series

The Sony Alpha will automatically apply a file number to each picture you take when this option is set to Series, using consecutive numbering for all your photos over a long period of time, spanning many different memory cards, and even if you reformat a card. Numbers are applied from 0001 to 9999, at which time the camera starts back at 0001. The camera keeps track of the last number used in its internal memory. So, you could take pictures numbered as high as 100-0240 on one card, remove the card and insert another, and the next picture will be numbered 100-0241 on the new card. Reformat either card, take a picture, and the next image will be numbered 100-0242. Use the Series option when you want all the photos you take to have consecutive numbers (at least, until your camera exceeds 9999 shots taken).

If you want to restart numbering back at 0001 on a more frequent basis, set the Reset option. In that case, the file number will be reset to 0001 *each* time you format a memory card or delete all the images in a folder, insert a different memory card, or change the folder name format (as described in the next menu entry).

Folder Name

Options: Standard form, Date form

Default: Standard form

If you have viewed one of your memory card's contents using a card reader, you noticed that the top-level folder on the card is always named DCIM. Inside that folder is another folder created by your camera. Different cameras use different folder names, and they can coexist on the same card. For example, if your memory card is removed from your Sony camera and used in, say, a camera from another vendor that also accepts Secure Digital or Memory Stick cards, the other camera will create a new folder using a different folder name within the DCIM directory.

By default, the Alpha creates its folders using a three-number prefix (starting with 100), followed by MSDCF. As each folder fills up with 999 images, a new folder with a prefix that's one higher (say, 101) is used. So, with the "Standard Form" the folders on your memory card will be named 100MSDCF, 101MSDCF, and so forth.

You can select Date Form instead, and the Alpha will use an *xxxymmdd* format, such as 10090204, where the 100 is the folder number, 9 is the last digit of the year, 02 is the month, and 04 is the day of that month. If you want your folder names to be more date-oriented, rather than generic, use the Date Form option instead of Standard Form.

Select Folder/New Folder

Options: Select Folder, Create New Folder

Default: None

Although your Alpha will create new folders automatically as needed, you can create a new folder at any time, and switch among available folders already created on your memory card. (But only, of course, if a memory card is installed in the camera.) This is an easy way to segregate photos by folder. For example, if you're on vacation, you can change the Folder Name convention to Date Form (described previously), and then deposit each day's shots into different folders, which you create with this menu entry.

- **Select folder.** To switch to a different folder (when more than one folder is available on your CF card), when you are using Standard Form folder naming, choose Select Folder from the menu. A scrolling list of available folders appears. Use the up/down controller keys to choose the folder you want, and press the center controller button to confirm your choice.
- **New folder.** To create a brand new folder, choose Select Folder/New Folder from Setup 2 menu. Press the center controller button, and a message like "101090114 folder created" appears on the LCD. Press the center button again to dismiss the screen and return to the menu.

Tip

Whoa! Sony has thrown you a curveball in this folder switching business. Note that if you are using Date Form naming, you can *create* folders using the date convention, but you can't switch among them—but only when Date Form is active. If you *do* want to switch among folders named using the date convention, you can do it. But you have to switch from Date Form back to Standard Form. *Then* you can change to any of the available folders (of either naming format). So, if you're on vacation, select Date Form, and then choose New Folder each day of your trip, if you like. But if, for some reason, you want to put some additional pictures in a different folder (say, you're revisiting a city and want the new shots to go in the same folder as those taken a few days earlier), you'll need to change to Standard Form, switch folders, and then resume shooting. Sony probably did this to preserve the "integrity" of the date/folder system, but it can be annoying.

USB Connection

Options: Mass storage, PTP

Default: Mass storage

This option, the first in the Setup 3 menu (see Figure 3.8), allows you to switch your USB connection protocol between the default Mass Storage setting (used when you transfer images from your camera to your computer), and PTP (Picture Transfer Protocol), which you'd use to connect your camera to a PictBridge-compatible printer. In Mass Storage mode, your camera appears to the computer as just another storage device, like a disk drive. You can drag and drop files between them. In PTP mode, the device you're connected to recognizes your camera as a camera and can communicate with it, which is what happens when you use a PictBridge printer.

Most of the time, you'll want to leave this setting at Mass Storage, changing it only when you're communicating with a PictBridge printer that requires a PTP connection.

Audio Signals

Options: On/Off

Default: On

The Sony Alpha's internal beeper provides a helpful chirp to signify various functions, such as the countdown of your camera's self-timer. You can switch it off if you want to avoid the beep because it's annoying, impolite, or distracting (at a concert or museum), or undesired for any other reason. (I've actually had new dSLR owners ask me how to turn off the "shutter sound" the camera makes; such an option was available in the point-and-shoot camera they'd used previously.) Select Audio Signals from the Setup 2 menu, choose On or Off, and press the center controller button.

Pixel Mapping (Alpha A390 Only)

Options: Remap, Cancel

Default: None

Sometimes good pixels go bad. Sometimes they're just made that way. We're talking here about the pixels on the Alpha's LCD screen, not sensor pixels. You're not likely to notice these errant pixels as you take photos, except when using Live View. You can reduce their effect by remapping the pixels shown on the LCD, so your Alpha will ignore them during display. Select this option and let your camera go to work, "removing" the bad pixels. This feature is not available, or needed with the A290, which does not have Live View.

Because pixel mapping affects *only* the pixels on the LCD, and then only when using Live View mode, this menu entry is available only when you have activated Live View.

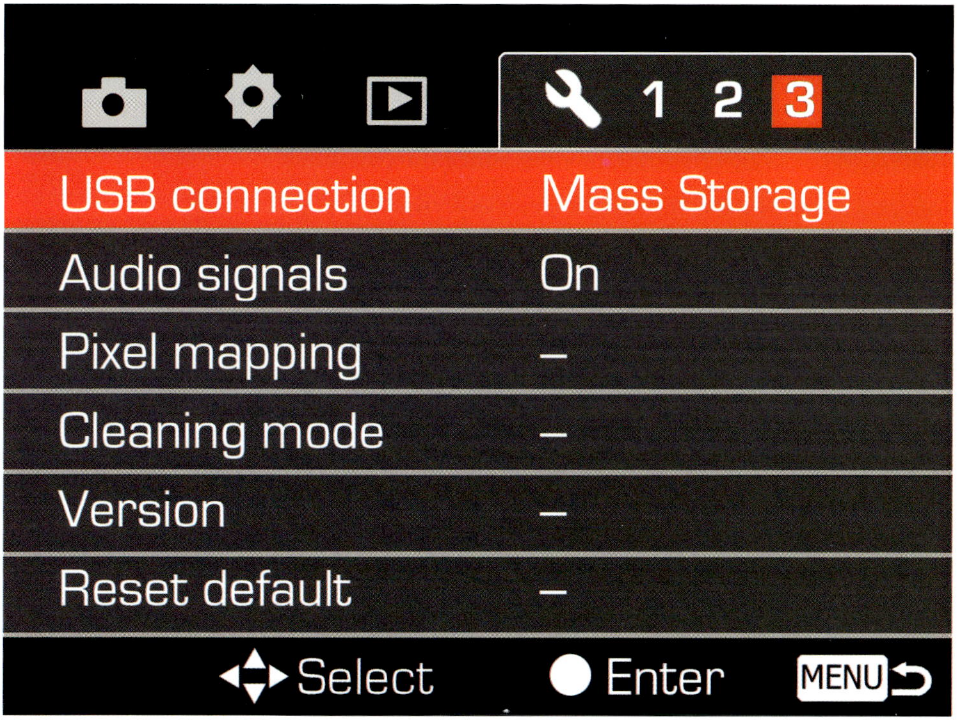

Figure 3.8 The Sony Alpha's Setup 3 menu.

Cleaning Mode

Options: OK (flip up mirror), Cancel

Default: None

One of the Sony Alpha's best features is the automatic sensor cleaning system that reduces or eliminates the need to clean your camera's sensor manually using brushes, swabs, or bulb blowers (you'll find instructions on how to do that in Chapter 9). Sony has applied anti-static coatings to the sensor and other portions of the camera body interior to counter charge build-ups that attract dust. A separate filter over the sensor vibrates ultrasonically each time the Alpha is powered off, shaking loose any dust, which is captured by a sticky strip beneath the sensor.

When it's time to clean the sensor manually, use this menu entry to lock up the mirror to provide access to the charge-coupled device (CCD). Use a fully charged battery or optional AC adapter and choose Cleaning mode from Setup 3 menu. A warning screen pops up "After cleaning turn camera off. Continue?" Choose OK and press the center controller button to move the mirror into its fully upright and locked position, after the Alpha makes one last stab at automatic cleaning and vibrates for a short time. Turn the camera off (as advised by the on-screen prompt) to return the mirror to its picture-taking position.

Version

Options: None

This entry displays the current firmware version installed in the camera. You'll find instructions in Chapter 9 for upgrading your firmware.

Reset Default

Options: Reset, Cancel Reset

Default: None

If you've made a lot of changes to your Alpha's settings, you may want to return to the factory settings so you can start over without manually going back through the menus and restoring everything. This menu selection lets you do that with the press of a few buttons.

Function Menus

It's time to drag out the Alpha's two Fn (Function) menus again, mentioned in Chapters 1 and 2, but not explained in a great amount of detail in either. That's because several of the functions deserve complete descriptions within the context of their respective applications. For example, Autofocus mode/AF area and Metering are best deferred to the chapters that explain those features in exhaustive detail. This section will provide an overview that points you to the parts of the book that do delve into the functions available from these menus.

The Shooting function menu appears when you press the Fn button when the camera is in Shooting mode (that is, you're not reviewing an image on the LCD) when using PSAM modes. If you are looking at a shot that's already been taken, the Playback Function menu appears instead. Each of the two menus has options that relate to their respective camera operational modes.

Shooting Function Menu

This menu (see Figure 3.9) has six functions:

- **Autofocus mode.** This entry summons a terse submenu that allows you to choose *when* the Alpha locks in focus, either AF-A (single autofocus), AF-C (continuous autofocus), or AF-A (automatic autofocus). These were described in Chapter 1, and will be explained more completely in the autofocus section of Chapter 5.

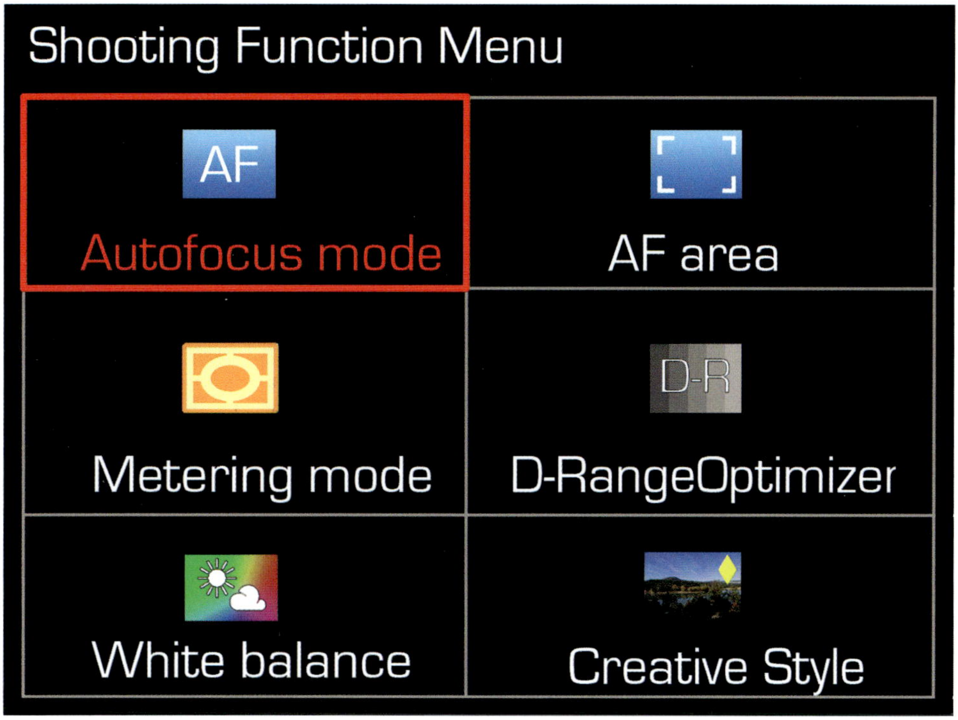

Figure 3.9 Shooting function menu.

- **AF area.** The Alpha includes nine autofocus sensors scattered about the central portion of the viewfinder. You can elect to have the Alpha always choose which of the sensors to use, you can select the sensor yourself, or use the center autofocus point (either always or only when you press the controller's center button). You'll find tips for choosing the best AF area mode, from among Wide, Spot, or Local, for the kind of shooting you are doing in Chapter 5.
- **Metering mode.** The metering mode determines what part of the image is used to determine correct exposure. The Alpha can be set to evaluate multiple points within the image, concentrate only on the center portion of the frame, or measure a small spot in the middle of the shot. You'll learn how metering mode affects exposure in the next chapter, which is devoted exclusively to exposure topics.
- **D-Range Optimizer.** The brightness/darkness range of many images is so broad that the sensor has difficulty capturing both the brightest highlight areas and the darkest shadow areas. The Alpha is able to expand its *dynamic range* using the D-Range Optimizer feature available in Standard and Advanced options from this menu entry. I'll provide tips and examples in the special "exposure" section, in Chapter 4.

- **White balance.** The different light sources you shoot under have differing color balances. Indoor light, for example, is much redder than outdoor illumination, which tends to have a bluish bias. The Alpha lets you choose the color/white balance that's appropriate, or can make this adjustment automatically. This aspect relates to exposure, covered in Chapter 4.
- **Creative Style.** This option gives you seven different combinations of contrast, saturation, and sharpness: Standard, Vivid, Portrait, Landscape, Night, Sunset, and B/W (black and white). You can apply Creative Styles *only* when you are using Program Auto, Aperture priority, Shutter priority, or Manual exposure modes.

I explain the "looks" of each of these styles in Chapter 5.

Playback Function Menu

The six options provided in this menu (see Figure 3.10) let you adjust or manipulate the images you've taken. These are all simple features, and don't need additional discussion beyond what I provide here. Your choices include:

- **Delete.** Use this to mark individual images or groups of images for removal.

  To use this function, select Marked images or All images from the Delete screen. If you choose Marked images, you'll be taken to an image review screen similar to the one for Specify printing. Press the center controller button to mark an image for deletion. A green trash can icon will be overlaid on the image. Use the left/right controller buttons to scroll back and forth among the remaining images on the card. Use the center controller button to mark any of those that you want. When finished, press the Fn button to see a screen asking you to confirm Delete or Cancel. Choose All images instead, and you'll see this same screen just before all the images on the card are removed.

- **Slide show.** You can view images stored in your camera one after another, in slide show fashion. This feature is especially useful when you have the Alpha connected to an external TV monitor. The submenu has only two options: you can choose a display interval of 1, 3, 5, 10, or 30 second intervals; and the display can be set to play just once, or to keep repeating. You might want to repeat the display if your camera is connected to an external TV at, say, a trade show, where your images can be shown continuously. (The optional AC adapter is also a good idea in this case.)

  During the slide show, you have several options:

  - **Pause.** Press the center controller button to pause the show at any point. Press again to resume.
  - **Forward/Back.** Press the left/right controller buttons to advance or move back.
  - **Stop.** Press the Playback button or press the shutter release to end the show immediately.

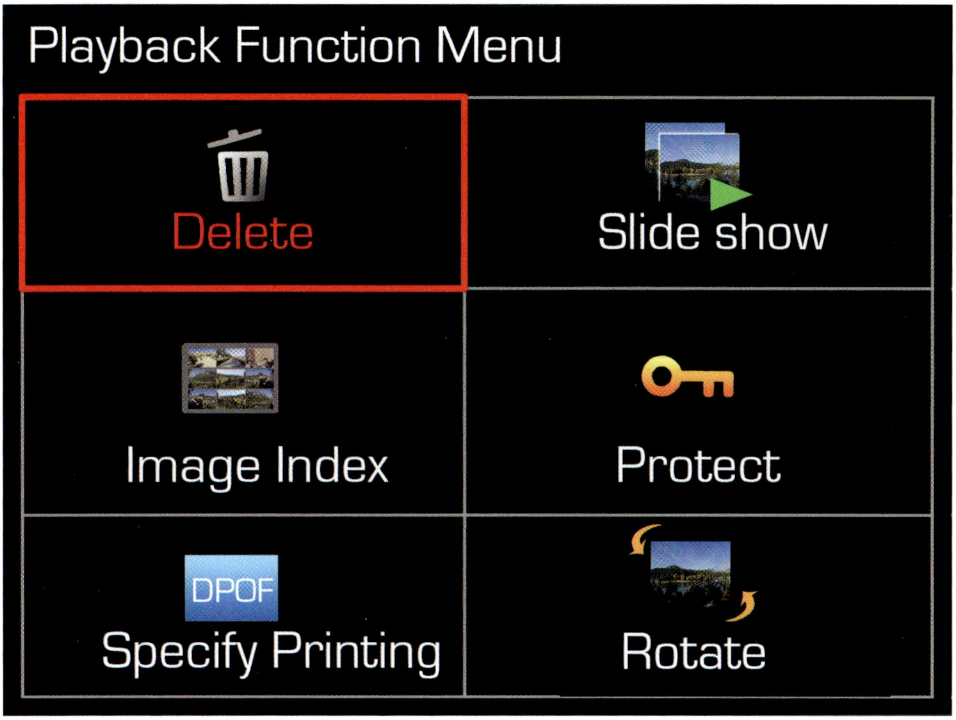

Figure 3.10 Playback function menu.

- **Image Index.** Select an image "proof sheet" of 4, 9, or 25 miniature images that will display on your screen. You can navigate among them with the controller directional buttons, and jump to any single image by pressing the center controller button. The image index is a fast way to advance to any image on your memory card.
- **Protect.** Use this option to mark images to protect them from accidental erasure. If you really want to get rid of a photo that has been protected, you'll need to unprotect it, or format your memory card. Choose Marked images to protect specific photos, All images to protect all the pictures on your memory card, and Cancel all to remove protection from all the photos on the card.

  When you choose Marked images, you'll be able to select individual shots using the type of screen and controls used to mark images using Delete, as described earlier in this section. The center controller button specifies which images should be marked.
- **Specify printing.** This entry takes you to the same menu already discussed in the Playback menu section earlier in this chapter.
- **Rotate.** Re-orients your images by 90 degrees each time you press the center controller button. When you're satisfied with the new orientation, press the Playback button to exit.

4

Getting the Right Exposure

When you bought your Sony Alpha DSLR-A390/A290, you probably thought your days of worrying about getting the correct exposure were over. To paraphrase an old Kodak tagline dating back to the 19th Century—the goal is, "you press the button, and the camera does the rest." For the most part, that's a realistic objective. The Alpha is one of the smartest cameras available when it comes to calculating the right exposure for most situations. You can generally choose one of the Scene modes, or spin the mode dial to Program (P), Aperture priority (A), or Shutter priority (S) and shoot away.

So, why am I including an entire chapter on exposure? As you learn to use your Alpha creatively, you're going to find that the right settings—as determined by the camera's exposure meter and intelligence—need to be *adjusted* to account for your creative decisions or special situations.

For example, when you shoot with the main light source behind the subject, you end up with *backlighting*, which can result in an overexposed background and/or an underexposed subject. The Sony Alpha recognizes backlit situations nicely, and can properly base exposure on the main subject, producing a decent photo. Features like D-Range Optimizer (first mentioned in Chapter 3) can fine-tune exposure to preserve detail in the highlights and shadows.

But what if you *want* to underexpose the subject, to produce a silhouette effect? Or, perhaps, you might want to flip up the Alpha's built-in flash unit to fill in the shadows on your subject. The more you know about how to use your Alpha, the more you'll run into situations where you want to creatively tweak the exposure to provide a different look than you'd get with a straight shot.

This chapter shows you the fundamentals of exposure, so you'll be better equipped to override the Sony Alpha's default settings when you want to, or need to. After all, correct exposure is one of the foundations of good photography, along with accurate focus and sharpness, appropriate color balance, freedom from unwanted noise and excessive contrast, as well as pleasing composition.

The Sony Alpha gives you a great deal of control over all of these, although composition is entirely up to you. You must still frame the photograph to create an interesting arrangement of subject matter, but all the other parameters are basic functions of the camera. You can let your Alpha set them for you automatically, you can fine-tune how the camera applies its automatic settings, or you can make them yourself, manually. The amount of control you have over exposure, sensitivity (ISO settings), color balance, focus, and image parameters like sharpness and contrast make the Alpha a versatile tool for creating images.

In the next few pages, I'm going to give you a grounding in one of those foundations, and explain the basics of exposure, either as an introduction or as a refresher course, depending on your current level of expertise. When you finish this chapter, you'll understand most of what you need to know to take well-exposed photographs creatively in a broad range of situations.

Getting a Handle on Exposure

In the most basic sense, exposure is all about light. Exposure can make or break your photo. Correct exposure brings out the detail in the areas you want to picture, providing the range of tones and colors you need to create the desired image. Poor exposure can cloak important details in shadow, or wash them out in glare-filled featureless expanses of white. However, getting the perfect exposure requires some intelligence—either that built into the camera, or the smarts in your head—because digital sensors can't capture all the tones we are able to see. If the range of tones in an image is extensive, embracing both inky black shadows and bright highlights, we often must settle for an exposure that renders most of those tones—but not all—in a way that best suits the photo we want to produce.

For example, look at the two typical tourist snapshots presented side by side in Figure 4.1. For the image on the left, the camera, set for Spot metering, calculated exposure based on the scene in the background that is visible through the archway. While the background is reasonably well exposed, the interior, statues, and ceiling overhead are quite underexposed. For the version at right, Spot metering was used to read the ceiling of the scene, producing a more detailed interior shot, but badly overexposing the exterior details. The camera's sensor simply can't capture detail in both dark areas and bright areas in a single shot.

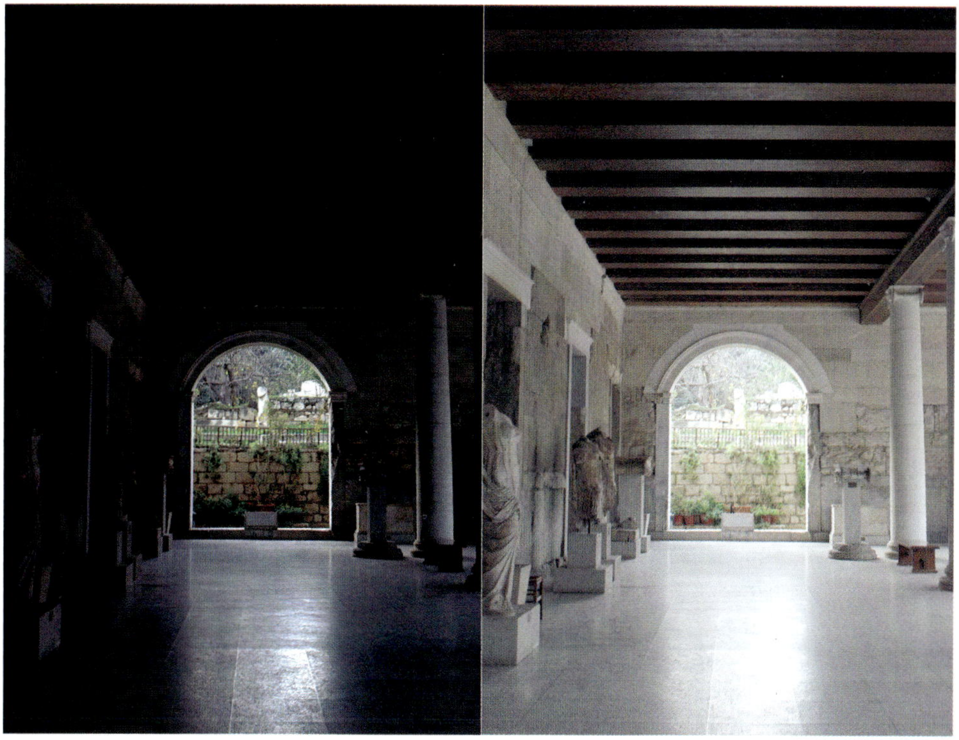

Figure 4.1
At left, the image is exposed for the background highlights, losing shadow detail. At right, the exposure captures detail in the shadows, but the background highlights are washed out.

The solution, in this particular case, was to resort to a technique called High Dynamic Range (HDR) photography, in which the two exposures from Figure 4.1 were combined in an image editor such as Photoshop, or a specialized HDR tool like Photomatix (about $100 from www.hdrsoft.com). The resulting shot is shown in Figure 4.2. I'll explain more about HDR photography later in this chapter. For now, though, I'm going to concentrate on showing you how to get the best exposures possible without resorting to such tools, using only the features of your Sony Alpha.

To understand exposure, you need to understand the six aspects of light that combine to produce an image. Start with a light source—the sun, an interior lamp, or the glow from a campfire—and trace its path to your camera, through the lens, and finally to the sensor that captures the illumination. Here's a brief review of the things within our control that affect exposure, listed in "chronological" order (that is, as the light moves from the subject to the sensor):

- **Light at its source.** Our eyes and our cameras—film or digital—are most sensitive to that portion of the electromagnetic spectrum we call *visible light.* That light has several important aspects that are relevant to photography, such as color and harshness (which is determined primarily by the apparent size of the light source as it illuminates a subject). But, in terms of exposure, the important attribute of a light source is its *intensity.* We may have direct control over intensity, which might be the

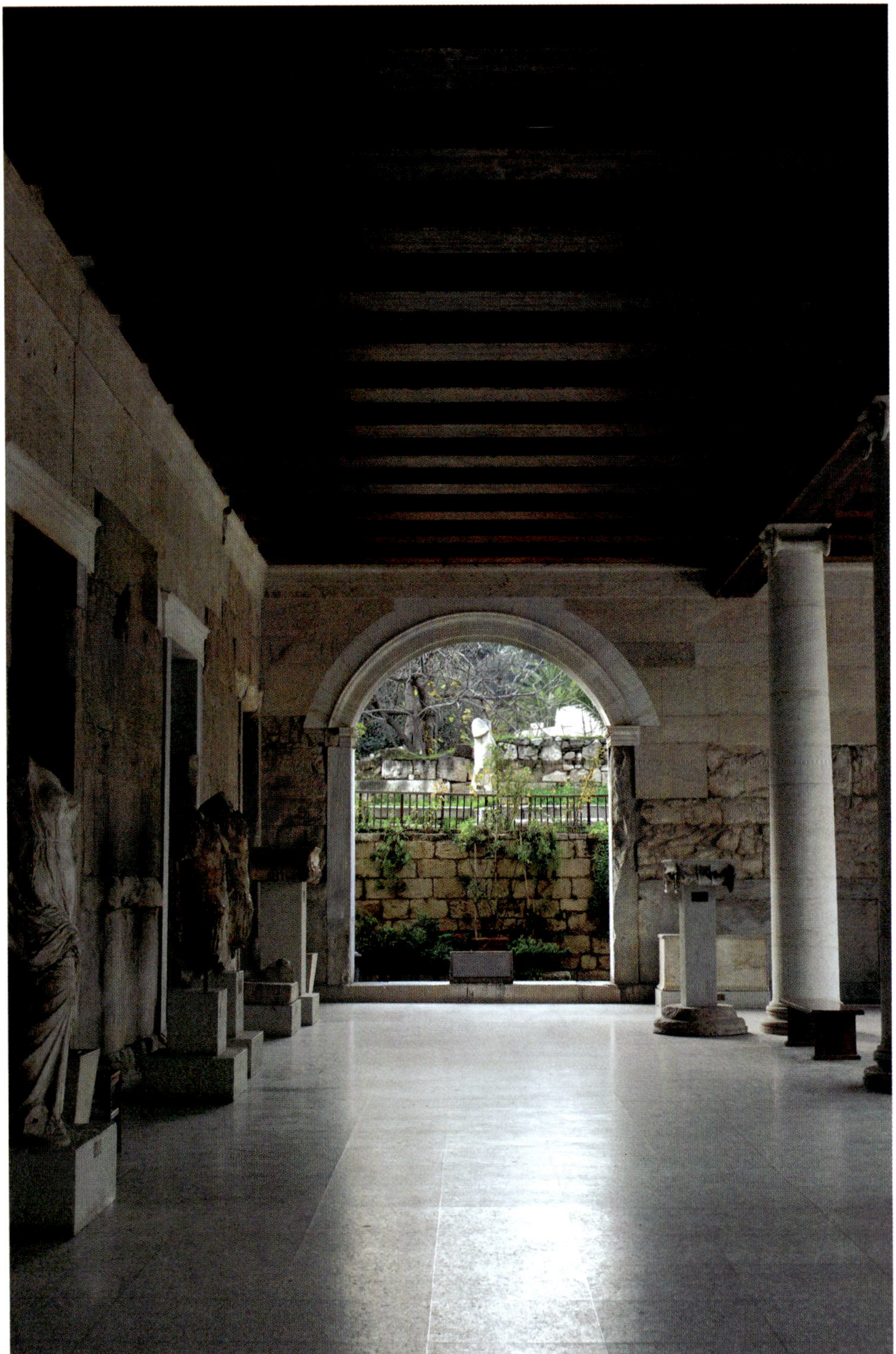

Figure 4.2
Combining the two exposures produces the best compromise image.

case with an interior light that can be brightened or dimmed. Or, we might have only indirect control over intensity, as with sunlight, which can be made to appear dimmer by introducing translucent light-absorbing or reflective materials in its path.

- **Light's duration.** We tend to think of most light sources as continuous. But, as you'll learn in Chapter 7, the duration of light can change quickly enough to modify the exposure, as when the main illumination in a photograph comes from an intermittent source, such as an electronic flash.
- **Light reflected, transmitted, or emitted.** Once light is produced by its source, either continuously or in a brief burst, we are able to see and photograph objects by the light that is reflected from our subjects towards the camera lens; transmitted (say, from translucent objects that are lit from behind); or emitted (by a candle or television screen). When more or less light reaches the lens from the subject, we need to adjust the exposure. This part of the equation is under our control to the extent we can increase the amount of light falling on or passing through the subject (by adding extra light sources or using reflectors), or by pumping up the light that's emitted (by increasing the brightness of the glowing object).
- **Light passed by the lens.** Not all the illumination that reaches the front of the lens makes it all the way through. Filters can remove some of the light before it enters the lens. Inside the lens barrel is a variable-sized diaphragm called an *aperture* that dilates and contracts to control the amount of light that enters the lens. You, or the Alpha's autoexposure system, can control exposure by varying the size of the aperture. The relative size of the aperture is called the *f/stop*. (See Figure 4.3.)
- **Light passing through the shutter.** Once light passes through the lens, the amount of time the sensor receives it is determined by the Alpha's shutter, which can remain open for as long as 30 seconds (or even longer if you use the Bulb setting) or as briefly as 1/4,000th second.
- **Light captured by the sensor.** Not all the light falling onto the sensor is captured. If the number of photons reaching a particular photosite doesn't pass a set threshold, no information is recorded. Similarly, if too much light illuminates a pixel in the sensor, then the excess isn't recorded or, worse, spills over to contaminate adjacent pixels. We can modify the minimum and maximum number of pixels that contribute to image detail by adjusting the ISO setting. At higher ISOs, the incoming light is amplified to boost the effective sensitivity of the sensor.

These four factors—quantity of light, light passed by the lens, the amount of time the shutter is open, and the sensitivity of the sensor—all work proportionately and reciprocally to produce an exposure. That is, if you double the amount of light, increase the aperture by one stop, make the shutter speed twice as long, or boost the ISO setting 2X, you'll get twice as much exposure. Similarly, you can increase any of these factors while decreasing one of the others by a similar amount to keep the same exposure.

F/STOPS AND SHUTTER SPEEDS

If you're *really* new to more advanced cameras (and I realize that some ambitious amateurs do purchase the Alpha as their first digital SLR), you might need to know that the lens aperture, or f/stop, is a ratio, much like a fraction, which is why f/2 is larger than f/4, just as 1/2 is larger than 1/4. However, f/2 is actually *four times* as large as f/4. (If you remember your high school geometry, you'll know that to double the area of a circle, you multiply its diameter by the square root of two: 1.4.)

Lenses are usually marked with intermediate f/stops that represent a size that's twice as much/half as much as the previous aperture. So, a lens might be marked:

f/2, f/2.8, f/4, f/5.6, f/8, f/11, f/16, f/22, with each larger number representing an aperture that admits half as much light as the one before, as shown in Figure 4.3.

Shutter speeds are actual fractions (of a second), but the numerator is omitted, so that 60, 125, 250, 500, 1,000, and so forth represent 1/60th, 1/125th, 1/250th, 1/500th, and 1/1,000th second. To avoid confusion, Sony Alpha uses quotation marks to signify longer exposures: 2", 2"5, 4", and so forth representing 2.0, 2.5, and 4.0-second exposures, respectively.

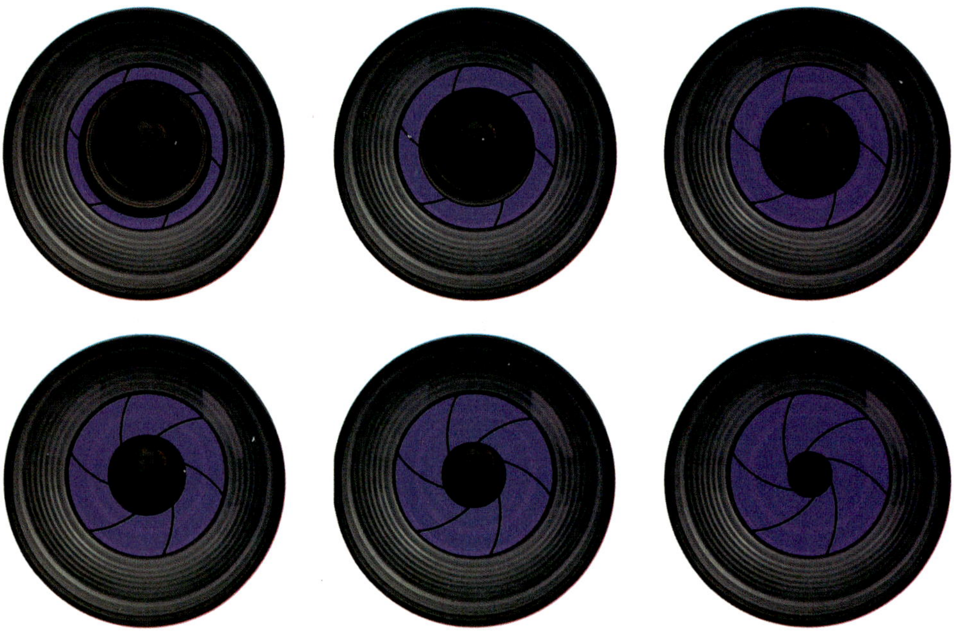

Figure 4.3
Top row (left to right): f/2, f/2.8, f/4; bottom row, f/5.6, f/8, f11.

Most commonly, exposure settings are made using the aperture and shutter speed, followed by adjusting the ISO sensitivity if it's not possible to get the preferred exposure (that is, the one that uses the "best" f/stop or shutter speed for the depth-of-field or action stopping we want). Table 4.1 shows equivalent exposure settings using various shutter speeds and f/stops.

When the Alpha is set for P mode, the metering system selects the correct exposure for you automatically. In Aperture priority (A) and Shutter priority (S) modes, you can change to an equivalent exposure, but only by adjusting either the aperture (the camera chooses the shutter speed) or shutter speed (the camera selects the aperture). I'll cover all these exposure modes later in the chapter.

Table 4.1 Equivalent Exposures

Shutter Speed	f/stop	Shutter Speed	f/stop
1/30th second	f/22	1/500th second	f/5.6
1/60th second	f/16	1/1,000th second	f/4
1/125th second	f/11	1/2,000th second	f/2.8
1/250th second	f/8	1/4,000th second	f/2

How the Sony Alpha Calculates Exposure

Your Alpha calculates exposure by measuring the light that passes through the lens using a metering pattern you can select (more on that later) and based on the assumption that each area being measured reflects about the same amount of light as a neutral gray card with approximately 18-percent reflectance. That assumption is necessary, because different subjects reflect different amounts of light. It's approximate because digital cameras are rarely calibrated for exactly 18-percent reflectance; a figure between 13-14 percent is more common.

In a photo containing a white cat and a dark gray cat, the white cat might reflect five times as much light as the gray cat. An exposure based on the white cat will cause the gray cat to appear to be black, while an exposure based on the gray cat will make the white cat appear washed out. Light-measuring devices handle this by assuming that the areas measured average the standard calibrated value in the neighborhood of 18-percent gray, a figure that's been used as a rough standard (as I noted, not all vendors calibrate their metering for exactly 18-percent gray) for many years. Black, white, and gray cats have been a standard metaphor for many years, as well, so I'm going to explain this concept using a different, and more cooperative, life form: peppers.

Figure 4.4 shows three peppers. The yellow peppers at top represent a white cat, or any object that is very light but contains detail that we want to see in the light areas. The red peppers in the middle are a stand-in for a gray cat, because it has most of its details in the middle tones. The green peppers serve as our black cat, because it is a dark object with detail in its shadows.

The colors confuse the issue, so I'm going to convert our color peppers to black-and-white. For the version shown in Figure 4.5, the exposure was optimized for the white (yellow) peppers, changing its tonal value to a medium, 18-percent gray. The dark (green) and medium-toned (red) peppers are now *too* dark. For Figure 4.6, the exposure was optimized for the dark (green) peppers, making most of their surface, now, fall into the middle-tone, 18-percent gray range. The yellow (light) and midtone (red) peppers are now too light.

The solution, of course, is to measure exposure from the object with the middle tones that most closely correspond to the 18-percent gray "standard." Do that, and you wind up with a picture that more closely resembles the original tonality of the red, yellow, and green peppers, and which looks, in black-and-white, like Figure 4.7.

In the real world, you could calculate exposure the hard way, and arrive at accurate settings by pointing your Alpha at an evenly lit object, such as an actual gray card or the palm of your hand (the backside of the hand is too variable). You'll need to increase the exposure by one stop in the latter case, because the human palm—of any ethnic group—reflects about twice as much light as a gray card. As you'll see, however, it's more practical to use your Alpha's system to meter the actual scene.

F/STOPS VERSUS STOPS

In photography parlance, *f/stop* always means the aperture or lens opening. However, for lack of a current commonly used word for one exposure increment, the term *stop* is often used. (In the past, EV served this purpose, but Exposure Value and its abbreviation has been inextricably intertwined with its use in describing Exposure Compensation.) In this book, when I say "stop" by itself (no *f/*), I mean one whole unit of exposure, and am not necessarily referring to an actual f/stop or lens aperture. So, adjusting the exposure by "one stop" can mean both changing to the next shutter speed increment (say, from 1/125th second to 1/250th second) or the next aperture (such as f/4 to f/5.6). Similarly, 1/3 stop or 1/2 stop increments can mean either shutter speed or aperture changes, depending on the context. Be forewarned.

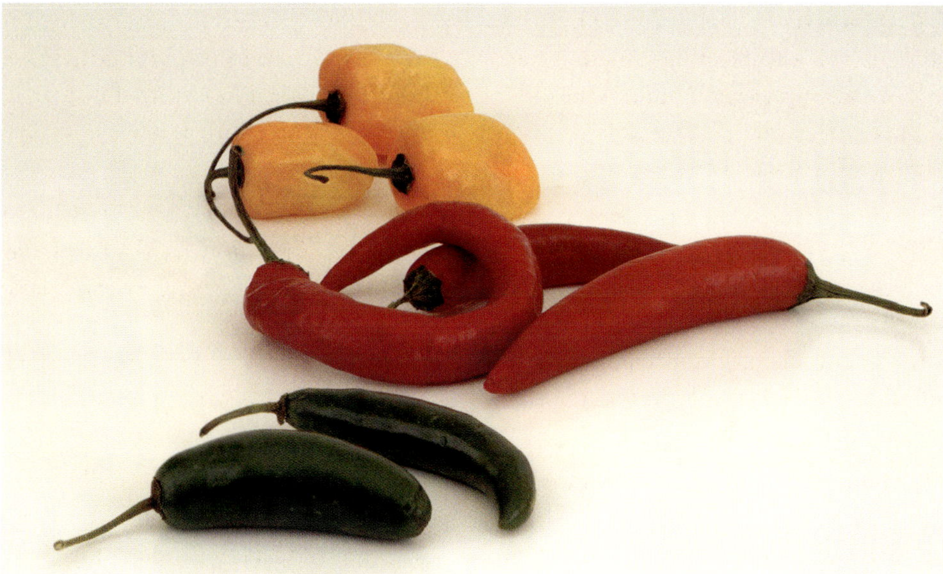

Figure 4.4 The yellow peppers, red peppers, and green peppers represent light, middle, and dark tones.

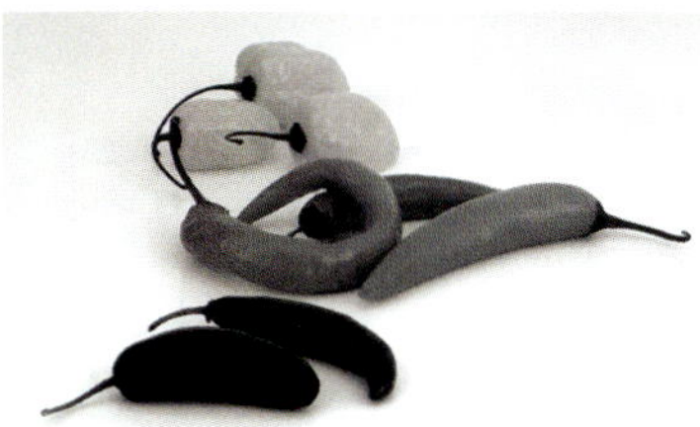

Figure 4.5 Exposing for the light-colored peppers at top renders the others excessively dark.

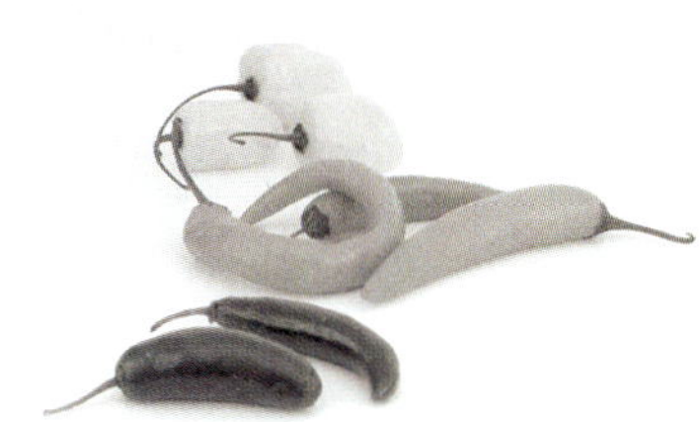

Figure 4.6 Exposing for the dark peppers (bottom) causes the other peppers to become too light.

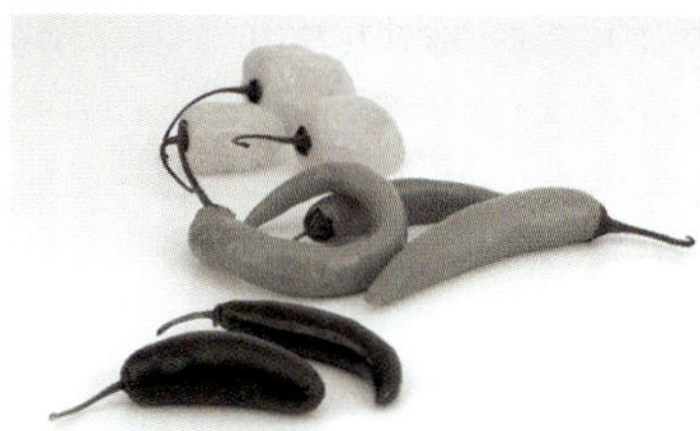

Figure 4.7 Exposing for the middle-toned red peppers produces an image in which the tones of all three subjects appear accurately.

In most cases, your camera's light meter will do a good job of calculating the right exposure, especially if you use the exposure tips in the next section. But if you want to double-check, or feel that exposure is especially critical, take the light reading off an object of known reflectance..

To meter properly, you'll want to choose both the *metering method* (how light is evaluated) and *exposure method* (how the appropriate shutter speeds and apertures are chosen). I'll describe both in the following sections.

Choosing a Metering Method

The Alpha has three different schemes for evaluating the light received by its exposure sensors. You can choose among them by pressing the Fn button and choosing Metering mode.

- **Multi segment.** The Alpha slices up the frame into 40 different zones, arranged in a honeycomb pattern, as shown in Figure 4.8. The camera evaluates the measurements to make an educated guess about what kind of picture you're taking, based on examination of exposure data derived from thousands of different real-world photos. For example, if the top sections of a picture are much lighter than the bottom portions, the algorithm can assume that the scene is a landscape photo with lots of sky. This mode is the best all-purpose metering method for most pictures.
- **Center weighted.** In this mode, the exposure meter emphasizes a zone in the center of the frame to calculate exposure, as shown in Figure 4.9, on the theory that, for most pictures, the main subject will be located in the center. Center-weighting works best for portraits, architectural photos, and other pictures in which the most important subject is located in the middle of the frame. As the name suggests, the light reading is *weighted* towards the central portion, but information is also used from the rest of the frame. If your main subject is surrounded by very bright or very dark areas, the exposure might not be exactly right. However, this scheme works well in many situations if you don't want to use one of the other modes.
- **Spot.** This mode confines the reading to a limited area in the center of the viewfinder, surrounded by the black dots representing the nine AF sensor points, as shown in Figure 4.10. This mode is useful when you want to base exposure on a small area in the frame. If that area is in the center of the frame, so much the better. If not, you'll have to make your meter reading and then lock exposure by pressing the shutter release halfway.

Choosing an Exposure Method

You'll find four methods for choosing the appropriate shutter speed and aperture semi-automatically or manually. Just spin the mode dial to choose the method you want to use (see Figure 4.11). Your choice of which is best for a given shooting situation will depend on things like your need for lots of (or less) depth-of-field, a desire to freeze action or allow motion blur, or how much noise you find acceptable in an image. Each of the Sony Alpha's exposure methods emphasizes one aspect of image capture or another. This section introduces you to all four. Scene modes will be discussed later.

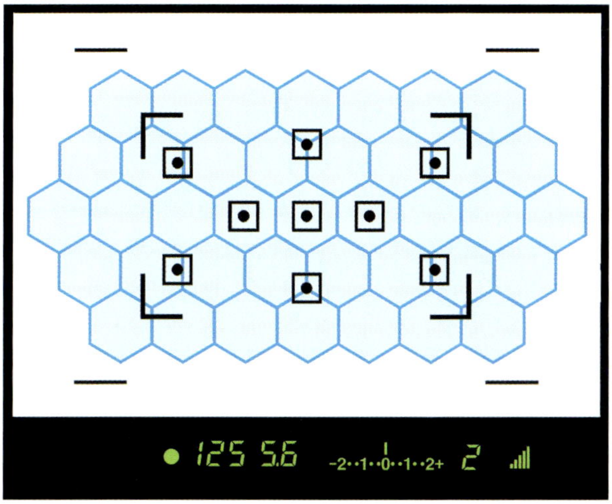

Figure 4.8
Multi segment metering uses 40 zones.

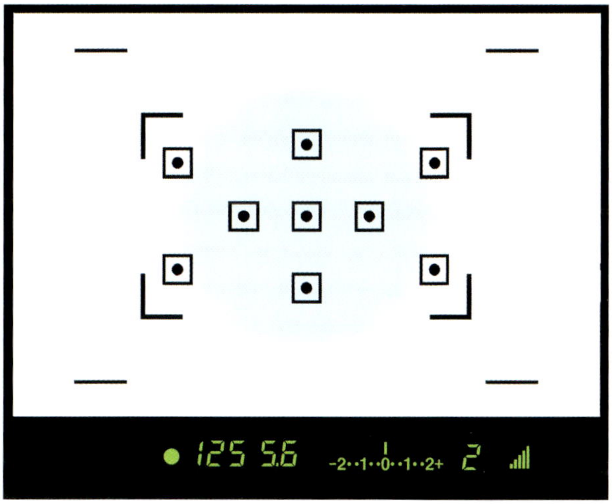

Figure 4.9
Center weighted metering calculates exposure based on the full frame, but emphasizes the center area.

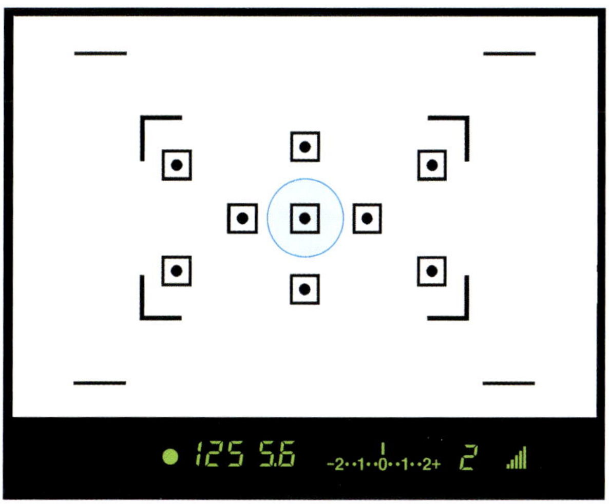

Figure 4.10
Spot metering calculates exposure based on a center spot that's only 3.5 percent of the image area.

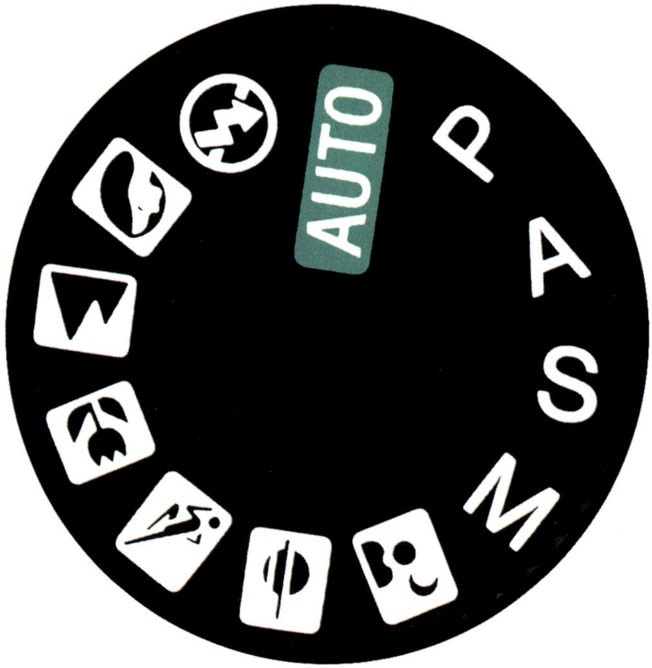

Figure 4.11
Choose exposure modes by spinning the mode dial.

Aperture Priority

In Aperture priority mode, you specify the lens opening used, and the Alpha selects the shutter speed. Aperture priority is especially good when you want to use a particular lens opening to achieve a desired effect. Perhaps you'd like to use the smallest f/stop possible to maximize depth-of-field in a close-up picture. Or, you might want to use a large f/stop to throw everything except your main subject out of focus, as in Figure 4.12. Maybe you'd just like to "lock in" a particular f/stop because it's the sharpest available aperture with that lens. Or, you might prefer to use, say, f/2.8 on a lens with a maximum aperture of f/1.4, because you want the best compromise between speed and sharpness.

Aperture priority can even be used to specify a *range* of shutter speeds you want to use under varying lighting conditions, which seems almost contradictory. But think about it. You're shooting a soccer game outdoors with a telephoto lens and want a relatively high shutter speed, but you don't care if the speed changes a little should the sun duck behind a cloud. Set your Alpha to A, and adjust the aperture until a shutter speed of, say, 1/1,000th second is selected at your current ISO setting. (In bright sunlight at ISO 400, that aperture is likely to be around f/11.) Then, go ahead and shoot, knowing that your Alpha will maintain that f/11 aperture (for sufficient depth-of-field as the soccer players move about the field), but will drop down to 1/750th or 1/500th second if necessary should the lighting change a little.

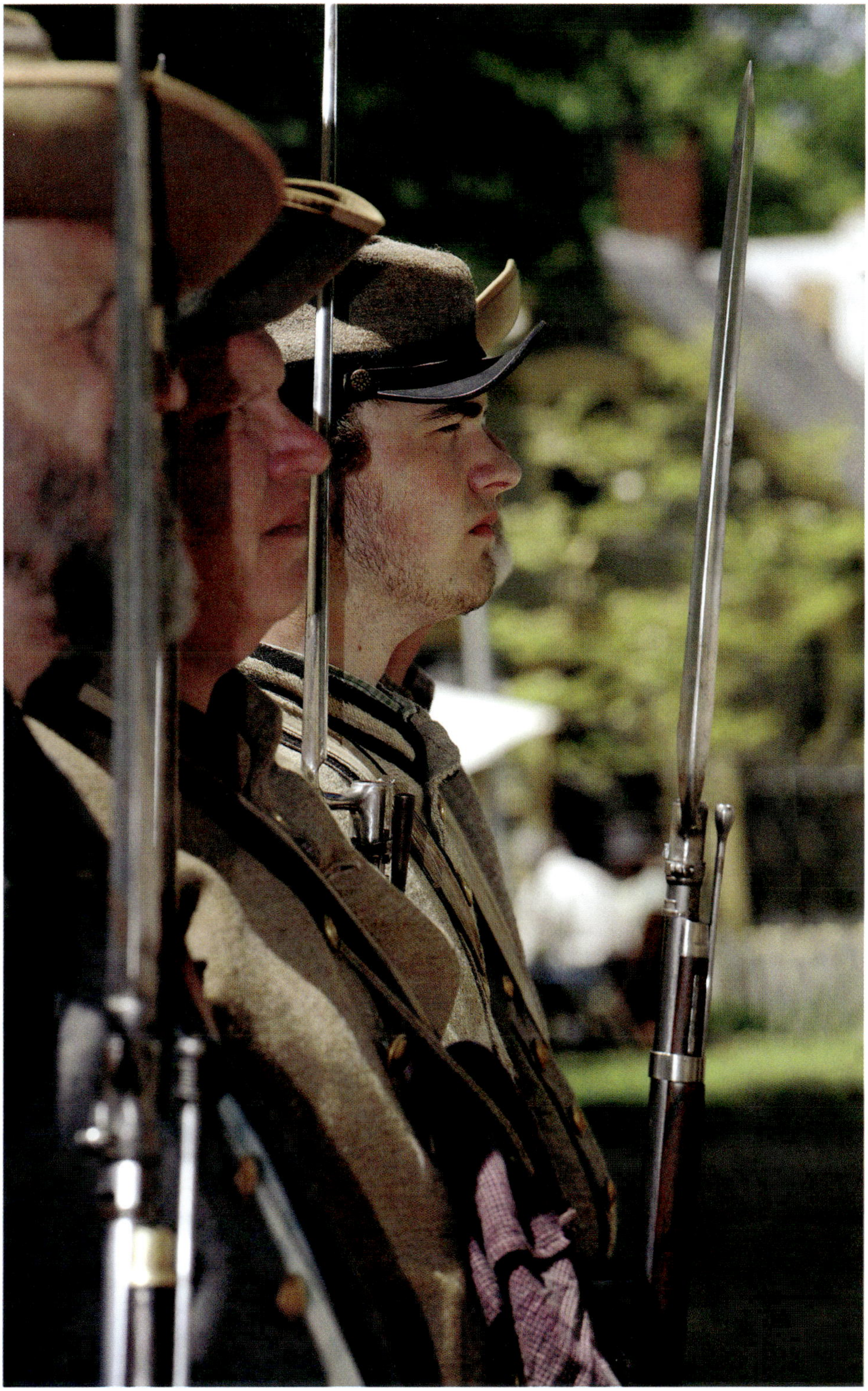

Figure 4.12
Use Aperture priority to "lock in" a large f/stop when you want to blur the background.

A blinking arrow on the EV scale on the LCD, or blinking camera shake warning icon in the viewfinder indicates that the Alpha is unable to select an appropriate shutter speed at the selected aperture and that over- and underexposure will occur at the current ISO setting. That's the major pitfall of using Aperture priority: you might select an f/stop that is too small or too large to allow an optimal exposure with the available shutter speeds. For example, if you choose f/2.8 as your aperture and the illumination is quite bright (say, at the beach or in snow), even your camera's fastest shutter speed might not be able to cut down the amount of light reaching the sensor to provide the right exposure. (The shutter speed indicator will blink if the camera is unable to select an appropriate shutter speed.) Or, if you select f/8 in a dimly lit room, you might find yourself shooting with a very slow shutter speed that can cause blurring from subject movement or camera shake. Aperture priority is best used by those with a bit of experience in choosing settings. Many seasoned photographers leave their Alpha set on Aperture priority all the time.

Shutter Priority

Shutter priority is the inverse of Aperture priority: you choose the shutter speed you'd like to use, and the camera's metering system selects the appropriate f/stop. Perhaps you're shooting action photos and you want to use the absolute fastest shutter speed

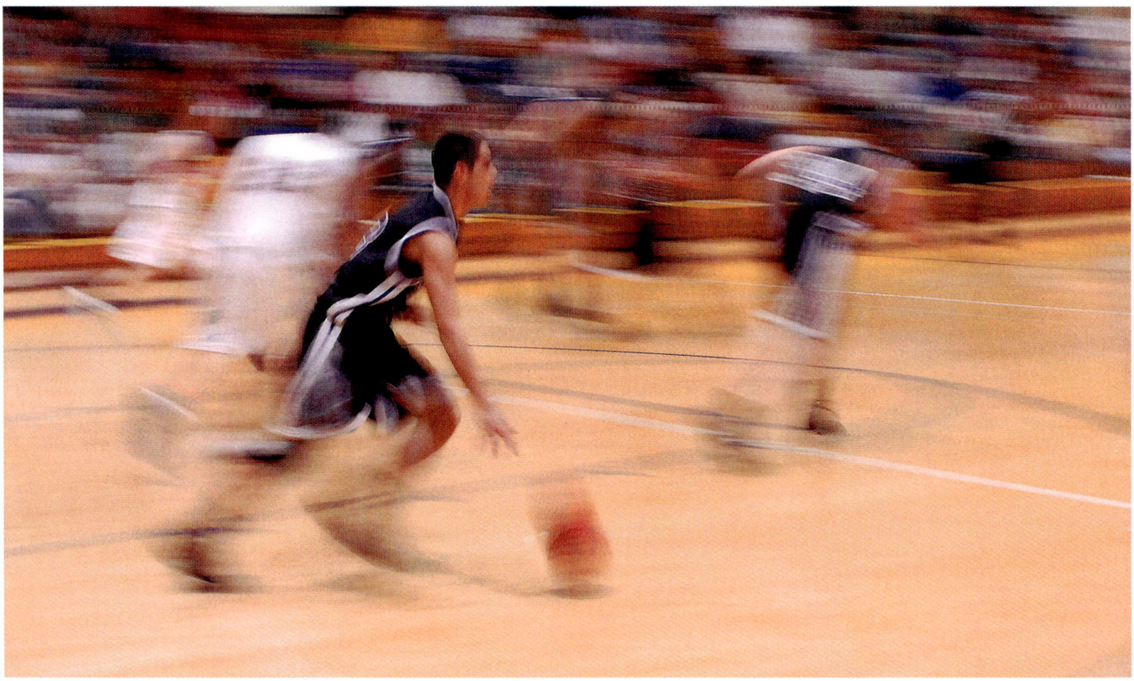

Figure 4.13 Lock the shutter at a slow speed to introduce blur into an action shot, as with this panned image of a basketball player.

available with your camera; in other cases, you might want to use a slow shutter speed to add some blur to a sports photo that would be mundane if the action were completely frozen (see Figure 4.13). Shutter priority mode gives you some control over how much action-freezing capability your digital camera brings to bear in a particular situation.

You'll also encounter the same problem as with Aperture priority when you select a shutter speed that's too long or too short for correct exposure under some conditions. I've shot outdoor soccer games on sunny Fall evenings and used Shutter priority mode to lock in a 1/1,000th second shutter speed, only to find my Alpha refused to shoot when the sun dipped behind some trees and there was no longer enough light to shoot at that speed, even with the lens wide open.

Like Aperture priority mode, it's possible to choose an inappropriate shutter speed. If that's the case, the maximum aperture of your lens (to indicate underexposure) or the minimum aperture (to indicate overexposure) will blink in the viewfinder and on the LCD.

Program Auto Mode

Program Auto mode (P) uses the Alpha's built-in smarts to select the correct f/stop and shutter speed using a database of picture information that tells it which combination of shutter speed and aperture will work best for a particular photo. If the correct exposure cannot be achieved at the current ISO setting, flashing arrows at the ends of the EV scale in the viewfinder and on your LCD, indicate under- or overexposure. If you're not using the Auto ISO setting, you can then boost or reduce the ISO to increase or decrease sensitivity.

Making Exposure Value Changes

Sometimes you'll want more or less exposure than indicated by the Sony Alpha's metering system. Perhaps you want to underexpose to create a silhouette effect, or overexpose to produce a high-key look. It's easy to use the Alpha's Exposure Compensation system to override the exposure recommendations. It's available in any exposure mode, including Scene modes, except Manual exposure.

Hold down the Exposure Compensation button (located on the back to the right of the optical viewfinder). Rotate the control dial to the right to make the image brighter (add exposure), and to the left to make the image darker (subtract exposure). The exposure scale in the viewfinder and on the LCD indicates the EV change you've made. The EV change you've made remains for the exposures that follow, until you manually zero out the EV setting with the Exposure Compensation button + control dial. As I noted, EV changes can't be made when using M; holding down the Exposure Compensation button while spinning the control dial changes the aperture.

Manual Exposure

Part of being an experienced photographer comes from knowing when to rely on your Sony Alpha's automation (including Auto, P mode, and Scene mode settings), when to go semi-automatic (with Shutter priority or Aperture priority), and when to set exposure manually (using M). Some photographers actually prefer to set their exposure manually, as the Alpha will be happy to provide an indication of when its metering system judges your manual settings provide the proper exposure, using the analog exposure scale at the bottom of the viewfinder and on the LCD.

Manual exposure can come in handy in some situations. You might be taking a silhouette photo and find that none of the exposure modes or EV correction features give you exactly the effect you want. For example, when I shot the windmill in Figure 4.14, there was no way any of my Sony Alpha's exposure modes would be able to interpret the scene the way I wanted to shoot it. So, I took a couple test exposures, and set the exposure manually to use the exact shutter speed and f/stop I needed. You might be working in a studio environment using multiple flash units. The additional flash are triggered by slave devices (gadgets that set off the flash when they sense the light from another flash, or, perhaps from a radio or infrared remote control). Your camera's exposure meter doesn't compensate for the extra illumination, and can't interpret the flash exposure at all, so you need to set the aperture manually.

Because, depending on your proclivities, you might not need to set exposure manually very often, you should still make sure you understand how it works. Fortunately, the Sony Alpha makes setting exposure manually very easy. Just set the mode dial to M, turn the control dial to set the shutter speed, and hold down the Exposure Compensation/AV (aperture value) button while rotating the control dial to adjust the aperture. Press the shutter release halfway, and the exposure scale in the viewfinder shows a secondary indicator that reveals how far your chosen setting diverges from the metered exposure.

Adjusting Exposure with ISO Settings

Another way of adjusting exposures is by changing the ISO sensitivity setting. Sometimes photographers forget about this option, because the common practice is to set the ISO once for a particular shooting session (say, at ISO 100 or 200 for bright sunlight outdoors, or ISO 800 when shooting indoors) and then forget about ISO. The reason for that is ISOs higher than ISO 100 or 200 are seen as "bad" or "necessary evils." However, changing the ISO is a valid way of adjusting exposure settings, particularly with the Sony Alpha, which produces good results at ISO settings that create grainy, unusable pictures with some other camera models.

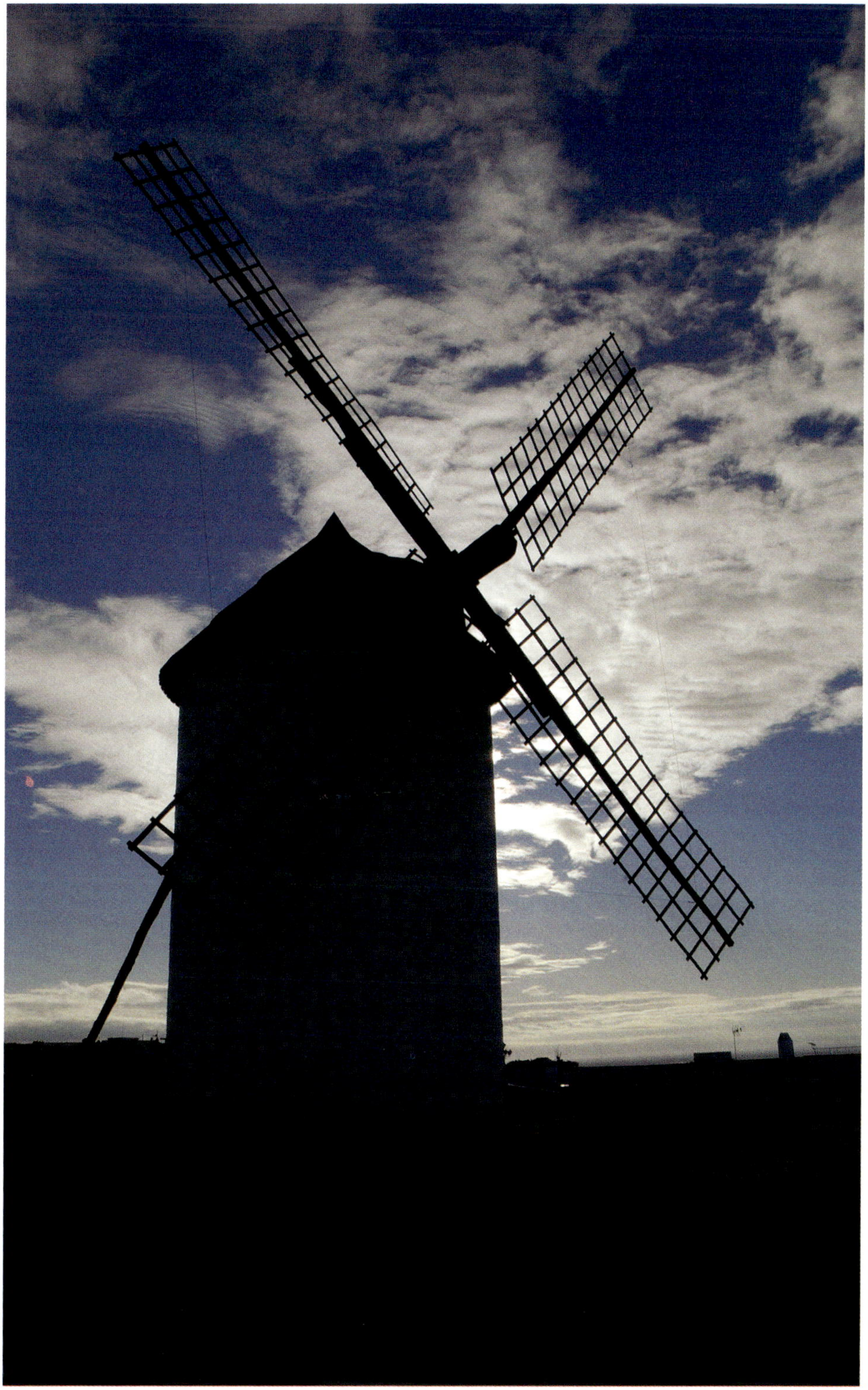

Figure 4.14
Manual mode allowed setting the exact exposure for this silhouette shot.

Indeed, I find myself using ISO adjustment as a convenient alternate way of adding or subtracting EV when shooting in Manual mode, and as a quick way of choosing equivalent exposures when in Automatic or Semi-automatic modes. For example, I've selected a manual exposure with both f/stop and shutter speed suitable for my image using, say, ISO 200. I can change the exposure in full-stop increments. The difference in image quality/noise at the base setting of ISO 200 is negligible if I dial in ISO 100 to reduce exposure a little, or change to ISO 400 to increase exposure. I keep my preferred f/stop and shutter speed, but still adjust the exposure.

Or, perhaps, I am using Shutter priority mode and the metered exposure at ISO 200 is 1/500th second at f/11. If I decide on the spur of the moment I'd rather use 1/500th second at f/8, I can press the ISO button, and spin the control dial to switch to ISO 100. Of course, it's a good idea to monitor your ISO changes, so you don't end up at ISO 1600 accidentally. ISO settings can, of course, also be used to boost or reduce sensitivity in particular shooting situations. The Sony Alpha can use ISO settings from ISO 100 up to 3200.

The camera can adjust the ISO automatically as appropriate for various lighting conditions. In Auto and Scene modes, ISO is normally set between ISO 100-800, but actually varies depending on the particular mode. When Auto ISO is chosen when using Program, Aperture priority, or Shutter priority modes, sensitivity will be set to ISO 100-400. If you want to use a higher ISO setting, you must select it manually. Auto ISO is not available when using Manual exposure.

Bracketing

Bracketing is a method for shooting several consecutive exposures using different settings, as a way of improving the odds that one will be exactly right. Before digital and electronic film cameras took over the universe, it was common to bracket exposures, shooting, say, a series of three photos at 1/125th second, but varying the f/stop from f/8 to f/11 to f/16. In practice, smaller than whole-stop increments were used for greater precision. Plus, it was just as common to keep the same aperture and vary the shutter speed, although in the days before electronic shutters, film cameras often had only whole increment shutter speeds available.

Today, cameras like the Alpha can bracket exposures much more precisely. When this feature is activated, the Alpha takes three consecutive photos: one at the metered "correct" exposure, one with less exposure, and one with more exposure, in your choice of 1/3 or 2/3 stop increments. Figure 4.15 shows an image with the metered exposure (center), flanked by exposures of 2/3 stop less (left), and 2/3 stop more (right).

Bracketing cannot be performed when using Auto or Scene exposure modes; you must be working with Program, Aperture priority, Shutter priority, or Manual exposure to use this feature. The Alpha cameras have just one exposure bracketing mode:

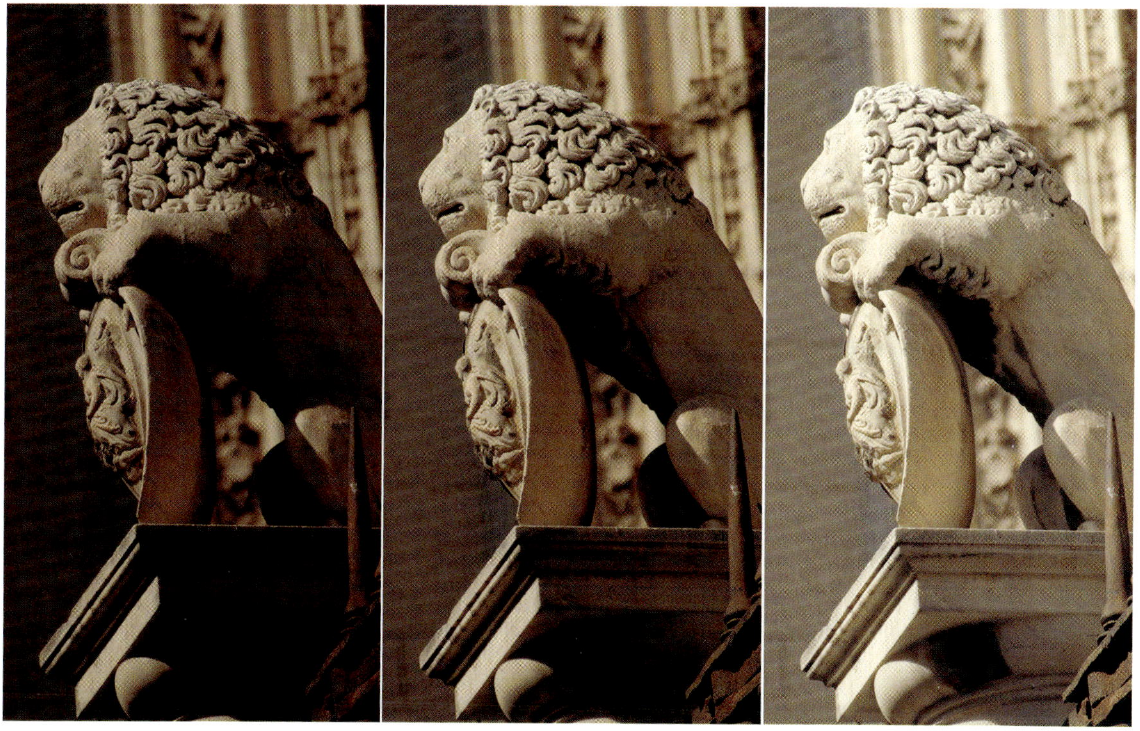

Figure 4.15 Metered exposure (center) accompanied by bracketed exposures of 2/3 stop less (left) and 2/3 stop more (right).

Continuous (BRK C), in which three exposures at the adjusted settings are taken if you hold down the shutter button. When bracket is set, a set of vertical lines appears above the center of the exposure scale in the viewfinder, showing how many shots remain to be shot in the set. When you begin, you'll see ||| (three lines), followed by ||, and then | as the bracket set is exposed. Here are some things to keep in mind:

- **Drive, he said.** You'll find the bracketing choice in the Drive menu. Press the Drive button (the left controller button) and choose BRK C. Then press the left/right directional buttons to switch between 0.3 and 0.7 bracket increments. Use 0.3 if you want to fine-tune exposure, or 0.7 if you'd like more dramatic changes between shots.
- **HDR isn't hard.** The 0.7 stop setting is the best choice if you plan to perform High Dynamic Range magic later on in Photoshop or another image editor. *Merge to HDR* (upgraded to a slightly more advanced *HDR Pro* feature in Photoshop CS5) allows you to combine three or more images with different exposures into one photo with an amazing amount of detail in both highlights and shadows. To get the best results, mount your camera on a tripod, shoot in RAW format, use BRK C, and set the exposure increment to 0.7 stops.

- **Adjust the base value.** You can bracket your exposures based on something other than the base (metered) exposure value. Make an adjustment for extra or less exposure with the Exposure Compensation button and control dial. Bracketing will be over, under, and equal to the *compensated* value.
- **What changes?** In Aperture priority mode, exposure bracketing will be achieved by changing the shutter speed; in Shutter priority mode, bracketing will be done using different f/stops; in Manual exposure mode, bracketing is applied using the shutter speed *unless* you press and hold the AEL button, in which case bracketing is done by changing the f/stop. In Program mode, the Alpha will use both shutter speed and aperture, as appropriate for your scene.
- **No Flash.** Automatic bracketing can't be used when working with the flash. The continuous shooting interval doesn't allow time for the flash to recycle between shots. Instead, you can use Flash Compensation, as described in Chapter 7, to bracket flash. Flash EV changes can be made plus or minus 2 EV in 1/3 EV steps, so you can manually select the Flash Compensation adjustments needed to simulate bracketing.

Dealing with Noise

Image noise is that random grainy effect that some like to use as a visual effect, but which, most of the time, is objectionable because it robs your image of detail even as it adds that "interesting" texture. Noise is caused by two different phenomena: high ISO settings and long exposures.

High ISO noise commonly appears when you raise your camera's sensitivity setting above ISO 400. With Sony cameras, which generally have good ISO noise characteristics, noise may become visible at ISO 800, and is usually fairly noticeable at ISO 1600 and ISO 3200. This kind of noise appears as a result of the amplification needed to increase the sensitivity of the sensor. While higher ISOs do pull details out of dark areas, they also amplify non-signal information randomly, creating noise. The Sony Alpha DSLR-A390/A290 automatically applies noise reduction that is strong enough to be visible as a reduction of sharpness in the image for any exposures taken when the ISO is set at ISO 1600 or ISO 3200. Figure 4.16 shows two pictures shot during different at-bats at the same baseball game. Both were exposed at ISO 1600, but with noise reduction applied in the version at top, and with no noise reduction at bottom. (I've exaggerated the differences between the two so the grainy/less grainy images are more evident on the printed page. The halftone screen applied to printed photos tends to mask these differences.)

A similar noisy phenomenon occurs during long time exposures, which allow more photons to reach the sensor, increasing your ability to capture a picture under low-light conditions. However, the longer exposures also increase the likelihood that some pixels will register random phantom photons, often because the longer an imager is "hot" the warmer it gets, and that heat can be mistaken for photons.

With a CCD like the one used in this Alpha series, the entire signal is conveyed off the chip and funneled through a single amplifier and analog-to-digital conversion circuit. Any noise introduced there is, at least, consistent. CMOS imagers found in some other

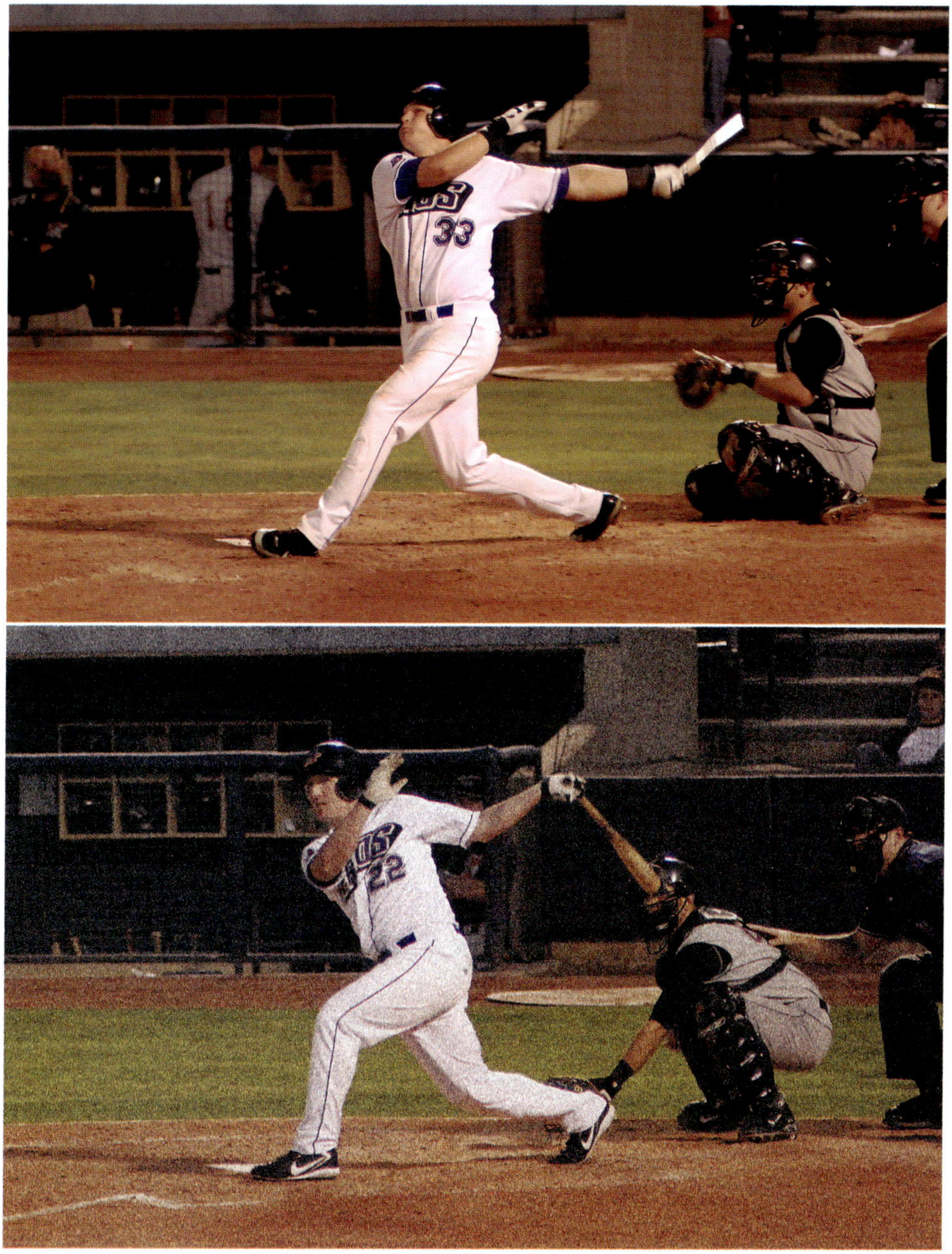

Figure 4.16 Noise reduction applied (top) produces a less grainy image than the version at bottom, which has no noise reduction.

Sony cameras, on the other hand, contain millions of individual amplifiers and A/D converters, all working in unison. Because all these circuits don't necessarily all process in precisely the same way all the time, they can introduce something called fixed-pattern noise into the image data. It's one kind of noise that your camera isn't subject to.

These Sony Alpha cameras perform long exposure noise reduction for any exposures longer than one full second. Fortunately, Sony's electronics geniuses have done an exceptional job minimizing noise. Even so, there are situations in which you might want to turn your camera's automatic noise reduction features on or off. For example, noise reduction can mask some detail as it removes random pixels from your image. Some of the image-making pixels are unavoidably vanquished at the same time. To enable/disable either type of noise reduction, navigate to Recording 2 menu and turn either Long exp. NR or High ISO NR on or off. Both types of NR are also disabled any time you are using continuous shooting or continuous bracketing, because noise reduction takes additional time that is not available when firing off continuous images.

You can also apply noise reduction to a lesser extent using Photoshop, and when converting RAW files to some other format, using your favorite RAW converter, or an industrial-strength product like Noise Ninja (www.picturecode.com) to wipe out noise after you've already taken the picture.

Fixing Exposures with Histograms

While you can often recover poorly exposed photos in your image editor, your best bet is to arrive at the correct exposure in the camera, minimizing the tweaks that you have to make in post-processing. However, you can't always judge exposure just by viewing the image on your Alpha's LCD after the shot is made. Nor can you get a 100-percent accurately exposed picture by using the Alpha's Live View feature. Ambient light may make the LCD difficult to see, and the brightness level you've set can affect the appearance of the playback image.

Instead, you can use a histogram, which is a chart displayed on the Sony Alpha's LCD that shows the number of tones being captured at each brightness level. You can use the information to provide correction for the next shot you take. The Alpha offers one histogram variation: one that shows overall brightness levels for an image and an alternate version that separates the red, green, and blue channels combined.

Both types are charts that include a representation of up to 256 vertical lines on a horizontal axis that show the number of pixels in the image at each brightness level, from 0 (black) on the left side to 255 (white) on the right. (The 2.7-inch LCD doesn't have enough pixels to show each and every one of the 256 lines, but, instead provides a representation of the shape of the curve formed.) The more pixels at a given level, the taller the bar at that position. If no bar appears at a particular position on the scale from left to right, there are no pixels at that particular brightness level.

A typical histogram produces a mountain-like shape, with most of the pixels bunched in the middle tones, with fewer pixels at the dark and light ends of the scale. Ideally, though, there will be at least some pixels at either extreme, so that your image has both a true black and a true white representing some details. Learn to spot histograms that represent over- and underexposure, and add or subtract exposure using an EV modification to compensate.

DISPLAYING HISTOGRAMS

To view histograms on your screen, press the DISP button while an image is shown on the LCD. Keep pressing the button until the histograms are shown. The histogram screen shows both brightness levels and levels for each of the red, green, and blue channels (Figure 4.17). During histogram display, you'll also see a thumbnail at the top left of the screen with your image displayed. An additional "live" histogram is available when using Live View mode on the A390. Note that Live View is possible only when using Program or Aperture priority modes; it cannot be used in Shutter priority or Manual exposure modes.

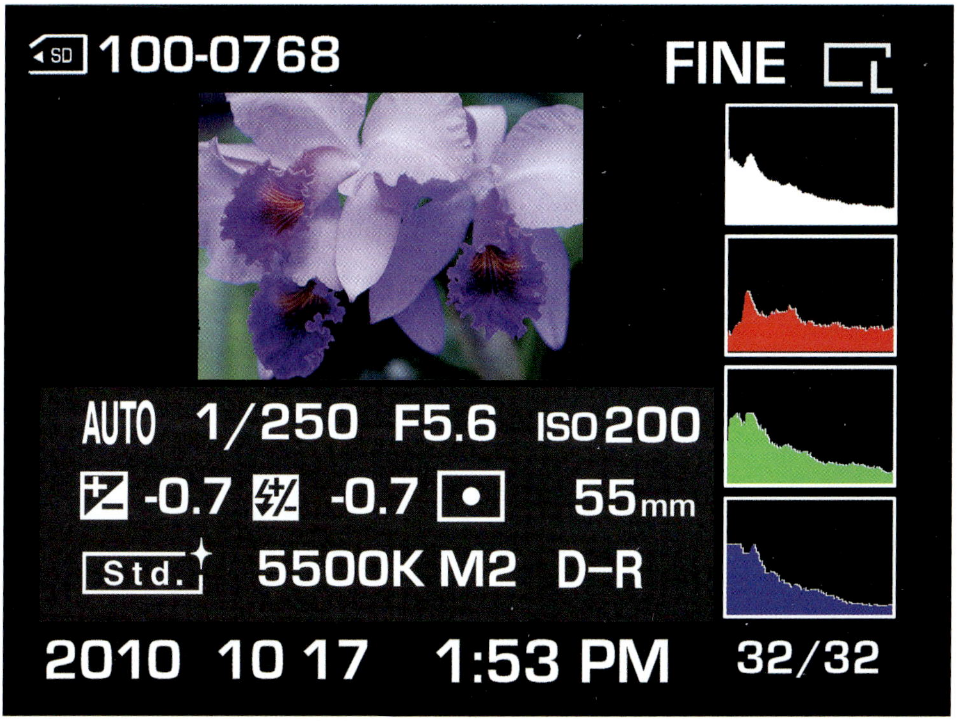

Figure 4.17 Histograms show the relationship of tones in an image, including brightness (top right), and red, green, and blue tones (middle and bottom right).

For example, Figure 4.18 shows the histogram for an image that is badly underexposed. You can guess from the shape of the histogram that many of the dark tones to the left of the graph have been clipped off. There's plenty of room on the right side for additional pixels to reside without having them become overexposed. Or, a histogram might look like Figure 4.19, which is overexposed. In either case, you can increase or decrease the exposure (either by changing the f/stop or shutter speed in Manual mode or by adding or subtracting an exposure compensation value in P, S, or A modes) to produce the corrected histogram shown in Figure 4.20, in which the tones "hug" the right side of the histogram to produce as many highlight details as possible. See "Making Exposure Value Changes," above for information on dialing in exposure compensation.

The histogram can also be used to aid in fixing the contrast of an image, although gauging incorrect contrast is more difficult. For example, if the histogram shows all the tones bunched up in one place in the image, the photo will be low in contrast. If the tones are spread out more or less evenly, the image is probably high in contrast. In either case, your best bet may be to switch to RAW (if you're not already using that format) so you can adjust contrast in post-processing.

Scene Modes

The final tools in your exposure repertoire are the seven Scene modes, which can automatically make all the basic settings needed for certain types of shooting situations, such as portraits, landscapes, close-ups, sports, night portraits, and "no-flash zone" pictures. These "autopilot" modes are especially useful when you suddenly encounter a picture-taking opportunity and don't have time to decide exactly which mode you want to use. Instead, you can spin the mode dial to the appropriate Scene mode and fire away, knowing that, at least, you have a fighting chance of getting a good or usable photo.

Scene modes are also helpful when you're just learning to use your Alpha. Once you've learned how to operate your camera, you'll probably prefer one of the PASM modes that provide more control over shooting options. The Scene modes may give you few options or none at all. The AF mode, drive mode, and metering mode are all set for you. Here are the modes available:

- **Auto.** This is the mode to use when you hand your camera to a total stranger and ask him or her to take your picture posing in front of the Eiffel Tower. All the photographer has to do is press the shutter release button. Every other decision is made by the camera's electronics.
- **Portrait.** This mode tends to use wider f/stops and faster shutter speeds, providing blurred backgrounds and images with no camera shake. If you hold the shutter release down, the Alpha will take a continuous sequence of photos, which can be useful in capturing fleeting expressions in portrait situations.

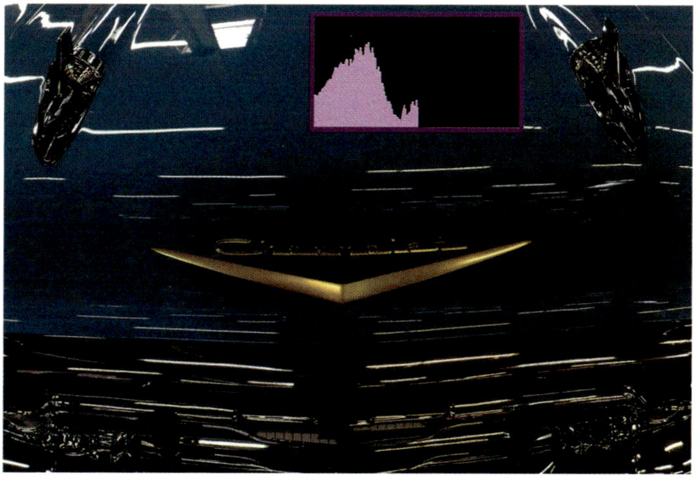

Figure 4.18
This histogram shows an underexposed image.

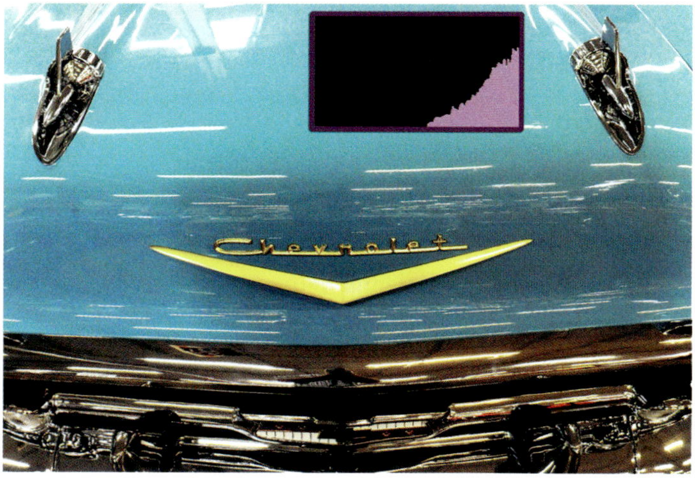

Figure 4.19
This histogram reveals that the image is overexposed.

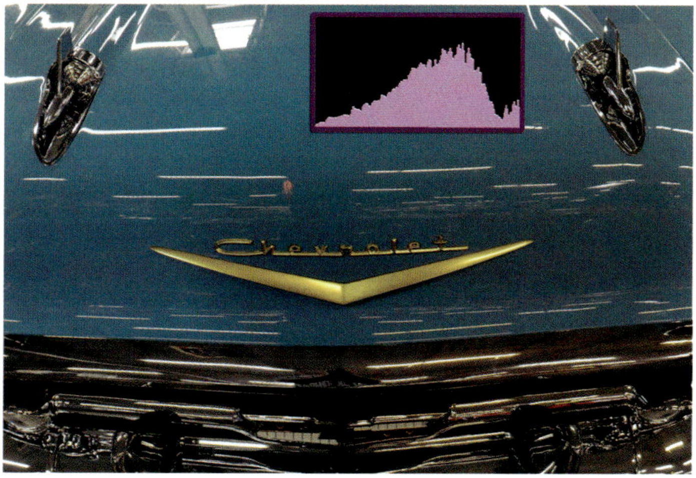

Figure 4.20
A histogram for a properly exposed image should look like this.

- **Landscape.** The Alpha tries to use smaller f/stops for more depth-of-field, and boosts saturation slightly for richer colors.
- **Macro.** This mode is similar to the Portrait setting, with wider f/stops to isolate your close-up subjects, and high shutter speeds to eliminate the camera shake that's accentuated at close focusing distances. However, if you have your camera mounted on a tripod or are using SteadyShot, you might want to use Aperture priority mode instead, so you can specify a smaller f/stop with additional depth-of-field.
- **Sports action.** In this mode, the Alpha tries to use high shutter speeds to freeze action, switches to Continuous drive mode to allow taking a quick sequence of pictures with one press of the shutter release, and uses Continuous Autofocus to continually refocus as your subject moves around in the frame. You can find more information on autofocus options in Chapter 5.
- **Sunset.** Increases saturation to emphasize the red tones of a sunrise or sunset. You can use exposure compensation to underexpose slightly to deepen colors, or overexpose to lighten them.
- **Night Portrait/Night View.** Combines flash with ambient light to produce an image that is mainly illuminated by the flash, but the background is exposed by the available light. This mode uses longer exposures, so a tripod, monopod, or SteadyShot is a must. To switch from Night Portrait to Night View mode, just set the Flash mode to Flash Off.
- **Flash Off.** Absolutely prevents the flash from flipping up and firing (like Flash Off in the Flash mode options menu, described in Chapter 7). You might want to use this mode in some situations, such as religious ceremonies, museums, classical music concerts, and your double-naught spy activities.

5

Advanced Techniques for Your Sony Alpha DSLR-A390/A290

Of the primary foundations of great photography, only one of them—the ability to capture a compelling image with a pleasing composition—takes a lifetime (or longer) to master. The art of *making* a photograph, rather than just *taking* a photograph, requires an aesthetic eye that sees the right angle for the shot, as well as a sense of what should be included or excluded in the frame; a knowledge of what has been done in the medium before (and where photography can be taken in the future); and a willingness to explore new areas. The more you pursue photography, the more you will learn about visualization and composition. When all is said and done, this is what photography is all about.

The other basics of photography—equally essential—involve more technical aspects: the ability to use your camera's features to produce an image with good tonal and color values; to achieve sharpness (where required) or unsharpness (when you're using selective focus); and mastering appropriate white/color balance. It's practical to learn these technical skills in a time frame that's much less than a lifetime, although most of us find there is always room for improvement. You'll find the basic information you need to become proficient in each of these technical areas in this book.

You've probably already spent a lot of time learning your Sony Alpha's basic features, and setting it up to take decent pictures automatically, with little input from you. It probably felt great to gain the confidence to snap off picture after picture, knowing that a large percentage of them were going to be well exposed, in sharp focus, and rich with color. The Sony dSLRs are designed to produce good, basic images right out of the box.

But after you were comfortable with your camera, you began looking for ways to add your own creativity to your shots. You explored ways of tweaking the exposure, using selective focus, and, perhaps, experimenting with the different looks that various lens zoom settings (*focal lengths*) could offer.

The final, and most rewarding, stage comes when you begin exploring advanced techniques that enable you to get stunning shots that will have your family, friends, and colleagues asking you, "How did you *do* that?" These more advanced techniques deserve an entire book of their own (and I have one for you called *Digital SLR Pro Secrets*, also from Course Technology). But there is plenty of room in this chapter to introduce you to some clever things you can do with your Sony Alpha dSLR that you might not have thought of.

Exploring Ultra-Fast Exposures

Fast shutter speeds stop action because they capture only a tiny slice of time. Electronic flash also freezes motion by virtue of its extremely short duration—as brief as 1/50,000th second or less. The Sony Alpha A390/A290 dSLRs have a top shutter speed of 1/4,000th second and their built-in flash units can give you these ultra-quick glimpses of moving subjects. An external flash, such as one of the Sony HVL-series strobes, offers even more versatility. You can read more about using electronic flash to stop action in Chapter 7.

In this chapter, I'm going to emphasize the use of short exposures to capture a moment in time. The Sony Alpha is fully capable of immobilizing all but the fastest movement using only its shutter speeds, which range all the way up to that impressive 1/4,000th second. Some cameras, such as the stablemate Alpha DSLR-A850, have speeds up to 1/8,000 second, but those ultra-fast shutters are generally overkill when it comes to stopping action, and rarely needed for achieving the exposure you desire. For example, the image shown in Figure 5.1 required a shutter speed of just 1/2,000th second to freeze the runner as she cleared the hurdles.

When it comes to stopping action, most sports can be frozen at 1/2,000th second or slower, and for many sports a shutter speed significantly slower than that is actually preferable—for example, to allow the wheels of a racing automobile or motorcycle, or the propeller on a classic aircraft, to blur realistically, a speed of 1/250th to 1/500th second might be appropriate.

In practice, shutter speeds faster than 1/4,000th second are rarely required. If you wanted to use an aperture of f/1.8 at ISO 100 outdoors in bright sunlight, say to throw a background out of focus with a wide aperture's shallow depth-of-field, a shutter speed of 1/4,000th second would more than do the job. You'd need a faster shutter speed only if you moved the ISO setting to a higher sensitivity, and you probably wouldn't do that if your goal were to use the widest f/stop possible. Under *less* than full sunlight, 1/4,000th second is more than fast enough for any conditions you're likely to encounter.

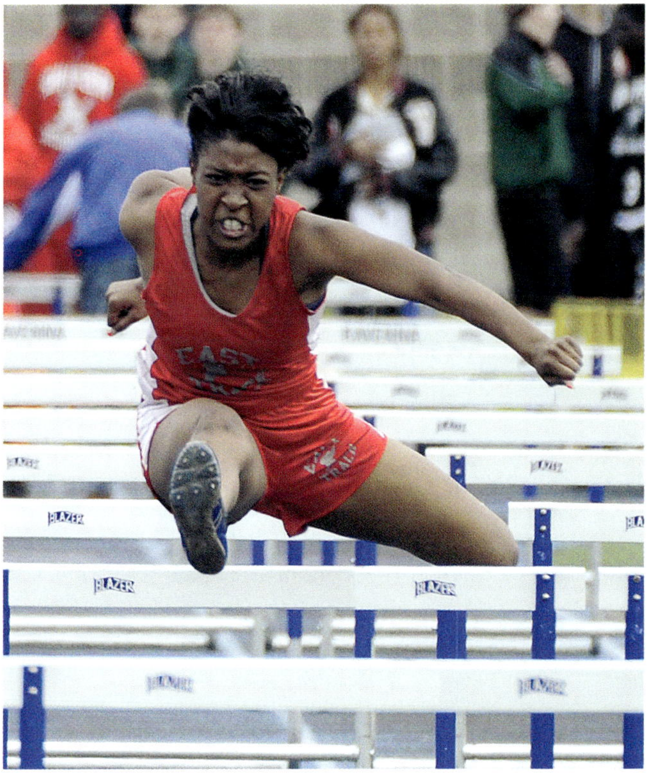

Figure 5.1
A shutter speed of 1/2,000th second will stop most action.

That's why electronic flash units work so well for high-speed photography when used as the only source of illumination: they provide both the effect of a very brief shutter speed and the high levels of light needed for an exposure.

Of course, as you'll see, the tiny slices of time extracted by the millisecond duration of an electronic flash exact a penalty. To use flash at its full power setting, you have to use a shutter speed equal to or slower than the *maximum sync speed* of your Alpha camera. With the A390/A290, the top speed usable for flash is 1/160th second (unless you're using the High-Speed Sync mode I'll describe in Chapter 7). The sync speed is the fastest speed at which the camera's focal plane shutter is completely open. At shorter speeds, the camera uses a "slit" passed in front of the sensor to make an exposure. The flash will illuminate only the portion of the slit exposed during the duration of the flash.

Indoors, that shutter speed limitation may cause problems: at 1/160th second, there may be enough existing ("ambient") light to cause ghost images. Outdoors, you may find it difficult to achieve a correct exposure. In bright sunlight at the lowest ISO settings available with the Alpha cameras, an exposure of 1/160th second at f/13 might be required. So, even if you want to use daylight as your main light source, and work with flash only as a fill for shadows, you can have problems. I'll explain the vagaries of electronic flash in more detail in Chapter 7.

You can have a lot of fun exploring the kinds of pictures you can take using very brief exposure times, whether you decide to take advantage of the action-stopping capabilities of your built-in or external electronic flash or work with the motion-freezing capabilities of Sony dSLR's faster shutter speeds (between 1/1,000th and 1/4,000th second). Here are a few ideas to get you started:

- **Take revealing images.** Fast shutter speeds can help you reveal the real subject behind the façade, by freezing constant motion to capture an enlightening moment in time. Legendary fashion/portrait photographer Philippe Halsman used leaping photos of famous people, such as the Duke and Duchess of Windsor, Richard Nixon, and Salvador Dali to illuminate their real selves. Halsman said, "*When you ask a person to jump, his attention is mostly directed toward the act of jumping and the mask falls so that the real person appears.*" Try some high-speed portraits of people you know in motion to see how they appear when concentrating on something other than the portrait.

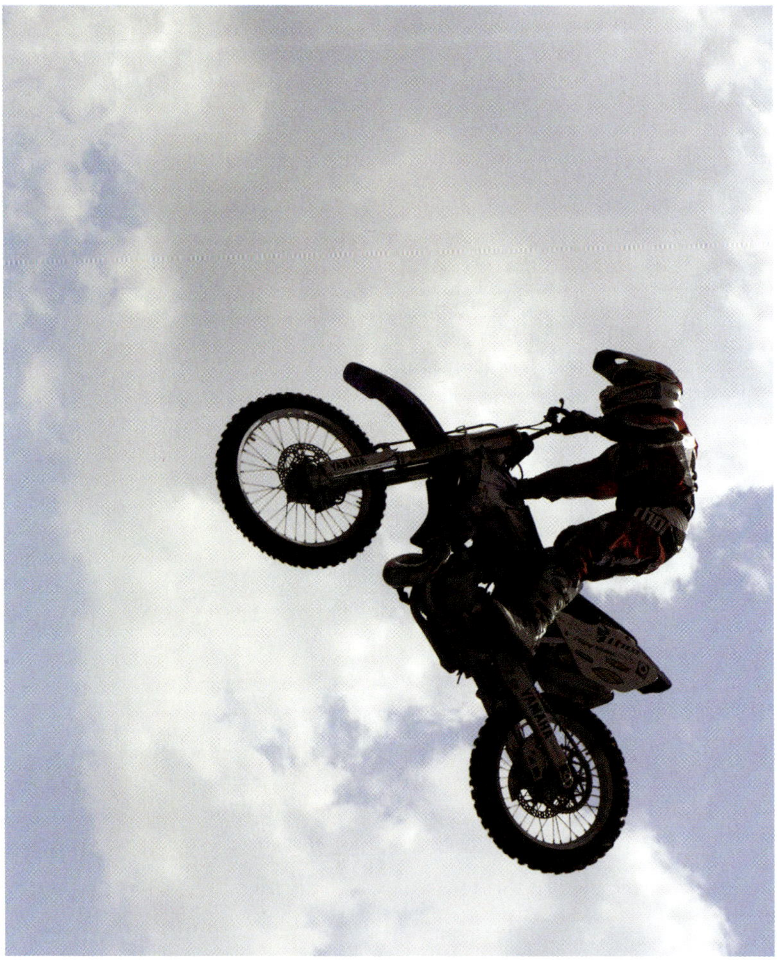

Figure 5.2
Freezing a leaping motocross rider in mid-air makes for an image that verges on the surreal.

- **Create unreal images.** High-speed photography can also produce photographs that show your subjects in ways that are quite unreal. A helicopter in mid-air with its rotors frozen or a motocross cyclist leaping over a ramp, but with all motion stopped so that the rider and machine look as if they were frozen in mid-air, make for an unusual picture. (See the silhouetted rider in Figure 5.2.) When we're accustomed to seeing subjects in motion, seeing them stopped in time can verge on the surreal.
- **Capture unseen perspectives.** Some things are *never* seen in real life, except when viewed in a stop-action photograph. M.I.T. professor Dr. Harold Edgerton's famous balloon burst photographs were only a starting point for the inventor of the electronic flash unit. Freeze a hummingbird in flight for a view of wings that never seem to stop. Or, capture the splashes as liquid falls into a bowl, as shown in Figure 5.3. No electronic flash was required for this image (and wouldn't have illuminated the water in the bowl as evenly). Instead, a clutch of high-intensity lamps and an ISO setting of 1600 allowed the Sony dSLR to capture this image at 1/2,000th second.

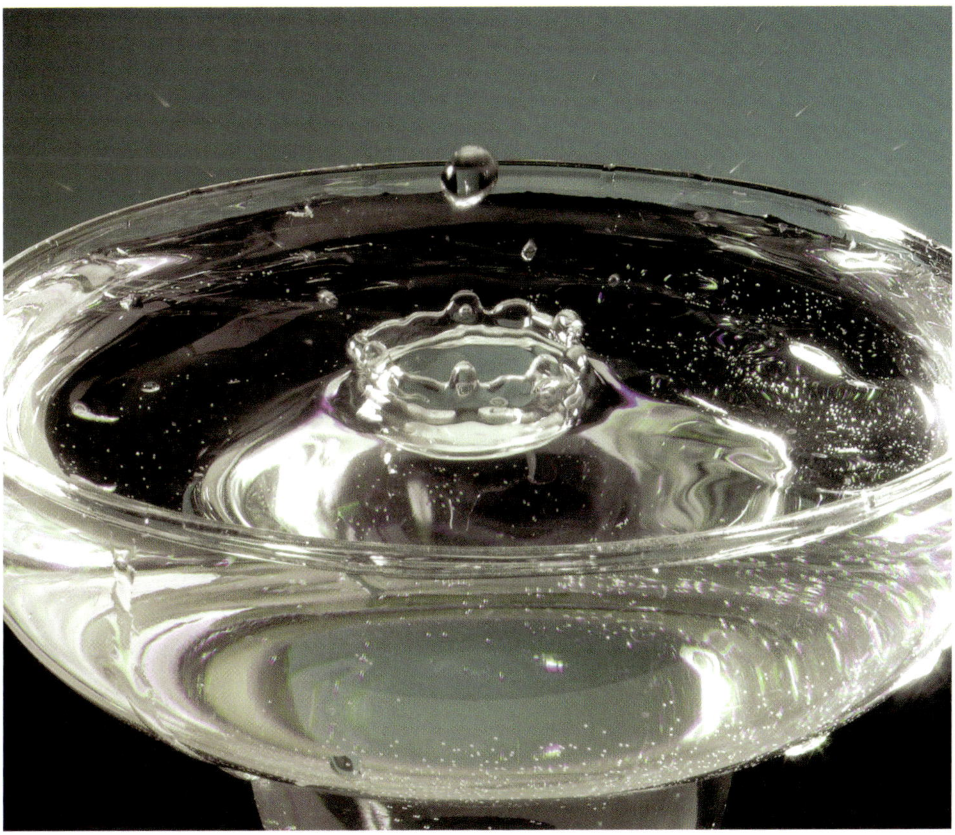

Figure 5.3
A large amount of artificial illumination and an ISO 1600 sensitivity setting allowed capturing this shot at 1/2,000th second without use of an electronic flash.

Long Exposures

Longer exposures are a doorway into another world, showing us how even familiar scenes can look much different when photographed over periods measured in seconds. At night, long exposures produce streaks of light from moving, illuminated subjects like automobiles or amusement park rides. Or, you can move the camera or zoom the lens to get interesting streaks from non-moving light sources, such as the holiday lights shown in Figure 5.4. Extra-long exposures of seemingly pitch-dark subjects can reveal interesting views using light levels barely bright enough to see by. At any time of day, including daytime (in which case you'll often need the help of neutral-density filters to make the long exposure practical), long exposures can cause moving objects to vanish entirely, because they don't remain stationary long enough to register in a photograph.

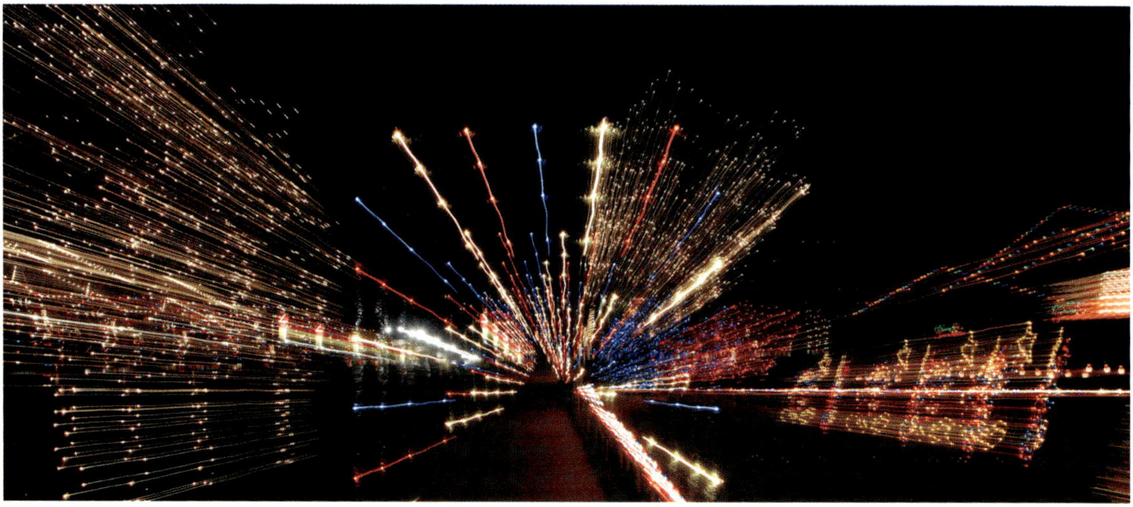

Figure 5.4 Zooming during exposure can produce interesting streaks of light.

Three Ways to Take Long Exposures

There are actually three common types of lengthy exposures: *timed exposures, bulb exposures,* and *time exposures.* The Sony dSLR offers only the first two, but once you understand all three, you'll see why Sony made the choices it did. Because of the length of the exposure, all of the following techniques should be used with a tripod to hold the camera steady.

- **Timed exposures.** These are long exposures from 1 second to 30 seconds, measured by the camera itself. To take a picture in this range, simply select Manual or Shutter priority modes and use the control dial to set the shutter speed to the length of time you want, choosing from preset speeds of 1.0, 1.3, 1.6, 2.0, 2.5, 3.2, 4.0, 5.0, 6.0, 8.0, 10.0, 13.0, 15.0, 20.0, 25.0, and 30.0 seconds. The advantage of timed exposures is that the camera does all the calculating for you. There's no need for a stopwatch. If you review your image on the LCD and decide to try again with the exposure doubled or halved, you can dial in the correct exposure with precision. The disadvantage of timed exposures is that you can't take a photo for longer than 30 seconds.

- **Bulb exposures.** This type of exposure is so-called because in the olden days the photographer squeezed and held an air bulb attached to a tube that provided the force necessary to keep the shutter open. Traditionally, a bulb exposure is one that lasts as long as the shutter release button is pressed; when you release the button, the exposure ends. To make a bulb exposure with the Sony Alpha, set the camera on Manual mode and use the control dial to select the shutter speed immediately after 30 seconds. BULB will be displayed on the LCD and buLb shown in the viewfinder. Then, press the shutter to start the exposure, and release it to close the shutter. If you'd like to minimize camera shake, you can use the self-timer or the Sony infrared remote control.
- **Time exposures.** This is a setting found on some cameras to produce longer exposures. With cameras that implement this option, the shutter opens when you press the shutter release button, and remains open until you press the button again. Usually, you'll be able to close the shutter using a mechanical cable release or, more commonly, an electronic release cable. The advantage of this approach is that you can take an exposure of virtually any duration without the need for special equipment. You can press the shutter release button, go off for a few minutes, and come back to close the shutter (assuming your camera is still there). The disadvantages of this mode are exposures must be timed manually, and with shorter exposures it's possible for the vibration of manually opening and closing the shutter to register in the photo. For longer exposures, the period of vibration is relatively brief and not usually a problem—and there is always the release cable option to eliminate photographer-caused camera shake entirely. While the Sony Alpha does not have a built-in time exposure capability, you can still get lengthy exposures using the RMT-DSLR1 Remote Commander, an infrared remote control that has a shutter lock button to hold the shutter open for the duration of your time exposure. This remote can also be used to control playback of your images when the Alpha is connected to an HDTV.

Working with Long Exposures

Because the Sony Alpha produces such good images at longer exposures, and there are so many creative things you can do with long exposure techniques, you'll want to do some experimenting. Get yourself a tripod or another firm support and take some test shots with long exposure noise reduction both enabled and disabled (to see whether you prefer low noise or high detail) and get started.

Here are some things to try:

- **Make people invisible.** One very cool thing about long exposures is that objects that move rapidly enough won't register at all in a photograph, while the subjects that remain stationary are portrayed in the normal way. That makes it easy to produce people-free landscape photos and architectural photos at night or, even, in full daylight if you use a neutral-density filter (or two or three) to allow an exposure of at least a few seconds. At ISO 100, f/22, and a pair of 8X (three-stop) neutral-density filters, you can use exposures of nearly two seconds; overcast days and/or even more neutral-density filtration would work even better if daylight people-vanishing is your goal. They'll have to be walking *very* briskly and across the field of view (rather than directly toward the camera) for this to work. At night, it's much easier to achieve this effect with the 20- to 30-second exposures that are possible.
- **Create streaks.** If you aren't shooting for total invisibility, long exposures with the camera on a tripod can produce some interesting streaky effects. Even a single 8X ND filter will let you shoot at f/22 and 1/6th second in daylight. Indoors, you can achieve interesting streaks with slow shutter speeds, as shown in Figure 5.5. I shot the ballet dancers using a 1/2 second exposure, triggering the shot at the beginning of a movement.

Tip

Neutral-density filters are gray (non-colored) filters that reduce the amount of light passing through the lens, without adding any color or effect of their own.

- **Produce light trails.** At night, car headlights, taillights, and other moving sources of illumination can generate interesting light trails. Your camera doesn't even need to be mounted on a tripod; handholding the Sony Alpha for longer exposures adds movement and patterns to your trails. If you're shooting fireworks, a longer exposure—with a tripod—may allow you to combine several bursts into one picture, as shown in Figure 5.6.
- **Blur waterfalls, etc.** You'll find that waterfalls and other sources of moving liquid produce a special type of long-exposure blur, because the water merges into a fantasy-like veil that looks different at different exposure times, and with different waterfalls. Cascades with turbulent flow produce a rougher look at a given longer exposure than falls that flow smoothly. Although blurred waterfalls have become almost a cliché, there are still plenty of variations for a creative photographer to explore, as you can see in Figure 5.7. For that shot, I incorporated the flowing stream in the background.

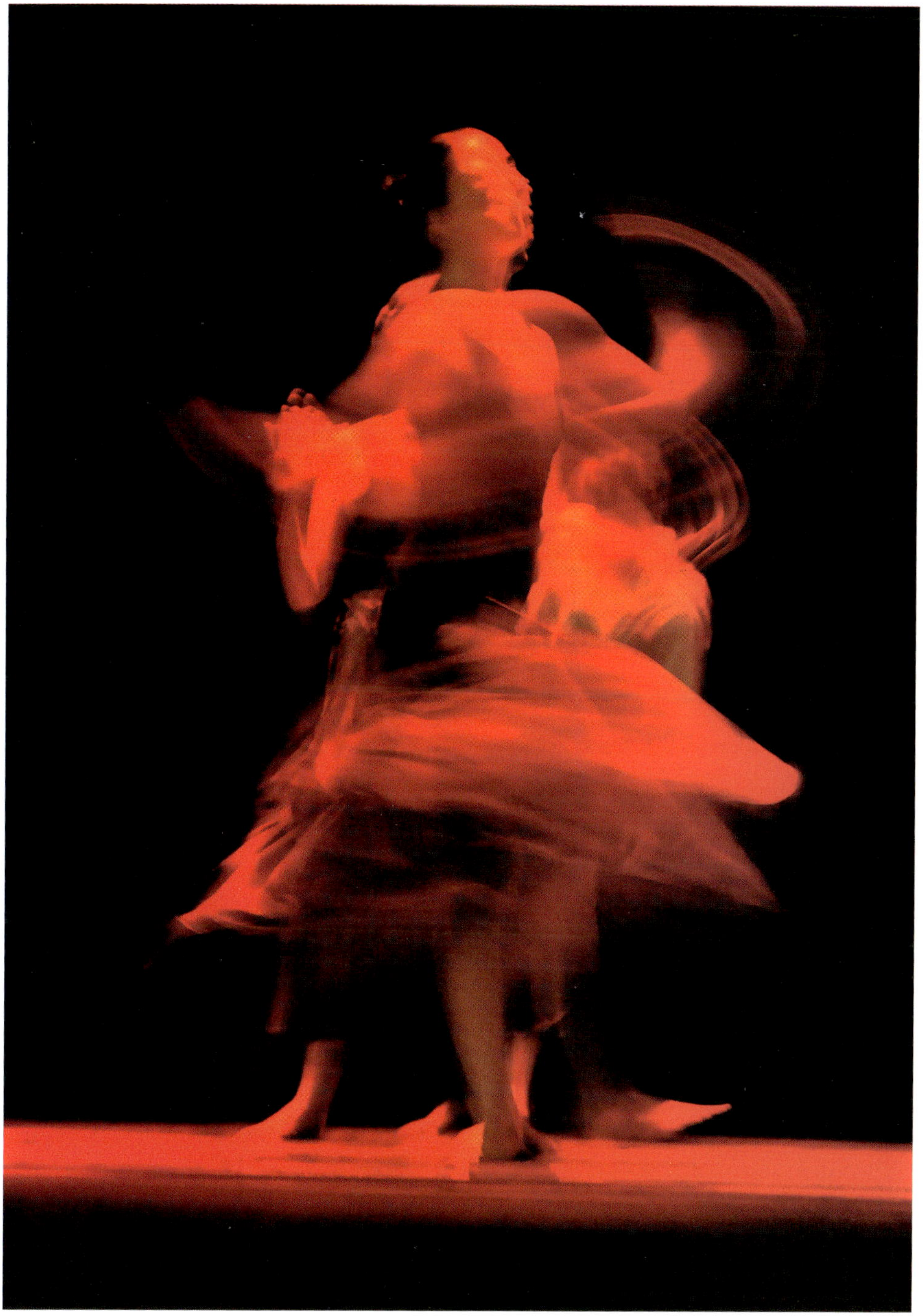

Figure 5.5
The shutter opened as the dancers began their movement from a standing position, and finished when they had bent over and paused.

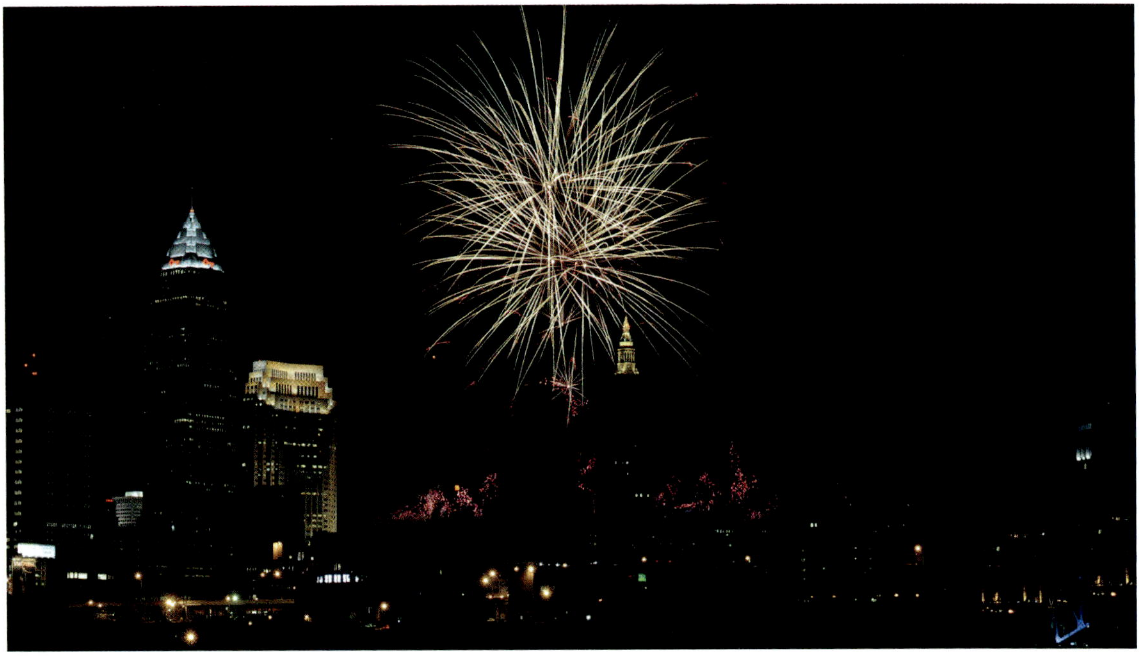

Figure 5.6 I caught the fireworks after a baseball game from a half-mile away, using a four-second exposure to capture several bursts in one shot.

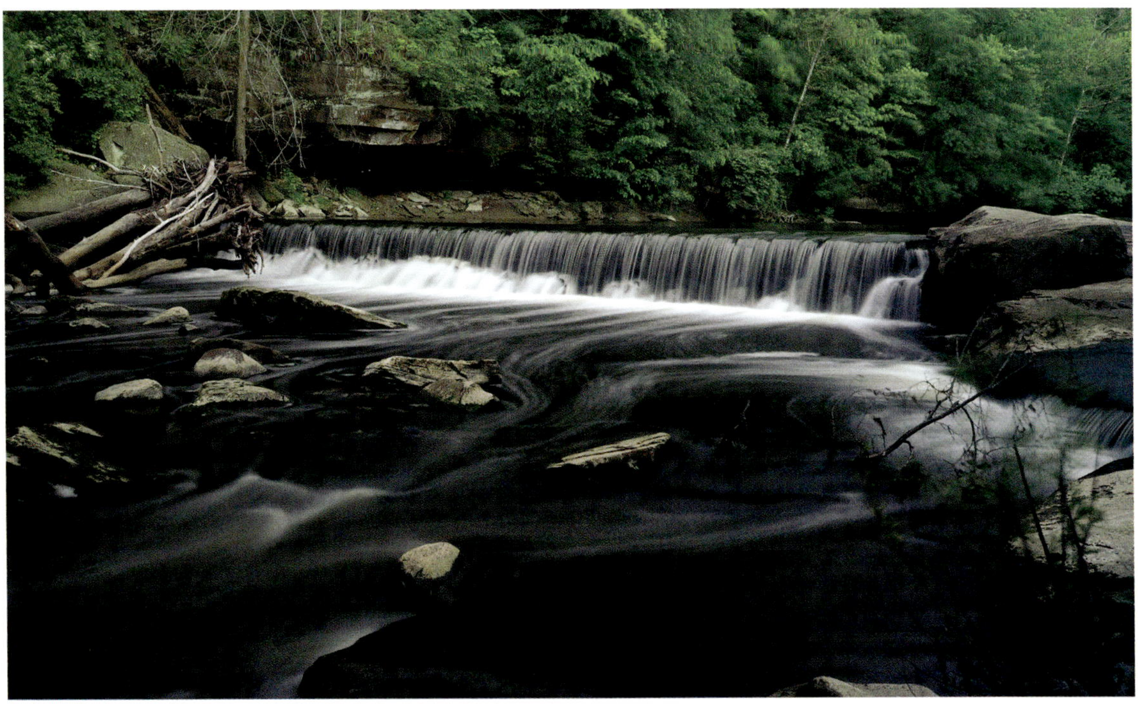

Figure 5.7 Long exposures can transform a waterfall and stream into a display of flowing silk.

- **Show total darkness in new ways.** Even on the darkest, moonless nights, there is enough starlight or glow from distant illumination sources to see by, and, if you use a long exposure, there is enough light to take a picture, too. I was visiting a lakeside park hours after sunset, but found that a one-second exposure at ISO 1600 revealed the scene shown in Figure 5.8, even though in real life, there was barely enough light to make out the boats in the distance. Although the photo appears as if it were taken at twilight or sunset, in fact the shot was made at 10 p.m.

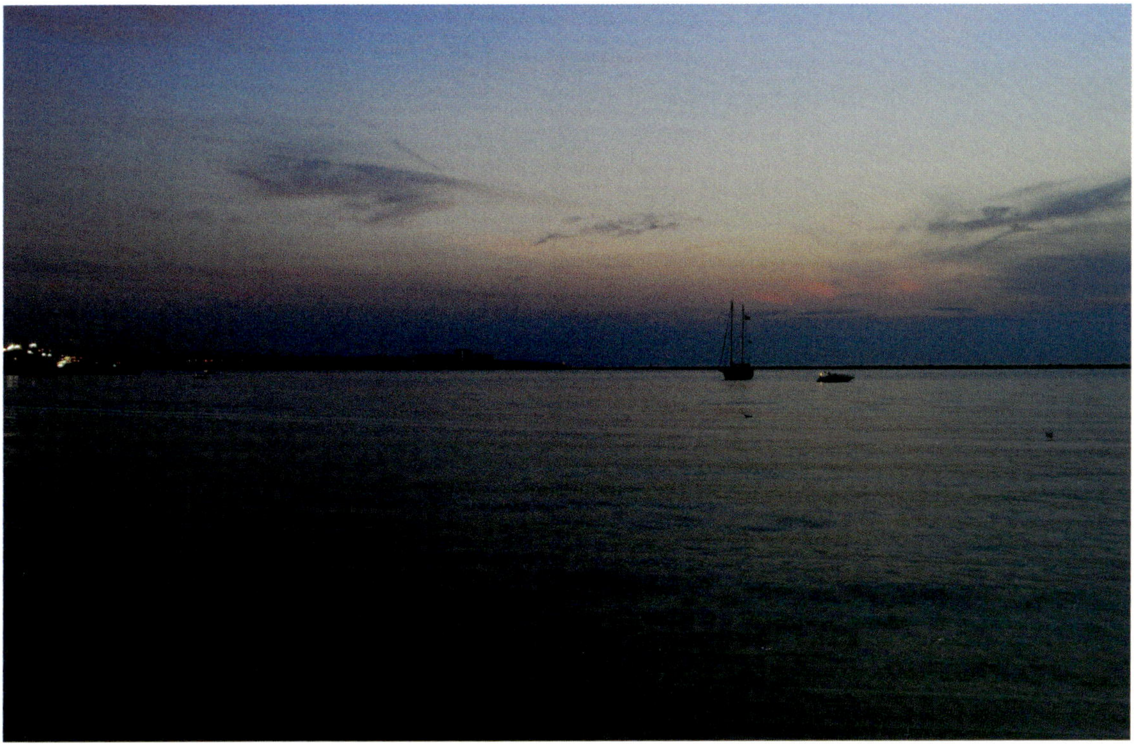

Figure 5.8 A long exposure transformed this night scene into a picture apparently taken at dusk.

Delayed Exposures

Sometimes it's desirable to have a delay of some sort before a picture is actually taken. Perhaps you'd like to get in the picture yourself, and would appreciate it if the camera waited 10 seconds after you press the shutter release to actually take the picture. Maybe you want to give a tripod-mounted camera time to settle down and damp any residual vibration after the release is pressed to improve sharpness for an exposure with a relatively slow shutter speed. It's possible you want to explore the world of time-lapse photography. The next sections present your delayed exposure options.

Self-Timer

The Sony dSLRs have a built-in self-timer with 10-second and 2-second delays. Activate the timer by pressing the Drive button (the left controller button) and then pressing the up/down controller buttons to choose the self-timer icon. Then, press the left/right controller buttons to toggle between 2-second and 10-second exposures. Press the center controller button to lock in your choice.

Then, press the shutter release button halfway to lock in focus on your subjects (if you're taking a self-portrait, focus on an object at a similar distance and use focus lock). When you're ready to take the photo, continue pressing the shutter release the rest of the way. The lamp on the front of the camera handgrip will blink slowly for eight seconds (when using the 10-second timer) and the beeper will chirp (if you haven't disabled it). During the final two seconds, the beeper sounds more rapidly and the lamp remains on until the picture is taken. (With the 2-second timer, you get 1.5-seconds of rapid chirping, followed by a longer beep just before the picture is taken.)

Getting into Focus

Prior to the invention of autofocus (in which Sony's predecessor Minolta was instrumental), focusing was always done manually. Honest. Even though viewfinders of film cameras were bigger and brighter than they are today, special focusing screens, magnifiers, and other gadgets were often used to help the photographer achieve correct focus. Imagine what it must have been like to focus manually under demanding, fast-moving conditions such as sports photography.

Learning to use the Sony dSLRs' modern autofocus system is easy, but you do need to fully understand how the system works to get the most benefit from it. Once you're comfortable with autofocus, you'll know when it's appropriate to use the manual focus option, too. The important thing to remember is that focus isn't absolute. For example, some things that look in sharp focus at a given viewing size and distance might not be in focus at a larger size and/or closer distance. In addition, the goal of optimum focus isn't always to make things look sharp. Not all of an image will be or should be sharp. Controlling exactly what is sharp and what is not is part of your creative palette. Use of depth-of-field characteristics to throw part of an image out of focus while other parts are sharply focused is one of the most valuable tools available to a photographer. But selective focus works only when the desired areas of an image are in focus properly. For the digital SLR photographer, correct focus can be one of the trickiest parts of the technical and creative process.

To make your job easier, the Sony Alpha A390/A290 dSLRs have a precision nine-point autofocus system that uses a separate sensor in the viewing system to measure the contrast of the image. When the contrast is highest at the active autofocus point(s), that part of the image is in sharp focus. The active focus points are actually nine sets of lines represented by boxes visible in the viewfinder (see Figure 5.9), and can be selected automatically by the camera, or manually by you, the photographer. The center autofocus point is of the advanced "cross" type (that is, it measures in both horizontal and vertical directions) that works with all Sony lenses having a maximum aperture of f/5.6 or larger, but has enhanced sensitivity when used with faster lenses.

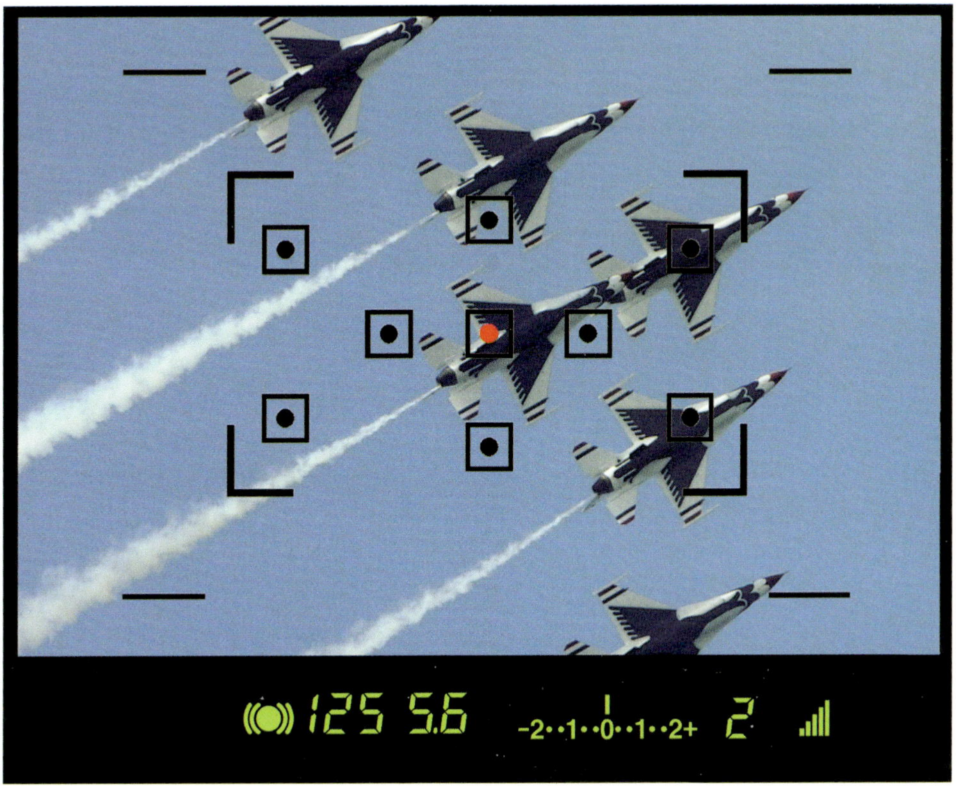

Figure 5.9
Any of the nine autofocus points can be selected by the photographer manually or by the camera automatically.

The camera also looks for these contrast differences among pixels to determine relative sharpness. There are two ways that sharp focus is determined:

Phase Detection

In this mode, the autofocus sampling area is divided into two halves by a lens in the sensor. The two halves are compared, much like (actually, exactly like) a two-window rangefinder used in surveying, weaponry, and non-SLR cameras like the venerable Leica M film models. The contrast between the two images changes as focus is moved in or out, until sharp focus is achieved when the images are "in phase," or lined up.

You can visualize how phase detection autofocus works if you look at Figures 5.10 and 5.11. (However, your camera's actual autofocus sensors don't look *anything* like this;

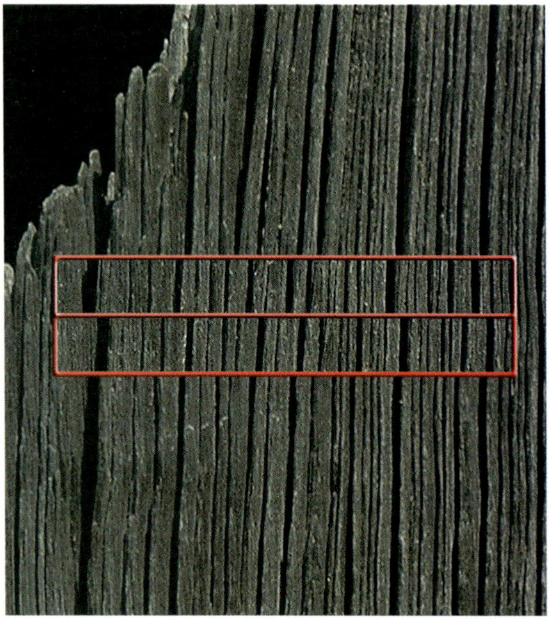

Figure 5.10 When an image is out of focus, the split lines don't align precisely.

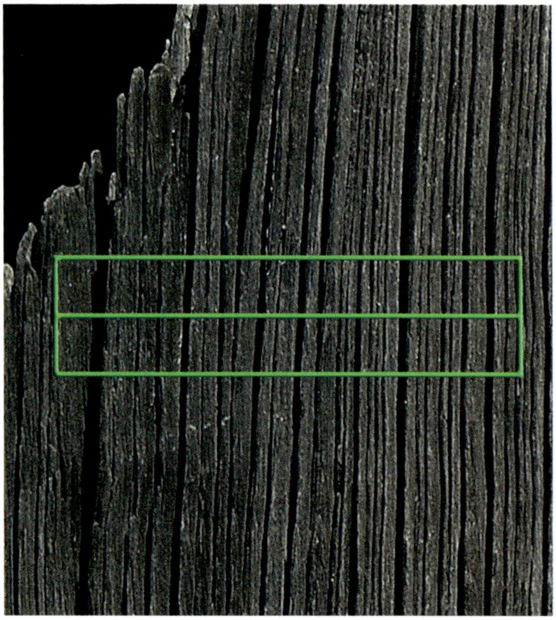

Figure 5.11 Using phase detection, the Alpha is able to align the features of the image and achieve sharp focus quickly.

I'm providing a greatly simplified view just for illustration.) In Figure 5.10, a typical horizontally oriented focus sensor is looking at a series of parallel vertical lines in a weathered piece of wood. The lines are broken into two halves by the sensor's rangefinder prism, and you can see that they don't line up exactly; the image is slightly out of focus.

Fortunately, the rangefinder approach of phase detection tells the Alpha exactly how out of focus the image is, and in which direction (focus is too near, or too far) thanks to the amount and direction of the displacement of the split image. The camera can quickly and precisely snap the image into sharp focus and line up the vertical lines, as shown in Figure 5.11. Of course, this scenario—vertical lines being interpreted by a horizontally oriented sensor—is ideal. When the same sensor is asked to measure focus for, say, horizontal lines that don't split up quite so conveniently, or, in the worst case, subjects such as the sky (which may have neither vertical or horizontal lines), focus can slow down drastically, or even become impossible.

Phase detection is the normal mode used by the Alpha for autofocus, in both Optical Viewfinder (OVF) and Live View modes (available only in the A390 model). (I'll tell you more about Live View later in this chapter.) As with any rangefinder-like function, accuracy is better when the "base length" between the two images is larger. (Think back to your high school trigonometry; you could calculate a distance more accurately when the separation between the two points where the angles were measured was greater.) For that reason, phase detection autofocus is more accurate with larger (wider) lens openings—especially those with maximum f/stops of f/2.8 or better—than with smaller lens openings, and may not work at all when the f/stop is smaller than f/5.6. As I noted, the Alpha is able to perform these comparisons very quickly.

Improved Cross-Type Focus Point

One improvement that new Sony Alpha owners sometimes overlook is the upgrade to a cross-type focus point at the center position. Why is this important? It helps to take a closer look at the phase detection system when presented with a non-ideal subject.

Figure 5.12 shows the same weathered wood pictured earlier, except in this case we've chosen to rotate the camera 90 degrees (say, because we want a vertically oriented composition). In the illustration, the image within the focus sensor's area is split in two and displaced slightly side-to-side, but the amount and direction of the misalignment is far from obvious. A horizontally oriented focus sensor will be forced to look for less obvious vertical lines to match up. Our best-case subject has been transformed into a *worst-case* subject for a horizontal focus sensor.

The value of the cross-type focus sensor, which can interpret contrast in both horizontal and vertical directions, can be seen in Figure 5.13. The horizontal lines are still giving the horizontal portion of the cross sensor fits, but the vertical bar can easily split and align the subject to achieve optimum focus. Cross-type sensors can handle horizontal and vertical lines with equal aplomb and, if you think about it, lines at any diagonal

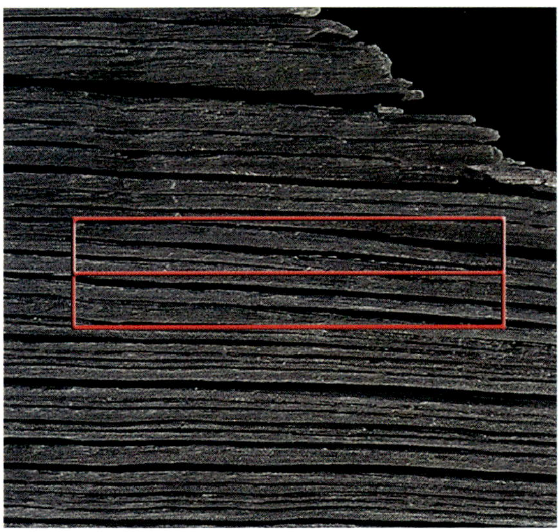

Figure 5.12 A horizontal focus sensor doesn't handle horizontal lines very well.

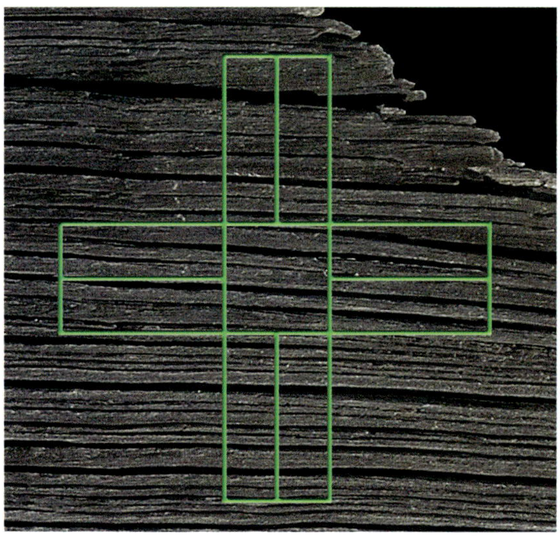

Figure 5.13 Cross-type sensors can evaluate contrast in both horizontal and vertical directions, as well as diagonally.

angle as well. In lower light levels, with subjects that were moving, or with subjects that have no pattern and less contrast to begin with, the cross-type sensor not only works faster but can focus subjects that a horizontal- or vertical-only sensor can't handle at all.

So, you can see that having a center cross-type focus sensor that is extra-sensitive with faster lenses is a definite advantage.

Contrast Detection

This is a slower mode, suitable for static subjects, and used by the Alpha only when you focus manually when using Live View mode. When autofocusing, the Alpha models that have Live View (A390) use the same phase detection system described earlier, using a novel approach—a second image sensor. I'll tell you about this sensor later in the chapter.

Contrast detection is what your eye uses to focus on the LCD in Live View, when you're focusing manually. It's a bit easier to understand, and is illustrated by Figure 5.14. At top in the figure, the transitions between the edges found in the image are soft and blurred because of the low contrast between them. Although the illustration uses the same vertical lines used with the phase detection example, the orientation of the features doesn't matter. The focus system looks only for contrast between edges, and those edges can run in any direction.

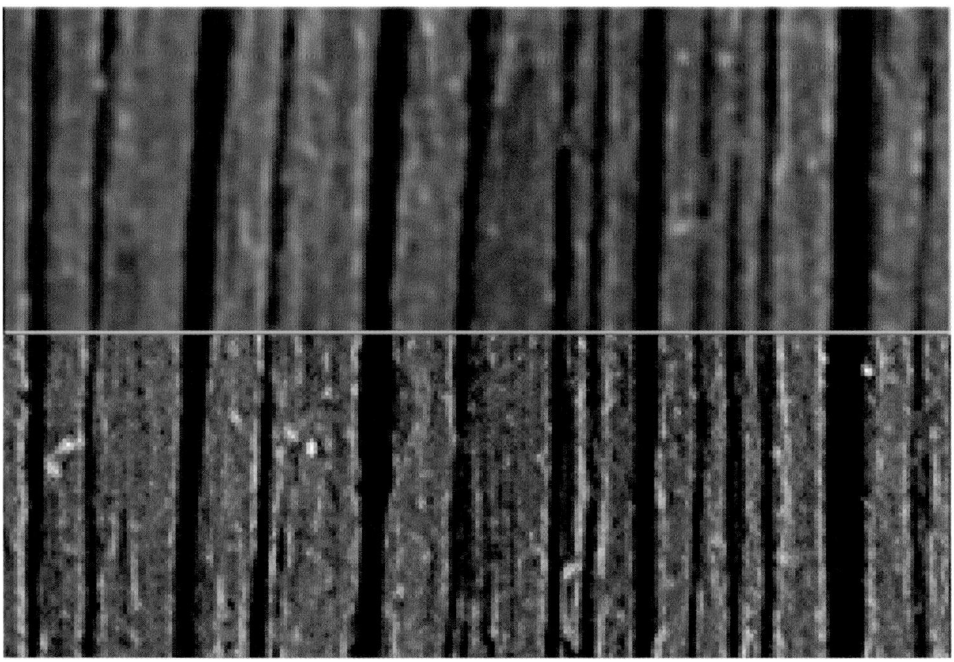

Figure 5.14
Manual focus in Contrast Detection mode allows you to evaluate the increase in contrast in the edges of subjects, starting with a blurry image (top) and producing a sharp, contrasty image (bottom).

At the bottom of Figure 5.14, the image has been brought into sharp focus, and the edges have much more contrast; the transitions are sharp and clear. Although this example is a bit exaggerated so you can see the results on the printed page, it's easy to understand that when maximum contrast in a subject is achieved, it can be deemed to be in sharp focus. Achieving focus with contrast detection is generally quite a bit slower, because you're doing it manually, but there are several advantages to this method:

- **Works with more image types.** Contrast detection doesn't require subject matter rotated 90 degrees from the sensor's orientation for you to use it to focus manually. Any subject that has edges will work.
- **Focus on any point.** While phase detection focus can be achieved *only* at the points that fall under one of the nine autofocus sensors, with contrast detection, any portion of the image can be used as you view the image. Focus is achieved with the actual sensor image, so focus point selection is simply a matter of choosing which part of the sensor image to use.
- **Potentially more accurate.** Phase detection can fall prey to the vagaries of uncooperative subject matter: if suitable lines aren't available, the system may have to hunt for focus or achieve less than optimal focus. Contrast detection is more clear-cut. Your eye can clearly see when the highest contrast has been achieved.

The Alpha's autofocus mechanism, like all such systems found in SLR cameras, evaluates the degree of focus, but, unlike the human eye, it is able to remember the progression perfectly, so that autofocus can lock in much more quickly and, with an image that has sufficient contrast, more precisely. Unfortunately, while the Alpha's focus system finds it easy to measure degrees of apparent focus at each of the focus points in the viewfinder, it doesn't really know with any certainty *which* object should be in sharpest focus. Is it the closest object? The subject in the center? Something lurking *behind* the closest subject? A person standing over at the side of the picture? Many of the techniques for using autofocus effectively involve telling the Sony Alpha exactly what it should be focusing on, by choosing a focus zone or by allowing the camera to choose a focus zone for you. I'll address that topic shortly.

As the camera collects focus information from the sensors, it then evaluates it to determine whether the desired sharp focus has been achieved. The calculations may include whether the subject is moving, and whether the camera needs to "predict" where the subject will be when the shutter release button is fully depressed and the picture is taken. The speed with which the camera is able to evaluate focus and then move the lens elements into the proper position to achieve the sharpest focus determines how fast the autofocus mechanism is.

Focus Modes

The Sony Alpha has three AF modes: Single-shot Autofocus (also known as Single Autofocus, or AF-S), Continuous Autofocus (or AF-C), and Automatic Autofocus (AF-A, which switches between the two as appropriate). I'll explain all of these in more detail later in this section.

MANUAL FOCUS

With Manual focus activated by sliding the switch on the lens or on the side of the camera body (the lens switch overrides the one on the body), your Sony Alpha lets you set the focus yourself. There are some advantages and disadvantages to this approach. While your batteries will last slightly longer in Manual focus mode, it will take you longer to focus the camera for each photo, a process that can be tricky. Modern digital cameras, even dSLRs, depend so much on autofocus that the viewfinders of models that have less than full-frame-sized sensors are no longer designed for optimum manual focus. Pick up any film camera and you'll see a bigger, brighter viewfinder with a focusing screen that's a joy to focus on manually. The DSLR-A290 offers .83X magnification, while the DSLR-A390 provides slightly less magnification of .74X life size. (That means that with a 50mm focal length, the image appears to be 83 and 74 percent of life size.)

Focus Pocus

Prior to the introduction of dSLR autofocus capabilities in the 1980s, back in the day of film cameras, focusing was always done manually. Honest. Even though viewfinders were bigger and brighter than they are today, special focusing screens, magnifiers, and other gadgets were often used to help the photographer achieve correct focus. Imagine what it must have been like to focus manually under demanding, fast-moving conditions such as sports photography. Minolta, which pioneered the technology now used in Sony Alpha cameras and lenses, was actually a pioneer in developing autofocus systems.

Manual focusing is problematic because our eyes and brains have poor memory for correct focus, which is why your eye doctor must shift back and forth between sets of lenses and ask "Does that look sharper—or was it sharper before?" in determining your correct prescription. Similarly, manual focusing involves jogging the focus ring back and forth as you go from almost in focus, to sharp focus, to almost focused again. The little clockwise and counterclockwise arcs decrease in size until you've zeroed in on the point of correct focus. As I mentioned earlier in this chapter, what you're looking for is the image with the most contrast between the edges of elements in the image.

The Sony Alpha's autofocus mechanism, like all such systems found in SLR cameras, also evaluates these increases and decreases in sharpness, but it is able to remember the progression perfectly, so that autofocus can lock in much more quickly and, with an image that has sufficient contrast, more precisely. Unfortunately, while the Sony Alpha's focus system finds it easy to measure degrees of apparent focus at each of the focus points in the viewfinder, it doesn't really know with any certainty *which object* should be in sharpest focus. Is it the closest object? The subject in the center? Something lurking *behind* the closest subject? A person standing over at the side of the picture? Using autofocus effectively involves telling the Sony dSLR exactly what it should be focusing on.

Adding Circles of Confusion

But there are other factors in play, as well. You know that increased depth-of-field brings more of your subject into focus. But more depth-of-field also makes autofocusing (or manual focusing) more difficult because the contrast is lower between objects at different distances. So, autofocus with a 200mm lens (or zoom setting) may be easier than at a 28mm focal length (or zoom setting) because the longer lens has less apparent depth-of-field. By the same token, a lens with a maximum aperture of f/1.8 will be easier to autofocus (or manually focus) than one of the same focal length with an f/4 maximum aperture, because the f/4 lens has more depth-of-field *and* a dimmer view. That's why lenses with a maximum aperture smaller than f/5.6 can give your Sony Alpha's autofocus system fits, because the largest f/stop is the lens opening the camera uses to focus.

To make things even more complicated, many subjects aren't polite enough to remain still. They move around in the frame, so that even if the Alpha is sharply focused on your main subject, it may change position and require refocusing. An intervening subject may pop into the frame and pass between you and the subject you meant to photograph. You (or the Alpha dSLR) have to decide whether to lock focus on this new subject, or remain focused on the original subject. Finally, there are some kinds of subjects that are difficult to bring into sharp focus because they lack enough contrast to allow the Sony Alpha's AF system (or our eyes) to lock in. Blank walls, a clear blue sky, or other subject matter may make focusing difficult.

If you find all these focus factors confusing, you're on the right track. Focus is, in fact, measured using something called a *circle of confusion.* An ideal image consists of zillions of tiny little points, which, like all points, theoretically have no height or width. There is perfect contrast between the point and its surroundings. You can think of each point as a pinpoint of light in a darkened room. When a given point is out of focus, its edges decrease in contrast and it changes from a perfect point to a tiny disc with blurry edges (remember, blur is the lack of contrast between boundaries in an image). (See Figure 5.15.)

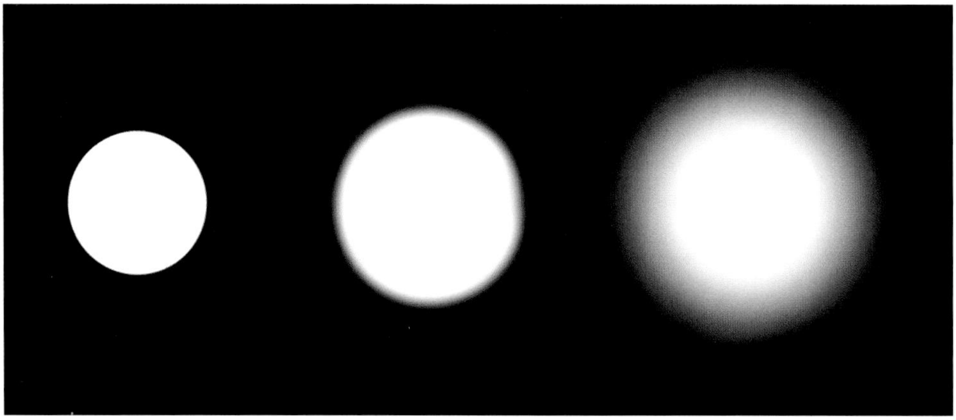

Figure 5.15
When a pinpoint of light (left) goes out of focus, its blurry edges form a circle of confusion (center and right).

If this blurry disc—the circle of confusion—is small enough, our eye still perceives it as a point. It's only when the disc grows large enough that we can see it as a blur rather than a sharp point that a given point is viewed as out of focus. You can see, then, that enlarging an image, either by displaying it larger on your computer monitor or by making a large print, also enlarges the size of each circle of confusion. Moving closer to the image does the same thing. So, parts of an image that may look perfectly sharp in a 5 × 7-inch print viewed at arm's length, might appear blurry when blown up to 11 × 14 and examined at the same distance. Take a few steps back, however, and it may look sharp again.

To a lesser extent, the viewer also affects the apparent size of these circles of confusion. Some people see details better at a given distance and may perceive smaller circles of confusion than someone standing next to them. For the most part, however, such differences are small. Truly blurry images will look blurry to just about everyone under the same conditions.

Technically, there is just one plane within your picture area, parallel to the back of the camera (or sensor, in the case of a digital camera), that is in sharp focus. That's the plane in which the points of the image are rendered as precise points. At every other plane in front of or behind the focus plane, the points show up as discs that range from slightly blurry to extremely blurry. In practice, the discs in many of these planes will still be so small that we see them as points, and that's where we get depth-of-field. Depth-of-field is just the range of planes that include discs that we perceive as points rather than blurred splotches. The size of this range increases as the aperture is reduced in size and is allocated roughly one-third in front of the plane of sharpest focus, and two-thirds behind it. The range of sharp focus is always greater behind your subject than in front of it—although in many cases, depth-of-field will be very shallow, as shown in Figure 5.16.

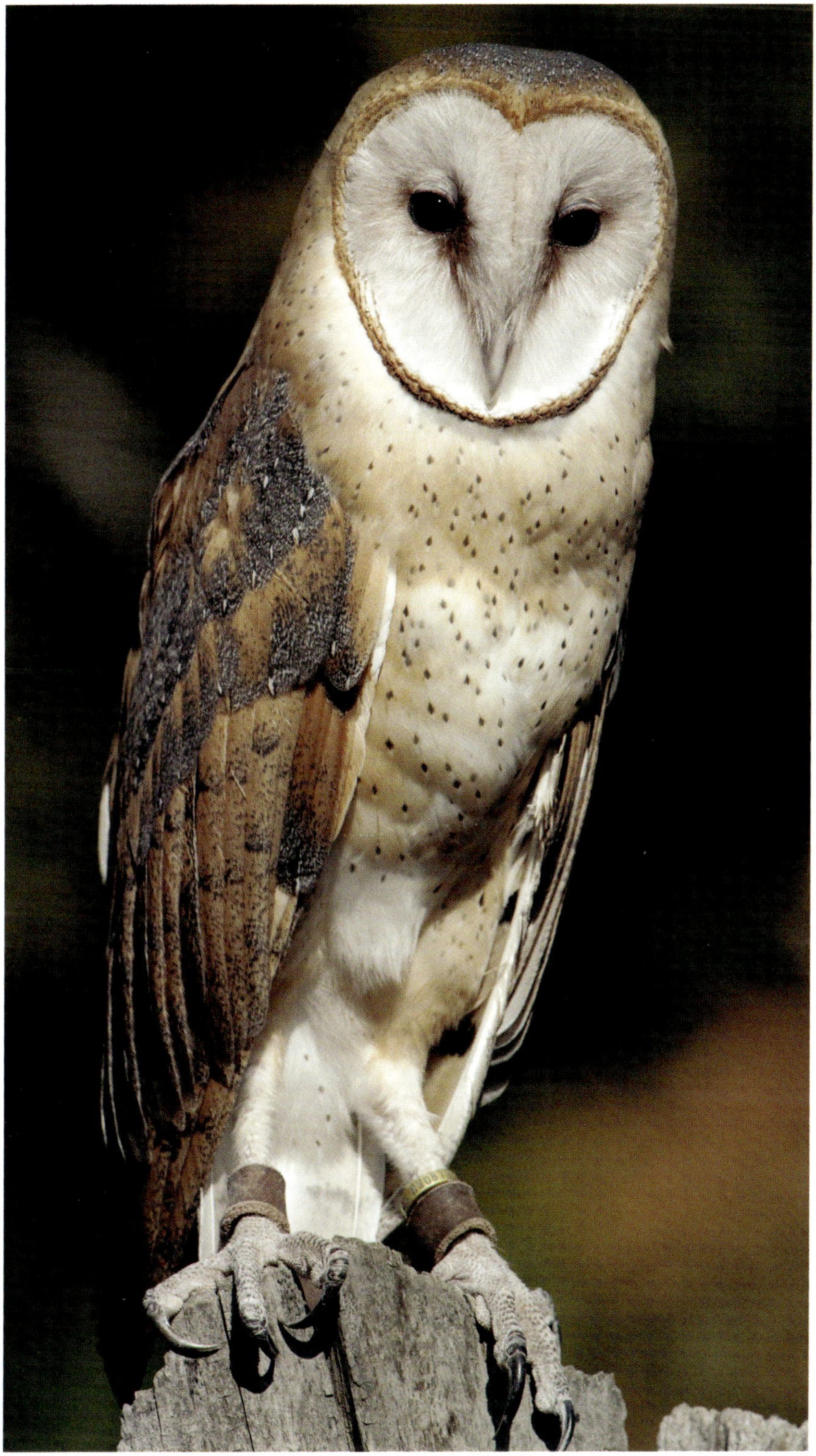

Figure 5.16
Only the owl is in focus, but the area behind him appears blurry because the depth-of-field is limited.

Making Sense of Focus Sensors

The number and type of autofocus sensors can affect how well the system operates. As I mentioned, the Sony A390 and A290 dSLRs have nine AF points. The Alpha DSLR-A850 has eleven AF points, and some cameras from other vendors have as many as 45-51 autofocus sensors. These focus sensors can consist of vertical or horizontal lines of pixels, cross-shapes, and often a mixture of these types within a single camera, although, as I mentioned, the Sony dSLR includes a cross-type sensor at the center position. The more AF points available, the more easily the camera can differentiate among areas of the frame, and the more precisely you can specify the area you want to be in focus if you're manually choosing a focus spot.

As the camera collects focus information from the sensors, it then evaluates it to determine whether the desired sharp focus has been achieved. The calculations may include whether the subject is moving, and whether the camera needs to "predict" where the subject will be when the shutter release button is fully depressed and the picture is taken. The speed with which the camera is able to evaluate focus and then move the lens elements into the proper position to achieve the sharpest focus determines how fast the autofocus mechanism is. Although your Sony Alpha will almost always focus more quickly than a human, there are types of shooting situations where that's not fast enough.

For example, if you're having problems shooting sports because the Sony Alpha's autofocus system manically follows each moving subject, a better choice might be to switch autofocus modes or shift into Manual and prefocus on a spot where you anticipate the action will be, such as a goal line or soccer net. At night football games, for example, when I am shooting with a telephoto lens almost wide open, I often focus manually on one of the referees who happens to be standing where I expect the action to be taking place (say, a halfback run or a pass reception). When I am less sure about what is going to happen, I may switch to Continuous (AF-C) Autofocus and let the camera decide.

Your Autofocus Mode Options

Choosing the right autofocus mode and the way in which focus points are selected is your key to success. Using the wrong mode for a particular type of photography can lead to a series of pictures that are all sharply focused—on the wrong subject. When I first started shooting sports with an autofocus SLR (back in the film camera days), I covered one game alternating between shots of base runners and outfielders with pictures of a promising young pitcher, all from a position next to the third base dugout. The base runner and outfielder photos were great, because their backgrounds didn't distract the autofocus mechanism. But all my photos of the pitcher had the focus tightly zeroed in on the fans in the stands behind him. Because I was shooting film instead of a digital camera, I didn't know about my gaffe until the film was developed. A simple change, such as locking in focus or focus zone manually, or even manually focusing, would have done the trick.

To save battery power, your Sony Alpha doesn't start to focus the lens until you partially depress the shutter release, or your face approaches the Eye-Start sensors (if you have that feature switched on). But, autofocus isn't some mindless beast out there snapping your pictures in and out of focus with no feedback from you after you press that button. There are several settings you can modify that return at least a modicum of control to you. Your first decision should be whether you set the Sony Alpha to Single-shot Autofocus (AF-S), Continuous Autofocus (AF-C), or Automatic Autofocus (AF-A). Press the Fn button (on the back of the camera, just above the controller) and use the left/right controller keys to select Autofocus mode, and then the up/down buttons to choose from among AF-S, AF-A, and AF-C. Press the center controller button to confirm your choice. (The AF/MF switch on the side of the camera does not need to be set to AF before you can change autofocus mode, but the mode will not be activated until you switch to AF mode.) Figure 5.17 shows the menu selections.

When the image under the current focus area (described later) is in sharp focus, the focus confirmation indicator in the viewfinder will glow a steady green; the camera is ready to shoot. If the green light framed by parentheses-like brackets is illuminated, focus is set, and the focus point will follow a moving subject. You can take a picture at

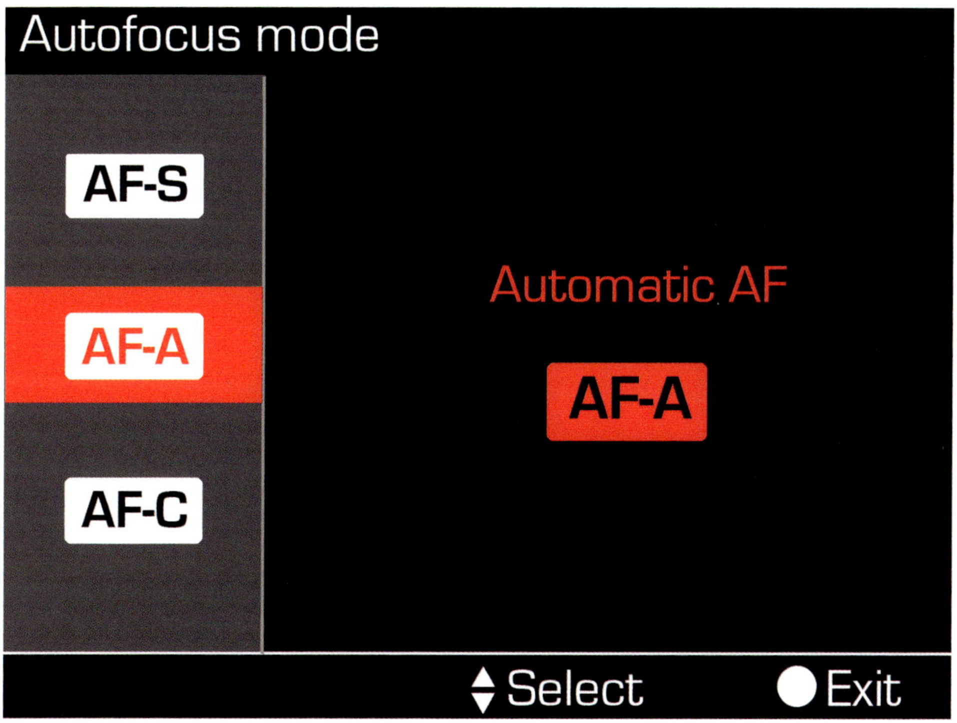

Figure 5.17 Press the up/down controller keys until the AF choice you want is selected.

any time. When only the green brackets are illuminated, the Alpha is still seeking focus, and the shutter is locked. A flashing indicator dot indicates that the Alpha is unable to focus. The shutter is locked. You may need to switch to Manual focus to get this shot.

Single-shot AF

In this mode, also called *Single Autofocus*, focus is set once and remains at that setting until the button is fully depressed, taking the picture, or until you release the shutter button without taking a shot. Activate by pressing the shutter release halfway down. For non-action photography, this setting is usually your best choice, as it minimizes out-of-focus pictures (at the expense of spontaneity). The drawback here is that you might not be able to take a picture at all while the camera is seeking focus; you're locked out until the autofocus mechanism is happy with the current setting. Single Autofocus is sometimes referred to as *focus priority* for that reason. Because of the small delay while the camera zeroes in on correct focus, you might experience slightly more shutter lag. This mode uses less battery power. When sharp focus is achieved, the selected focus point will flash red in the viewfinder, and the focus confirmation light at the lower left will glow.

Continuous AF

This mode is the mode to use for sports and other fast-moving subjects. In this mode, once the shutter release is partially depressed, the camera sets the focus but continues to monitor the subject, so that if it moves or you move, the lens will be refocused to suit. Focus and exposure aren't really locked until you press the shutter release down all the way to take the picture. As I mentioned, the focus confirmation indicator in the viewfinder is flanked by parentheses-like brackets, which indicates that the image is in focus, but the Alpha will change focus as your subject moves. (The central indicator disappears while searching for focus, but the brackets remain.) Continuous Autofocus uses the most battery power, because the autofocus system operates as long as the shutter release button is partially depressed.

Continuous AF uses a technology called *predictive AF*, which allows the camera to calculate the correct focus if the subject is moving toward or away from the camera at a constant rate. It uses either the automatically selected AF point or the point you select manually to set focus.

Automatic AF

This setting is actually a combination of the first two. When selected, the camera focuses using Single-shot AF and locks in the focus setting. But, if the subject begins moving, it will switch automatically to Continuous AF and change the focus to keep the subject sharp. Automatic AF is a good choice when you're shooting a mixture of action pictures and less dynamic shots and want to use Single-shot AF when possible. The camera will default to that mode, yet switch automatically to Continuous AF when it would be useful for subjects that might begin moving unexpectedly.

Setting the AF Area

You can specify which of the nine focus points the Sony dSLR uses to calculate correct focus, or allow the camera to select the point for you. Note that the Alpha A290/A390 cameras have the autofocus points clustered within the square brackets in the center of the screen, which indicate the general AF area. That means that you (or the camera) can focus only on subjects that fall under one of the autofocus marks. To focus somewhere else in the frame, you'll need to place your subject under the appropriate autofocus area, focus, and then lock focus by pressing the shutter release button halfway. You can then reframe your photo with the focus locked in.

There are three AF area options, shown in Figure 5.18. Press the Fn button, navigate to the AF area selection, press the controller button, and select one of these three choices. Press the controller button again to confirm.

- **Wide.** The Alpha chooses the appropriate focus zone from the nine AF areas on the screen. However, you can switch to the center (Spot) focus zone by pressing the center controller button.
- **Spot.** The Alpha always uses the center, cross-type focus zone to calculate correct focus.
- **Local.** Use the controller buttons to move the focus zone among the nine available zones. Press the center controller button to switch to the center, cross-type focus sensor quickly.

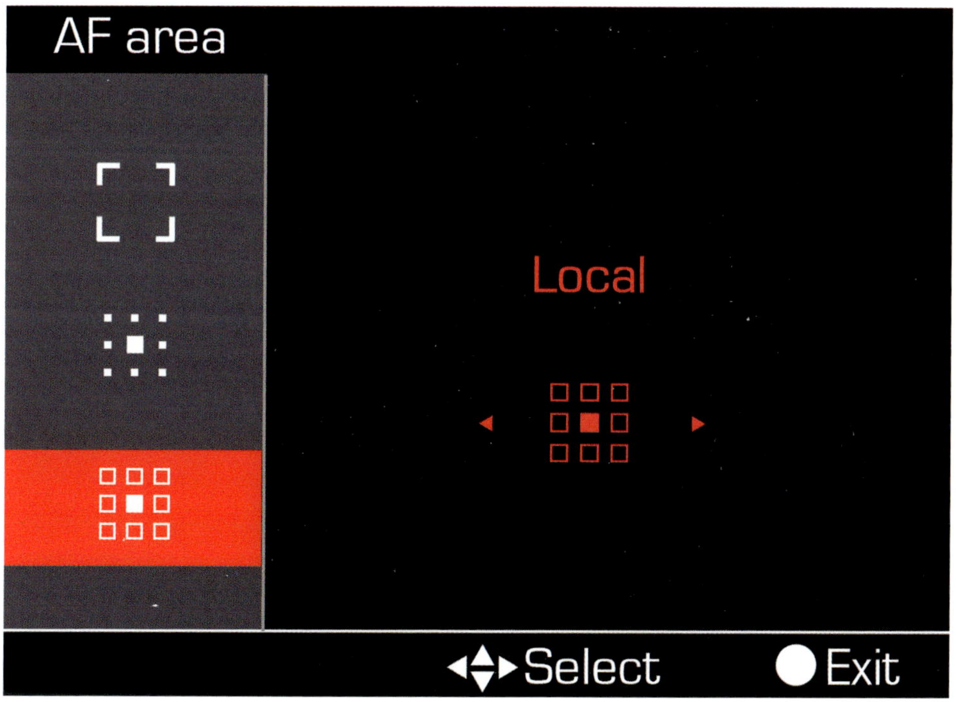

Figure 5.18 Choose from Wide (the Alpha selects one of the nine AF areas), Spot (only the center focus spot is used), or, the selected setting, Local (you can choose which area to use).

Continuous Shooting

The Sony dSLR's continuous shooting modes remind me how far digital photography has brought us. The first accessory I purchased when I worked as a sports photographer some years ago was a motor drive for my film SLR. It enabled me to snap off a series of shots at a three frames-per-second rate, which came in very handy when a fullback broke through the line and headed for the end zone. Even a seasoned action photographer can miss the decisive instant when a crucial block is made, or a baseball superstar's bat shatters and pieces of cork fly out. Continuous shooting simplifies taking a series of pictures, either to ensure that one has more or less the exact moment you want to capture or to capture a sequence that is interesting as a collection of successive images.

The Sony Alpha's "motor drive" capabilities are, in some ways, much superior to what you get with a film camera. For one thing, a motor-driven film camera can eat up film at an incredible pace, which is why many of them are used with cassettes that hold hundreds of feet of film stock. At three frames per second (typical of film cameras), a short burst of a few seconds can burn up as much as half of an ordinary 36-exposure roll of film. Digital cameras like the Alpha, in contrast, have reusable "film," at a slightly slower 2.5 fps shooting rate, so if you waste a few dozen shots on non-decisive moments, you can erase them and shoot more.

The increased capacity of digital film cards gives you a prodigious number of frames to work with. At a baseball game I covered earlier this year, I took more than 1,000 images in a couple hours. Yet, even with my Alpha DSLR-A390's 14-megapixel resolution I was able to cram 750 JPEG Fine images on a single 4GB Secure Digital or Memory Stick card. That's a lot of shooting. Given an average burst of about eight frames per sequence (nobody really takes 15-20 shots or more of one play in a baseball game), I was able to capture 38 different sequences before I needed to swap cards. Figure 5.19

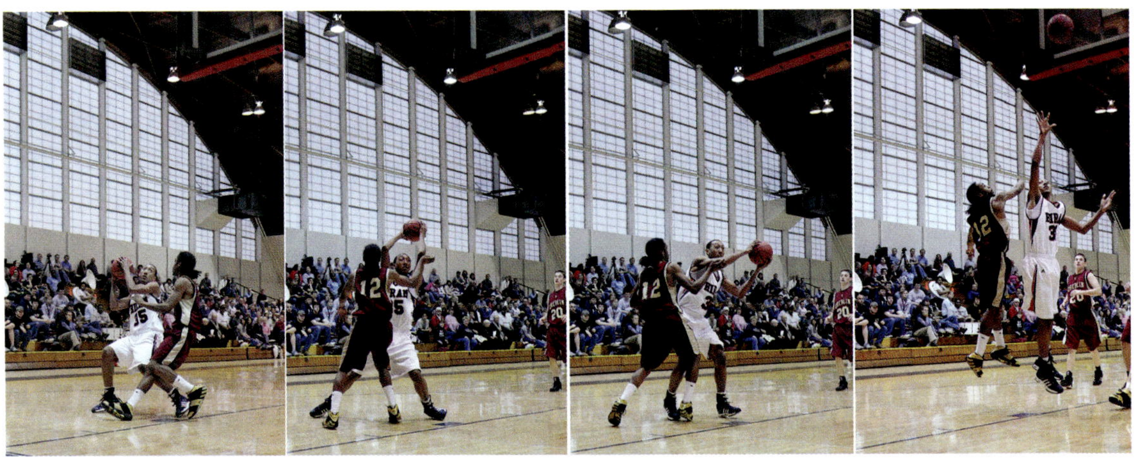

Figure 5.19 Continuous shooting allows you to capture an entire sequence of exciting moments as they unfold.

shows a typical short burst of four shots taken at 2.5 fps at a basketball game as a player drove in for a lay-up.

On the other hand, for some sports (such as football) the longer bursts came in handy, because running and passing plays often last 5 to 10 seconds, and change in character as the action switches from the quarterback dropping back to pass or hand off the ball, then to the receiver or running back trying to gain as much yardage as possible.

To use the Sony Alpha's Continuous Shooting mode, press the Drive button (the left controller key). Then navigate down the list with the up/down controller keys until the Continuous Adv. (continuous advance) mode is selected. Press the center controller button to confirm your choice. (See Figure 5.20.) When you partially depress the shutter button, the viewfinder will display a number representing the maximum number of shots you can take at the current quality settings at the Alpha's 2.5 frames per second burst rate.

To increase this number, reduce the image quality setting by switching to JPEG Standard, only (from JPEG+RAW), to a lower JPEG quality setting, or reduce the Sony Alpha's resolution from L (14 MP) to M (7.7 MP) or S (3.5 MP). The reason the size of your bursts is limited is that continuous images are first shuttled into the Sony Alpha's internal memory buffer, then doled out to the memory card as quickly as they can be written to the card. Technically, the Sony Alpha takes the RAW data received from the

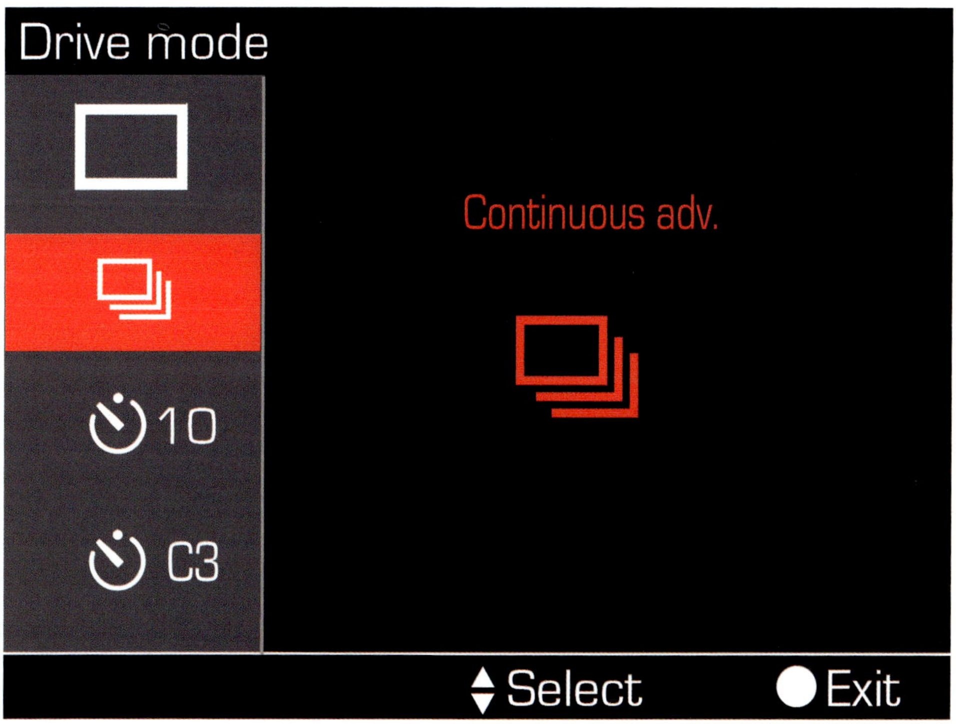

Figure 5.20
Press the Drive button and use the up/down controller keys to select Continuous Shooting.

digital image processor and converts it to the output format you've selected—either JPEG or RAW—and deposits it in the buffer ready to store on the card.

This internal "smart" buffer can suck up photos much more quickly than the memory card and, indeed, some memory cards are significantly faster or slower than others. When the buffer fills, you can't take any more continuous shots until the Sony Alpha has written some of them to the card, making more room in the buffer. (You should keep in mind that faster memory cards write images more quickly, freeing up buffer space faster.)

Setting Image Parameters

You can fine-tune the images that you take in several different ways. For example, if you don't want to choose a predefined white balance, you can set a custom white balance based on the illumination of the site where you'll be taking photos, or choose a white balance based on color temperature. With the Creative Style options, you can set up customized saturation, contrast, and sharpness for various types of pictures. This section shows you how to use the available image parameters.

Customizing White Balance

Back in the film days, color films were standardized, or balanced, for a particular "color" of light. Digital cameras like the Sony dSLR use a "white balance" that is, ideally, correctly matched to the color of light used to expose your photograph. The right white balance is measured using a scale called *color temperature.* Color temperatures were assigned by heating a mythical "black body radiator" and recording the spectrum of light it emitted at a given temperature in degrees Kelvin. So, daylight at noon has a color temperature in the 5,500 to 6,000 degree range. Indoor illumination is around 3,400 degrees. Hotter temperatures produce bluer images (think blue-white hot), whereas cooler temperatures produce redder images (think of a dull-red glowing ember). Because of human nature, though, bluer images are actually called "cool" (think wintry day) and redder images are called "warm" (think ruddy sunset), even though their color temperatures are reversed.

If a photograph is exposed indoors under warm illumination with a digital camera sensor balanced for cooler daylight, the image will appear much too reddish. An image exposed outdoors with the white balance set for incandescent illumination will seem much too blue. These color casts may be too strong to remove in an image editor from JPEG files, although if you shoot RAW you can change the WB setting to the correct value when you import the image into your editor.

Mismatched white balance settings are easier to achieve accidentally than you might think, even for experienced photographers. I'd just arrived at a concert after shooting some photos indoors with electronic flash and had manually set WB for flash. Then, as the concert began, I resumed shooting using the incandescent stage lighting—which looked white to the eye—and ended up with a few shots like Figure 5.21. Eventually, I caught the error during picture review, and changed my white balance. Another time, I was shooting outdoors, but had the camera white balance still set for incandescent illumination. The excessively blue image shown in Figure 5.22 resulted. (I suppose I should salvage my reputation as a photo guru by admitting that both these images were taken "incorrectly" deliberately, as illustrations for this book; in real life, I'm excessively attentive to how my white balance is set. You do believe me, don't you?)

The Auto White Balance (AWB) setting, available by pressing the Fn key and navigating to the White Balance menu, examines your scene and chooses an appropriate value based on your scene and the colors it contains. However, the Sony Alpha's selection process is far from foolproof. Under bright lighting conditions, it may evaluate the colors in the image and still assume the light source is daylight and balance the picture accordingly, even though, in fact, you may be shooting under extremely bright incandescent illumination. In dimmer light, the camera's electronics may assume that the illumination is tungsten, and if there are lots of reddish colors present, set color balance for that. Sony notes that with mercury vapor or sodium lamps, correct white balance is virtually impossible to achieve; use of flash is recommended instead, or shoot in RAW and make your corrections when importing the file into your image editor.

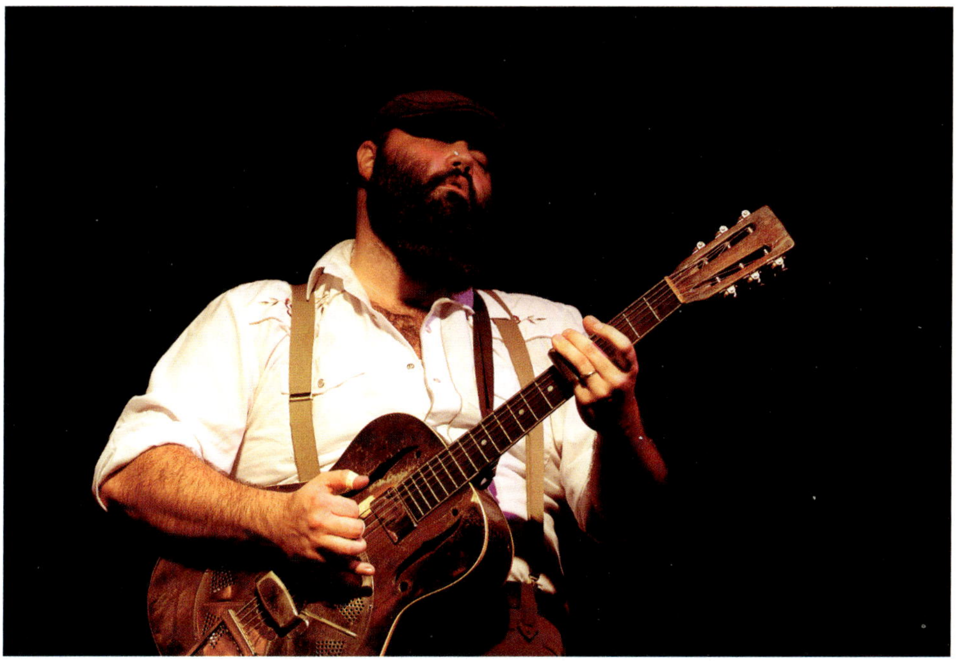

Figure 5.21
An image exposed indoors with the WB set for daylight or electronic flash will appear too reddish.

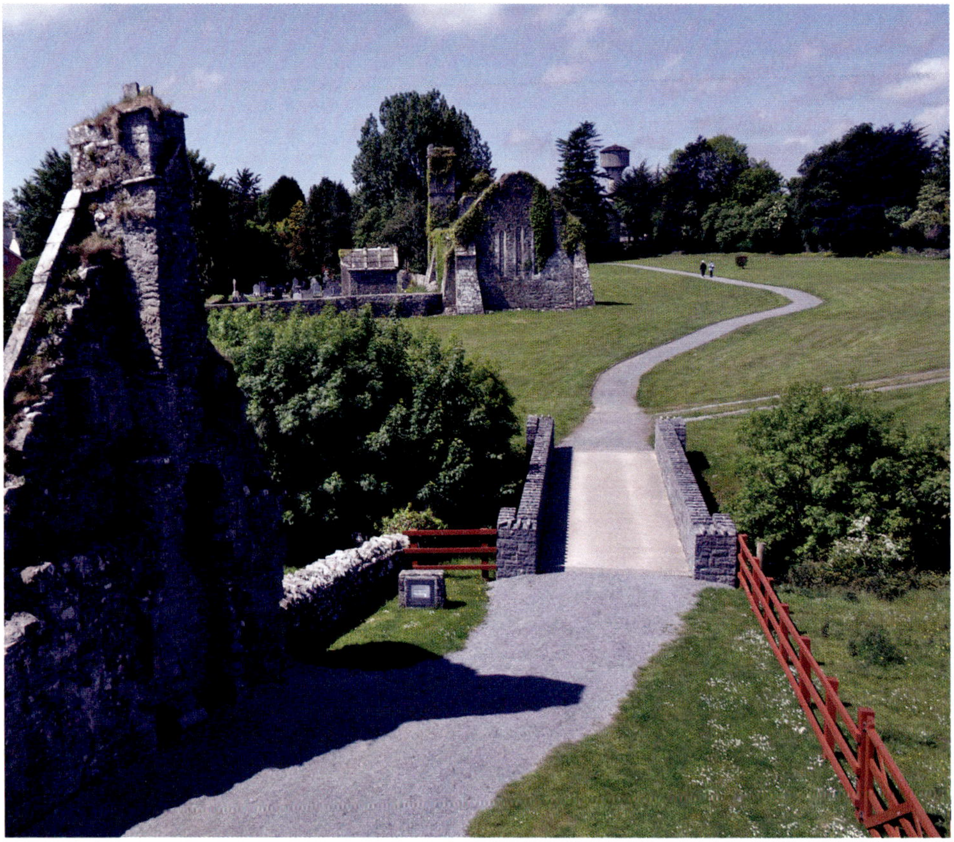

Figure 5.22
An image exposed under daylight illumination with the WB set for tungsten illumination will appear too blue.

Of course, flash isn't completely consistent in white balance, either. However, some electronic flash units, such as the Sony HVL-series dedicated flash units, can report to the camera the particular white balance that they are outputting, since a flash's color temperature can vary depending on how brief the flash exposure is. The Alpha can adjust its own white balance setting automatically, based on the information it receives from the flash.

The other presets in the WB list apply specific lighting conditions. You can choose from Daylight, Shade, Cloudy, Tungsten, Fluorescent, and Flash. All but Flash are shown in Figure 5.23 (it's scrolled off the bottom). When any of these other than AWB are selected, you can fine-tune the white balance by pressing the left/right controller buttons. Pressing the right button makes the image more reddish; the left button makes the image bluer. You can choose plus/minus 3 increments (although Sony doesn't reveal exactly what those increments are). If you want to be precise, you'll need to use the Color Temperature option, described shortly.

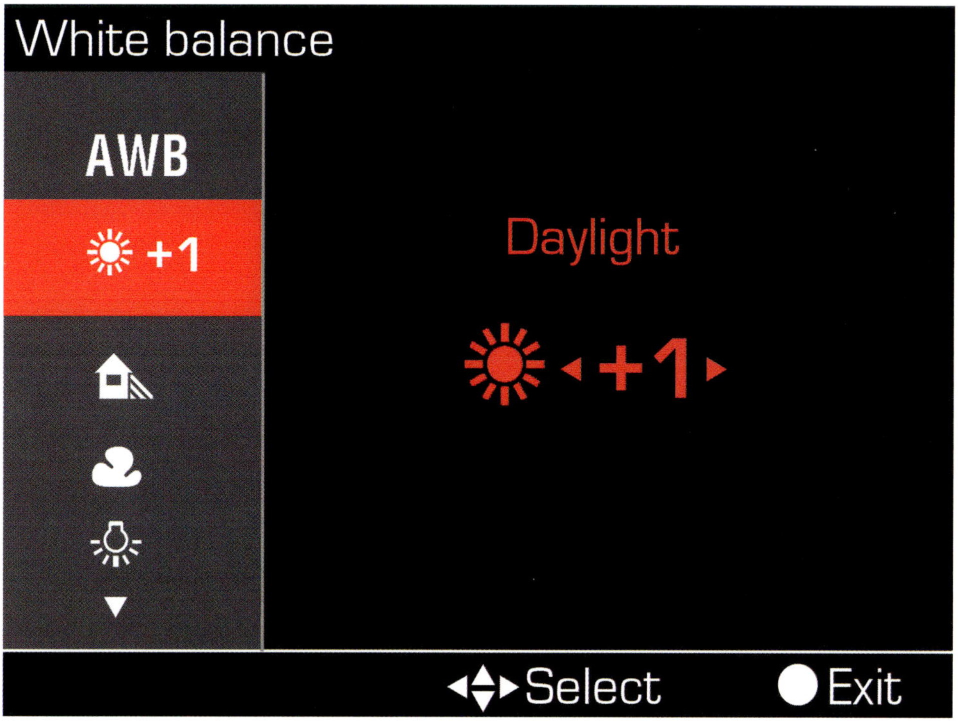

Figure 5.23 Your white balance preset selections include (top to bottom): Automatic, Daylight, Shade, Cloudy, and Incandescent, plus (not shown) Fluorescent, Flash, and Custom.

The Daylight setting sets WB to 5,200K, while the Shade setting uses a much bluer 7,000K. The chief difference between direct daylight and shade or even tungsten light sources is nothing more than the proportion of red and blue light. The spectrum of colors is continuous, but it is biased toward one end or the other.

However, some types of fluorescent lights produce illumination that has a severe deficit in certain colors, such as only *particular* shades of red. If you looked at the spectrum or rainbow of colors encompassed by such a light source, it would have black bands in it, representing particular wavelengths of light that are absent. You can't compensate for this deficiency by adding all tones of red. That's why the fluorescent setting of your Sony Alpha may provide less than satisfactory results with some kinds of fluorescent bulbs. If you take many photographs under a particular kind of non-compatible fluorescent light, you might want to investigate specialized fluorescent light filters for your lenses, available from camera stores, or learn how to adjust for various sources in your image editor. However, you might also get acceptable results using the choice on the WB list. The final choice is Custom (which allows you to use specific white balances you've captured).

Setting a Custom White Balance

Setting a custom white balance expressly for the scene you want to shoot may be the most accurate way of getting the right color balance. It's easy to do with the Sony Alpha DSLR-A390/A290. Just follow these steps:

1. Press the Fn button, and then use the controller up/down/left/right keys to navigate to the White Balance menu selection. Press the center controller button to produce the White Balance menu.
2. Scroll down the list of white balance options until the Custom entry is highlighted. Press the right controller key to move the highlighting over to the "business" side of the menu.
3. Point the camera at a neutral white object large enough to fill the center of the frame in the viewfinder.
4. Press the center controller button. A message will appear on the LCD: SET. Press shutter to calibrate.
5. Press the shutter release. The picture you took, as well as the custom white balance calculated appear on the LCD.
6. Press the center controller button to return to the recording information display.

The Alpha A390 and A290 will retain the custom setting you just captured until you repeat the process to replace the setting with a new one. Thereafter, you can activate this custom setting by scrolling down to Custom in the White Balance menu and pressing the center controller button to confirm your choice.

Image Processing

As I mentioned in Chapter 3, the Sony Alpha cameras offer several ways of customizing the rendition of your images. You can use the Dynamic Range Optimizer (aka, D-Range Optimizer and DRO), or specify certain changes to contrast, saturation, and sharpness in the Creative Style menu. The functions are available by pressing the Fn button with the Alpha set on P, S, A, or M.

D-Range Optimizer

This innovative tool helps you adjust the relative brightness range of your JPEG images as they are taken. The DRO has no effect on RAW images. To apply dynamic range effects to these files, use the bundled Image Data Converter SR program described in Chapter 8.

The DRO choice, available by pressing the Fn button and choosing D-RangeOptimizer (shown in the menu as one word) from the functions menu, has three settings: Off, Standard, and Advanced, giving you the results illustrated in Figure 5.24. These options work as follows:

- **Off.** No optimization. You're on your own. But if you have the foresight to shoot RAW+JPEG, you can apply DRO effects to your image when converting it with the Image Data Converter SR software, as I mentioned earlier. Use this setting when shooting subjects of normal contrast, or when you want to capture an image just as you see it, without modification by the camera.
- **D-R (Standard).** In this mode, the Alpha examines your photograph, and if there is a great deal of contrast between light and dark areas, the digital image processor reduces the contrast of the entire image. Use this option if you are shooting into the sun, or have a scene with bright/dark areas scattered throughout. This function is, more or less, an automatic contrast control.
- **D-R+ (Advanced).** In this mode, the Alpha dives into your image, looking at various small areas to examine the contrast of highlights and shadows, making modifications to each section to produce the best combination of brightness and tones with detail.

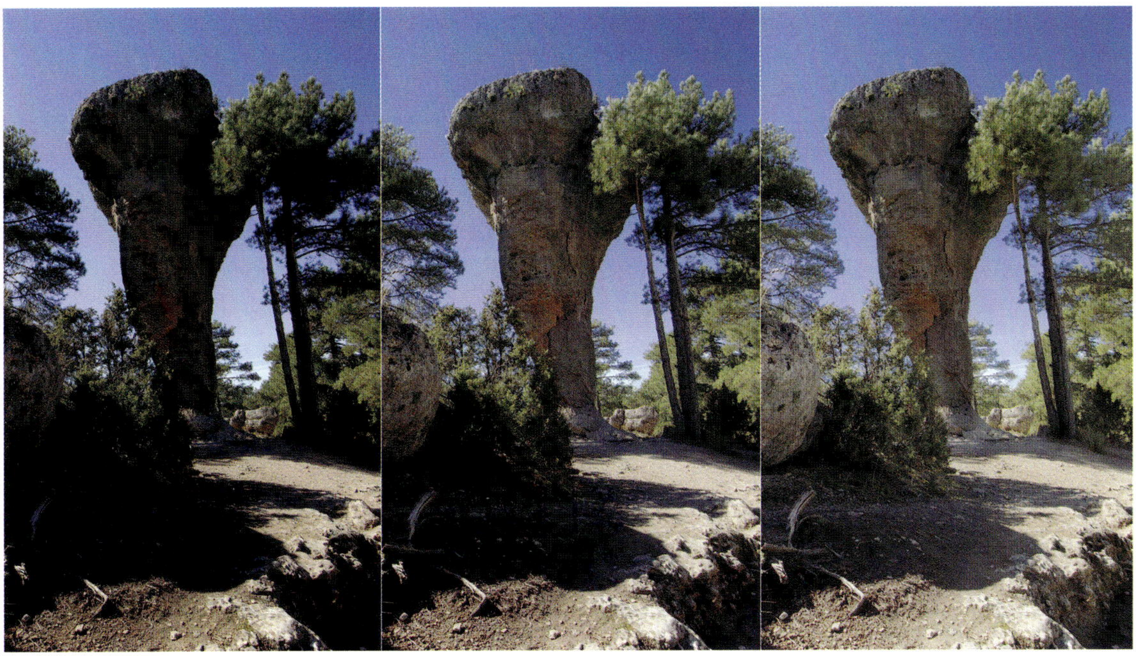

Figure 5.24 DRO off (left), D-R Standard (middle), and D-R+ (right), provide progressively more dynamic range optimization.

Using Creative Styles

This option, found in the Shooting Functions menu (except when using Scene modes), gives you eight different combinations of contrast, saturation, and sharpness: Standard, Vivid, Portrait, Landscape, Night, Sunset, B/W (black-and-white), and Adobe RGB. Those are useful enough that you should make them a part of your everyday toolkit. You can apply Creative Styles *only* when you are not using one of the Alpha's Scene modes. (That is, you're shooting in Program, Aperture priority, Shutter priority, or Manual exposure modes.) But wait, as they say, there's more. When working with Creative Styles, you can *adjust* those parameters within each preset option to fine-tune the rendition. First, look at the "stock" creative styles:

- **Standard.** This is, as you might expect, your default setting, with a good compromise of sharpness, color saturation, and contrast. Choose this, and your photos will have excellent colors, a broad range of tonal values, and standard sharpness that avoids the "oversharpened" look that some digital pictures acquire.
- **Vivid.** If you want more punch in your images, with richer colors, heightened contrast that makes those colors stand out, and moderate sharpness, this setting is for you. It's good for flowers, seaside photos, any picture with expanses of blue sky, and on overcast days where a punchier image can relieve the dullness.
- **Portrait.** Unless you're shooting a clown, you don't want overly vivid colors in your portraits. Nor do you need lots of contrast to emphasize facial flaws and defects. This setting provides realistic, muted skin tones, and a softer look that flatters your subjects.
- **Landscape.** As with the Vivid setting, this option boosts saturation and contrast to give you rich scenery and purple mountain majesties, even when your subject matter is located far enough from your camera that distant haze might otherwise be a problem. There's extra sharpness, too, to give you added crispness when you're shooting Fall colors.
- **Night.** This setting boosts the contrast to produce a more realistic night scene. If your available darkness shots are coming out a little blah, give this creative style a try.
- **Sunset.** Accentuates the red tones found in sunrise and sunset pictures.
- **B/W.** If you're shooting black-and-white photos in the camera, this setting allows you to change the contrast and sharpness (only).

To customize any of these settings, highlight the style you want to change on the menu, and press the right key to move over to the "business" side again. Then, use the left/right controller keys to choose from (left to right) contrast, saturation, and sharpness. With the parameter you want to modify highlighted, press the up/down controller keys to choose plus or minus 3 increments. (See Figure 5.25.)

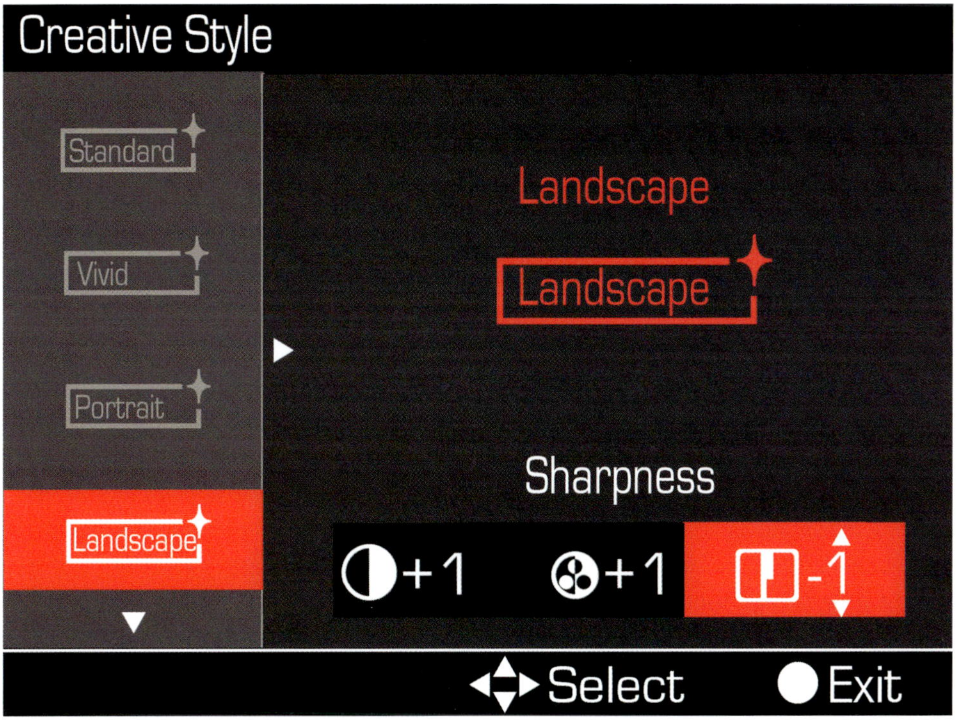

Figure 5.25 You can customize the sharpness, contrast, and color saturation of any of the Creative Styles.

Here is a summary of how the parameters you can change with Creative Styles affect your images:

- **Sharpness.** Increases or decreases the contrast of the edge outlines in your image, making the photo appear more or less sharp, depending on whether you've selected 0 (no sharpening), +3 (extra sharpening), to –3 (softening). Remember that boosting sharpness also increases the overall contrast of an image, so you'll want to use this parameter in conjunction with the contrast parameter with caution.
- **Contrast.** Compresses the range of tones in an image (increase contrast from 0 to +3) or expands the range of tones (from 0 to –3) to decrease contrast. Higher contrast images tend to lose detail in both shadows and highlights, while lower contrast images retain the detail but appear more flat and have less snap.
- **Color saturation.** You can adjust the richness of the color from low saturation (0 to –3) to high saturation (0 to +3). Lower saturation produces a muted look that can be more realistic for certain kinds of subjects, such as humans. Higher saturation produces a more vibrant appearance, but can be garish and unrealistic if carried too far. Boost your saturation if you want a vivid image, or to brighten up pictures taken on overcast days. As I noted, this setting cannot be changed for the B/W Creative Style.

Working with Live View

The Alpha A390 (but not the A290) has an absolutely brilliant Live View mode. I've used Live View with other cameras, including models from Nikon and Canon, and by comparison, the Alpha A390 has absolutely done it right. Only the Live View system found in Olympus's E-series cameras comes close.

Live View is one of those features that experienced SLR users (especially those dating from the film era) sometimes think they don't need—until they try it. Live View is also one of those features (like truly "silent" shooting, without any shutter click) that point-and-shoot refugees are surprised that digital SLRs (until recently) have lacked. Digital SLRs have actual, mechanical shutters that can't be completely silenced, as can be done with point-and-shoot cameras. I've fielded almost as many queries from those who want to know how to preview their images on the LCD—just as they did with their point-and-shoot cameras. Indeed, many P & S models don't even *have* optical viewfinders, engendering a whole generation of amateur photographers who think the only way to frame and compose an image is to hold the camera out at arm's length so the back-panel LCD can be viewed more easily.

While dSLR veterans didn't really miss what we've come to know as Live View, it was at least, in part, because they didn't have it and couldn't miss what they never had. After all, why would you eschew a big, bright, magnified through-the-lens optical view that showed depth-of-field fairly well, and which was easily visible under virtually all ambient light conditions? LCD displays, after all, were small, tended to wash out in bright light, and didn't really provide you with an accurate view of what your picture was going to look like.

There were technical problems, as well. Real-time previews theoretically disabled a dSLR's autofocus system, as focus was achieved by measuring phase contrast through the optical viewfinder, which is blocked when the mirror is flipped up for a live view. Extensive previewing had the same effect on the sensor as long exposures: the sensor heated up, producing excess noise. Pointing the camera at a bright light source when using a real-time view could damage the sensor. The list of potential problems goes on and on.

That was then. This is now.

Here's a list of the improvements Sony offers over some (or most) other Live View features from other vendors.

- **Separate Live View sensor.** Sony places a CCD imaging sensor in the optical viewing system that's used only for Live View. A tilting mirror directs incoming light either to the Live View sensor or the optical viewfinder. One significant benefit of this approach is that the imaging sensor remains covered by the shutter until the instant you take a picture, and can't overheat (increasing visual noise) or be damaged by extra bright light. (Which is the case with cameras that use the imaging sensor to provide a Live View.) Of course, the display of the image produced by the CCD sensor shows only 90 percent of the sensor's full image, but then, the optical viewfinder shows only a 95 percent view. Because a second imaging sensor is used, the Alpha can apply the same phase detection process to autofocusing the image as it uses when viewing through the optical viewfinder (OVF). You can still use contrast detection visually to focus manually. One other difference the separate Live View sensor creates is that, when using Live View, multi-segment metering actually measures 1200 different metering zones—not just the 40 used when measuring exposure through the optical viewfinder. That's because the entire second imaging sensor itself, rather than a limited metering sensor in the optical viewing system, can be used to evaluate exposure.

- **Bright view.** Olympus also uses a separate Live View sensor, but uses a half-silvered mirror to direct only part of the light to it. Because the Sony camera's Live View sensor receives 100 percent of the light, the view is bright and clear.
- **Simple activation.** To turn on Live View, just slide the Live View/OVF (Optical Viewfinder) switch forward. Some other cameras have special procedures you must follow to switch to Live View. Some have a "mode" dial that must be rotated, and if you want to use continuous shooting (which is another position on the mode dial) with Live View, you have to activate the drive mode using an additional menu. With the Sony, you just turn Live View on or off, as needed.
- **Tilting LCD.** The tilting 2.7-inch LCD of the Alpha A390 lets you use Live View in one of its most useful modes—to view, in real-time, an image that is inconvenient to view through the optical viewfinder. Nikon and Canon Live View modes display on a fixed LCD, so when you raise the camera up, or lower it, you can't really see the LCD preview anymore.
- **Fast autofocus.** Earlier in this chapter I compared fast "phase detection" autofocus to slower "contrast detection" autofocus, which is used in point-and-shoot cameras, and is offered as one of the focusing modes for Live View with cameras like the Canon and Nikon. Because it uses a second sensor for Live View, the Sony can use the faster phase detection system regardless of mode. Other cameras may need to flip the mirror back up, interrupting the Live View, if you want to use phase detection instead of their default contrast detection. So, with those cameras you have your choice of relatively slow autofocus (with multiple mirror flips) or even slower autofocus. Sony's method is better.

There are a couple things I *don't* like about Sony's Live View mode, and the most serious drawback is the cluttered screen, as you can see in Figure 5.26. (You can remove some of the extraneous information by pressing the DISP button.) Information that normally would be shown on the LCD when you remove your eye from the optical viewfinder is overlaid on the Live View screen. In addition, the Sony Live View doesn't have a conventional provision for zooming in on a portion of the screen for manual focus (or for checking autofocus), unlike some other cameras. You have to use the Smart Teleconverter button to zoom in by factors of 1.4X and 2.0X. The Alpha's Continuous Shooting mode drops from 2.5 to 2 fps when using Live View, but that's likely to be a concern only when you're shooting sports or bracketing in Live View mode. And keep in mind, that, like most Live View implementations, Sony's really increases the amount of battery power the camera consumes (possibly as much as, or more than using the built-in electronic flash).

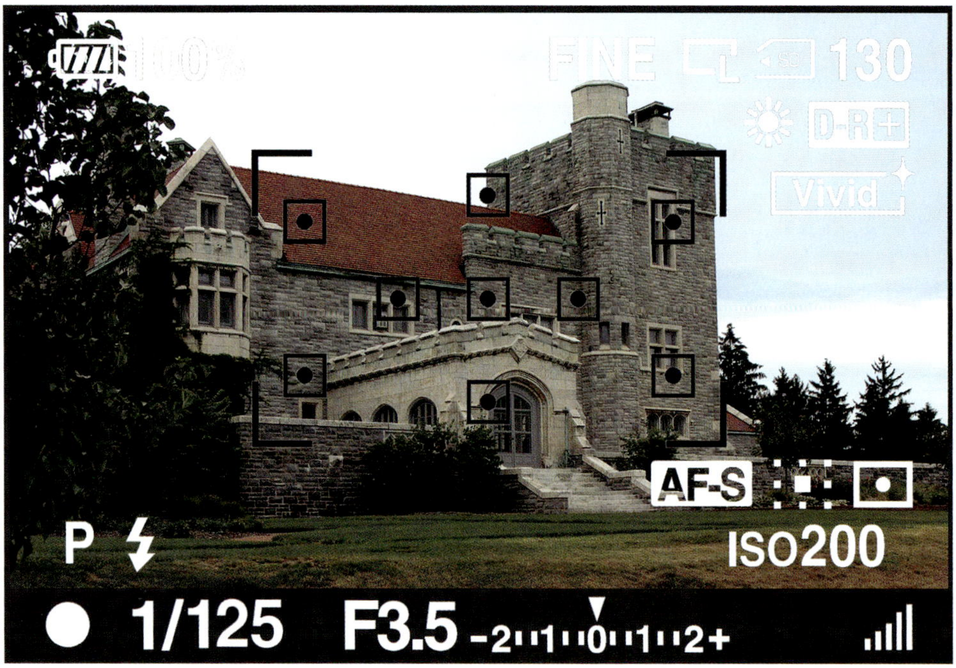

Figure 5.26
Sony's Live View is great, but the cluttered LCD screen can be annoying.

What You Can/Cannot Do with Live View

You may not have considered just what you can do with Live View, because the capability is so novel. But once you've played with it, you'll discover dozens of applications for this capability, as well as a few things that you can't do. Here's a list of Live View considerations.

- **Preview your images on a TV.** Connect your Sony dSLR to a television using the video cable, and you can preview your image on a large screen.
- **Preview remotely.** Extend the cable between the camera and TV screen, and you can preview your images some distance away from the camera.
- **Continuous shooting.** You can shoot bursts of images using Live View, but at the slower frame rate I mentioned.
- **Shoot from tripod or handheld.** Of course, holding the camera out at arm's length to preview an image is poor technique, and will introduce a lot of camera shake. If you want to use Live View for handheld images, make sure SteadyShot is turned on and/or use a high shutter speed. A tripod is a better choice if you are in an environment where it's convenient (or permissible) to use one.
- **Watch your power.** As I mentioned, Live View uses a lot of juice and will deplete your battery rapidly. Sony estimates that you can get 430 shots per battery charge when using Live View, compared to 730 shots when using the optical viewfinder.

6

Working with Lenses

Although it's sometimes alarming for those of us who have been taking pictures a very long time, the recent tendency for larger companies to absorb smaller vendors has paid some big dividends, most notably in the huge selection of lenses available for the relatively new Sony Alpha dSLR camera line.

In my youth, I managed a camera store for a while, and had access to a broad range of different models, and so used both Konica and Minolta cameras for many years—dating back to the Konica Autoreflex T (the first SLR with autoexposure/through-the-lens metering) and the legendary Minolta SRT-101. Only a few years into the digital SLR era, the two companies joined forces as Konica Minolta, and in turn saw their technology eventually taken over by Sony in 2006. Bye-bye Konica Minolta 7D, hello Sony Alpha models, like the company's first entry, the Alpha DSLR-A100, each with a legacy of hundreds of lenses from the sorely missed Minolta lineup.

Thanks to the head start provided by Konica and Minolta (and boosted by Minolta-compatible lenses from third parties), your Sony Alpha A390/A290 cameras can be used with a very broad range of high-quality lenses, suitable for a user base that extends from novice photo enthusiasts to advanced amateur and professional photographers. It's this mind-bending assortment of high-quality lenses available to enhance the capabilities of cameras like the Sony Alpha DSLR-A390 and A290 that make the camera line so attractive. Hundreds of current and older lenses introduced by Minolta, Sony, and third-party vendors since the late 1980s can be used to give you a wider view, bring distant subjects closer, let you focus closer, shoot under lower light conditions, or provide a more detailed, sharper image for critical work. Other than the sensor itself, the lens you choose for your dSLR is the most important component in determining image quality and perspective of your images.

This chapter explains how to select the best lenses for the kinds of photography you want to do.

But Don't Forget the Crop Factor

From time to time you've heard the term *crop factor*, and you've probably also heard the term *lens multiplier factor*. Both are misleading and inaccurate terms used to describe the same phenomenon: the fact that cameras like the Sony Alpha (and most other affordable digital SLRs) provide a field of view that's smaller and narrower than that produced by certain other (usually much more expensive) cameras, when fitted with exactly the same lens.

Figure 6.1 quite clearly shows the phenomenon at work. The outer rectangle, marked 1X, shows the field of view you might expect with a 50mm lens mounted on a so-called "full-frame" digital model like the Alpha A850, or a 35mm film camera, like the 1985 Minolta Maxxum 7000 (which happened to be the first SLR to feature both autofocus and motorized advance, something we take for granted in the digital SLR age). The rectangle marked 1.5X shows the field of view you'd get with that 50mm lens installed on a Sony Alpha. It's easy to see from the illustration that the 1X rendition provides a wider, more expansive view, while the other view is, in comparison, *cropped*.

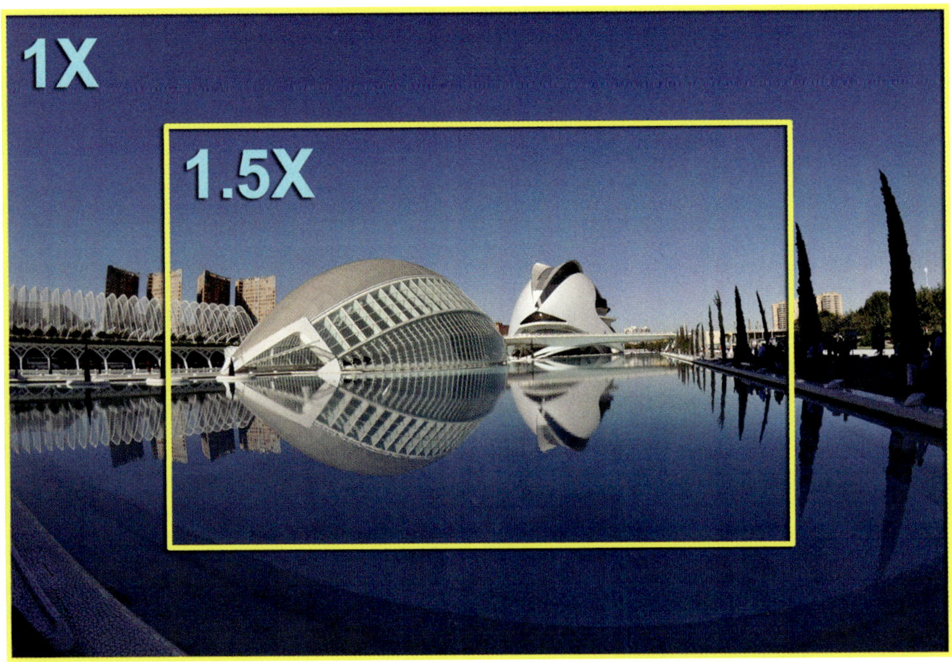

Figure 6.1
Sony offers digital SLRs with full-frame (1X) views, as well as 1.5X crops.

The cropping effect is produced because the sensors of the Alpha A390/A290 are smaller than the sensors of a full-frame camera. The "full-frame" camera has a sensor that's the size of the standard 35mm film frame, 24mm × 36mm. Your Sony Alpha's sensor does *not* measure 24mm × 36mm; instead, it specs out at roughly 24 × 16mm (there is a difference of a few tenths of a millimeter in each direction among the three Alpha models), or about 66 percent of the area of a full-frame sensor, as shown by the yellow boxes in the figure. You can calculate the relative field of view by dividing the focal length of the lens by .667. Thus, a 100mm lens mounted on a Sony Alpha has the same field of view as a 150mm lens on a full-frame camera like the A850. We humans tend to perform multiplication operations in our heads more easily than division, so such field of view comparisons are usually calculated using the reciprocal of .667—1.5—so we can multiply instead. (100 / .667=150; 100 × 1.5=150.)

This translation is generally useful only if you're accustomed to using full-frame cameras (usually of the film variety) and want to know how a familiar lens will perform on a digital camera. I strongly prefer *crop factor* to *lens multiplier*, because nothing is being multiplied; a 100mm lens doesn't "become" a 150mm lens—the depth-of-field and lens aperture remain the same. (I'll explain more about these later in this chapter.) Only the field of view is cropped. But the term *crop factor* isn't much better, as it implies that the 24 × 36mm frame is "full" and anything else is "less." I get e-mails all the time from photographers who point out that they own full-frame cameras with 36mm × 48mm sensors (like the Mamiya 645ZD or Hasselblad H3D-39 medium format digitals). By their reckoning, the "half-size" sensors found in full-frame cameras like the Sony Alpha DSLR-A850 are "cropped."

If you're accustomed to using full-frame film cameras, you might find it helpful to use the crop factor "multiplier" to translate a lens's real focal length into the full-frame equivalent, even though, as I said, nothing is actually being multiplied. Throughout most of this book, I've been using actual focal lengths and not equivalents, except when referring to specific wide-angle or telephoto focal length ranges and their fields of view.

Your First Lens

The Sony Alpha is most frequently purchased with a lens, often the SAL-1855 DT 18-55mm f/3.5-5.6 zoom lens, which adds only about $100 to the price tag of the body alone, and is thus an irresistible bargain. You can also buy one of the Alpha bodies alone if you already have some lenses. So, you'll need to make a decision about what lens to buy, or decide what other kind of lenses you need to fill out your complement of Sony optics. This section will cover "first lens" concerns, while later in the chapter we'll look at "add-on lens" considerations.

When deciding on a first lens, there are several factors you'll want to consider:

- **Cost.** Even with two low-cost camera bodies to choose from, you might have stretched your budget a bit to purchase your Sony Alpha, so you might want to keep the cost of your first lens fairly low. Fortunately, there are excellent lenses available that will add from $100 to $300 to the price of your camera if purchased at the same time. Others cost a little more, but have very desirable features.
- **Zoom range.** If you have only one lens, you'll want a fairly long zoom range to provide as much flexibility as possible. Once you "graduate" from the 18-55mm kit lens, you'll find several other (pricey) options. For example, one of the most popular basic lenses for the Alpha, the DT 18-250mm f/3.5-6.3 and DT 18-200mm f/3.5-6.3 optics have 11.0X to an astounding 13.8X zoom ranges, with both extending from moderate wide-angle/normal out to long telephoto. These lenses are fine for everyday shooting, portraits, and some types of sports. They're not cheap, starting at about $529, but may be worth the cost to you if such a long range is desirable.
- **Adequate maximum aperture.** You'll want an f/stop of at least f/3.5 to f/4 for shooting under fairly low light conditions. The thing to watch for is the maximum aperture when the lens is zoomed to its telephoto end. You may end up with no better than an f/5.6 maximum aperture if you buy a kit lens. That's not great, but you can often live with it.
- **Image quality.** Your starter lens should have good image quality, because that's one of the primary factors that will be used to judge your photos. Even at a low price, the 18-70mm lens sold with the Alpha as a kit includes extra-low dispersion glass and aspherical elements that minimize distortion and chromatic aberration; it's plenty sharp enough for most applications.
- **Size matters.** A good walking-around lens is compact in size and light in weight.
- **Fast/close focusing.** Your first lens should have a speedy autofocus system. Close focusing (to 12 inches or closer) will let you use your basic lens for some types of macro photography.

You can find comparisons of the lenses discussed in the next section. I'll provide my recommendations.

Buy Now, Expand Later

The Alpha is commonly available with several good, basic lenses that can serve you well as a "walk-around" lens (one you keep on the camera most of the time, especially when you're out and about without your camera bag). The number of options available to you is actually quite amazing when you consider third-party lenses, even if your budget is limited to about $100-$400 for your first lens. The most popular starter lens Sony offers for the Alpha is shown in Figure 6.2.

Sony's best-bet first lenses are as follows:

- **Sony SAL-1855 DT 18-55mm f/3.5-5.6 zoom lens.** This lens is sharp, small in size, and is fast enough at the wide-angle end of its zoom range for most available light shooting. Priced at $200 if purchased separately, this lens is an all-around good choice.
- **Sony SAL-24105 24-105mm f/3.5-4.5 zoom lens.** This discontinued lens is more expensive at about $470, but, if you can find one, may be a smarter choice if you intend to shoot indoor or outdoor sports. It's faster at its longest focal length, and provides the equivalent of a moderate wide angle to short telephoto 5X zoom in one compact lens.
- **Sony SAL-18250 18-250mm f/3.5-6.3 high magnification zoom lens.** If you have $550 to spare, this lens is truly a do-everything lens with a near-14X zoom range that takes you from true wide angle to long telephoto in one swoop. It's great for sports, landscapes, and portraits, even though a bit slow at f/6.3 at the telephoto end. Sony also offers the similar, slightly smaller SAL-18200 18-200mm f/3.5-6.3 lens for $50 less.

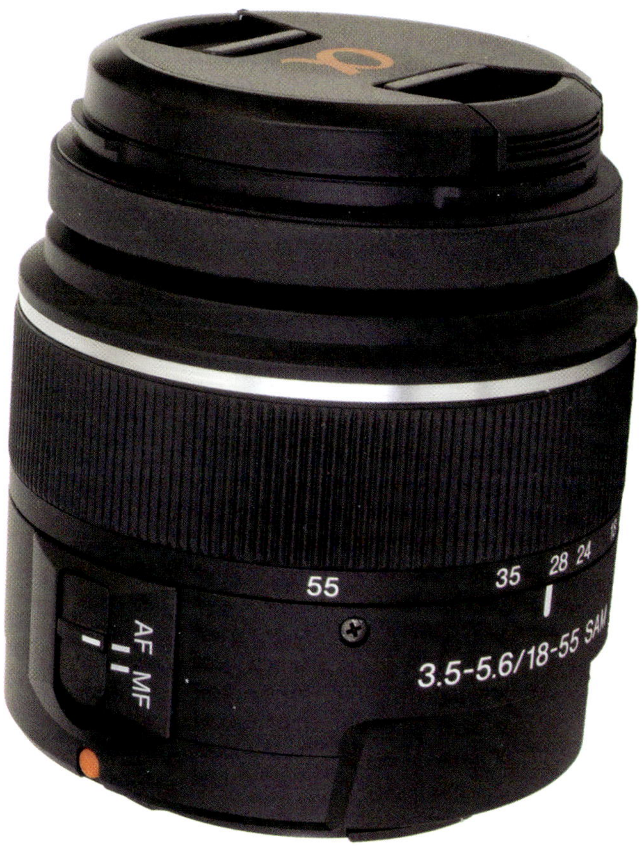

Figure 6.2
This 18-55mm lens is the most popular starter lens for Sony Alpha digital SLRs.

- **Sony SAL-16105 DT 16-105mm f/3.5-5.6 zoom lens.** Slightly wider and with twice as much telephoto reach as the kit lens, this one will let you shoot landscapes, portraits, and some sports with equal ease, and is more compact than the 18-250/18-200 tandem, while still being affordable to the serious photographer at $600. It focuses as close as 1.25 feet. This is another upgrade from the kit lens that serious photographers will appreciate.
- **Sony SAL-1680Z Carl Zeiss Vario-Sonnar T* DT 16-80mm f/3.5-4.5 zoom lens.** Slightly wider and longer than the kit lens, and a tad faster when fully zoomed, this one should be your first "pro" lens. It has the famed Carl Zeiss image quality and rugged mechanics. Buy this if you're looking to work your lenses hard without compromising quality, and are willing to compromise your budget with its $750 pricetag.
- **Sony SAL-55200 DT 55-200mm f/4-5.6 telephoto zoom lens.** One main advantage of this lens is its low cost—about $230. Mated with the 18-55mm kit lens, you're covered for focal lengths from wide to long telephoto at a very attractive price.
- **Sony SAL-75300 75-300mm f/4.5-5.6 telephoto zoom lens.** This is another $250 bargain, but sacrifices some of the short telephoto range (55-70mm) for a longer reach, out to a long 300mm. (Remember, a 300mm focal length on an Alpha is the equivalent of 450mm on a full-frame camera—truly super-telephoto range.) This is a compact lens (weighing just 18 ounces) that also can be used with any full-frame camera Sony might introduce in the future. It focuses as close as 5 feet at 300mm, which allows you to shoot skittish creatures (and humans) from a non-threatening distance.

Your Second (and Third...) Lens

There are really only two advantages to owning just a single lens. One of them is creativity. Keeping one set of optics mounted on your Alpha all the time forces you to be especially imaginative in your approach to your subjects. I once visited Europe with only a single camera body and a 35mm f/2 lens. The experience was actually quite exciting, because I had to use a variety of techniques to allow that one lens to serve for landscapes, available light photos, action, close-ups, portraits, and other kinds of images. Sony makes an excellent "35mm" lens (actually, it's the SAL-20F28 20mm f/2.8 wide-angle lens, which provides the equivalent field of view on the Alpha cameras). At around $600, this lens is expensive—and very sharp. It focuses down to 9.5 inches, and would be perfect for my Europe experiment today, although my personal choice would be the sublime SAL-35F15G 35mm f/1.4 lens, which is a little longer and a lot more expensive at $1,369.

Of course, it's more likely that your "single" lens is actually a zoom, which is, in truth, many lenses in one, taking you from, say, 18mm to 55mm (or some other range) with a rapid twist of the zoom ring. You'll still find some creative challenges when you stick to a single zoom lens's focal lengths.

The second advantage of the unilens camera is only a marginal technical benefit since the introduction of the Sony Alpha. If you don't exchange lenses, the chances of dust and dirt getting inside your Alpha and settling on the sensor are reduced (but *not* eliminated entirely). Although I've known some photographers who minimized the number of lens changes they made for this very reason, reducing the number of lenses you work with is not a productive or rewarding approach for most of us. The Alpha's automatic sensor cleaning feature has made this "advantage" much less significant than it was in the past.

It's more likely that you'll succumb to the malady known as *Lens Lust*, which is defined as an incurable disease marked by a significant yen for newer, better, longer, faster, sharper, anything-er optics for your camera. (And, it must be noted, this disease can *cost* you significant yen—or dollars, or whatever currency you use.) In its worst manifestations, sufferers find themselves with lenses that have overlapping zoom ranges or capabilities, because one or the other offers a slight margin in performance or suitability for specific tasks. When you find yourself already lusting after a new lens before you've really had a chance to put your latest purchase to the test, you'll know the disease has reached the terminal phase.

What Lenses Can Do for You

A saner approach to expanding your lens collection is to consider what each of your options can do for you and then choosing the type of lens that will really boost your creative opportunities. Here's a general guide to the sort of capabilities you can gain by adding a lens to your repertoire.

- **Wider perspective.** Your 18-55mm f/3.5-5.6 lens has served you well for moderate wide-angle shots. Now you find your back is up against a wall and you *can't* take a step backwards to take in more subject matter. Perhaps you're standing on the rim of the Grand Canyon, and you want to take in as much of the breathtaking view as you can. You might find yourself just behind the baseline at a high school basketball game and want an interesting shot with a little perspective distortion tossed in the mix. There's a lens out there that will provide you with what you need, such as the SAL-1118 DT 11-18mm f/4.5-5.6 super-wide zoom lens or SAL-16F28 16mm f/2.8 fisheye lens. Your extra-wide choices may not be abundant, but they are there. Figure 6.3 shows the perspective you get from an ultrawide-angle lens.

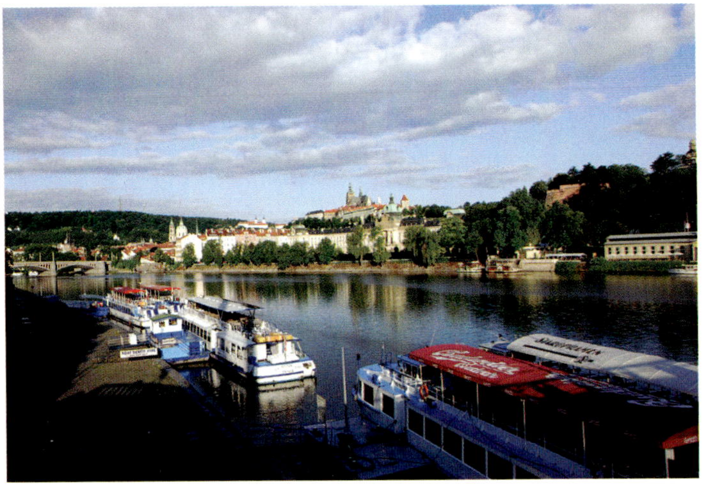

Figure 6.3
An ultrawide-angle lens provided this view of a castle in Prague.

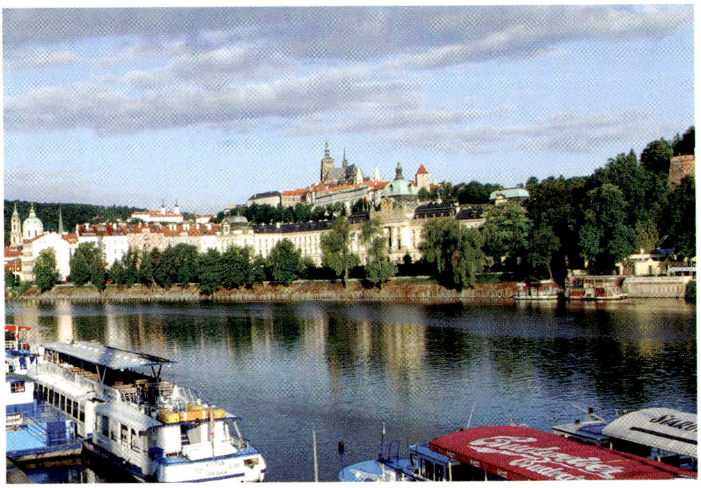

Figure 6.4
This photo, taken from roughly the same distance shows the view using a short telephoto lens.

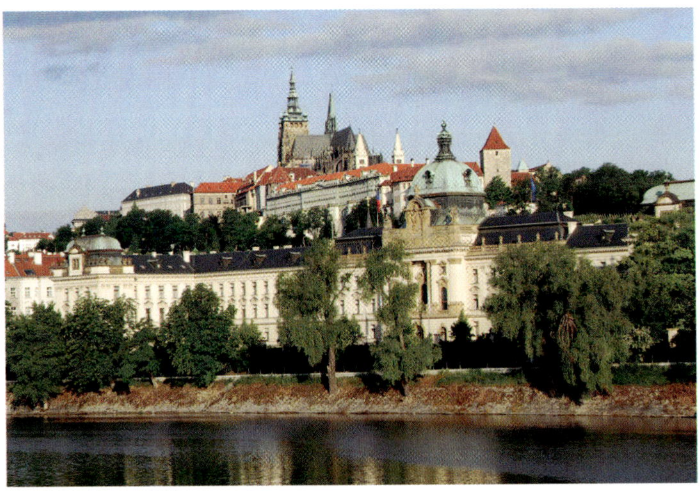

Figure 6.5
A longer telephoto lens captured this closer view from approximately the same shooting position.

- **Bring objects closer.** A long lens brings distant subjects closer to you, offers better control over depth-of-field, and avoids the perspective distortion that wide-angle lenses provide. They compress the apparent distance between objects in your frame. In the telephoto realm, Sony is right in the ballgame, with lenses like the telephoto zooms I mentioned earlier to some super high-end models like the SAL-70200G 70-200mm f/2.8 G-series telephoto zoom. (You'll pay $1,800 for this baby.) Remember that the Sony Alpha's crop factor narrows the field of view of all these lenses, so your 70-200mm lens looks more like a 105mm-300mm zoom through the viewfinder. Figures 6.4 and 6.5 were taken from the same position as Figure 6.3, but with an 85mm and 500mm lens, respectively.
- **Bring your camera closer.** Sony has three excellent close-up lenses, the SAL-30M28 30mm f/2.8 macro lens, the SAL-50M28 50mm f/2.8 macro lens, and the SAL-100M28 100mm f/2.8 macro lens. The 30mm lens is most reasonably priced at $200 (very inexpensive for a true macro), but paying $479 with the 50mm lens, or $679 for the 100mm version is not out of order for someone who wants to shoot close-up subjects but wants to stay farther away from a subject to provide more flexibility in lighting and enough distance to avoid spooking small wildlife.
- **Look sharp.** Many lenses, particularly the higher-priced Sony optics, are prized for their sharpness and overall image quality. While your run-of-the-mill lens is likely to be plenty sharp for most applications, the very best optics are even better over their entire field of view (which means no fuzzy corners), are sharper at a wider range of focal lengths (in the case of zooms), and have better correction for various types of distortion. That, along with a constant f/2.8 aperture, is why the 70-200mm f/2.8 lens I mentioned earlier sells for $1,800.
- **More speed.** Your basic telephoto lens might have the perfect focal length and sharpness for sports photography, but the maximum aperture won't cut it for night baseball or football games, or, even, any sports shooting in daylight if the weather is cloudy or you need to use some ungodly fast shutter speed, such as 1/4,000th second. You might be happier with the Carl Zeiss SAL-135F18Z 135mm f/1.8 lens (if money is no object, it costs $1,400). But there are lower-cost fast lens options, such as the SAL-50F14 50mm f/1.4 lens ($350), which might be suitable for indoor sports such as basketball or volleyball. (See Figure 6.6.)

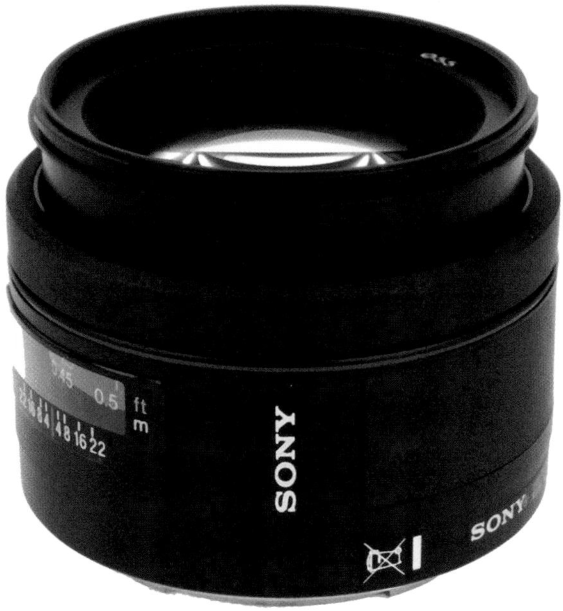

Figure 6.6
A fast prime lens offers f/stops as large as the f/1.4 available with this 50mm optic.

Zoom or Prime?

Zoom lenses have changed the way serious photographers take pictures. One of the reasons that I own 12 SLR film bodies is that in ancient times it was common to mount a different fixed focal length prime lens on various cameras and take pictures with two or three cameras around your neck (or tucked in a camera case) so you'd be ready to take a long shot or an intimate close-up or wide-angle view on a moment's notice, without the need to switch lenses. It made sense (at the time) to have a half-dozen or so bodies (two to use, one in the shop, one in transit, and a couple backups). Zoom lenses of the time had a limited zoom range, were heavy, and not very sharp (especially when you tried to wield one of those monsters handheld).

That's all changed today. Lenses like the sharp Sony lenses I've already described, including the top-of-the-line Carl Zeiss optics, have zoom ranges up to 13.8X, and are light in weight. The best zooms might seem expensive, but they are actually much less costly than the six or so lenses replaced. When selecting between zoom and prime lenses, there are several considerations to ponder. Here's a checklist of the most important factors. I already mentioned image quality and maximum aperture earlier, but those aspects take on additional meaning when comparing zooms and primes.

- **Logistics.** As prime lenses offer just a single focal length, you'll need more of them to encompass the full range offered by a single zoom. More lenses mean additional slots in your camera bag, and extra weight to carry. Even so, you might be willing to carry an extra prime lens or two in order to gain the speed or image quality that lens offers.

- **Image quality.** Prime lenses usually produce better image quality at their focal length than even the most sophisticated zoom lenses at the same magnification. Zoom lenses, with their shifting elements and f/stops that can vary from zoom position to zoom position, are in general more complex to design than fixed focal length lenses. That's not to say that the very best prime lenses can't be complicated as well. However, the exotic designs, aspheric elements, and other tweaks can be applied to improving the quality of the lens, rather than wasting a lot of it on compensating for problems caused by the zoom process itself.
- **Maximum aperture.** Because of the same design constraints, zoom lenses usually have smaller maximum apertures than prime lenses, and the most affordable zooms have a lens opening that grows effectively smaller as you zoom to the telephoto position. The difference in lens speed verges on the ridiculous at some focal lengths. For example, the 18mm-55mm basic zoom gives you an 83.5mm f/5.6 lens when zoomed all the way out, while prime lenses in approximately that focal length commonly have f/1.8 or faster maximum apertures. Indeed, the fastest Sony lenses are all primes, and if you require speed, a fixed focal length lens is what you should rely on.
- **Speed.** Using prime lenses takes time and slows you down. It takes a few seconds to remove your current lens and mount a new one, and the more often you need to do that, the more time is wasted. If you choose not to swap lenses, when using a fixed focal length lens you'll still have to move closer or farther away from your subject to get the field of view you want. A zoom lens allows you to change magnifications and focal lengths with the twist of a ring and generally saves a great deal of time.

Categories of Lenses

Lenses can be categorized by their intended purpose—general photography, macro photography, and so forth—or by their focal length. The range of available focal lengths is usually divided into three main groups: wide-angle, normal, and telephoto. Prime lenses fall neatly into one of these classifications. Zooms can overlap designations, with a significant number falling into the catchall wide-to-telephoto zoom range. This section provides more information about focal length ranges, and how they are used.

Any lens with an equivalent focal length of 10mm to 20mm is said to be an *ultrawide-angle lens*; from about 20mm to 40mm (equivalent) is said to be a *wide-angle lens. Normal lenses* have a focal length roughly equivalent to the diagonal of the film or sensor, in millimeters, and so fall into the range of about 45mm to 60mm (on a full-frame camera). *Telephoto lenses* usually fall into the 75mm and longer focal lengths, while those from about 300mm-400mm and longer often are referred to as *super-telephotos.*

Using Wide-Angle and Wide-Zoom Lenses

To use wide-angle prime lenses and wide zooms, you need to understand how they affect your photography. Here's a quick summary of the things you need to know.

- **More depth-of-field.** Practically speaking, wide-angle lenses offer more depth-of-field at a particular subject distance and aperture. (But see the sidebar below for an important note.) You'll find that helpful when you want to maximize sharpness of a large zone, but not very useful when you'd rather isolate your subject using selective focus (telephoto lenses are better for that).
- **Stepping back.** Wide-angle lenses have the effect of making it seem that you are standing farther from your subject than you really are. They're helpful when you don't want to back up, or can't because there are impediments in your way.
- **Wider field of view.** While making your subject seem farther away, as implied above, a wide-angle lens also provides a larger field of view, including more of the subject in your photos.
- **More foreground.** As background objects retreat, more of the foreground is brought into view by a wide-angle lens. That gives you extra emphasis on the area that's closest to the camera. Photograph your home with a normal lens/normal zoom setting, and the front yard probably looks fairly conventional in your photo (that's why they're called "normal" lenses). Switch to a wider lens and you'll discover that your lawn now makes up much more of the photo. So, wide-angle lenses are great when you want to emphasize that lake in the foreground, but problematic when your intended subject is located farther in the distance.
- **Super-sized subjects.** The tendency of a wide-angle lens to emphasize objects in the foreground, while de-emphasizing objects in the background, can lead to a kind of size distortion that may be more objectionable for some types of subjects than others. Shoot a bed of flowers up close with a wide angle, and you might like the distorted effect of the larger blossoms nearer the lens. Take a photo of a family member with the same lens from the same distance, and you're likely to get some complaints about that gigantic nose in the foreground.
- **Perspective distortion.** When you tilt the camera so the plane of the sensor is no longer perpendicular to the vertical plane of your subject, some parts of the subject are now closer to the sensor than they were before, while other parts are farther away. So, buildings, flagpoles, or NBA players appear to be falling backwards (building shown in Figure 6.7). While this kind of apparent distortion (it's not caused by a defect in the lens) can happen with any lens, it's most apparent when a wide angle is used.

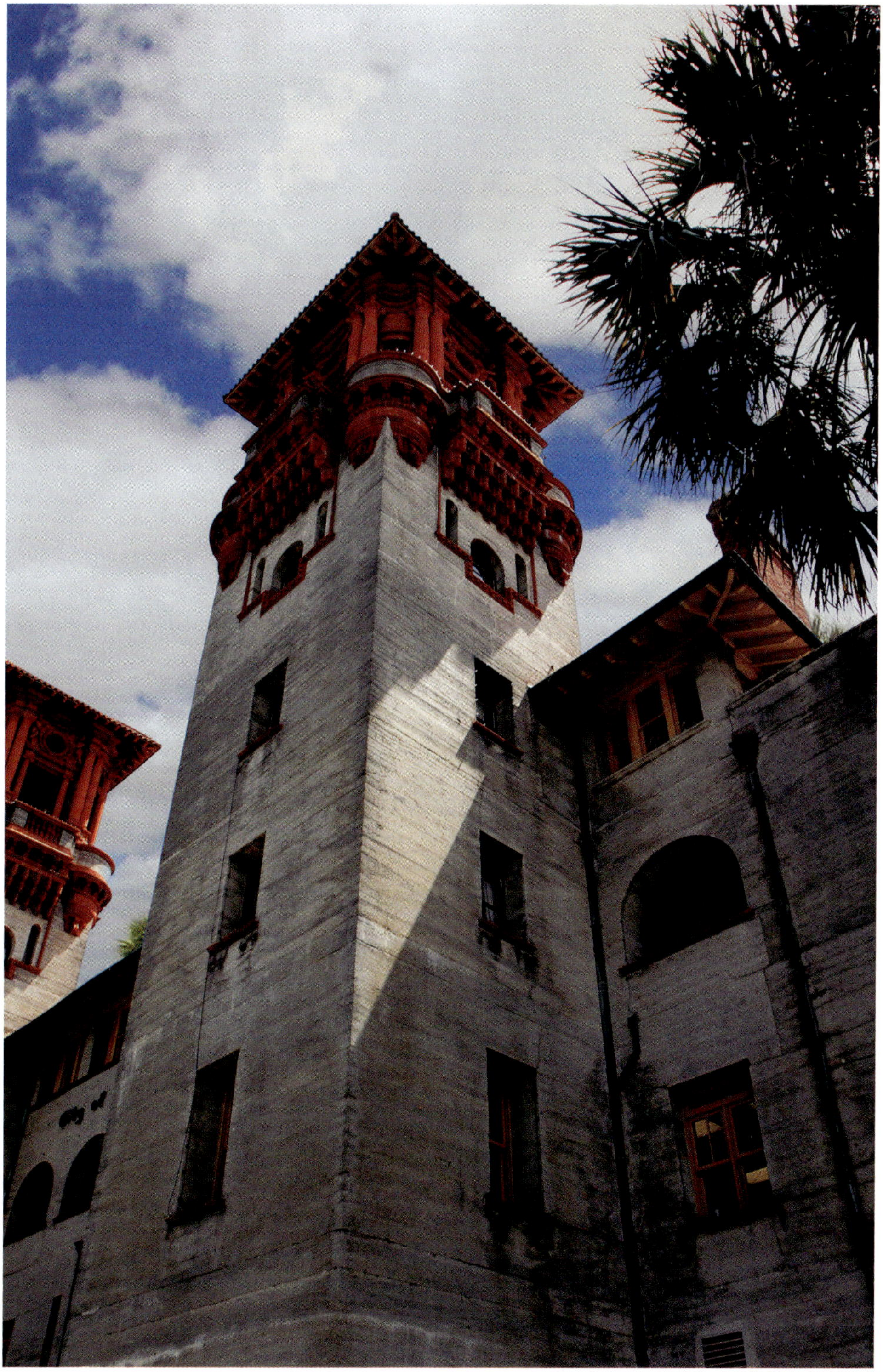

Figure 6.7
Tilting the camera produces this "falling back" look in architectural photos.

- **Steady cam.** You'll find that it is easier to handhold a wide-angle lens at slower shutter speeds, without need for SteadyShot, than it is a telephoto lens. The reduced magnification of the wide-lens or wide-zoom setting doesn't emphasize camera shake like a telephoto lens does.
- **Interesting angles.** Many of the factors already listed combine to produce more interesting angles when shooting with wide-angle lenses. Raising or lowering a telephoto lens a few feet probably will have little effect on the appearance of the distant subjects you're shooting. The same change in elevation can produce a dramatic effect for the much-closer subjects typically captured with a wide-angle lens or wide-zoom setting.

DOF IN DEPTH

The DOF advantage of wide-angle lenses is diminished when you enlarge your picture; believe it or not, a wide-angle image enlarged and cropped to provide the same subject size as a telephoto shot would have the *same* depth-of-field. Try it: take a wide-angle photo of a friend from a fair distance, and then zoom in to duplicate the picture in a telephoto image. Then, enlarge the wide shot so your friend is the same size in both. The wide photo will have the same depth-of-field (and will have much less detail, too).

Avoiding Potential Wide-Angle Problems

Wide-angle lenses have a few quirks that you'll want to keep in mind when shooting so you can avoid falling into some common traps. Here's a checklist of tips for avoiding common problems:

- **Symptom: converging lines.** Unless you want to use wildly diverging lines as a creative effect, it's a good idea to keep horizontal and vertical lines in landscapes, architecture, and other subjects carefully aligned with the sides, top, and bottom of the frame. That will help you avoid undesired perspective distortion. Sometimes it helps to shoot from a slightly elevated position so you don't have to tilt the camera up or down.
- **Symptom: color fringes around objects.** Lenses are often plagued with fringes of color around backlit objects, produced by *chromatic aberration*, which comes in two forms: *longitudinal/axial*, in which all the colors of light don't focus in the same plane; and *lateral/transverse*, in which the colors are shifted to one side. Axial chromatic aberration can be reduced by stopping down the lens, but transverse

chromatic aberration cannot. Better quality lenses reduce both types of imaging defect; it's common for reviews to point out these failings, so you can choose the best performing lenses that your budget allows.

- **Symptom: lines that bow outward.** Some wide-angle lenses cause straight lines to bow outwards, with the strongest effect at the edges. In fisheye (or *curvilinear*) lenses, this defect is a feature, as you can see in Figure 6.8. When distortion is not desired, you'll need to use a lens that has corrected barrel distortion. Manufacturers like Sony do their best to minimize or eliminate it (producing a *rectilinear* lens), often using *aspherical* lens elements (which are not cross-sections of a sphere). You can also minimize barrel distortion simply by framing your photo with some extra space all around, so the edges where the defect is most obvious can be cropped out of the picture.

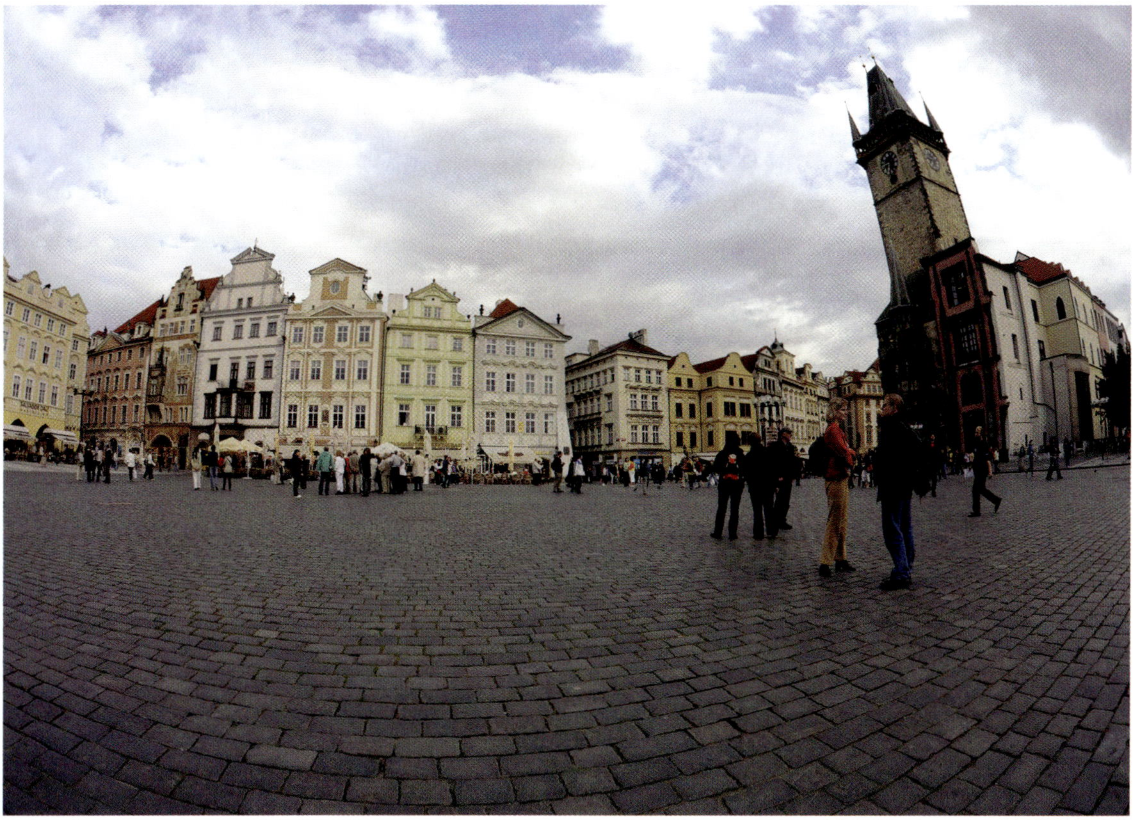

Figure 6.8 Many wide-angle lenses cause lines to bow outwards towards the edges of the image; with a fisheye lens, this tendency is considered an interesting feature.

- **Symptom: dark corners and shadows in flash photos.** The Sony Alpha's built-in electronic flash is designed to provide even coverage for fairly wide lenses. If you use a wider lens, you can expect darkening, or *vignetting*, in the corners of the frame. At wider focal lengths, the lens hood of some lenses (my 16mm-80mm f/3.5-4.5 zoom lens is a prime offender) can cast a semi-circular shadow in the lower portion of the frame when using the built-in flash. Sometimes removing the lens hood or zooming in a bit can eliminate the shadow. Mounting an external flash unit can solve both problems. Its higher vantage point eliminates the problem of lens hood shadow, too.
- **Symptom: light and dark areas when using polarizing filter.** If you know that polarizers work best when the camera is pointed 90 degrees away from the sun and have the least effect when the camera is oriented 180 degrees from the sun, you know only half the story. With lenses having a focal length of 10mm to 18mm (the equivalent of 16mm-28mm), the angle of view (107 to 75 degrees diagonally, or 97 to 44 degrees horizontally) is extensive enough to cause problems. Think about it: when a 10mm lens is pointed at the proper 90-degree angle from the sun, objects at the edges of the frame will be oriented at 135 to 41 degrees, with only the center at exactly 90 degrees. Either edge will have much less of a polarized effect. The solution is to avoid using a polarizing filter with lenses having an actual focal length of less than 18mm (or 28mm equivalent).

Using Telephoto and Tele-Zoom Lenses

Telephoto lenses also can have a dramatic effect on your photography, and Sony is especially strong in the long-lens arena, with lots of choices in many focal lengths and zoom ranges. You should be able to find an affordable telephoto or tele-zoom to enhance your photography in several different ways. Here are the most important things you need to know. In the next section, I'll concentrate on telephoto considerations that can be problematic—and how to avoid those problems.

- **Selective focus.** Long lenses have reduced depth-of-field within the frame, allowing you to use selective focus to isolate your subject. You can open the lens up wide to create shallow depth-of-field, or close it down a bit to allow more to be in focus. The flip side of the coin is that when you *want* to make a range of objects sharp, you'll need to use a smaller f/stop to get the depth-of-field you need. Like fire, the depth-of-field of a telephoto lens can be friend or foe. (See Figure 6.9.)

- **Getting closer.** Telephoto lenses bring you closer to wildlife, sports action, and candid subjects. No one wants to get a reputation as a surreptitious or "sneaky" photographer (except for paparazzi), but when applied to candids in an open and honest way, a long lens can help you capture memorable moments while retaining enough distance to stay out of the way of events as they transpire.
- **Reduced foreground/increased compression.** Telephoto lenses have the opposite effect of wide angles: they reduce the importance of things in the foreground by squeezing everything together. This compression even makes distant objects appear to be closer to subjects in the foreground and middle ranges. You can use this effect as a creative tool.

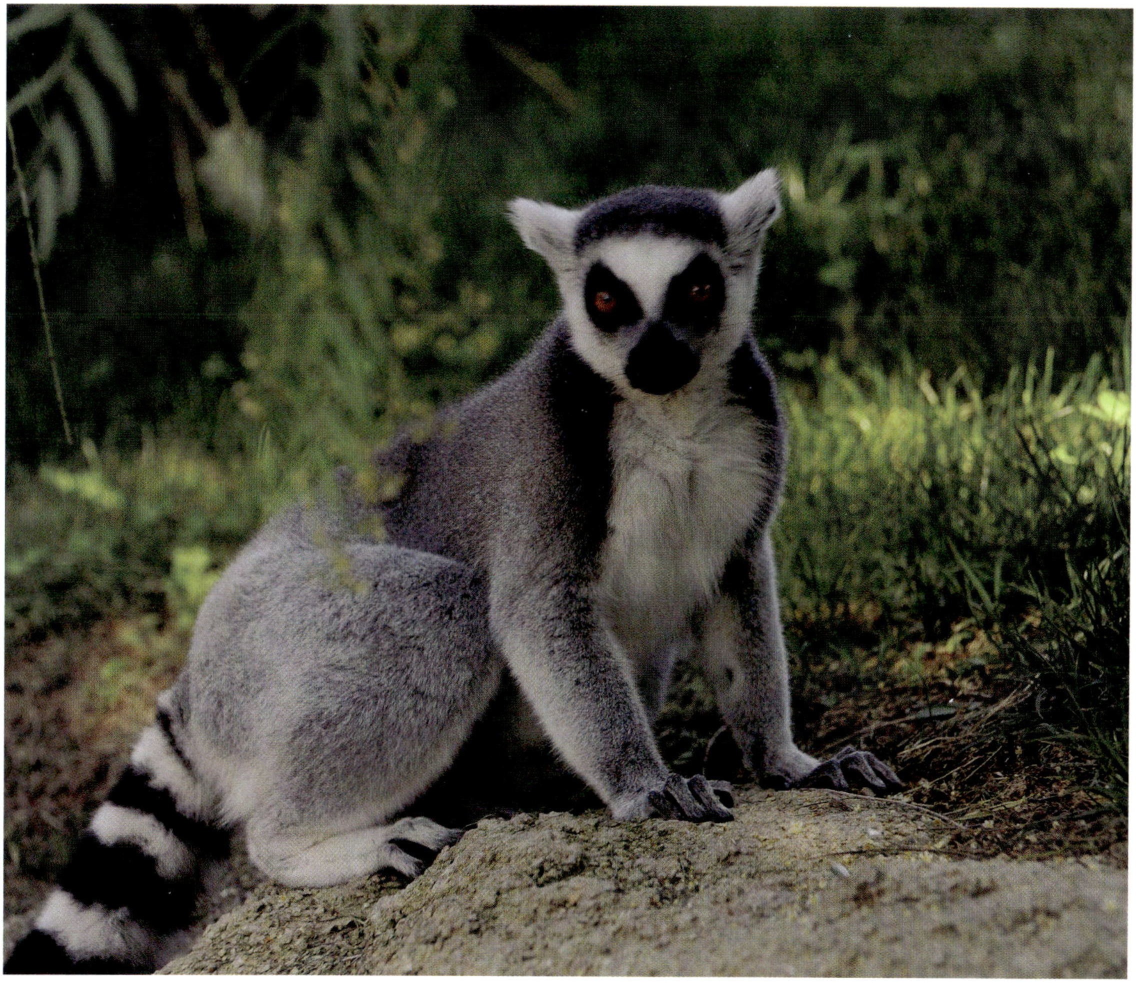

Figure 6.9 A wide f/stop helped isolate this lemur from its background.

- **Accentuates camera shakiness.** Telephoto focal lengths hit you with a double-whammy in terms of camera/photographer shake. The lenses themselves are bulkier, more difficult to hold steady, and may even produce a barely perceptible seesaw rocking effect when you support them with one hand halfway down the lens barrel. Telephotos also magnify any camera shake. It's no wonder that image stabilization like SteadyShot is especially popular among those using longer lenses.
- **Interesting angles require creativity.** Telephoto lenses require more imagination in selecting interesting angles, because the "angle" you do get on your subjects is so narrow. Moving from side to side or a bit higher or lower can make a dramatic difference in a wide-angle shot, but raising or lowering a telephoto lens a few feet probably will have little effect on the appearance of the distant subjects you're shooting.

Avoiding Telephoto Lens Problems

Many of the "problems" that telephoto lenses pose are really just challenges and not that difficult to overcome. Here is a list of the seven most common picture maladies and suggested solutions.

- **Symptom: flat faces in portraits.** Head-and-shoulders portraits of humans tend to be more flattering when a focal length of 50mm to 85mm is used. Longer focal lengths compress the distance between features like noses and ears, making the face look wider and flat. A wide-angle might make noses look huge and ears tiny when you fill the frame with a face. So stick with 50mm to 85mm focal lengths or zoom settings, going longer only when you're forced to shoot from a greater distance, and wider only when shooting three-quarters/full-length portraits, or group shots.
- **Symptom: blur due to camera shake.** First, make sure you have SteadyShot turned on! Then, if possible, use a higher shutter speed (boosting ISO if necessary), or mount your camera on a tripod, monopod, or brace it with some other support. Of those three solutions, only the second will reduce blur caused by *subject* motion; SteadyShot or a tripod won't help you freeze a racecar in mid-lap.
- **Symptom: color fringes.** Chromatic aberration is the most pernicious optical problem found in telephoto lenses. There are others, including spherical aberration, astigmatism, coma, curvature of field, and similarly scary-sounding phenomena. The best solution for any of these is to use a better lens that offers the proper degree of correction, or stop down the lens to minimize the problem. But that's not always possible. Your second-best choice may be to correct the fringing in your favorite RAW conversion tool or image editor. Photoshop's Lens Correction filter offers sliders that minimize both red/cyan and blue/yellow fringing.

- **Symptom: lines that curve inwards.** Pincushion distortion is found in many telephoto lenses. You might find after a bit of testing that it is worse at certain focal lengths with your particular zoom lens. Like chromatic aberration, it can be partially corrected using tools like Photoshop's Lens Correction filter.
- **Symptom: low contrast from haze or fog.** When you're photographing distant objects, a long lens shoots through a lot more atmosphere, which generally is muddied up with extra haze and fog. That dirt or moisture in the atmosphere can reduce contrast and mute colors. Some feel that a skylight or UV filter can help, but this practice is mostly a holdover from the film days. Digital sensors are not sensitive enough to UV light for a UV filter to have much effect. So you should be prepared to boost contrast and color saturation in your Picture Styles menu or image editor if necessary.
- **Symptom: low contrast from flare.** Lenses are furnished with lens hoods for a good reason: to reduce flare from bright light sources at the periphery of the picture area, or completely outside it. Because telephoto lenses often create images that are lower in contrast in the first place, you'll want to be especially careful to use a lens hood to prevent further effects on your image (or shade the front of the lens with your hand).
- **Symptom: dark flash photos.** Edge-to-edge flash coverage isn't a problem with telephoto lenses as it is with wide angles. The shooting distance is. A long lens might make a subject that's 50 feet away look as if it's right next to you, but your camera's flash isn't fooled. You'll need extra power for distant flash shots, and probably more power than your Alpha's built-in flash provides unless you increase the ISO setting to ISO 3200.

Telephotos and Bokeh

Bokeh describes the aesthetic qualities of the out-of-focus parts of an image and whether out-of-focus points of light—circles of confusion—are rendered as distracting fuzzy discs or smoothly fade into the background. *Boke* is a Japanese word for "blur," and the h was added to keep English speakers from rendering it monosyllabically to rhyme with *broke*. Although bokeh is visible in blurry portions of any image, it's of particular concern with telephoto lenses, which, thanks to the magic of reduced depth-of-field, produce more obviously out-of-focus areas.

Bokeh can vary from lens to lens, or even within a given lens depending on the f/stop in use. Bokeh becomes objectionable when the circles of confusion are evenly illuminated, making them stand out as distinct discs, or, worse, when these circles are darker in the center, producing an ugly "doughnut" effect. A lens defect called spherical aberration may produce out-of-focus discs that are brighter on the edges and darker in the center, because the lens doesn't focus light passing through the edges of the lens exactly as it does light going through the center. (Mirror or *catadioptric* lenses also produce this effect.)

Other kinds of spherical aberration generate circles of confusion that are brightest in the center and fade out at the edges, producing a smooth blending effect, as you can see at right in Figure 6.10. Ironically, when no spherical aberration is present at all, the discs are a uniform shade, which, while better than the doughnut effect, is not as pleasing as the bright center/dark edge rendition. The shape of the disc also comes into play, with round smooth circles considered the best, and nonagonal or some other polygon (determined by the shape of the lens diaphragm) considered less desirable. Most Sony lenses have near-circular irises, producing very pleasing bokeh.

If you plan to use selective focus a lot, you should investigate the bokeh characteristics of a particular lens before you buy. Sony user groups and forums will usually be full of comments and questions about bokeh, so the research is fairly easy.

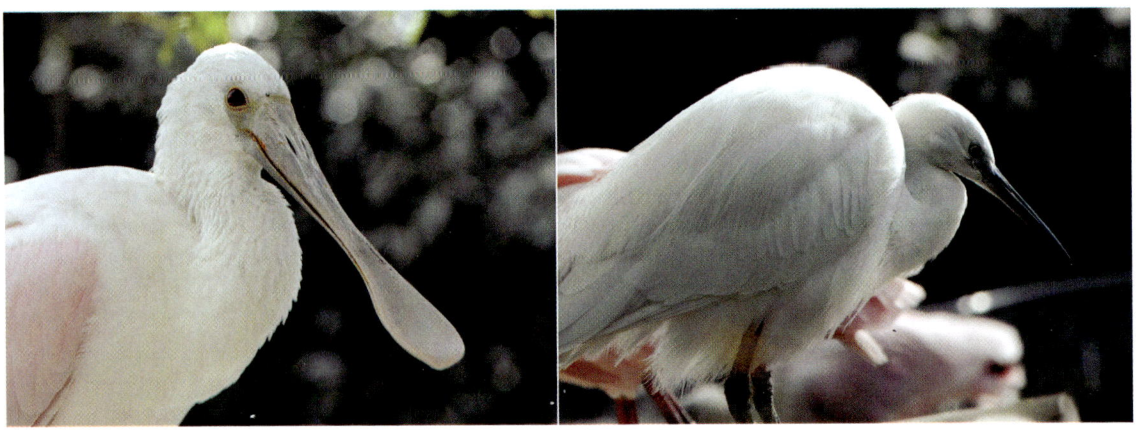

Figure 6.10 Bokeh is less pleasing when the discs are prominent (left), and less obtrusive when they blend into the background (right).

Add-ons and Special Features

Once you've purchased your telephoto lens, you'll want to think about some appropriate accessories for it. There are some handy add-ons available that can be valuable. Here are a couple of them to think about.

Lens Hoods

Lens hoods are an important accessory for all lenses, but they're especially valuable with telephotos. As I mentioned earlier, lens hoods do a good job of preserving image contrast by keeping bright light sources outside the field of view from striking the lens and, potentially, bouncing around inside that long tube to generate flare that, when coupled with atmospheric haze, can rob your image of detail and snap. In addition, lens hoods serve as valuable protection for that large, vulnerable, front lens element. It's easy to forget that you've got that long tube sticking out in front of your camera and accidentally whack the front of your lens into something. It's cheaper to replace a lens hood than it is to have a lens repaired, so you might find that a good hood is valuable protection for your prized optics.

When choosing a lens hood, it's important to have the right hood for the lens, usually the one offered for that lens by Sony or the third-party manufacturer. You want a hood that blocks precisely the right amount of light: neither too much light nor too little. A hood with a front diameter that is too small can show up in your pictures as vignetting. A hood that has a front diameter that's too large isn't stopping all the light it should. Generic lens hoods may not do the job.

When your telephoto is a zoom lens, it's even more important to get the right hood, because you need one that does what it is supposed to at both the wide-angle and telephoto ends of the zoom range. Lens hoods may be cylindrical, rectangular (shaped like the image frame), or petal shaped (that is, cylindrical, but with cutout areas at the corners that correspond to the actual image area). Lens hoods should be mounted in the correct orientation (a bayonet mount for the hood usually takes care of this).

Telephoto Extenders

Telephoto extenders, like the SAL-14TC 1.4X G-series tele-converter lens and SAL-20TC 2.0X G-series tele-converter lens multiply the actual focal length of your lens, giving you a longer telephoto for much less than the price of a lens with that actual focal length. These extenders fit between the lens and your camera and contain optical elements that magnify the image produced by the lens. Available in 1.4X and 2.0X configurations from Sony, an extender transforms, say, a 200mm lens into a 300mm or 400mm optic, respectively. Given the Alpha's crop factor, your 200mm lens now has the same field of view as a 450mm or 600mm lens on a full-frame camera. At around $450 each, they're quite a bargain, aren't they?

Actually, there are some downsides. While extenders retain the closest focusing distance of your original lens, autofocus is maintained only if the lens's original maximum aperture is f/4 or larger (for the 1.4X extender) or f/2.8 or larger (for the 2X extender). The components reduce the effective aperture of any lens they are used with, by one f/stop with the 1.4X extender, and 2 f/stops with the 2X extender.

Macro Focusing

Some telephotos and telephoto zooms available for the Sony Alpha have particularly close focusing capabilities, making them *macro* lenses. Of course, the object is not necessarily to get close (get too close and you'll find it difficult to light your subject). What you're really looking for in a macro lens is to magnify the apparent size of the subject in the final image. Camera-to-subject distance is most important when you want to back up farther from your subject (say, to avoid spooking skittish insects or small animals). In that case, you'll want a macro lens with a longer focal length to allow that distance while retaining the desired magnification.

Sony makes three lenses with official macro designations, all f/2.8 optics in 30mm, 50mm, and 100mm focal lengths. You'll also find macro lenses, macro zooms, and other close-focusing lenses available from Sigma, Tamron, and Tokina. If you want to focus closer with a macro lens, or any other lens, you can add an accessory called an *extension tube*, like the one shown in Figure 6.11. These add-ons move the lens farther from the focal plane, allowing it to focus more closely. You can also buy add-on close-up lenses, which look like filters, and allow lenses to focus more closely.

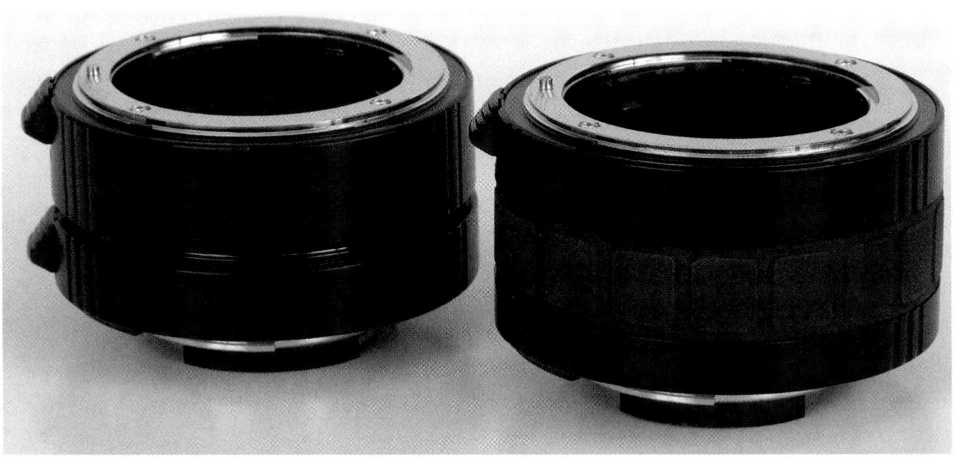

Figure 6.11
Extension tubes enable any lens to focus more closely to the subject.

SteadyShot and Your Lenses

Vendors like Nikon and Canon sell special lenses with anti-shake features built in. With your Sony Alpha A390/A290, *every* lens you own has image stabilization. SteadyShot provides you with camera steadiness that's the equivalent of at least two or three shutter speed increments. This extra margin can be invaluable when you're shooting under dim lighting conditions or handholding a long lens for, say, wildlife photography. Perhaps that shot of a foraging deer calls for a shutter speed of 1/1,000th second at f/5.6 with your lens. Relax. You can shoot at 1/250th second at f/11 and get virtually the same results, as long as the deer doesn't decide to bound off.

Or, maybe you're shooting a high school play without a tripod or monopod, and you'd really, really like to use 1/15th second at f/4. Assuming the actors aren't flitting around the stage at high speed, your wide-angle lens (or wide-angle zoom at the wide angle position) can grab the shot for you. However, keep these facts in mind:

- **SteadyShot doesn't stop action.** Unfortunately, no stabilization is a panacea to replace the action-stopping capabilities of a higher shutter speed. Image stabilization applies only to camera shake. You still need a fast shutter speed to freeze action. SteadyShot works great in low light, when you're using long lenses, and for macro photography. It's not always the best choice for action photography, unless there's enough light to allow a sufficiently high shutter speed. If so, stabilization can make your shot even sharper.
- **Stabilization might slow you down.** The process of adjusting the sensor to counter camera shake takes time, just as autofocus does, so you might find that SteadyShot adds to the lag between when you press the shutter and when the picture is actually taken. That's another reason why image stabilization might not be a good choice for sports.
- **Use when appropriate.** Sometimes, stabilization produces worse results if used while you're panning. You might want to switch off IS when panning or when your camera is mounted on a tripod.
- **Do you need SteadyShot at all?** Remember that an inexpensive monopod might be able to provide the same additional steadiness as SteadyShot. If you're out in the field shooting wild animals or flowers and think a tripod isn't practical, try a monopod first.

7

Making Light Work for You

Successful photographers and artists have an intimate understanding of the importance of light in shaping an image. Rembrandt was a master of using light to create moods and reveal the character of his subjects. Artist Thomas Kinkade's official tagline is "Painter of Light." The late Dean Collins, co-founder of Finelight Studios, revolutionized how a whole generation of photographers learned and used lighting. It's impossible to underestimate how the use of light adds to—and how misuse can detract from—your photographs.

All forms of visual art use light to shape the finished product. Sculptors don't have control over the light used to illuminate their finished work, so they must create shapes using planes and curved surfaces so that the form envisioned by the artist comes to life from a variety of viewing and lighting angles. Painters, in contrast, have absolute control over both shape and light in their work, as well as the viewing angle, so they can use both the contours of their two-dimensional subjects and the qualities of the "light" they use to illuminate those subjects to evoke the image they want to produce.

Photography is a third form of art. The photographer may have little or no control over the subject (other than posing human subjects) but can often adjust both viewing angle *and* the nature of the light source to create a particular compelling image. The direction and intensity of the light sources create the shapes and textures that we see. The distribution and proportions determine the contrast and tonal values: whether the image is stark or high key, or muted and low in contrast. The colors of the light (because even "white" light has a color balance that the sensor can detect), and how much of those colors the subject reflects or absorbs, paint the hues visible in the image.

As a Sony Alpha photographer, you must learn to be a painter and sculptor of light if you want to move from *taking* a picture to *making* a photograph. This chapter provides an introduction to using the two main types of illumination: *continuous* lighting (such as daylight, incandescent, or fluorescent sources) and the brief, but brilliant snippets of light we call *electronic flash.*

Continuous Illumination versus Electronic Flash

Continuous lighting is exactly what you might think: uninterrupted illumination that is available all the time during a shooting session. Daylight, moonlight, and the artificial lighting encountered both indoors and outdoors count as continuous light sources (although all of them can be "interrupted" by passing clouds, solar eclipses, a blown fuse, or simply by switching off a lamp). Indoor continuous illumination includes both the lights that are there already (such as incandescent lamps or overhead fluorescent lights indoors) and fixtures you supply yourself, including photoflood lamps or reflectors used to bounce existing light onto your subject.

The surge of light we call electronic flash is produced by a burst of photons generated by an electrical charge that is accumulated in a component called a *capacitor* and then directed through a glass tube containing xenon gas, which absorbs the energy and emits the brief flash. Electronic flash is notable because it can be much more intense than continuous lighting, lasts only a brief moment, and can be much more portable than supplementary incandescent sources. It's a light source you can carry with you and use anywhere.

Indeed, your Sony Alpha DSLR-A390/A290 has a flip-up electronic flash unit built in, as shown in Figure 7.1. But you can also use an external flash, either mounted on the Alpha's accessory shoe or used off-camera and linked with a cable or triggered by a slave light (which sets off a flash when it senses the firing of another unit). Studio flash units are electronic flash, too, and aren't limited to "professional" shooters, as there are economical "monolight" (one-piece flash/power supply) units available in the $200 price range. Those who want to set up a home studio can buy a couple to store in a closet and use to set up a home studio, or use as supplementary lighting when traveling away from home. (You'll need the FA-ST1AM sync terminal adapter for any flash unit that uses a PC-type connection.)

There are advantages and disadvantages to each type of illumination. Here's a quick checklist of pros and cons:

- **Lighting preview—Pro: continuous lighting.** With continuous lighting, such as incandescent lamps or daylight (see Figure 7.2), you always know exactly what kind of lighting effect you're going to get and, if multiple lights are used, how they will interact with each other. With electronic flash, the general effect you're going to see

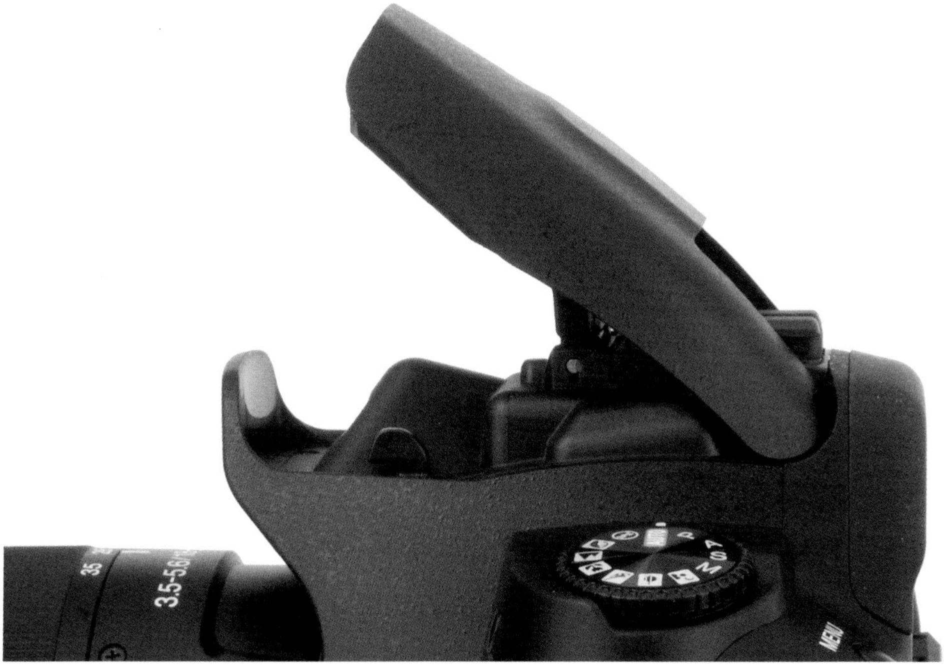

Figure 7.1 One form of light that's always available is the flip-up flash on your Sony Alpha.

may be a mystery until you've built some experience, and you may need to review a shot on the LCD, make some adjustments, and then reshoot to get the look you want. (In this sense, a digital camera's review capabilities replace the Polaroid test shots pro photographers relied on in decades past.)

- **Lighting preview—Con: electronic flash.** While some external flash have a modeling light function (consisting of a series of low-powered bursts that flash for a period of time), your Alpha lacks such a capability in its internal flash, and, in any case, this feature is no substitute for continuous illumination, or an always-on modeling lamp like that found in studio flash. As the number of flash units increases, lighting previews, especially if you want to see the proportions of illumination provided by each flash, grow more complex.
- **Exposure calculation—Pro: continuous lighting.** Your Alpha has no problem calculating exposure for continuous lighting, because the lighting remains constant and can be measured through a sensor that interprets the light reaching the viewfinder. The amount of light available just before the exposure will, in almost all cases, be the same amount of light present when the shutter is released. The Alpha's Spot metering mode can be used to measure and compare the proportions of light in the highlights and shadows, so you can make an adjustment (such as using more or less fill light) if necessary. You can even use a handheld light meter to measure the light yourself.

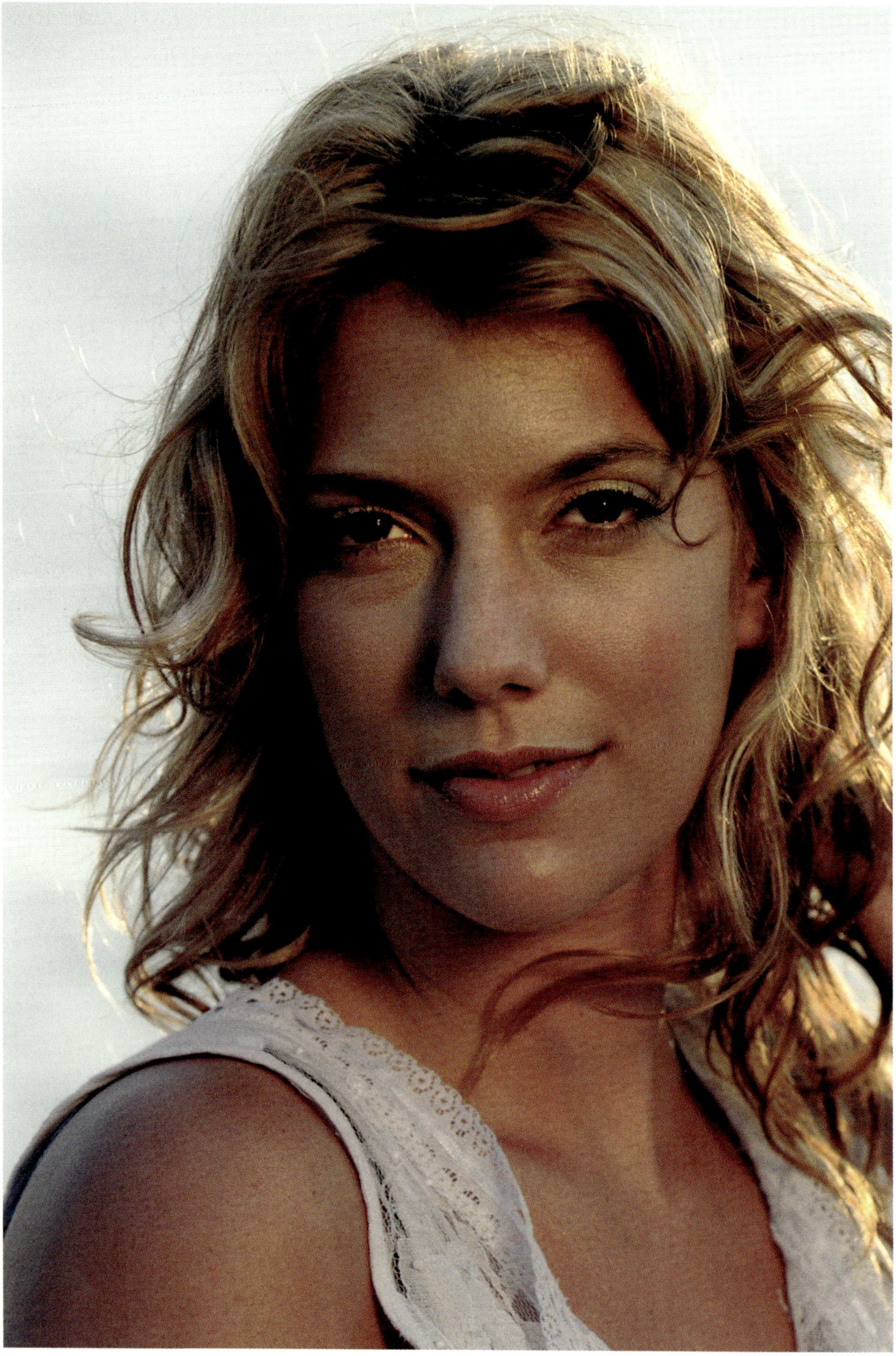

Figure 7.2
You always know how the lighting will look when using continuous illumination.

- **Exposure calculation—Con: electronic flash.** Electronic flash illumination doesn't exist until the flash fires, and so it can't be measured by the Alpha's exposure sensor when the mirror is flipped up during the exposure. Instead, the light must be measured by metering the intensity of a pre-flash triggered an instant before the main flash, as it is reflected back to the camera and through the lens. The Alpha cameras actually have two exposure measuring modes using the pre-flash: the ADI (Advanced Distance Integration) flash mode, which adds in distance information to calculate flash exposure, and Pre-Flash TTL, which uses only the information from the pre-flash reflected back to the camera from the subject. If you have a do-it-yourself bent, there are handheld flash meters, too, including models that measure both flash and continuous light.
- **Evenness of illumination—Pro/con: continuous lighting.** Of continuous light sources, daylight, in particular, provides illumination that tends to fill an image completely, lighting up the foreground, background, and your subject almost equally. Shadows do come into play, of course, so you might need to use reflectors or fill-in light sources to even out the illumination further, but barring objects that block large sections of your image from daylight, the light is spread fairly evenly. Indoors, however, continuous lighting is commonly less evenly distributed. The average living room, for example, has hot spots and dark corners. But on the plus side, you can *see* this uneven illumination and compensate with additional lamps.
- **Evenness of illumination—Con: electronic flash.** Electronic flash units, like continuous light sources such as lamps that don't have the advantage of being located 93 million miles from the subject, suffer from the effects of their proximity. The *inverse square law*, first applied to both gravity and light by Sir Isaac Newton, dictates that as a light source's distance increases from the subject, the amount of light reaching the subject falls off proportionately to the square of the distance. In plain English, that means that a flash or lamp that's eight feet away from a subject provides only one-quarter as much illumination as a source that's four feet away (rather than half as much). (See Figure 7.3.) This translates into relatively shallow "depth-of-light."
- **Action stopping—Con: continuous lighting.** Action stopping with continuous light sources is completely dependent on the shutter speed you've dialed in on the camera. And the speeds available are dependent on the amount of light available and your camera's ISO sensitivity setting. Outdoors in daylight, there will probably be enough sunlight to let you shoot at 1/2,000th second and f/6.3 with a non-grainy sensitivity setting of ISO 400. That's a fairly useful combination of settings if you're not using a super-telephoto with a small maximum aperture. But inside, the reduced illumination quickly has you pushing your Sony Alpha to its limits. For example, if you're shooting indoor sports, there probably won't be enough available light to allow you to use a 1/2,000th second shutter speed (although I

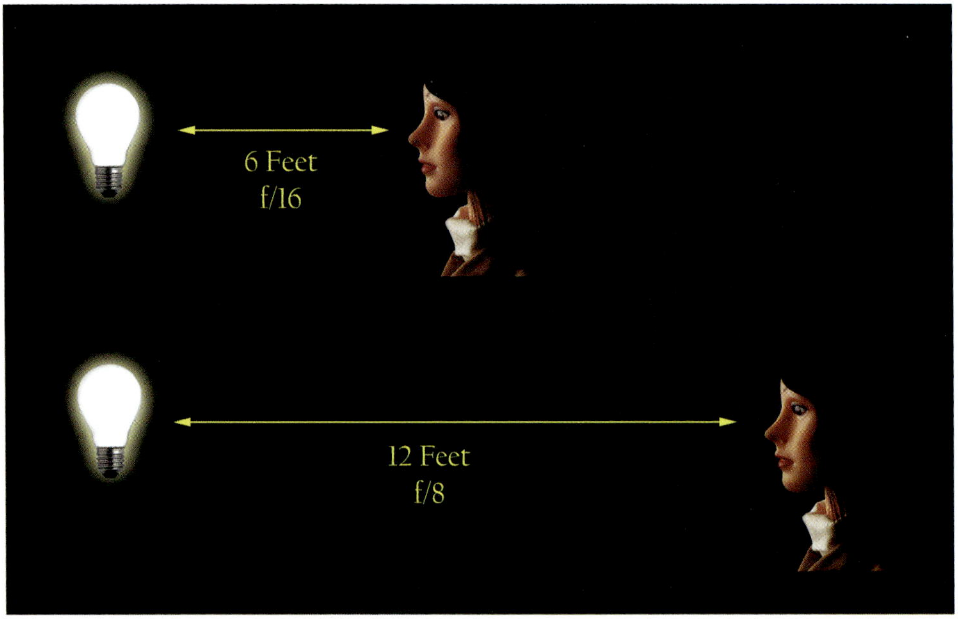

Figure 7.3
A light source that is twice as far away provides only one-quarter as much illumination.

routinely shoot indoor basketball at ISO 1600 and 1/500th second at f/4). In many indoor sports situations, you may find yourself limited to 1/500th second or slower.

- **Action stopping—Pro: electronic flash.** When it comes to the ability to freeze moving objects in their tracks, the advantage goes to electronic flash. The brief duration of electronic flash serves as a very high "shutter speed" when the flash is the main or only source of illumination for the photo. Your Sony Alpha's shutter speed may be set for 1/160th second during a flash exposure, but if the flash illumination predominates, the *effective* exposure time will be the 1/1,000th to 1/50,000th second or less duration of the flash, as you can see in Figure 7.4, because the flash unit reduces the amount of light released by cutting short the duration of the flash. The only fly in the ointment is that, if the ambient light is strong enough, it may produce a secondary "ghost" exposure, as I'll explain later in this chapter.
- **Cost—Pro: continuous lighting.** Incandescent or fluorescent lamps are generally much less expensive than external electronic flash units, which can easily cost several hundred dollars. I've used everything from desktop high-intensity lamps to reflector floodlights for continuous illumination at very little cost. There are lamps made especially for photographic purposes, too, priced up to $50 or so. Maintenance is economical, too; many incandescent or fluorescents use bulbs that cost only a few dollars.

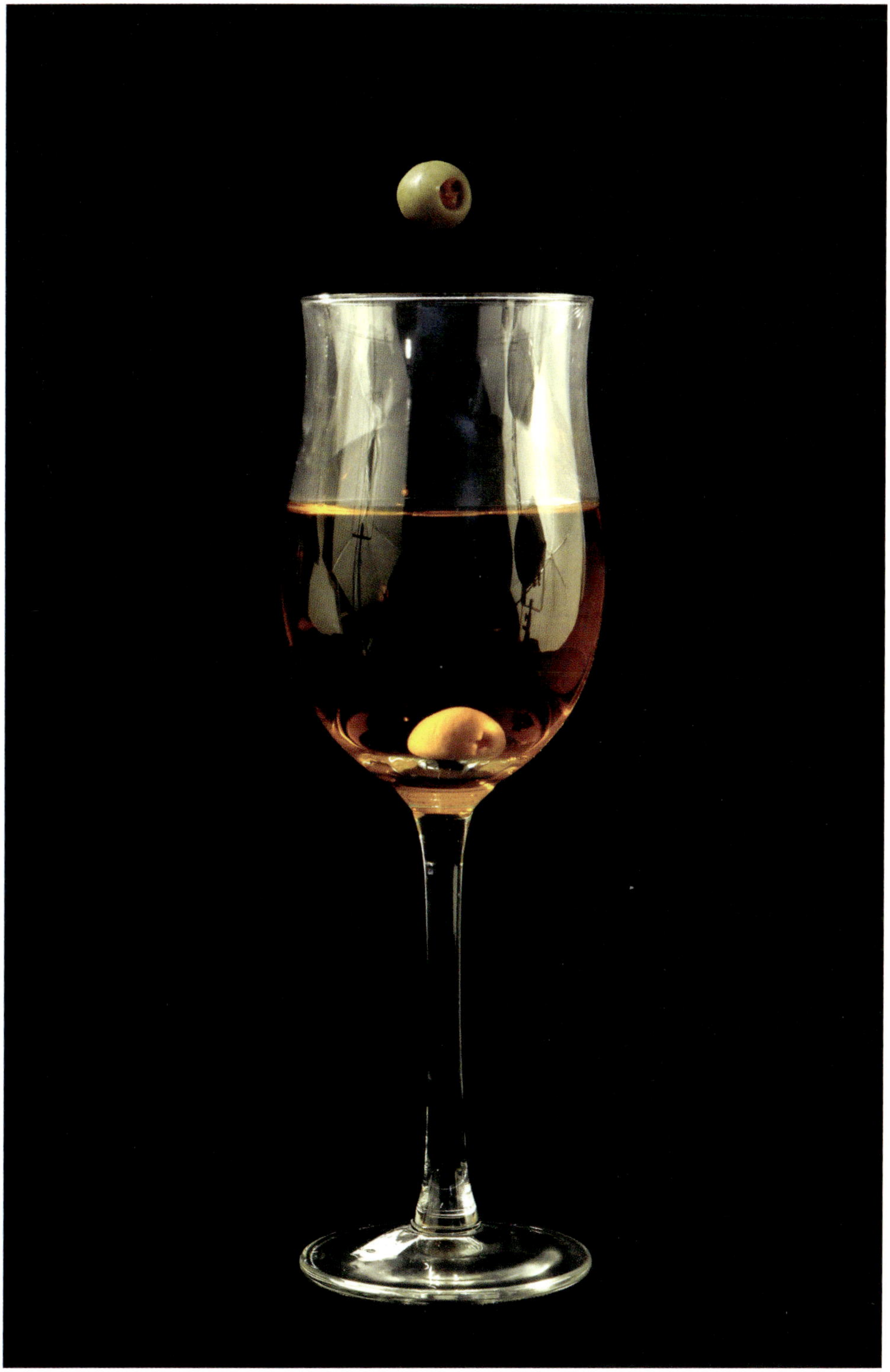

Figure 7.4
Electronic flash can freeze almost any action.

- **Cost—Con: electronic flash.** Electronic flash units aren't particularly cheap. The lowest-cost dedicated flash designed specifically for the Sony dSLRs (the HVL-F20AM) is about $129. Such units are limited in features, however, and intended for those with entry-level cameras. Plan on spending some money to get the features that a sophisticated electronic such as the HVL-F58AM flash offers.
- **Flexibility—Con: continuous lighting.** Because incandescent and fluorescent lamps are not as bright as electronic flash, the slower shutter speeds required (see "Action stopping," above) mean that you may have to use a tripod more often, especially when shooting portraits. The incandescent variety of continuous lighting gets hot, especially in the studio, and the side effects range from discomfort (for your human models) to disintegration (if you happen to be shooting perishable foods like ice cream).
- **Flexibility—Pro: electronic flash.** Electronic flash's action-freezing power allows you to work without a tripod in the studio (and elsewhere), adding flexibility and speed when choosing angles and positions. Flash units can be easily filtered, and, because the filtration is placed over the light source rather than the lens, you don't need to use high quality filter material. For example, Roscoe or Lee lighting gels, which may be too flimsy to use in front of the lens, can be mounted or taped in front of your flash with ease.

Continuous Lighting Basics

While continuous lighting and its effects are generally much easier to visualize and use than electronic flash, there are some factors you need to take into account, particularly the color temperature of the light. (Color temperature concerns aren't exclusive to continuous light sources, of course, but the variations tend to be more extreme and less predictable than those of electronic flash.)

Color temperature, in practical terms, is how "bluish" or how "reddish" the light appears to be to the digital camera's sensor. Indoor illumination is quite warm, comparatively, and appears reddish to the sensor. Daylight, in contrast, seems much bluer to the sensor. Our eyes (our brains, actually) are quite adaptable to these variations, so white objects don't appear to have an orange tinge when viewed indoors, nor do they seem excessively blue outdoors in full daylight. Yet, these color temperature variations are real and the sensor is not fooled. To capture the most accurate colors, we need to take the color temperature into account in setting the color balance (or *white balance*) of the Alpha—either automatically using the camera's smarts or manually using our own knowledge and experience.

Color temperature can be confusing, because of a seeming contradiction in how color temperatures are named: warmer (more reddish) color temperatures (measured in degrees Kelvin) are the *lower* numbers, whereas cooler (bluer) color temperatures are *higher* numbers. It might not make sense to say that 3,400K is warmer than 6,000K, but that's the way it is. If it helps, think of a glowing red ember contrasted with a white-hot welder's torch, rather than fire and ice.

The confusion comes from physics. Scientists calculate color temperature from the light emitted by a mythical object called a black body radiator, which absorbs all the radiant energy that strikes it, and reflects none at all. Such a black body not only *absorbs* light perfectly, but it *emits* it perfectly when heated (and since nothing in the universe is perfect, that makes it mythical).

At a particular physical temperature, this imaginary object always emits light of the same wavelength or color. That makes it possible to define color temperature in terms of actual temperature in degrees on the Kelvin scale that scientists use. Incandescent light, for example, typically has a color temperature of 3,200K to 3,400K. Daylight might range from 5,500K to 6,000K. Each type of illumination we use for photography has its own color temperature range—with some cautions. The next sections will summarize everything you need to know about the qualities of these light sources.

Daylight

Daylight is produced by the sun, and so is moonlight (which is just reflected sunlight). Daylight is present, of course, even when you can't see the sun. When sunlight is direct, it can be bright and harsh. If daylight is diffused by clouds, softened by bouncing off objects such as walls or your photo reflectors, or filtered by shade, it can be much dimmer and less contrasty.

Daylight's color temperature can vary quite widely. It is highest (most blue) at noon when the sun is directly overhead, because the light is traveling through a minimum amount of the filtering layer we call the atmosphere. The color temperature at high noon may be 6,000K. At other times of day, the sun is lower in the sky and the particles in the air provide a filtering effect that warms the illumination to about 5,500K for most of the day. Starting an hour before dusk and for an hour after sunrise, the warm appearance of the sunlight is even visible to our eyes when the color temperature may dip to 5,000-4,500K, as shown in Figure 7.5.

Because you'll be taking so many photos in daylight, you'll want to learn how to use or compensate for the brightness and contrast of sunlight, as well as how to deal with its color temperature. I'll provide some hints later in this chapter.

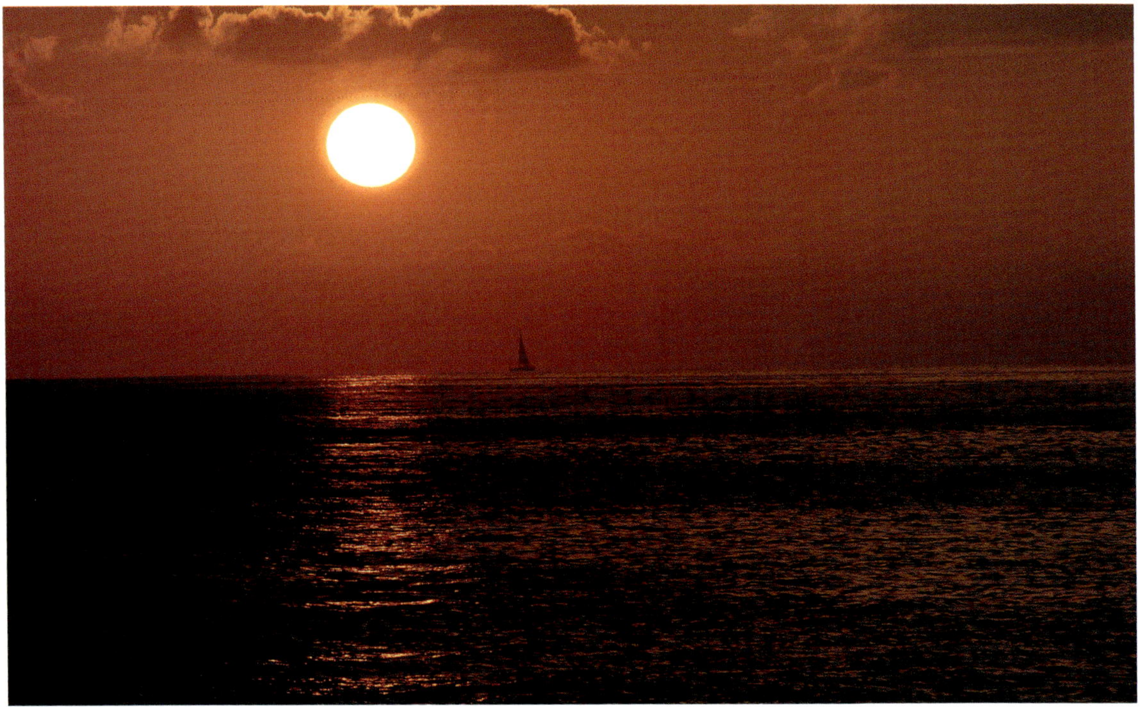

Figure 7.5 At dawn and dusk, the color temperature of the sky may dip as low as 4,500K.

Incandescent/Tungsten Light

The term incandescent or tungsten illumination is usually applied to the direct descendents of Thomas Edison's original electric lamp. Such lights consist of a glass bulb that contains a vacuum, or is filled with a halogen gas, and contains a tungsten filament that is heated by an electrical current, producing photons and heat. Tungsten-halogen lamps are a variation on the basic light bulb, using a more rugged (and longer-lasting) filament that can be heated to a higher temperature, housed in a thicker glass or quartz envelope, and filled with iodine or bromine ("halogen") gases. The higher temperature allows tungsten-halogen (or quartz-halogen/quartz-iodine, depending on their construction) lamps to burn "hotter" and whiter. Although popular for automobile headlamps today, they've also been popular for photographic illumination.

Although incandescent illumination isn't a perfect black body radiator, it's close enough that the color temperature of such lamps can be precisely calculated (about 3,200-3,400K, depending on the type of lamp) and used for photography without concerns about color variation (at least, until the very end of the lamp's life).

The other qualities of this type of lighting, such as contrast, are dependent on the distance of the lamp from the subject, type of reflectors used, and other factors that I'll explain later in this chapter.

Fluorescent Light/Other Light Sources

Fluorescent light has some advantages in terms of illumination, but some disadvantages from a photographic standpoint. This type of lamp generates light through an electrochemical reaction that emits most of its energy as visible light, rather than heat, which is why the bulbs don't get as hot. The type of light produced varies depending on the phosphor coatings and type of gas in the tube. So, the illumination fluorescent bulbs produce can vary widely in its characteristics.

That's not great news for photographers. Different types of lamps have different "color temperatures" that can't be precisely measured in degrees Kelvin, because the light isn't produced by heating. Worse, fluorescent lamps have a discontinuous spectrum of light that can have some colors missing entirely. A particular type of tube can lack certain shades of red or other colors (see Figure 7.6), which is why fluorescent lamps and other alternative technologies such as sodium-vapor illumination can produce ghastly looking human skin tones. Their spectra can lack the reddish tones we associate with healthy skin and emphasize the blues and greens popular in horror movies.

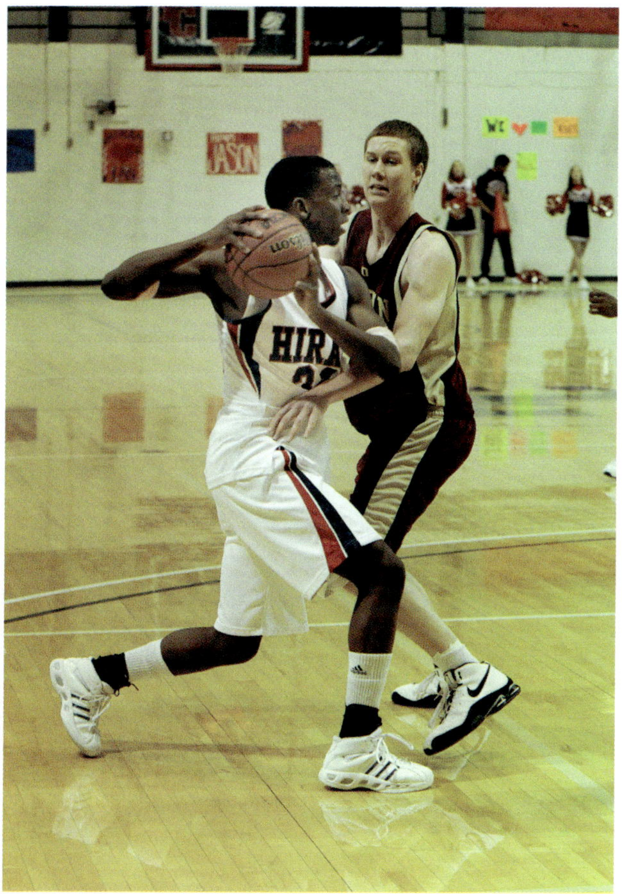

Figure 7.6
The fluorescent lighting in this gym added a distinct greenish cast to the image.

Adjusting White Balance

I showed you how to adjust white balance in Chapter 5, using the Alpha's built-in presets and custom balance.

In most cases, however, the Sony Alpha will do a good job of calculating white balance for you, so Auto can be used as your choice most of the time. Use the preset values or set a custom white balance that matches the current shooting conditions when you need to. The only really problematic light sources are likely to be fluorescents. Vendors, such as GE and Sylvania, may actually provide a figure known as the *color rendering index* (or CRI), which is a measure of how accurately a particular light source represents standard colors, using a scale of 0 (some sodium-vapor lamps) to 100 (daylight and most incandescent lamps). Daylight fluorescents and deluxe cool white fluorescents might have a CRI of about 79 to 95, which is perfectly acceptable for most photographic applications. Warm white fluorescents might have a CRI of 55. White deluxe mercury vapor lights are less suitable with a CRI of 45, while low-pressure sodium lamps can vary from CRI 0-18.

Remember that if you shoot RAW, you can specify the white balance of your image when you import it into Photoshop, Photoshop Elements, or another image editor using your preferred RAW converter, including Image Data Converter SR. Although color-balancing filters that fit on the front of the lens exist, they are primarily useful for film cameras, because film's color balance can't be tweaked as extensively as that of a sensor.

Electronic Flash Basics

Until you delve into the situation deeply enough, it might appear that serious photographers have a love/hate relationship with electronic flash. You'll often hear that flash photography is less natural looking, and that the built-in flash in most cameras should never be used as the primary source of illumination because it provides a harsh, garish look. Indeed, most "pro" cameras don't have a built-in flash at all. Available ("continuous") lighting is praised, and built-in flash photography seems to be roundly denounced.

In truth, however, the bias is against *bad* flash photography. Indeed, flash has become the studio light source of choice for pro photographers, because it's more intense (and its intensity can be varied to order by the photographer), freezes action, frees you from using a tripod (unless you want to use one to lock down a composition), and has a snappy, consistent light quality that matches daylight. (While color balance changes as the flash duration shortens, some Sony flash units can communicate to the camera the exact white balance provided for that shot.) And even pros will cede that the built-in flash of the Sony Alpha has some important uses as an adjunct to existing light, particularly to fill in dark shadows.

But electronic flash isn't as inherently easy to use as continuous lighting. As I noted earlier, electronic flash units are more expensive, don't show you exactly what the lighting effect will be, unless you use a second source called a *modeling light* for a preview (some flashes, such as the HVL-F58AM have pulsed light rudimentary modeling light capabilities built in), and the exposure of electronic flash units is more difficult to calculate accurately.

How Electronic Flash Works

The bursts of light we call electronic flash are produced by a flash of photons generated by an electrical charge that is accumulated in a component called a *capacitor* and then directed through a glass tube containing xenon gas, which absorbs the energy and emits the brief flash. For the pop-up flash built into the Sony Alpha, the full burst of light lasts about 1/1,000th second and provides enough illumination to shoot a subject 10 feet away at f/4 using the ISO 100 setting. In a more typical situation, you'd use ISO 200, f/5.6 to f/8 and photograph something 8 to 10 feet away. As you can see, the built-in flash is somewhat limited in range and not your best choice when photographing distant subjects. You'll see why external flash units are often a good idea in some situations later in this chapter.

The electronic flash you use will be built-in, connected to the camera by slipping it onto the hot shoe, or connected by a cable and adapter, such as the Sony FA-ST1AM (very expensive at $179) or more affordable adapters from third parties, such as the Seagull SC-5 (available on Amazon.com and other websites). In all cases, the flash is triggered at the instant of exposure, during a period when the sensor is fully exposed by the shutter.

As I mentioned earlier in this book, the Alpha has a vertically traveling shutter that consists of two curtains. The first curtain opens and moves to the opposite side of the frame, at which point the shutter is completely open. The flash can be triggered at this point (so-called *first-curtain sync*), making the flash exposure. Then, after a delay that can vary from 30 seconds to 1/160th second (with the Sony Alpha A390/A290 models; other cameras may sync at a faster or slower speed), a second curtain begins moving across the sensor plane, covering up the sensor again. If the flash is triggered just before the second curtain starts to close, then *second-curtain sync* is used. In both cases, though, a shutter speed of 1/160th second is the maximum that can be used to take a photo.

Figure 7.7 illustrates how this works, with a fanciful illustration of a generic shutter (your Alpha's shutter does *not* look like this, and some vertically traveling shutters move bottom to top rather than the top-to-bottom motion shown). Both curtains are tightly closed at upper left. At upper right, the first curtain begins to move downwards, starting to expose a narrow slit that reveals the sensor behind the shutter. At lower left, the first curtain moves downward farther until, as you can see at lower right in the figure, the sensor is fully exposed.

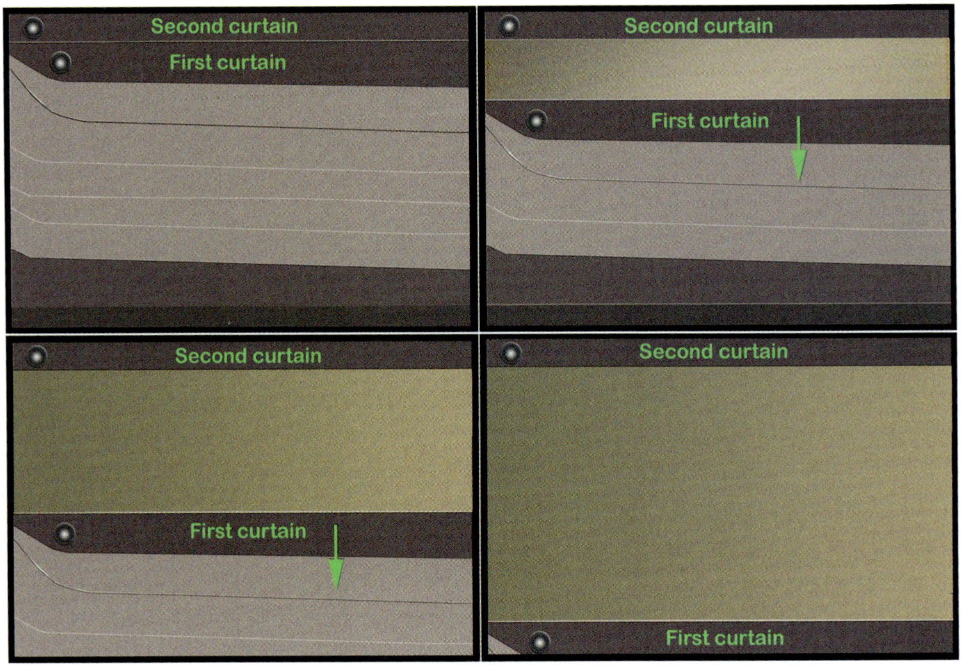

Figure 7.7
A focal plane shutter has two curtains, the lower, or first curtain, and an upper, second curtain.

When first-curtain sync is used, the flash is triggered at the instant that the sensor is completely exposed. The shutter then remains open for an additional length of time (from 30 seconds to 1/160th second), and the second curtain begins to move downward, covering the sensor once more. When second-curtain sync is activated, the flash is triggered *after* the main exposure is over, just before the second curtain begins to move downward.

I first mentioned flash sync mode in Chapter 2. The Alpha cameras always default to front/first-curtain sync unless you explicitly select another mode using the Flash mode screen (press the Flash/right directional button on the controller pad to access). Auto flash mode is blocked when using P, S, A, or M modes.

Avoiding Sync Speed Problems

Using a shutter speed faster than 1/160th second can cause problems. Triggering the electronic flash only when the shutter is completely open makes a lot of sense if you think about what's going on. To obtain shutter speeds faster than 1/160th second, the Alpha exposes only part of the sensor at one time, by starting the second curtain on its journey before the first curtain has completely opened. That effectively provides a briefer exposure as the slit of the shutter passes over the surface of the sensor. If the flash were to fire during the time when the first and second curtains partially obscured the sensor, only the slit that was actually open would be exposed.

You'd end up with only a narrow band, representing the portion of the sensor that was exposed when the picture is taken. For shutter speeds *faster* than 1/160th second, the second curtain begins moving *before* the first curtain reaches the bottom of the frame. As a result, a moving slit—the width of the distance between the first and second curtains—exposes one portion of the sensor at a time as it moves from the top to the bottom. Figure 7.8 shows three views of our typical (but imaginary) focal plane shutter. At left is pictured the closed shutter; in the middle version you can see the first curtain has moved down about 1/4 of the distance down from the top, and in the right-hand version, the second curtain has started to "chase" the first curtain across the frame towards the bottom.

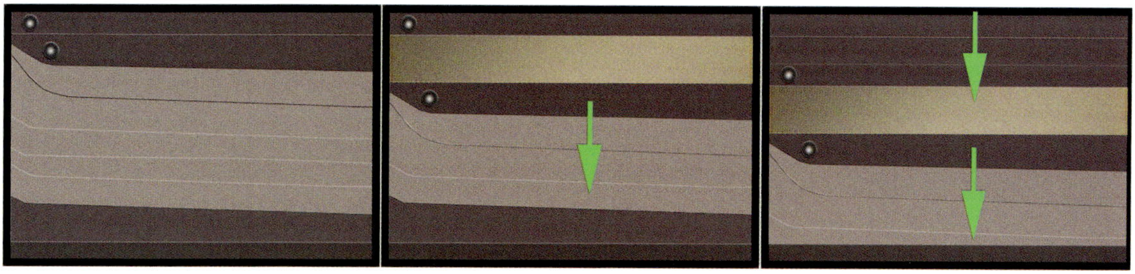

Figure 7.8 A closed shutter (left); partially open shutter as the first curtain begins to move downwards (middle); only part of the sensor is exposed as the slit moves (right).

If the flash is triggered while this slit is moving, only the exposed portion of the sensor will receive any illumination. You end up with a photo like the one shown in Figure 7.9. Note that a band across the bottom of the image is black. That's a shadow of the second shutter curtain, which had started to move when the flash was triggered. Sharp-eyed readers will wonder why the black band is at the *bottom* of the frame rather than at the top, where the second curtain begins its journey. The answer is simple: your lens flips the image upside down and forms it on the sensor in a reversed position. You never notice that, because the camera is smart enough to show you the pixels that make up your photo in their proper orientation during picture review. But this image flip is why, if your sensor gets dirty and you detect a spot of dust in the upper half of a test photo, if cleaning manually, you need to look for the speck in the *bottom* half of the sensor.

I generally end up with sync speed problems only when shooting in the studio, using studio flash units rather than my Alpha's built-in flash or a Sony dedicated unit. That's because if you're using either type of "smart" flash, the camera knows that a strobe is attached, and remedies any unintentional goof in shutter speed settings. If you happen to set the Alpha's shutter to a faster speed in S or M mode, the camera will automatically adjust the shutter speed down to 1/160th second as soon as you flip up the flash (or prevent you from choosing a faster speed if the flash is already up). In A, P, or any of the Scene modes, where the Alpha selects the shutter speed, it will never choose a shutter speed higher than 1/160th second when using flash.

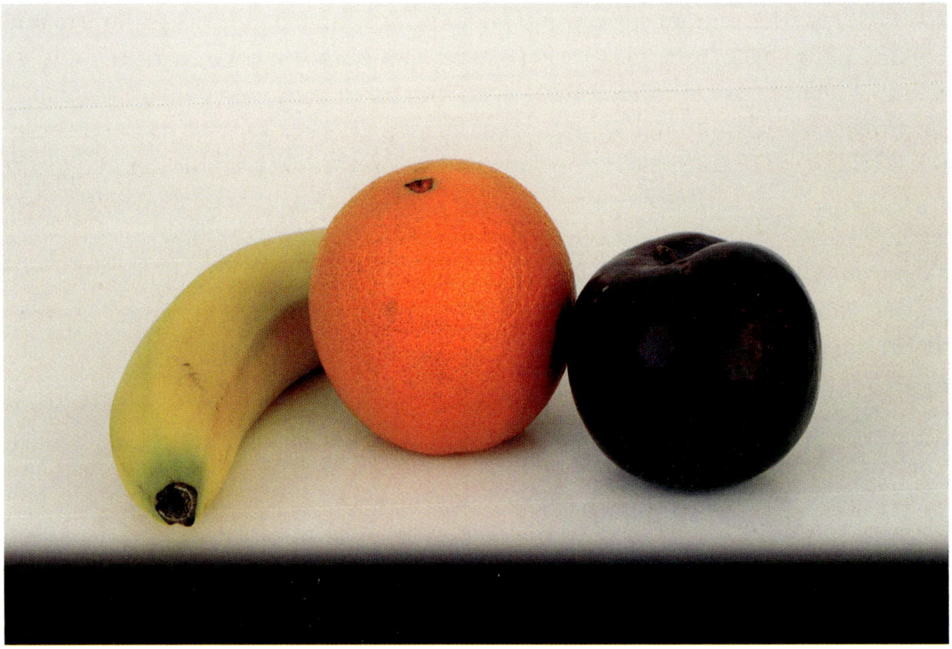

Figure 7.9
If a shutter speed faster than 1/160th second is used, you can end up photographing only a portion of the image.

But when using a non-dedicated flash, such as a studio unit plugged into the Alpha's hot shoe connector equipped with an adapter, the camera has no way of knowing that a flash is connected, so shutter speeds faster than 1/160th second can be set inadvertently.

Note that the Alpha can use a feature called *high-speed sync* that allows shutter speeds faster than 1/160th second with certain external dedicated Sony flash units. When using high-speed sync, the flash fires a continuous serious of bursts at reduced power for the entire duration of the exposure, so that the illumination is able to expose the sensor as the slit moves.

HS sync is set using the controls that adjust the compatible external flash units, which include the HVL-F58AM and HVL-F42AM. You'll find complete instructions accompanying those flash units. You'll also need to set your Alpha for high-speed sync; it appears as an H option in the Flash menu (press the Flash button/right directional button on the controller pad) when (and only when) a compatible flash unit is attached.

Ghost Images

The difference might not seem like much, but whether you use first-curtain sync (the default setting) or rear-curtain sync (an optional setting) can make a significant difference to your photograph *if the ambient light in your scene also contributes to the image.* At faster shutter speeds, particularly 1/160th second, there isn't much time for the ambient light to register, unless it is very bright. It's likely that the electronic flash will provide almost all the illumination, so first-curtain sync or second-curtain sync isn't very important.

However, at slower shutter speeds, or with very bright ambient light levels, there is a significant difference, particularly if your subject is moving, or the camera isn't steady. In any of those situations, the ambient light will register as a second image accompanying the flash exposure, and if there is movement (camera or subject), that additional image will not be in the same place as the flash exposure. It will show as a ghost image and, if the movement is significant enough, as a blurred ghost image trailing in front of or behind your subject in the direction of the movement.

As I mentioned earlier, when you're using first-curtain sync, the flash goes off the instant the shutter opens, producing an image of the subject on the sensor. Then, the shutter remains open for an additional period (which can be from 30 seconds to 1/160th second). If your subject is moving, say, towards the right side of the frame, the ghost image produced by the ambient light will produce a blur on the right side of the original subject image, making it look as if your sharp (flash-produced) image is chasing the ghost. For those of us who grew up with lightning-fast superheroes that always left a ghost trail *behind them*, that looks unnatural (see Figure 7.10).

So, Sony provides rear (second) curtain sync to remedy the situation. In that mode, the shutter opens, as before. The shutter remains open for its designated duration, and the ghost image forms. If your subject moves from the left side of the frame to the right side, the ghost will move from left to right, too. *Then*, about 1.5 milliseconds before the second shutter curtain closes, the flash is triggered, producing a nice, sharp flash image *ahead* of the ghost image. Voilà! We have monsieur *le Flash* outrunning his own trailing image. I'll show you how to make these settings later in this section.

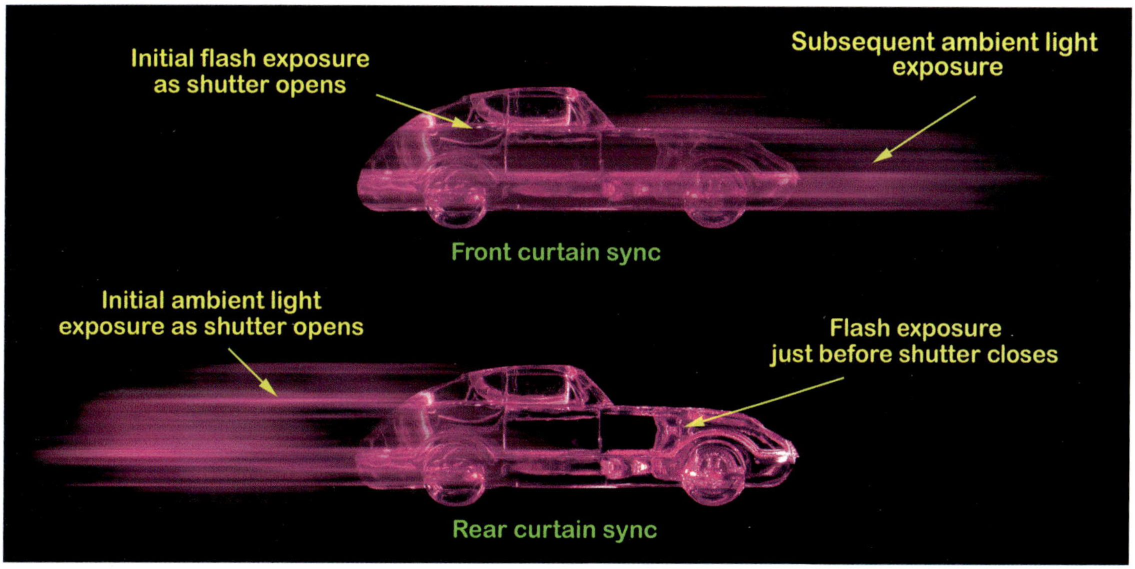

Figure 7.10 Front-curtain sync produces an image that trails in front of the flash exposure (top), whereas rear-curtain sync creates a more "natural looking" trail behind the flash image (bottom).

EVERY WHICH WAY, INCLUDING UP

Note that, although I describe the ghost effect in terms of subject matter that is moving left to right in a horizontally oriented composition, it can occur in any orientation, and with the subject moving in *any* direction. (Try photographing a falling rock, if you can, and you'll see the same effect.) Nor are the ghost images affected by the fact that modern shutters travel vertically rather than horizontally. Secondary images are caused between the time the first curtain fully opens, and the second curtain begins to close. The direction of travel of the shutter curtains, or the direction of your subject, does not matter.

Determining Exposure

Calculating the proper exposure for an electronic flash photograph is a bit more complicated than determining the settings by continuous light. The right exposure isn't simply a function of how far away your subject is, even though the inverse square law I mentioned does have an effect: the farther away the subject is, the less light is available for the exposure. The Alpha can calculate distance if you're using a lens with "DT" in its name (these lenses transmit distance codes to the camera), based on the autofocus distance that's locked in just prior to taking the picture.

But, of course, flash exposure isn't based on distance alone. Various objects reflect more or less light at the same distance so, obviously, the camera needs to measure the amount of light reflected back and through the lens. Yet, as the flash itself isn't available for measuring until it's triggered, the Alpha has nothing to measure.

The solution is to fire the flash twice. The initial shot is a pre-flash that can be analyzed, then followed by a main flash that's given exactly the calculated intensity needed to provide a correct exposure. As a result, the primary flash may be longer for distant objects and shorter for closer subjects, depending on the required intensity for exposure. This through-the-lens evaluative flash exposure system when coupled with distance information from a DT lens is called *ADI flash exposure* (ADI stands for Advanced Distance Integration), and it operates whenever the pop-up internal flash is used, or you have attached a Sony dedicated flash unit to the Alpha, and a DT lens.

Guide Numbers

Guide numbers, usually abbreviated GN, are a way of specifying the power of an electronic flash in a way that can be used to determine the right f/stop to use at a particular shooting distance and ISO setting. In fact, before automatic flash units became prevalent, the GN was actually used to do just that. A GN is usually given as a pair of numbers for both feet and meters that represent the range at ISO 100. For example, the Sony Alpha's built-in flash has a GN of 10/40 (meters/feet) at ISO 100. To calculate the right exposure at that ISO setting, you'd divide the guide number by the distance to arrive at the appropriate f/stop.

Using the Alpha's built-in flash as an example, at ISO 100 with its GN of 40, if you wanted to shoot a subject at a distance of 10 feet, you'd use f/4 (40 divided by 10). At 7 feet, an f/stop of f/5.7 (round down to f/5.6) would be used. Some quick mental calculations with the GN will give you any particular electronic flash's range. You can easily see that the built-in flash would begin to peter out at about 14 feet, where you'd need an aperture of f/2.8 at ISO 100. Of course, in the real world you'd probably bump the sensitivity up to a setting of ISO 400 so you could use a more practical f/5.6 at that distance.

Today, guide numbers are most useful for comparing the power of various flash units. You don't need to be a math genius to see that an electronic flash with a GN of, say, 58/190 would be *a lot* more powerful than your built-in flash (at ISO 100, you could use f/14 instead of f/2.8 at 14 feet).

Using the Built-In Flash

The Sony Alpha's built-in flash is a handy accessory because it is available as required, without the need to carry an external flash around with you constantly. This section explains how to use the flip-up flash.

Your Alpha automatically pops up the built-in flash when there is insufficient light and you are using Auto, Portrait, Macro, and Night View/Night Scene modes. In PASM modes (Program, Aperture priority, Shutter priority, and Manual), you'll need to flip up the flash manually, unless you've chosen Fill-Flash mode. In other modes that do not pop up the flash, including Flash Off mode, the flash will not pop up. If the flash is already up, because you switched to a non-flash mode from a PASM, or if you have set Flash Off as the flash mode using the right controller button, the flash will not fire.

For example, the flash doesn't pop up in Landscape mode because the flash doesn't have enough reach to have much effect for pictures of distant vistas in any case; nor does the flash pop up automatically in Sports mode, because you'll often want to use shutter speeds faster than 1/160th second and/or be shooting subjects that are out of flash range. Pop-up flash is disabled in Flash Off mode for obvious reasons.

If you happen to be shooting a landscape photo and do want to use flash (say, to add some illumination to a subject that's closer to the camera), or you want flash with your sports photos, or you *don't* want the flash popping up all the time when using one of the other Scene modes, switch to an appropriate PASM mode and use that instead.

When using a flash-compatible mode with the built-in flash, if you want the Alpha to issue a few additional low-light pre-flashes prior to taking the picture, turn the feature on with the Red eye reduc. option in Custom 1 menu.

When using Semi-automatic or Manual exposure modes (or any Scene mode in which flash is used), if Red-eye reduction is turned on in the Recording menu (as described in Chapter 3), the red-eye reduction flash will emit as you press down the shutter release to take the picture, theoretically causing your subjects' irises to contract (if they are looking toward the camera), and thereby reducing the red-eye effect in your photograph, all without overexposing the subject.

Setting Flash Modes

To set the various flash modes, press the Flash button (right controller button) and choose:

- **Flash Off.** The flash never fires; this may be useful in museums, concerts, or religious ceremonies where electronic flash would prove disruptive.
- **Auto Flash.** The flash fires as required, depending on lighting conditions.
- **Fill-Flash.** The Alpha balances the available illumination with flash to provide a balanced lighting effect.
- **Slow Sync.** The Alpha combines flash with slow shutter speeds, so that the subject can be illuminated by flash, but the longer shutter speed allows the ambient light to illuminate the background.
- **Rear Sync.** Fires the flash at the end of the exposure, producing more "realistic" "ghost" images, as described earlier in this chapter.
- **Wireless Flash.** The internal flash triggers compatible external flash units without the need for a connecting cord.
- **H (High-Speed Sync).** Available only when the HVF-F56AM or HVF-F42AM flash units are attached, it allows synchronizing those flashes at shutter speeds higher than 1/160th second.

Flash Exposure Compensation

It's important to keep in mind how the Alpha cameras' exposure compensation system (discussed in Chapter 4) works when you're using electronic flash. To activate exposure compensation for both flash and continuous light sources, choose Flash compens. from the Recording 1 menu. The Flash compens. screen appears (see Figure 7.11), with its plus/minus scale. Use the left/right controller keys to add or subtract exposure. Pressing the right button adds exposure to an image; pressing the left button subtracts exposure. This function is not available when using Auto or Scene exposure modes, nor when you have used the Flash Off option from the Flash menu. Flash exposure compensation affects only the flash, and not continuous light sources, when chosen from the Recording menu. If the camera is set to P, S, A, or M modes, you'll see both flash and continuous lighting compensation represented by separate arrows along the exposure scale. Continuous lighting compensation can be set separately by pressing the Exposure button while rotating the control dial counterclockwise to reduce exposure, and clockwise to increase exposure.

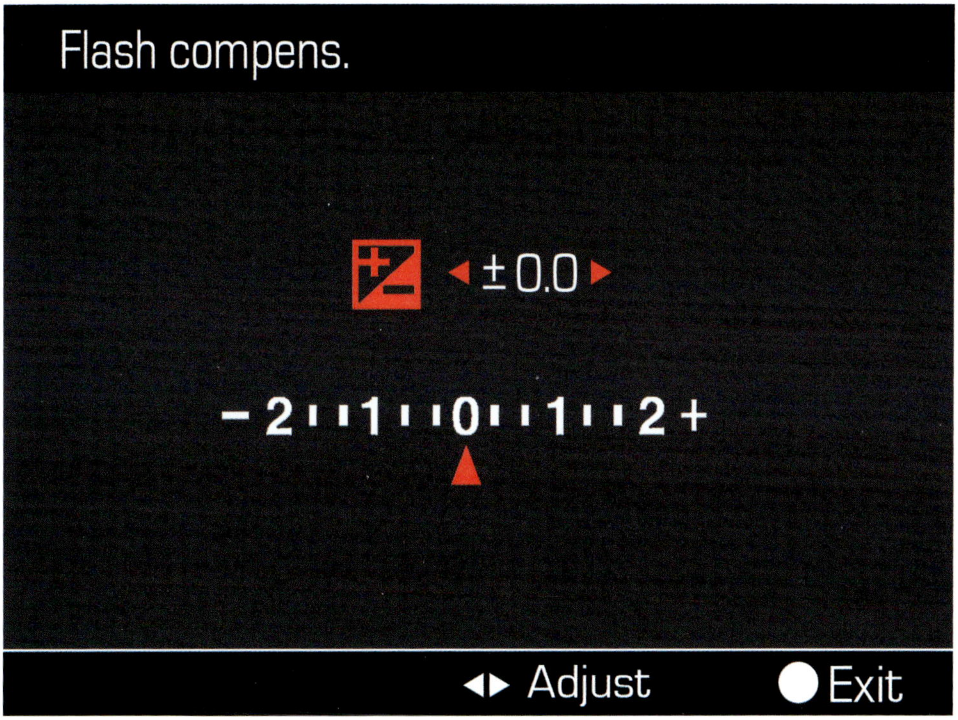

Figure 7.11 Adjust flash exposure using this screen.

Using the External Electronic Flash

Sony currently offers several accessory electronic flash units for the Sony Alpha cameras. They can be mounted to the flash accessory shoe, or used off-camera with a dedicated cord that plugs into the flash shoe to maintain full communications with the camera for all special features. The beefier units range from the HVL-F58AM (see Figure 7.12), which can correctly expose subjects up to 17 feet away at f/11 and ISO 100, to the (discontinued) HVL-F36AM, which is good out to 11 feet at f/11 and ISO 100. (You'll get greater ranges at even higher ISO settings, of course.) A very inexpensive and useful unit, the $129 HVL-F20AM, was introduced at the same time as this Alpha series. There is also an electronic flash unit, the HVL-RLAM Alpha Ring Light, specifically for specialized close-up flash photography.

HVL-F58AM Flash Unit

This $499 flagship of the Sony accessory flash line is the most powerful unit the company offers, with an ISO 100 guide number of 58/190 (meters/feet). Guide numbers are a standard way of specifying the power of a flash in manual, non-autoexposure mode. Divide the guide number by the distance to determine the correct f/stop. With a GN of 190, you would use f/19 at 10 feet (190 divided by 10), or f/8.5 at 20 feet.

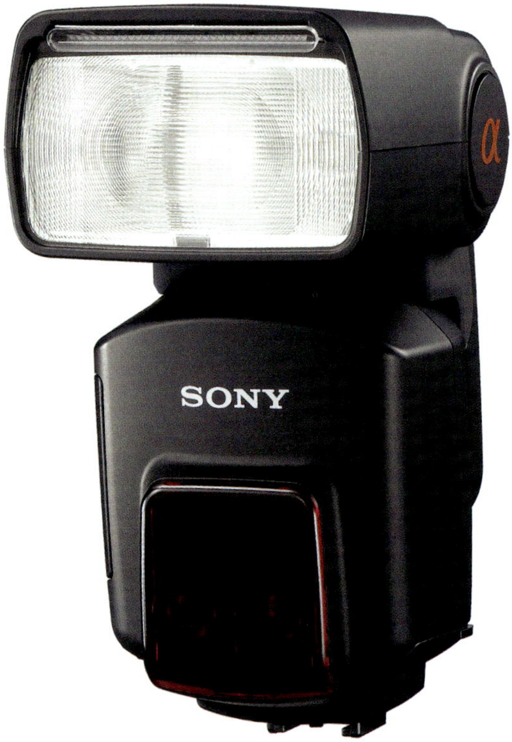

Figure 7.12
The Sony HVL-F58AM is a top-of-the-line external flash unit for the Alpha.

This flash automatically adjusts for focal length settings from 24mm to 105mm, and a built-in slide-out diffuser panel boosts wide-angle coverage to 16mm. You can zoom coverage manually, if you like. There's also a slide-out "white card" that reflects some light forward even when bouncing the flash off the ceiling, to fill in shadows or add a catch light in the eyes of your portrait subjects.

Bouncing is particularly convenient and effective, thanks to what Sony calls a "quick shift bounce" system. This configuration is particularly effective when shooting vertical pictures. With most other on-camera external flash units, as soon as you turn the camera vertically, the flash is oriented vertically, too, whether you're using direct flash or bouncing off the ceiling (or, wall, when the camera is rotated). The HVL-58AM's clever pivoting system allows re-orienting the flash when the camera is in the vertical position, so flash coverage is still horizontal, and can be tilted up or down for ceiling bounce.

The 15.6 ounce unit uses convenient AA batteries in a four-pack, but can also be connected to the FA-EB1AM external battery adapter (you just blew another $250), which has room for 6 AA batteries for increased capacity and faster recycling. The flash automatically communicates white balance information to your camera, allowing the Alpha to adjust WB to match the flash output.

You can even simulate a modeling light effect. A test button on the back of the flash unit can be rotated for flash mode (one test flash, with no modeling light); three low-power flashes at a rate of two flashes per second, as a rough guide; and a more useful (but more power-consuming) mode that flashes for 40 flashes per second for 4 seconds (160 continuous mini-bursts in all). This switch also has a HOLD position that locks all flash operations except for the LCD data display on the flash, and the test button. Use this when you want to take a few pictures without flash, but don't want to turn off your flash or change its settings.

The HVL-F58AM can function as a main flash, or be triggered wirelessly by another compatible flash unit. The pre-flash from the second "main" flash is used to trigger the remote, wireless flash unit that has been removed or disconnected from the camera. When using flash wirelessly, Sony recommends rotating the unit so that the flashtube is pointed where you want the light to go, but the front (light sensor) of the flash is directed at the flash mounted on the camera. In wireless mode, you can control up to three groups of flashes, and specify the output levels for each group, giving you an easy way to control the lighting ratios of multiple flash units.

Those who are frustrated by an inability to use a shutter speed faster than 1/160th second will love the High Speed Sync (HSS) mode offered by this unit, the HVL-F42AM, and the discontinued HVL-F36AM flash. When activated, you can take flash pictures at any shutter speed from 1/500th to 1/4,000th second! For example, if you want to use a high shutter speed and a very wide aperture to apply selective focus to a subject, HSS is one way to avoid overexposure when using flash. The mode button on the back of the flash is used to choose either TTL or Manual flash exposure. Once the flash mode is chosen, then use the Select button and flash plus/minus keys to activate HSS mode. HSS appears on the data panel of the flash, and an indicator appears on the camera's LCD monitor. (Note: HSS is not available when using the 2-second self-timer or rear-sync mode.)

Keep in mind that because less than the full duration of the flash is being used to expose each portion of the image as it is exposed by the slit passing in front of the sensor, the effective flash range of this "reduced" output is smaller. In addition, HSS cannot be used when using multiple flash or left/right/up bounce flash. (If you're pointing the flash downwards, say, at a close-up subject, HSS can be used.)

Another feature I like is the HVL-F58AM's multiple flash feature, which allows you to create interesting stroboscopic effects with several images of the same subject presented in the same frame, as you can see in Figure 7.13. If you want to shoot subjects at distances of more than a few feet, however, you'll need to crank up the ISO setting of your Alpha, as the output of each strobe burst is significantly less than when using the flash for single shots.

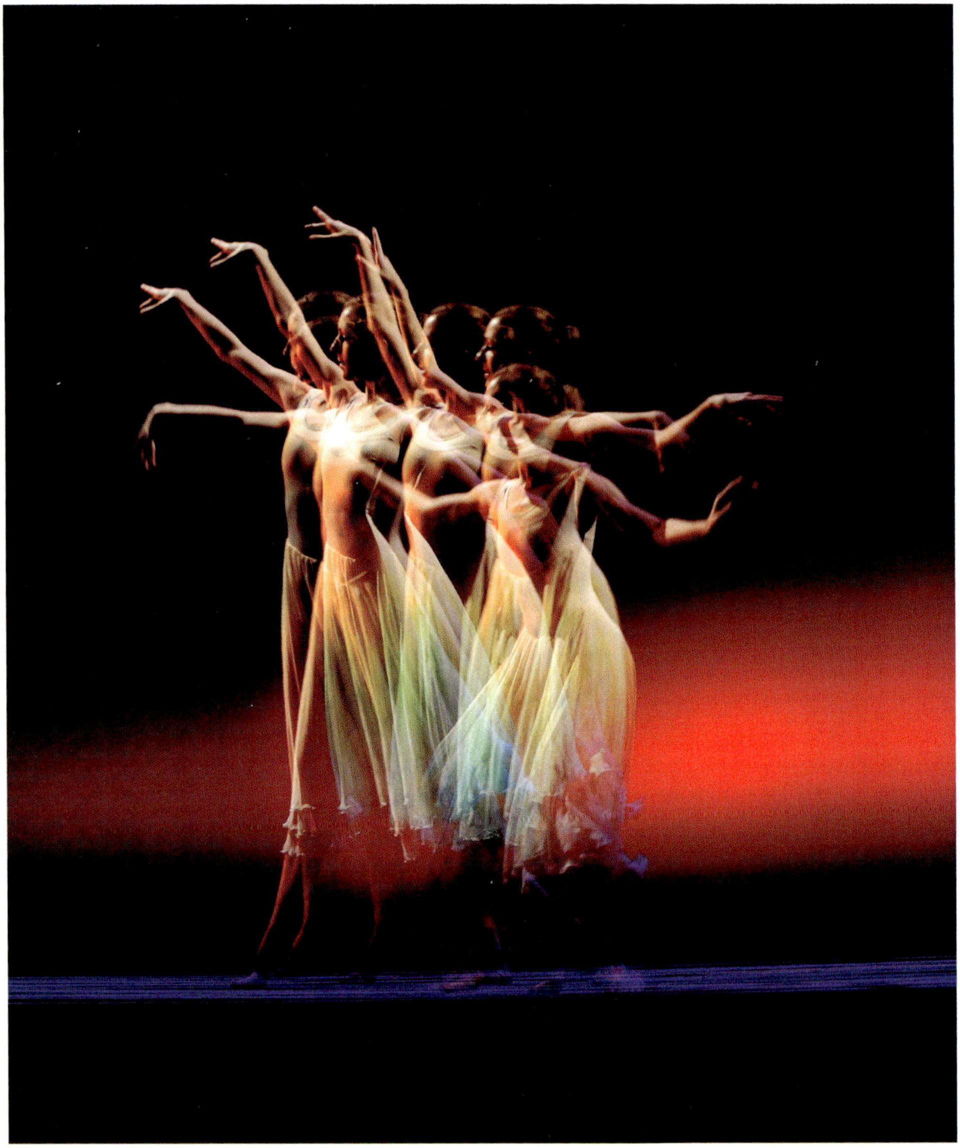

Figure 7.13
Stroboscopic lighting allows taking several pictures in one frame.

HVL-F42AM Flash Unit

This less pricey ($299) electronic flash shares many of the advanced features of the HVL-F42AM, but has a lower guide number of 42/138 (meters/feet). (By now, you've figured out that the number in Sony's electronic flash units represent the GN in meters, so the power rating of the HVL-F36AM, described next, will not come as a surprise to you.)

The shared features include high-speed sync, automatic white balance adjustment, and automatic zoom with the same coverage from 24-105mm (16mm with the slide-out diffuser). This unit also can be used in wireless mode to operate other Sony strobes using a pre-flash signal. Bounce flash swiveling is still versatile, with adjustable angles of 90 degrees up, 90 degrees left, and 180 degrees right, so you can reflect your flash off ceilings, walls, or persons wearing large items of clothing in light colors. The HVL-F42AM is a tad lighter than its bigger sibling, at 12 ounces.

HVL-F36AM Flash Unit

Although discontinued, you can easily find this versatile flash available online or in used condition. The guide number for this lower cost ($199) Sony flash unit is (surprise!) 36/118 (meters/feet). Although (relatively) tiny at 9 ounces, you still get some big-flash features, such as wireless operation, auto zoom, and high-speed sync capabilities. Bounce flash flexibility is reduced a little, with no swiveling from side to side and only a vertical adjustment of up to 90 degrees available. Like its four siblings, this one uses four AA batteries.

HVL-F20AM Flash Unit

This is the least expensive Sony flash (see Figure 7.14), designed to appeal to the budget conscious, especially those who need just a bit of a boost for fill flash, or want a small unit (just 3.2 ounces) on their camera. It has a guide number of 20/66 (meters/feet) at

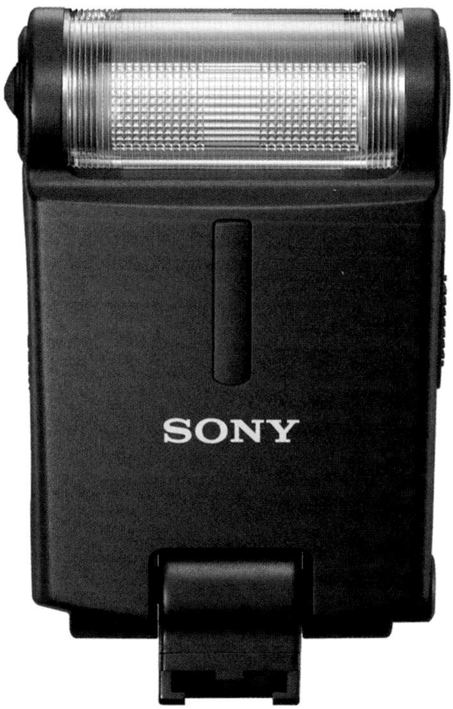

Figure 7.14 The HVL-F20AM flash unit is compact and inexpensive.

ISO 100, and features simplified operation. For example, there's a switch on the side of the unit providing Indoor and Outdoor settings (the Indoor setting tilts the flash upwards to provide bounce light; with the Outdoor setting, the flash fires directly at your subject). There are special modes for wide-angle shooting (use the built-in diffuser to spread the flash's coverage to that of a 27mm lens) or choose the Tele position to narrow the flash coverage to that of a 50mm lens for illuminating more distant subjects. While it's handy for fill flash, owners of an Alpha A550 or A500 will probably want a more powerful unit as their main electronic flash.

More Advanced Lighting Techniques

As you advance in your Sony Alpha photography, you'll want to learn more sophisticated lighting techniques, using more than just straight-on flash, or using just a single flash unit. Entire books have been written on lighting techniques. (If you're *really* into complex lighting setups, you might want to check out my book, *David Busch's Quick Snap Guide to Lighting*, available from the same folks who brought you this guidebook.) I'm going to provide a quick introduction to some of the techniques you should be considering.

Diffusing and Softening the Light

Direct light can be harsh and glaring, especially if you're using the flash built into your camera, or an auxiliary flash mounted in the hot shoe and pointed directly at your subject. The first thing you should do is stop using direct light (unless you're looking for a stark, contrasty appearance as a creative effect). There are a number of simple things you can do with both continuous and flash illumination.

- **Use window light.** Light coming in a window can be soft and flattering, and a good choice for human subjects. Move your subject close enough to the window that its light provides the primary source of illumination. You might want to turn off other lights in the room, particularly to avoid mixing daylight and incandescent light (see Figure 7.15).
- **Use fill light.** Your Alpha's built-in flash makes a perfect fill-in light for the shadows, brightening inky depths with a kicker of illumination (see Figure 7.16).
- **Bounce the light.** All the Sony flashes have a swivel that allows them to be pointed up at a ceiling for a bounce light effect. As I noted, two of them let you bounce the light off a wall. You'll want the ceiling or wall to be white or have a neutral gray color to avoid a color cast.

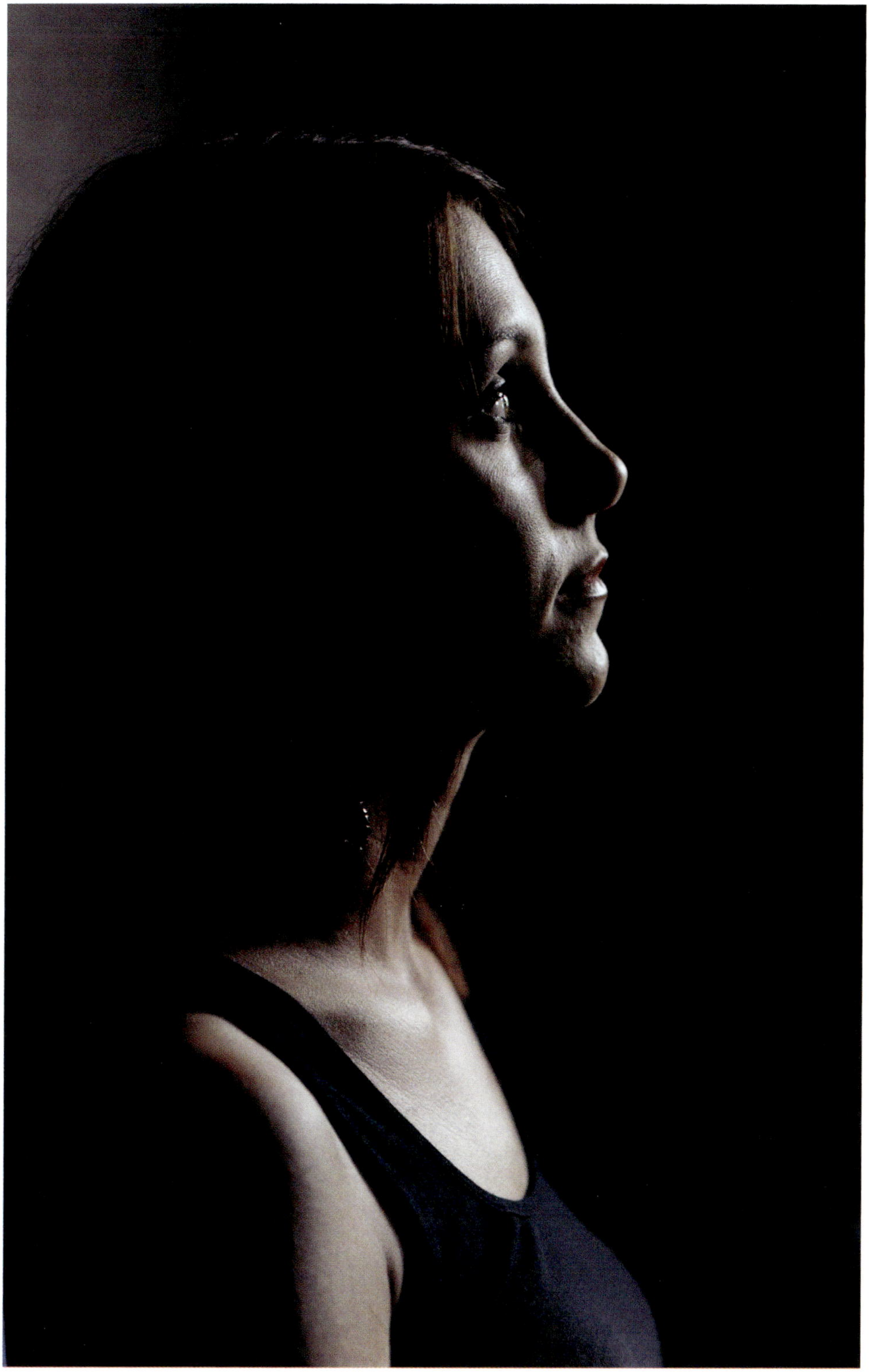

Figure 7.15
Window light makes the perfect diffuse illumination for informal soft-focus portraits like this one.

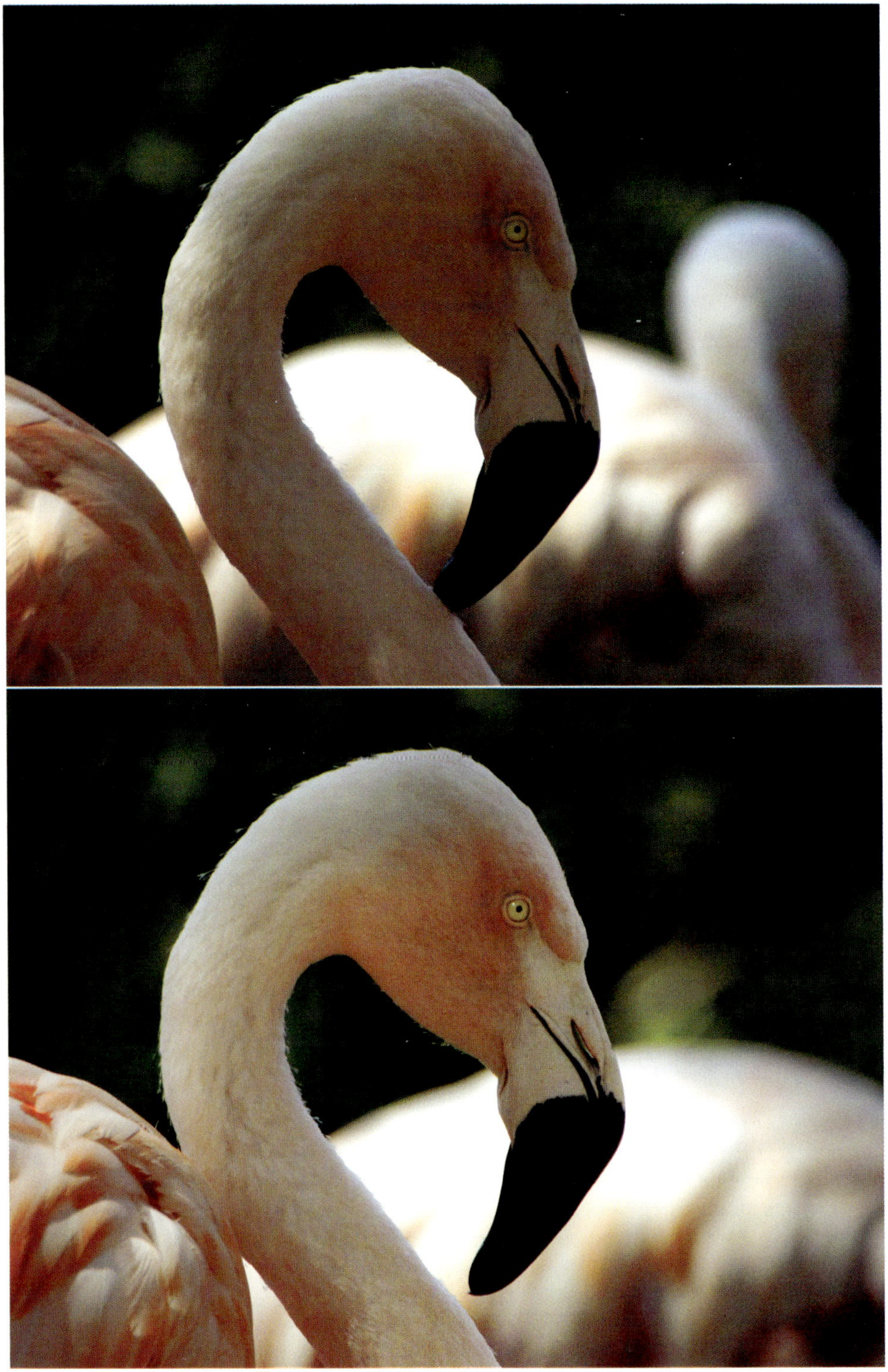

Figure 7.16
The flamingo (top) was in shadow. Fill flash (bottom) brightened up the bird, while adding a little catch light to its eye.

- **Use reflectors.** Another way to bounce the light is to use reflectors or umbrellas that you can position yourself to provide a greater degree of control over the quantity and direction of the bounced light. Good reflectors can be pieces of foamboard, Mylar, or a reflective disk held in place by a clamp and stand. Although some expensive umbrellas and reflectors are available, spending a lot isn't necessary. A simple piece of white foamboard does the job beautifully. Umbrellas have the advantage of being compact and foldable, while providing a soft, even kind of light. They're relatively cheap, too, with a good 40-inch umbrella available for as little as $20.
- **Use a diffuser.** Stofen (www.stofen.com) makes a clip-on diffuser for Sony HVL-series flash units. This simple device (see Figure 7.17) creates a softer light for direct flash or bounce.
- **Try a soft box.** Inexpensive attachments like the one shown in Figure 7.18 can provide the equivalent of a miniature photo studio "soft box," although in a much smaller, more convenient size.

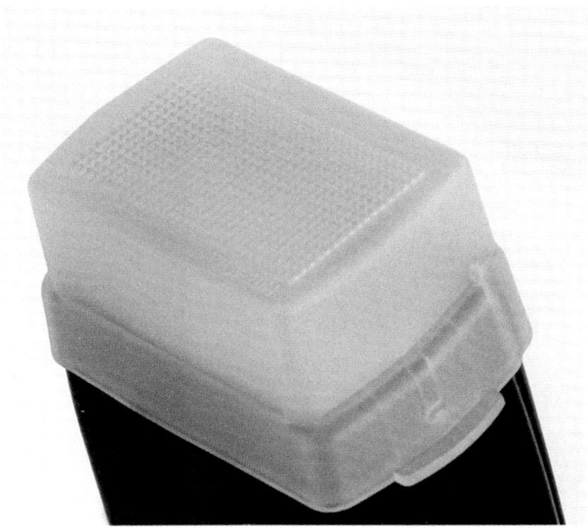

Figure 7.17 Sto-fen's Omni-Bounce diffuser is available for Sony electronic flash units.

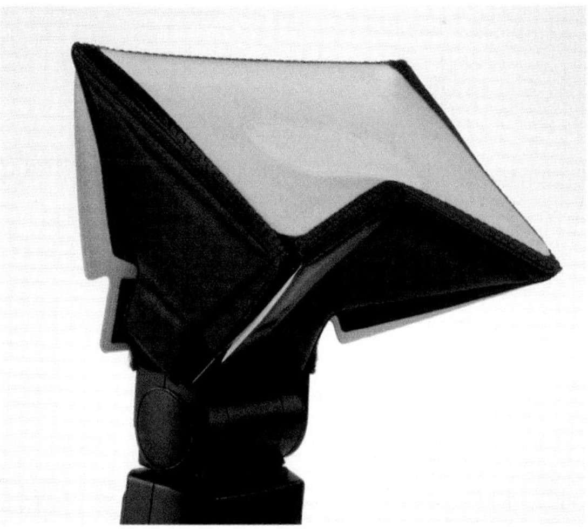

Figure 7.18 Soft boxes use Velcro strips to attach them to third-party flash units (like the one shown) or any Sony external flash.

Using Multiple Light Sources

Once you gain control over the qualities and effects you get with a single light source, you'll want to graduate to using multiple light sources. Using several lights allows you to shape and mold the illumination of your subjects to provide a variety of effects, from backlighting to side lighting to more formal portrait lighting. You can start simply with several incandescent light sources, bounced off umbrellas or reflectors that you construct. Or you can use more flexible multiple electronic flash setups.

Effective lighting is the one element that differentiates great photography from candid or snapshot shooting. Lighting can make a mundane subject look a little more glamorous; it can make subjects appear to be soft when you want a soft look, or bright and sparkly when you want a vivid look, or strong and dramatic if that's what you desire. As you might guess, having control over your lighting means that you probably can't use the lights that are already in the room. You'll need separate, discrete lighting fixtures that can be moved, aimed, brightened, and dimmed on command.

Selecting your lighting gear will depend on the type of photography you do, and the budget you have to support it. It's entirely possible for a beginning Alpha photographer to create a basic, inexpensive lighting system capable of delivering high-quality results for a few hundred dollars, just as you can spend megabucks ($1,000 and up) for a sophisticated lighting system.

Basic Flash Setups

If you want to use multiple electronic flash units, the Sony flash units in wireless mode will serve admirably. The two higher-end models can be used with Sony's wireless feature, which allows you to set up to three separate groups of flash units (several flashes can be included in each group) and trigger them using a master flash and the camera. Just set up one master unit and arrange the compatible slave units around your subject. You can set the relative power of each unit separately, thereby controlling how much of the scene's illumination comes from the main flash, and how much from the auxiliary flash units, which can be used as fill flash, background lights, or, if you're careful, to illuminate the hair of portrait subjects.

Studio Flash

If you're serious about using multiple flash units, a studio flash setup might be more practical. The traditional studio flash is a multi-part unit, consisting of a flash head that mounts on your light stand, and is tethered to an AC (or sometimes battery) power supply. A single power supply can feed two or more flash heads at a time, with separate control over the output of each head.

When they are operating off AC power, studio flash don't have to be frugal with the juice, and are often powerful enough to illuminate very large subjects or to supply lots and lots of light to smaller subjects. The output of such units is measured in watt seconds (ws), so you could purchase a 200ws, 400ws, or 800ws unit, and a power pack to match.

Their advantages include greater power output, much faster recycling, built-in modeling lamps, multiple power levels, and ruggedness that can stand up to transport, because many photographers pack up these kits and tote them around as location lighting rigs. Studio lighting kits can range in price from a few hundred dollars for a set of lights, stands, and reflectors, to thousands for a high-end lighting system complete with all the necessary accessories.

A more practical choice these days are *monolights* (see Figure 7.19), which are "all-in-one" studio lights that sell for about $200-$400. They have the flash tube, modeling light, and power supply built into a single unit that can be mounted on a light stand. Monolights are available in AC-only and battery-pack versions, although an external battery eliminates some of the advantages of having a flash with everything in one unit. They are very portable, because all you need is a case for the monolight itself, plus the stands and other accessories you want to carry along. Because these units are so popular with photographers who are not full-time professionals, the lower-cost monolights are often designed more for lighter duty than professional studio flash. That doesn't mean they aren't rugged; you'll just need to handle them with a little more care, and, perhaps, not expect them to be used eight hours a day for weeks on end. In most other respects, however, monolights are the equal of traditional studio flash units in terms of fast recycling, built-in modeling lamps, adjustable power, and so forth. As I mentioned earlier, you'll need a sync terminal adapter for any flash unit that uses a PC-type connection.

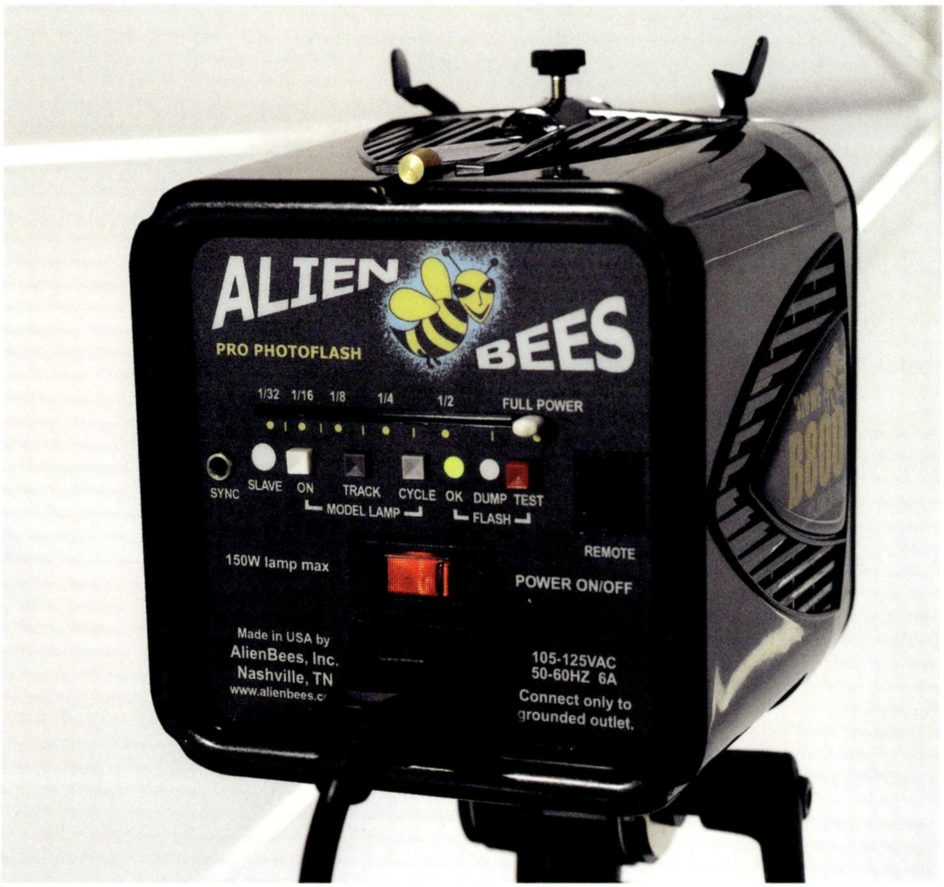

Figure 7.19
All-in-one "monolights" contain flash, power supply, and a modeling light in one compact package (umbrella not included).

Other Lighting Accessories

Once you start working with light, you'll find there are plenty of useful accessories that can help you. Here are some of the most popular that you might want to consider.

Soft Boxes

Soft boxes are large square or rectangular devices that may resemble a square umbrella with a front cover, and produce a similar lighting effect. They can extend from a few feet square to massive boxes that stand five or six feet tall—virtually a wall of light. With a flash unit or two inside a soft box, you have a very large, semi-directional light source that's very diffuse and very flattering for portraiture and other people photography.

Soft boxes are also handy for photographing shiny objects. They not only provide a soft light, but if the box itself happens to reflect in the subject (say you're photographing a chromium toaster), the box will provide an interesting highlight that's indistinct and not distracting.

You can buy soft boxes, like the one shown in Figure 7.20, or make your own. Some lengths of friction-fit plastic pipe and a lot of muslin cut and sewed just so may be all that you need.

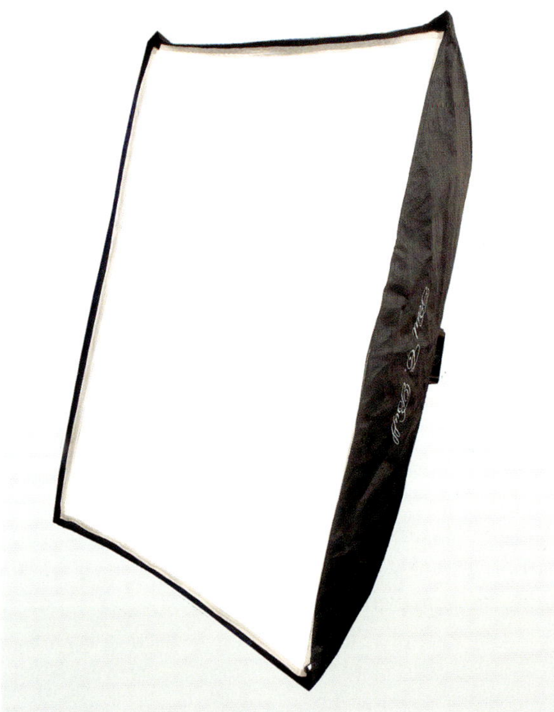

Figure 7.20
Soft boxes provide a large, diffuse light source.

Light Stands

Both electronic flash and incandescent lamps can benefit from light stands. These are lightweight, tripod-like devices (but without a swiveling or tilting head) that can be set on the floor, tabletops, or other elevated surfaces and positioned as needed. Light stands should be strong enough to support an external lighting unit, up to and including a relatively heavy flash with soft box or umbrella reflectors. You want the supports to be capable of raising the lights high enough to be effective. Look for light stands capable of extending six to seven feet high. The nine-foot units usually have larger, steadier bases, and extend high enough that you can use them as background supports. You'll be using these stands for a lifetime, so invest in good ones. I bought the light stand shown in Figure 7.21 when I was in college, and I have been using it for decades.

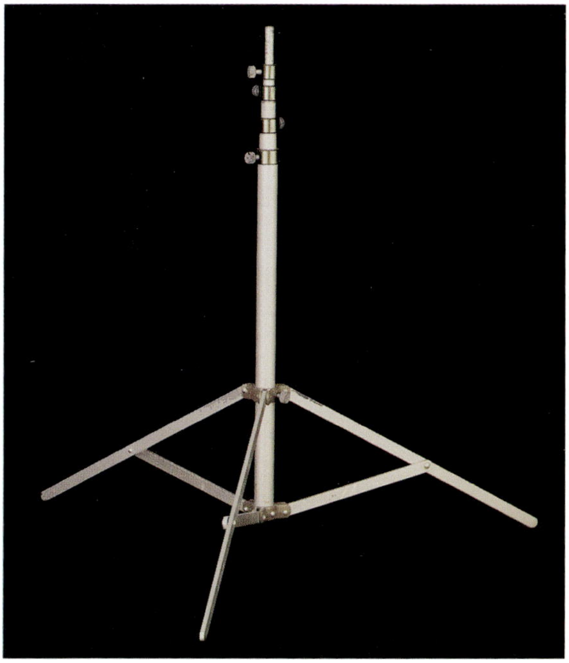

Figure 7.21 Light stands can hold lights, umbrellas, backdrops, and other equipment.

Backgrounds

Backgrounds can be backdrops of cloth, sheets of muslin you've painted yourself using a sponge dipped in paint, rolls of seamless paper, or any other suitable surface your mind can dream up. Backgrounds provide a complementary and non-distracting area behind subjects (especially portraits) and can be lit separately to provide contrast and separation that outlines the subject, or which helps set a mood.

I like to use plain-colored backgrounds for portraits, and white seamless backgrounds for product photography. You can usually construct these yourself from cheap materials and tape them up on the wall behind your subject, or mount them on a pole stretched between a pair of light stands.

Snoots and Barn Doors

These fit over the flash unit and direct the light at your subject. Snoots are excellent for converting a flash unit into a hair light, whereas barn doors give you enough control over the illumination by opening and closing their flaps that you can use another flash as a background light, with the capability of feathering the light exactly where you want it on the background. Barn doors are shown in Figure 7.22.

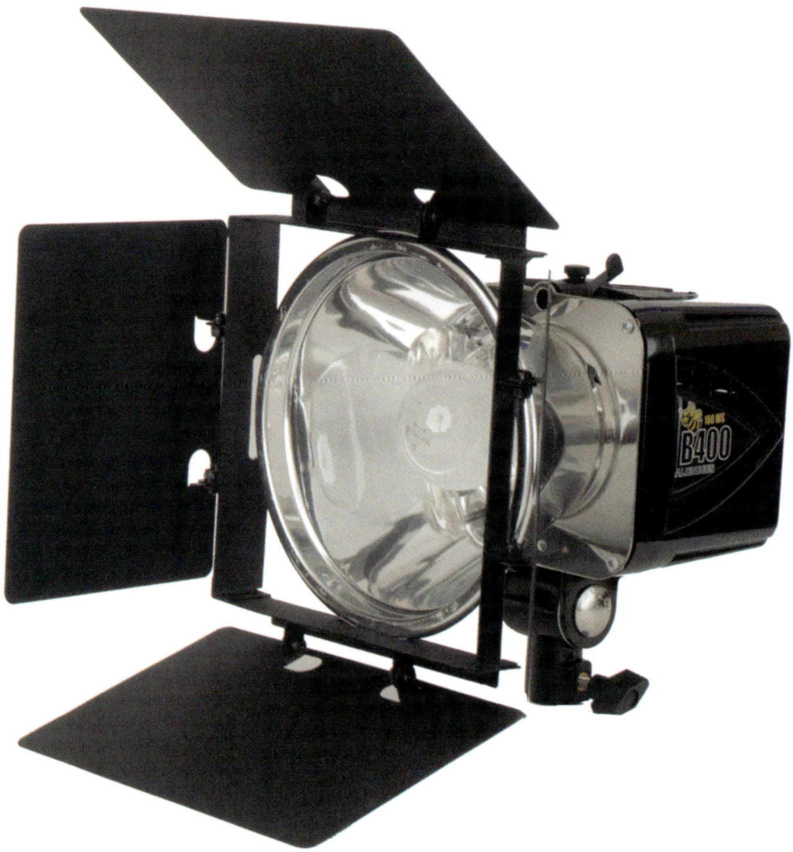

Figure 7.22
Barn doors allow you to modulate the light from a flash or lamp, and they are especially useful for hair lights and background lights.

8

Downloading and Editing Your Images

Taking the picture is only half the work and, in some cases, only half the fun. After you've captured some great images and have them safely stored on your Sony Alpha's memory card, you'll need to transfer them from your camera and memory card to your computer, where they can be organized, fine-tuned in an image editor, and prepared for web display, printing, or some other final destination.

Fortunately, there are lots of software utilities and applications to help you do all these things. This chapter will introduce you to a few of them. Don't expect a lot of "how-to-do-it" or instructions on using the software itself. This is primarily a *camera* guide, rather than a software manual. My intent in this chapter is to let you know what options are available, to help you choose what is right for you.

What's in the Box?

Sony includes three basic software utilities with the Alpha DSLR-A390/A290. They are the Picture Motion Browser (compatible with Windows only), Image Data Lightbox SR (for Windows and Macs), and Image Data Converter SR (supplied for both Windows and Mac operating systems). Install them using the CD supplied with the camera. Picture Motion Browser is an importing utility that collects images into folders and offers some simple editing capabilities for making minor fixes. Image Data Lightbox is a more advanced image browsing and workflow manager, while Image Data Converter SR is a sophisticated tool for importing and manipulating RAW images.

Picture Motion Browser

This tool, supplied with a variety of Sony cameras, camcorders, and other imaging devices, works with both still images and video files. It is available for Windows only, but Mac users can get most of its functions in iPhoto, and can import images to their computer by dragging and dropping image files as described in the "Transferring Your Photos" section that follows. Once you've imported/registered images with this browser, they are displayed either in a folder view (see Figure 8.1) or in a calendar view that arranges the photos by the date they were taken.

Double-click a thumbnail to display it in an editing window (see Figure 8.2), along with tools for trimming, rotating, adjusting brightness and contrast, enhancing or reducing saturation, adjusting sharpness, manipulating tonal curves, and activating red-eye reduction. You can also put the date on your photo. Picture Motion Browser can display all

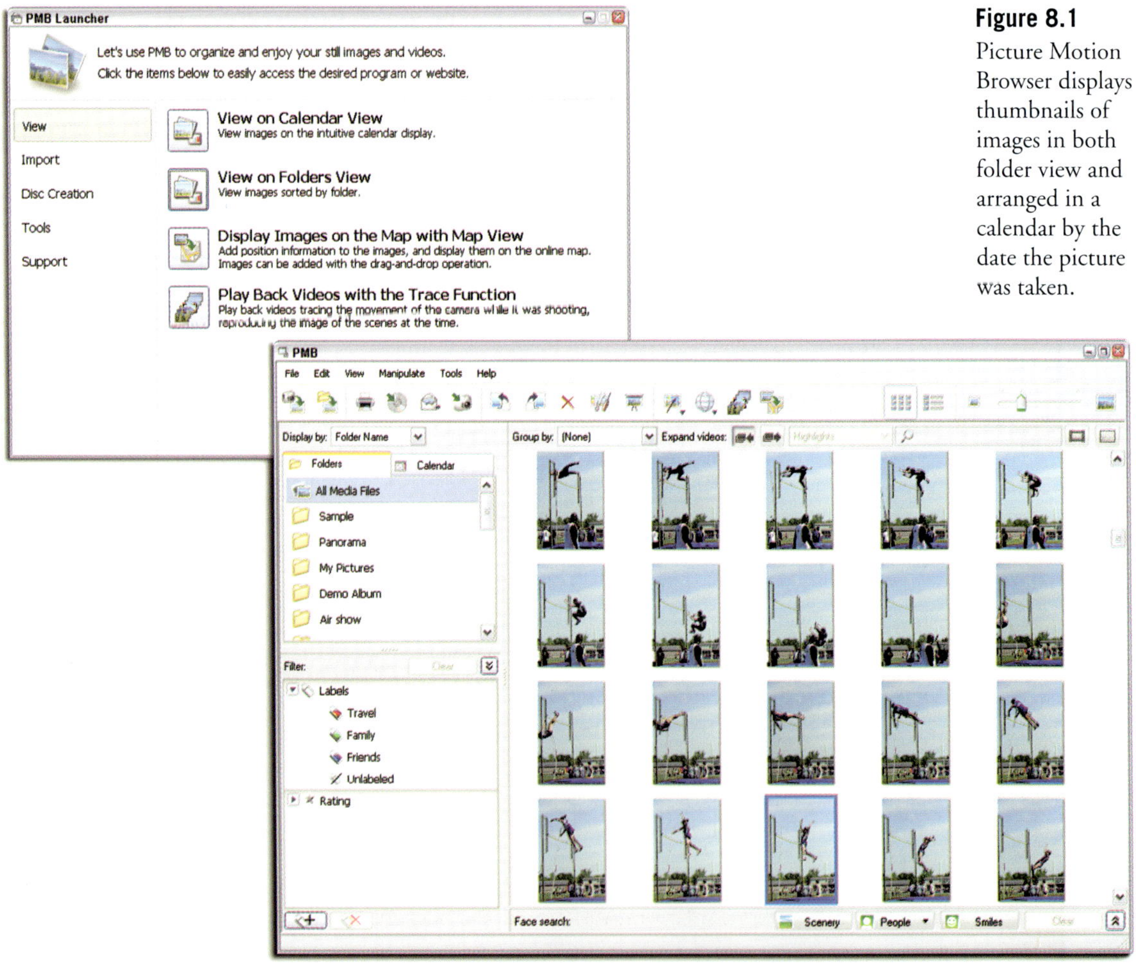

Figure 8.1
Picture Motion Browser displays thumbnails of images in both folder view and arranged in a calendar by the date the picture was taken.

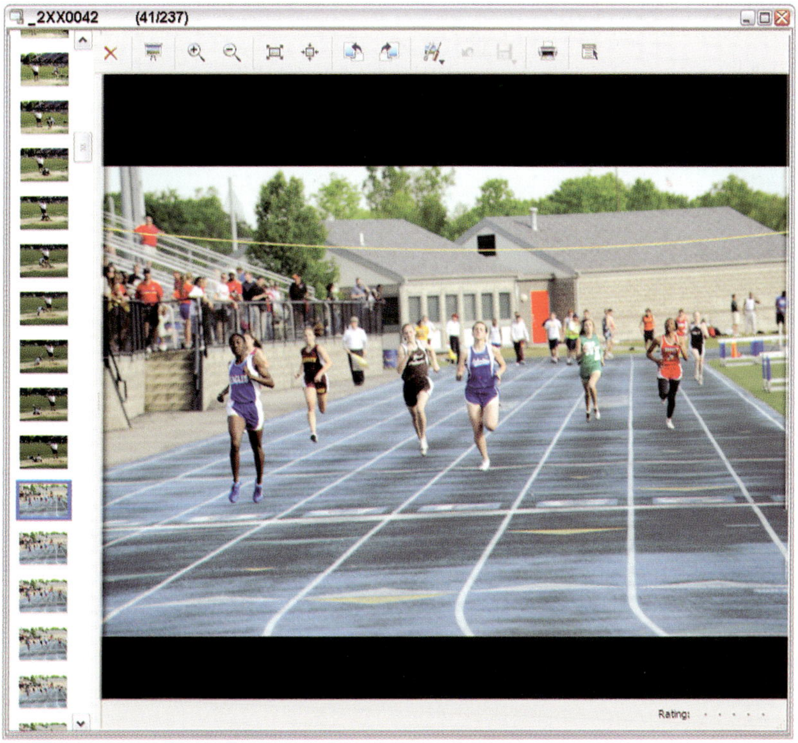

Figure 8.2
Simple editing fixes can be applied within Picture Motion Browser.

the photos in a folder as a slide show, burn them to a CD or DVD, and mark them for printing or e-mailing.

Picture Motion Browser has a photo-downloading utility that you can activate or deactivate in the Tools menu. As images are imported, they are moved into a folder within your My Pictures folder and are named after the import date, or deposited in a folder with a different name that you specify.

Image Data Lightbox SR

This is a newer application than Picture Motion Browser and is better for viewing, sorting, and comparing images than the older program. It's no Adobe Lightroom (or Apple Aperture, for that matter), but the price—free—is right. The application lets you compare images, even when still in RAW format, and apply star ratings, so you can segregate your best shots from a group of similar images (as shown in Figure 8.3) while you manage your photo library. You can choose to view the images as all thumbnails or in the Preview Display format, which features a line of images and one large image. It includes tools for creating image collections, batch printing, and converting photos to JPEG or TIFF format. To manipulate RAW files, you need Image Data Converter SR, discussed next.

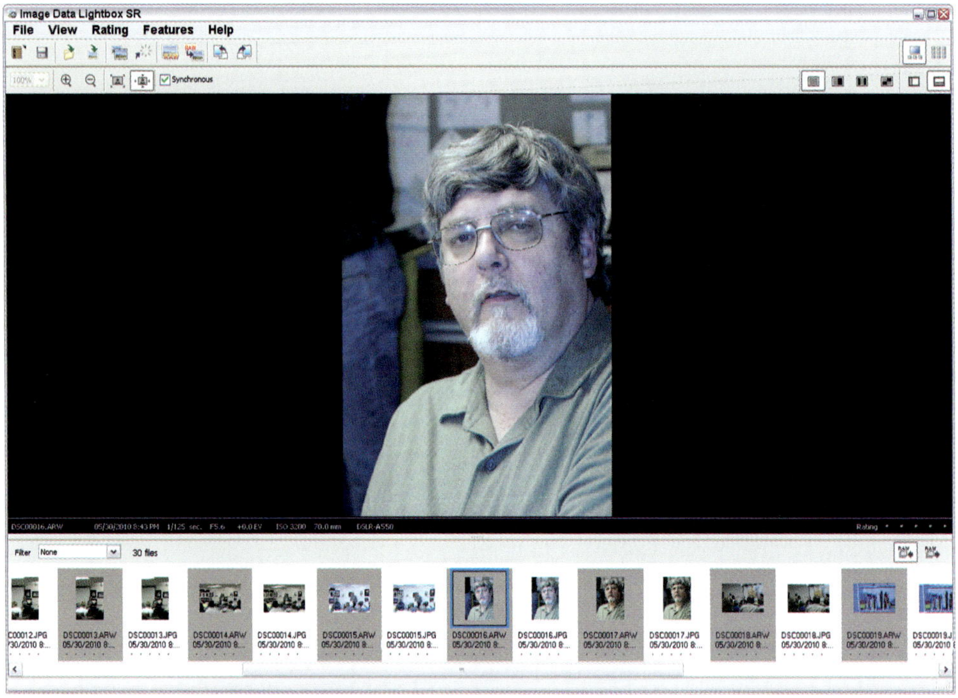

Figure 8.3
Image Data Lightbox SR helps you manage your picture collection.

Image Data Converter SR

This RAW converter is Sony's equivalent of Adobe Camera Raw, except that as your .arw files are converted, they can be transferred to the image editor of your choice, such as Corel Paint Shop Pro, rather than just to Adobe Photoshop or Photoshop Elements.

Like all RAW converters, Image Data Converter SR (see Figure 8.4) enables you to change any of the settings you could have made in the camera, plus modify a selection of additional settings, such as tonal curves, that you can't normally adjust when you take the photo. Making these changes after the picture is taken enables you to fine-tune your images, correct errors you might have made when you shot the photo, and fix things such as color balance that the camera (or you) might have set incorrectly.

This program includes four Adjustment Palettes that enable you to invoke specific dialog boxes with sliders and other adjustments. For example, there are separate exposure value (EV) adjustment settings, contrast and saturation settings, and a three-channel histogram, which can, optionally, display separate red, green, and blue histograms rather than the simple brightness (luminance) histogram shown in the camera.

Palette 1 is used for adjusting and setting white balance, color correction, hue, and saturation; Palette 2 is used to modify exposure, contrast, D-Range Optimizer, and other settings; Palette 3 makes it easy to set Creative Style adjustments, and specify sharpness, noise reduction, and picture effects, etc.; Palette 4 is where you'll find controls for display area, histograms, and tone curves.

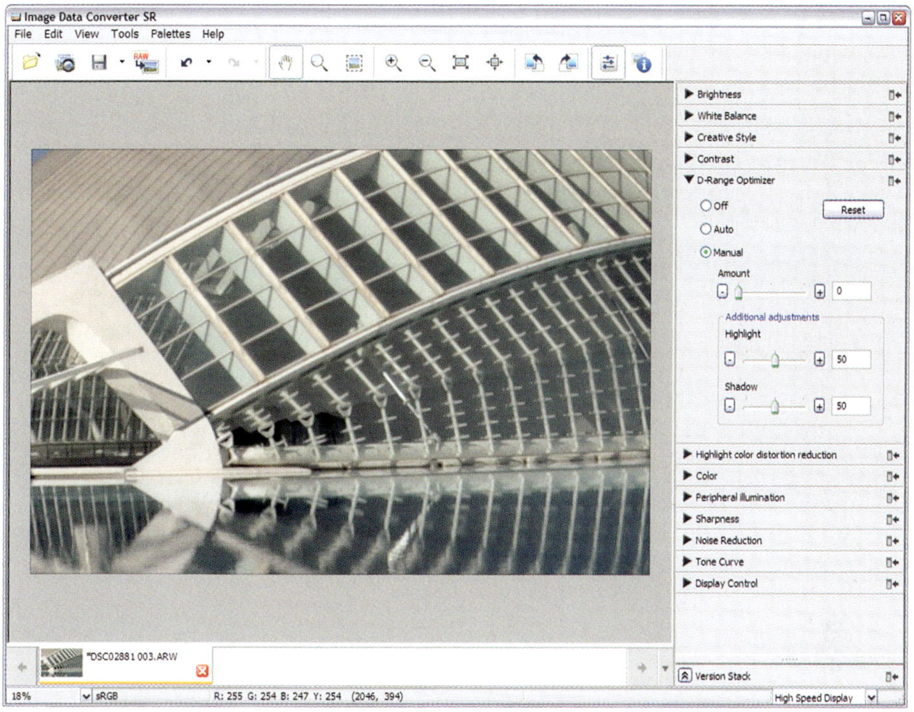

Figure 8.4
Image Data Converter SR lets you manage any of the in-camera settings as RAW files are imported—as well as many other options.

The Image Properties dialog box, shown in Figure 8.5, has an icon you can click to view a complete listing of all the settings you applied when you originally took the photo, such as lens, f/stop, shutter speed, ISO setting, and metering mode. These can all be changed within Image Data Converter SR as the files are imported for your image editor.

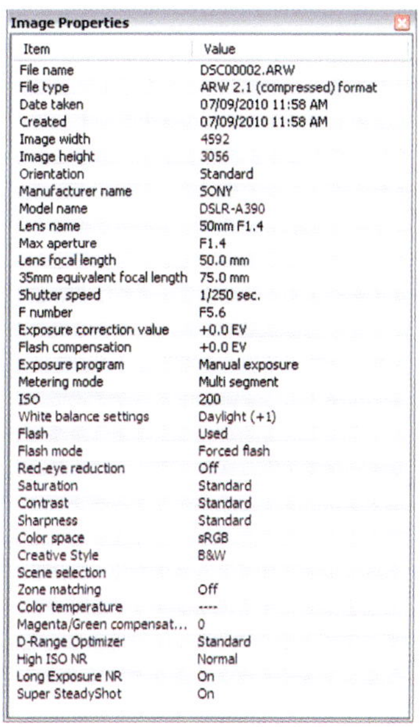
Image Properties

Item	Value
File name	DSC00002.ARW
File type	ARW 2.1 (compressed) format
Date taken	07/09/2010 11:58 AM
Created	07/09/2010 11:58 AM
Image width	4592
Image height	3056
Orientation	Standard
Manufacturer name	SONY
Model name	DSLR-A390
Lens name	50mm F1.4
Max aperture	F1.4
Lens focal length	50.0 mm
35mm equivalent focal length	75.0 mm
Shutter speed	1/250 sec.
F number	F5.6
Exposure correction value	+0.0 EV
Flash compensation	+0.0 EV
Exposure program	Manual exposure
Metering mode	Multi segment
ISO	200
White balance settings	Daylight (+1)
Flash	Used
Flash mode	Forced flash
Red-eye reduction	Off
Saturation	Standard
Contrast	Standard
Sharpness	Standard
Color space	sRGB
Creative Style	B&W
Scene selection	
Zone matching	Off
Color temperature	----
Magenta/Green compensat...	0
D-Range Optimizer	Standard
High ISO NR	Normal
Long Exposure NR	On
Super SteadyShot	On

Figure 8.5
Check out your original settings in the Image Properties dialog box.

Transferring Your Photos

While it's rewarding to capture some great images and have them ensconced in your camera, eventually you'll be transferring them to your laptop or PC, whether you're using a Windows or Macintosh machine. You have four options for image transfer: direct transfer over a USB cable; automated transfer using a card reader and transfer software such as the Sony Import Media Files utility that is a part of the Picture Motion Browser and Image Data Converter SR applications; Adobe Photoshop Elements Photo Downloader; or manual transfer using drag and drop from a memory card inserted in a card reader.

If you want to transfer your photos directly from your Sony Alpha camera to your computer, you'll first need to visit Setup 3 menu and make sure that the USB connection option is set to Mass Storage. That allows your computer to recognize the memory card in your computer as just another external drive, as if the camera were a hard drive or thumb/flash drive. While this method consumes a lot more battery power than the card reader option discussed later, and may be quite a bit slower, it is convenient (assuming you have the USB cable handy) and easy. Just follow these steps:

1. With the Alpha's USB connection option set to Mass Storage, turn the camera and computer on.
2. Open the memory card door and plug the smaller connector of the USB cable into the camera. Then, plug the larger cable plug into a USB socket on your computer.
3. If you're using Windows, its Autoplay Wizard may pop up (see Figure 8.6), offering a selection of downloading utilities (including the Windows Scanner and Camera Wizard, Adobe Photo Downloader, and the Media Importer). Choose one. Mac OS X offers similar options.

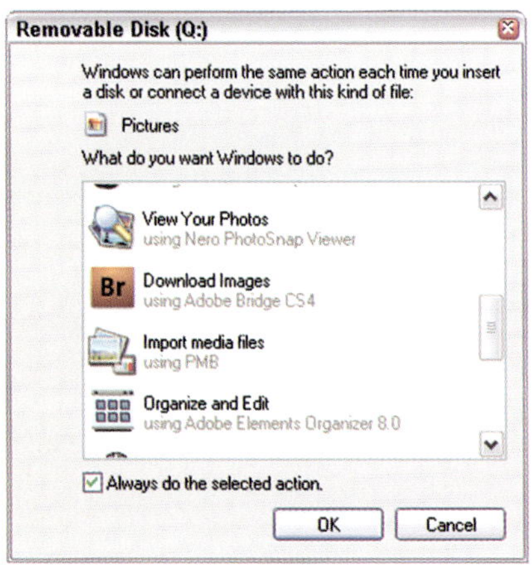

Figure 8.6 Windows Autoplay Wizard allows you to choose which utility to use to transfer your photos.

4. Use the options in the downloading utility you selected. You may be able to specify automatic red-eye correction, rename your files, place your files in a folder you select, or even view thumbnails of the available images so you download only the ones you want.
5. Activate the download process.

Using a Card Reader and Software

You can also use a memory card reader and software to transfer photos and automate the process using any of the downloading applications available with your computer. The process is similar to downloading directly from the camera, except that you must remove the memory card from the Alpha camera and insert it into a memory card reader attached to your computer.

Where USB-to-computer transfers are limited to the speed of your USB connection, card readers can be potentially much faster. This method is more frugal in its use of your camera's battery and can be faster if you have a speedy USB 2.0 or (some day soon) USB 3.0 card reader attached to an appropriate port.

The installed software automatically remains in memory as you work, and it recognizes when a memory card is inserted in your card reader; you don't have to launch it yourself. You'll see the Import Media Files dialog box (see Figure 8.7), or, sometimes, several competing downloaders will pop up at once. If that happens, you may want to disable the superfluous downloaders so your utility of choice will take precedence.

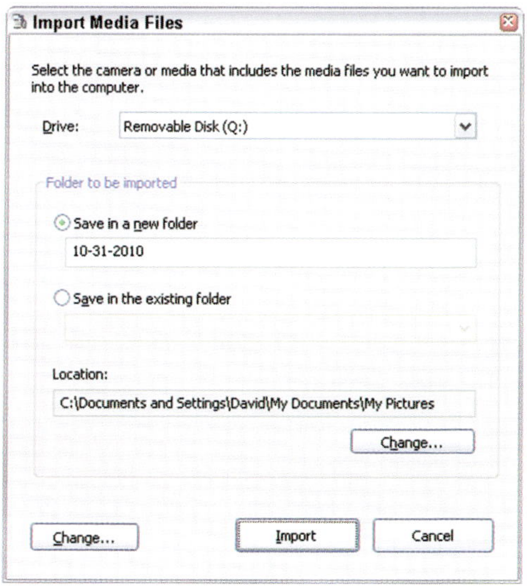

Figure 8.7 The Import Media Files utility is installed automatically with the Sony software suite.

With Photoshop Elements 8.0's Photo Downloader, you can choose basic options, such as file renaming and folder location, and then click Get Photos to begin the transfer of all images immediately. (See Figure 8.8.) Or choose Advanced Dialog for additional options, such as the ability to select which images to download from the memory card by marking them on a display of thumbnails. You can select other options, such as Automatically Fix Red Eyes, or insert a copyright notice of your choice. Start the download by clicking Get Photos, and a confirmation dialog box like the one in Figure 8.9 shows the progress.

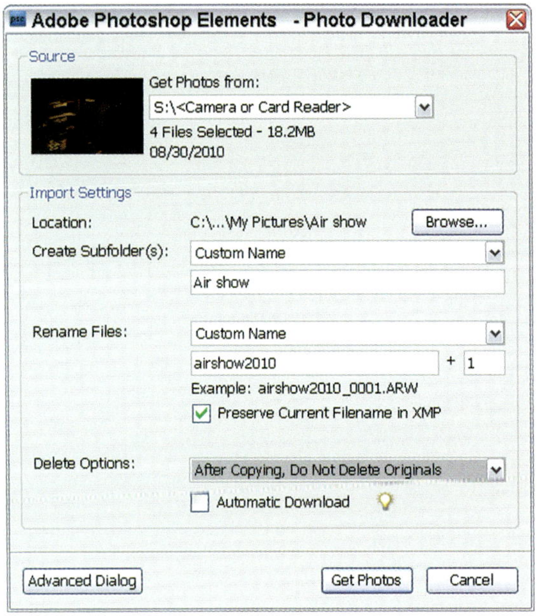

Figure 8.8 With Basic view activated, Photoshop Elements' Photo Downloader allows you to choose a filename and destination for your photos.

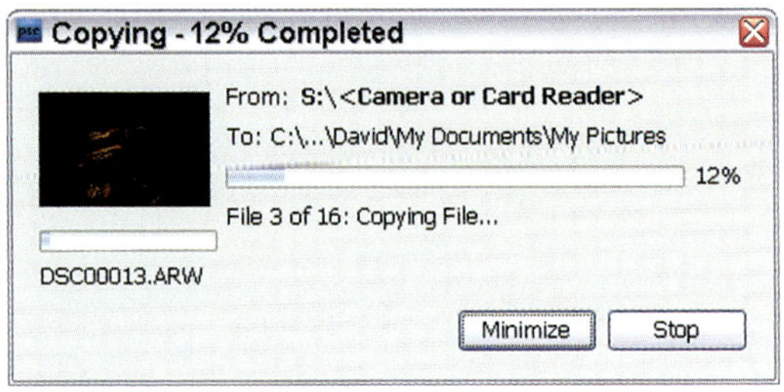

Figure 8.9 The Photo Downloader's confirmation dialog box shows the progress as images are transferred.

Dragging and Dropping

The final way to move photos from your memory card to your computer is the old-fashioned way: manually dragging and dropping the files from one window on your computer to another. The procedure works pretty much the same whether you're using a Mac or a PC.

1. Remove the memory card from the Sony Alpha and insert it in your memory card reader.
2. Using Windows Explorer, My Computer, Computer, or your Mac desktop, open the icon representing the memory card, which appears on your desktop as just another disk drive.

3. Open a second window representing the folder on your computer that you want to use as the destination for the files you are copying or moving.
4. Drag and drop the files from the memory card window to the folder on your computer. You can select individual files, press Ctrl/Command+A to select all the files, or Ctrl/Command+click to select multiple files.

Editing Your Photos

Image manipulation tasks fall into several categories. You might want to fine-tune your images, retouch them, change color balance, composite several images together, and perform other tasks we know as image editing, with a program like Adobe Photoshop, Photoshop Elements, or Corel Photo Paint.

You might want to play with the settings in RAW files, too, as you import them from their .arw state into an image editor. There are specialized tools expressly for tweaking RAW files, ranging from Sony's own Digital Image Converter to Adobe Camera Raw, and PhaseOne's Capture One Pro (C1 Pro). A third type of manipulation is the specialized task of noise reduction, which can be performed within Photoshop, Adobe Camera Raw, or tools like Bibble Professional. There are also specialized tools just for noise reduction, such as Noise Ninja (also included with Bibble) and Neat Image.

Each of these utilities and applications deserves a chapter of its own, so I'm simply going to enumerate some of the most popular image editing and RAW conversion programs here and tell you a little about what they do.

Image Editors

Image editors are general-purpose photo-editing applications that can do color correction, tonal modifications, retouching, combining of several images into one, and usually include tools for working with RAW files and reducing noise. So, you'll find programs like those listed here good for all-around image manipulation. The leading programs are as follows:

Adobe Photoshop/Photoshop Elements. Photoshop is the serious photographer's number one choice for image editing, and Elements is an excellent option for those who need most of Photoshop's power, but not all of its professional-level features. Both Photoshop and Elements editors use the latest version of Adobe's Camera Raw plug-in, which makes it easy to adjust things like color space profiles, color depth (either 8 bits or 16 bits per color channel), image resolution, white balance, exposure, shadows, brightness, sharpness, luminance, and noise reduction. One plus with the Adobe products is that they are available in identical versions for both Windows and Macs.

Corel Photo Paint. This is the image-editing program that is included in the popular CorelDRAW Graphics suite. Although a Mac version was available in the past, this is exclusively a Windows application today. It's a full-featured photo retouching and image-editing program with selection, retouching, and painting tools for manual image manipulations, and it also includes convenient automated commands for a few common tasks, such as red-eye removal. Photo Paint accepts Photoshop plug-ins to expand its assortment of filters and special effects.

Corel Paint Shop Pro. This is a general-purpose Windows-only image editor that has gained a reputation as the "poor man's Photoshop" for providing a substantial portion of Photoshop's capabilities at a fraction of the cost. It includes a nifty set of wizard-like commands that automate common tasks, such as removing red eye and scratches, as well as filters and effects, which can be expanded with other Photoshop plug-ins.

Corel Painter. Here's another image-editing program from Corel for both Mac and Windows. This one's strength is in mimicking natural media, such as charcoal, pastels, and various kinds of paint. Painter includes a basic assortment of tools that you can use to edit existing images, but the program is really designed for artists to use in creating original illustrations. As a photographer, you might prefer another image editor, but if you like to paint on top of your photographic images, nothing else really does the job of Painter.

Corel PhotoImpact. Corel finally brought one of the last remaining non-Adobe image editors into its fold when it acquired PhotoImpact. This is a general-purpose photo-editing program for Windows with a huge assortment of brushes for painting, retouching, and cloning in addition to the usual selection, cropping, and fill tools. If you frequently find yourself performing the same image manipulations on a number of files, you'll appreciate PhotoImpact's batch operations. Using this feature, you can select multiple image files and then apply any one of a long list of filters, enhancements, or auto-process commands to all the selected files.

RAW Utilities

Your software choices for manipulating RAW files are broader than you might think. Camera vendors always supply a utility to read their cameras' own RAW files, but sometimes, particularly with those point-and-shoot cameras that can produce RAW files, the options are fairly limited.

Because in the past digital camera vendors offered RAW converters that weren't very good, there is a lively market for third-party RAW utilities available at extra cost. The third-party solutions are usually available as standalone applications (often for both Windows and Macintosh platforms), as Photoshop-compatible plug-ins, or both.

Because the RAW plug-ins displace Photoshop's own RAW converter, I tend to prefer to use most RAW utilities in standalone mode. That way, if I choose to open a file directly in Photoshop, it automatically opens using Photoshop's fast and easy-to-use Adobe Camera Raw (ACR) plug-in. If I have more time or need the capabilities of another converter, I can load that, open the file, and make my corrections there. Most are able to transfer the processed file directly to Photoshop even if you aren't using plug-in mode.

The latest version of Photoshop includes a built-in RAW plug-in that is compatible with the proprietary formats of a growing number of digital cameras, both new and old, and it's continually updated to embrace any new cameras that are introduced. This plug-in also works with Photoshop Elements.

To open a RAW image in Photoshop, just follow these steps (Elements users can use much the same workflow, although fewer settings are available):

1. Transfer the .arw images from your camera to your computer's hard drive.
2. In Photoshop, choose Open from the File menu, or use Bridge.
3. Select an .arw image file. The Adobe Camera Raw plug-in will pop up, showing a preview of the image, like the one shown in Figure 8.10.

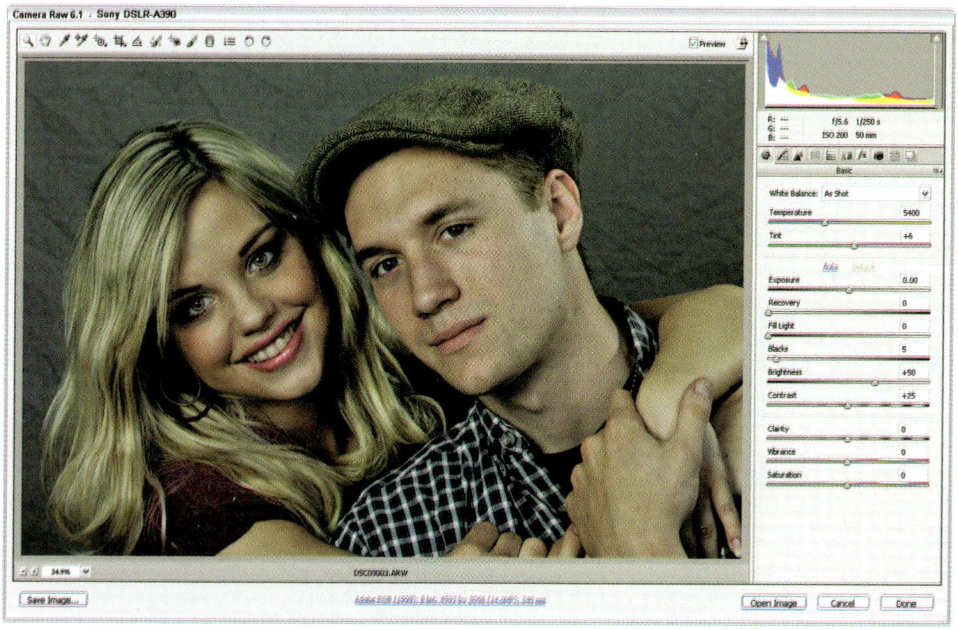

Figure 8.10
The basic ACR dialog box looks like this when processing a single image.

4. If you like, use one of the tools found in the toolbar at the top left of the dialog box. From left to right, they are as follows:
   - **Zoom.** The Camera Raw zoom tool operates just like the Zoom tool in Photoshop.
   - **Hand.** Use like the Hand tool in Photoshop.
   - **White Balance.** Click an area in the image that should be neutral gray or white to set the white balance quickly.
   - **Color Sampler.** Use to determine the RGB values of areas you click with this eyedropper.
   - **Crop.** Pre-crop the image so that only the portion you specify is imported into Photoshop. This option saves time when you want to work on a section of a large image, and you don't need the entire file.
   - **Straighten.** Drag in the preview image to define what should be a horizontal or vertical line, and ACR will realign the image to straighten it.
   - **Retouch.** Use to heal or clone areas you define.
   - **Red-Eye Removal.** Quickly zap red pupils in your human subjects.
   - **ACR Preferences.** Produces a dialog box of Adobe Camera Raw preferences.
   - **Rotate Counterclockwise.** Rotates counterclockwise in 90-degree increments with a click.
   - **Rotate Clockwise.** Rotates clockwise in 90-degree increments with a click.
5. Using the Basic tab, you can have ACR show you red and blue highlights in the preview that indicate shadow areas that are clipped (too dark to show detail) and light areas that are blown out (too bright). Click the triangles in the upper-left corner of the histogram display (shadow clipping) and upper-right corner (highlight clipping) to toggle these indicators on or off.
6. Also in the Basic tab you can choose white balance, either from the drop-down list or by setting a color temperature and green/magenta color bias (tint) using the sliders.
7. Other sliders are available to control exposure, recovery, fill light, blacks, brightness, contrast, vibrance, and saturation. A checkbox can be marked to convert the image to grayscale.
8. Make other adjustments (described in more detail below).
9. ACR makes automatic adjustments for you . You can click Default and make the changes for yourself, or click the Auto link (located just above the Exposure slider) to reapply the automatic adjustments after you've made your own modifications.

10. If you've marked more than one image to be opened, the additional images appear in a "filmstrip" at the left side of the screen. You can click on each thumbnail in the filmstrip in turn and apply different settings to each.
11. Click Open image/Open image(s) into Photoshop using the settings you've made. You can also click Save or Done to save the changes you've made *without* opening the file in your image editor.

The Basic tab is displayed by default when the ACR dialog box opens, and it includes most of the sliders and controls you'll need to fine-tune your image as you import it into Photoshop. These include

- **White Balance.** Leave it As Shot or change to a value such as Daylight, Cloudy, Shade, Tungsten, Fluorescent, or Flash. If you like, you can set a custom white balance using the Temperature and Tint sliders.
- **Exposure.** This slider adjusts the overall brightness and darkness of the image.
- **Recovery.** Restores detail in the red, green, and blue color channels.
- **Fill Light.** Reconstructs detail in shadows.
- **Blacks.** Increases the number of tones represented as black in the final image, emphasizing tones in the shadow areas of the image.
- **Brightness.** This slider adjusts the brightness and darkness of an image.
- **Contrast.** Manipulates the contrast of the midtones of your image.
- **Convert to Grayscale.** Mark this box to convert the image to black-and-white.
- **Vibrance.** Prevents over-saturation when enriching the colors of an image.
- **Saturation.** Manipulates the richness of all colors equally, from zero saturation (gray/black, no color) at the –100 setting to double the usual saturation at the +100 setting.

Additional controls are available on the Tone Curve, Detail, HSL/Grayscale, Split Toning, Lens Corrections, Camera Calibration, and Presets tabs, shown in Figure 8.11. The Tone Curve tab can change the tonal values of your image. The Detail tab lets you adjust sharpness, luminance smoothing, and apply color noise reduction. The HSL/Grayscale tab offers controls for adjusting hue, saturation, and lightness and converting an image to black-and-white. Split Toning helps you colorize an image with sepia or cyanotype (blue) shades. The Lens Corrections tab has sliders to adjust for chromatic aberrations and vignetting. The Camera Calibration tab provides a way for calibrating the color corrections made in the Camera Raw plug-in. The Presets tab (not shown) is used to load settings you've stored for reuse.

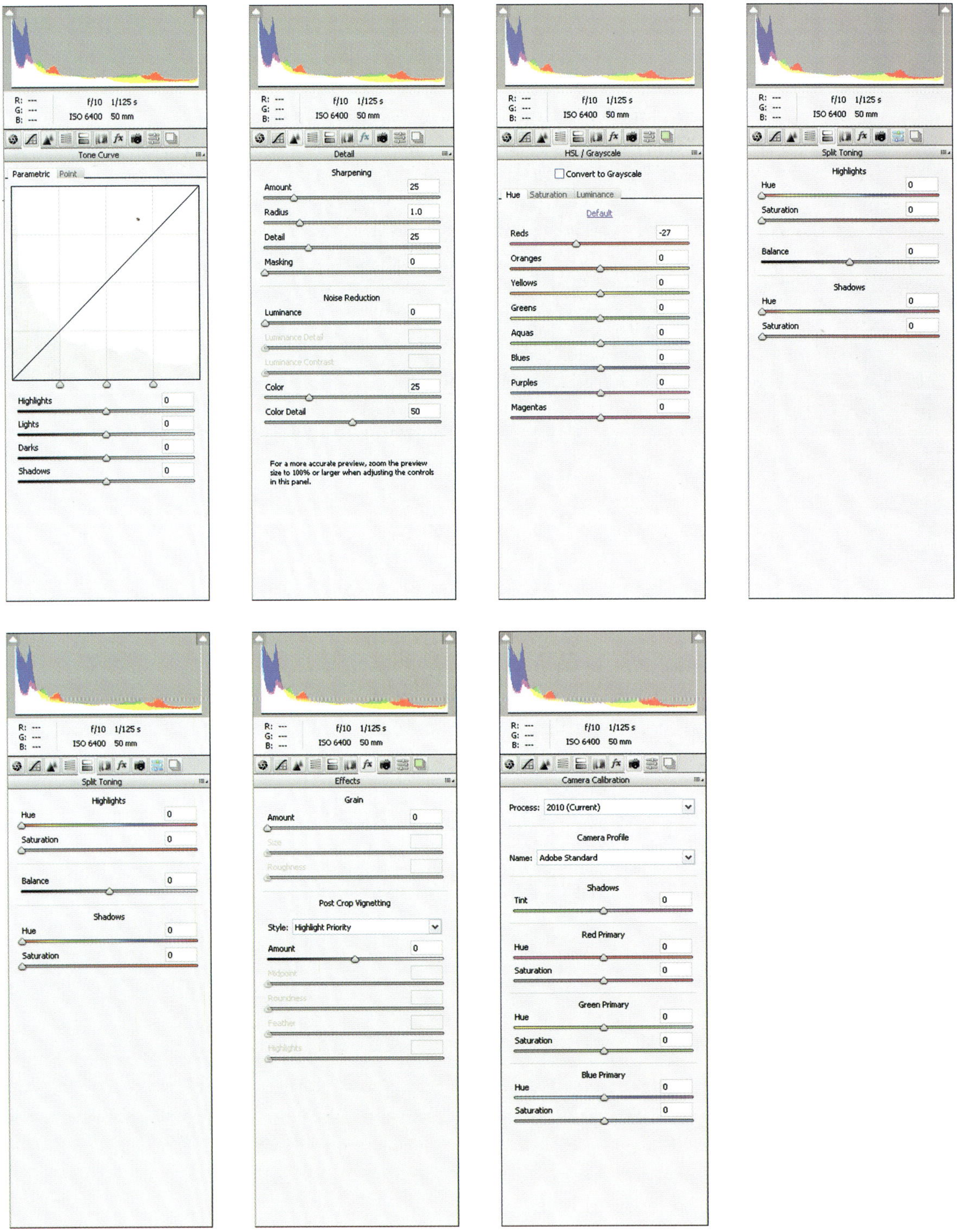

Figure 8.11 More controls are available within the additional tabbed dialog boxes in Adobe Camera Raw.

9

Sony Alpha DSLR-A390/A290: Troubleshooting and Prevention

One of the nice things about modern electronic cameras like the A390/A290 series is that they have fewer mechanical moving parts to fail, so they are less likely to "wear out." No film transport mechanism, no wind lever or motor drive, no complicated mechanical linkages from camera to lens to physically stop down the lens aperture. Instead, tiny, reliable motors are built into each lens (and you lose the use of only that lens should something fail), and one of the few major moving parts in the camera itself is a lightweight mirror (its small size one of the advantages of the Alpha's 1.5X crop factor) that flips up and down with each shot when you're not shooting in Live View mode on the A390 model.

Of course, the camera also has a moving shutter that can fail, but the shutter is built rugged enough that you can expect it to last 100,000 shutter cycles or more. Unless you're shooting sports in continuous mode day in and day out, the shutter on your Alpha is likely to last as long as you expect to use the camera.

The only other things on the camera that move are switches, dials, buttons, the flip-up electronic flash, and the door that slides open to allow you to remove and insert the memory card. Unless you're extraordinarily clumsy or unlucky and manage to give your built-in flash a good whack while it is in use, there's not a lot that can go wrong mechanically with your Sony Alpha.

On the other hand, one of the chief drawbacks of modern electronic cameras is that they are modern *electronic* cameras. Your Alpha is fully dependent on its battery. Without it, the camera can't be used. There are numerous other electrical and electronic connections in the camera (many connected to those mechanical switches and dials), and components like the tilting 2.7-inch color LCD on the A390 that can potentially fail or suffer damage. The camera also relies on its "operating system," or *firmware*, which can be plagued by bugs that cause unexpected behavior. Luckily, electronic components are generally more reliable and trouble-free, especially when compared to their mechanical counterparts from the pre-electronic film camera days. (Film cameras of the last 10 to 20 years have had almost as many electronic features as digital cameras, but, believe it or not, there were whole generations of film cameras that had *no* electronics or batteries.)

Digital cameras have problems unique to their breed, too—the most troublesome being the need to clean the sensor of dust and grime periodically. This chapter will show you how to diagnose problems, fix some common ills, and, importantly, learn how to avoid them in the future.

Updating Your Firmware

As I said, the firmware in your Sony Alpha is the camera's operating system, which handles everything from menu display (including fonts, colors, and the actual entries themselves), what languages are available, and even support for specific devices and features. Upgrading the firmware to a new version makes it possible to add new features while fixing some of the bugs that sneak in.

The exact changes made to the firmware are generally spelled out in the firmware release announcement. You can examine the remedies provided and decide if a given firmware patch is important to you. If not, you can usually safely wait a while before going through the bother of upgrading your firmware—at least long enough for the early adopters to report whether the bug fixes have introduced new bugs of their own. Each new firmware release incorporates the changes from previous releases, so if you skip a minor upgrade you should have no problems.

WARNING

Use a fully charged battery to ensure that you'll have enough power to operate the camera for the entire upgrade. Moreover, you should not turn off the camera while your old firmware is being overwritten. Don't open the memory card door or do anything else that might disrupt operation of the Alpha while the firmware is being installed.

To see which firmware version is currently installed in your camera, venture to the Setup 3 menu, select Version, and press the center button. A screen pops up with the name of your camera and firmware version, as shown in Figure 9.1. Press the center controller button or the MENU button to dismiss this screen. Write down the firmware version installed in your camera, and then check to see if a firmware update is available.

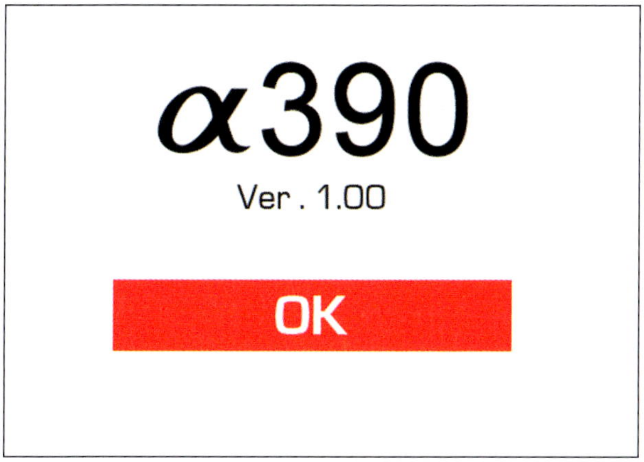

Figure 9.1 Press the MENU button and DISP buttons to show the current firmware version in your camera.

To do that, visit the Sony support site at www.esupport.sony.com. The support page provides updates and information about a huge range of Sony products, but there is a Search box you can use to jump directly to the page for your particular camera. I've found that all you need to enter is "DSLR-A390," "DSLR- ," or "DSLR-A290" to get to the correct page. There, you'll find a notice listing "Hot Topics" and other support information. If new firmware is available, it will be listed as a link under the "Hot Topics" display. Follow the links and download the update, if one is available. The latest firmware for this Alpha series is Version 1.0.

Then follow these steps:

1. **Put the firmware software in a separate directory or folder.** It will have a name like DSCA390v11.exe (for Windows computers) or DSCA390v11.zip (for Mac OS).
2. **Extract the firmware file.** Go to the directory/folder where the firmware download was placed and extract the DSCA390.APP (or DSC .APP or DSCA290.APP) by double-clicking the file you downloaded. The .APP file extension may not be displayed if your computer has been set to hide extensions of known file types.
3. **Format a Secure Digital or Memory Stick card.** Format the memory card *in the camera* and *not* in your computer.

4. **Copy the firmware to the CF card.** Use a card reader or USB cable linked to your camera and computer to copy the firmware to the top (root) directory/folder of your memory card. If using the USB cable, make sure the USB Connection has been set to Mass Storage in Setup 2 menu.
5. **Turn off power and make sure fully charged battery is installed.**
6. **Install firmware.** With the memory card containing the firmware update in the camera, hold down the MENU button and slide the Power switch on the back of the camera to the ON position. Continue to hold down the MENU button until the confirmation window appears.
7. **Activate installation.** Use the controller keys to highlight OK, and press the center controller button to begin the update. A screen indicating that the update is complete will appear, and the camera will restart.
8. **Check update.** Turn off the camera; then switch it on again. Press the MENU button, followed by the DISP button to see that the firmware has been correctly updated.

Protecting Your LCD

The 2.7-inch color LCD on the back of your Sony Alpha almost seems like a target for banging, scratching, and other abuse, especially when it is swiveled up or down for viewing from high or low vantage points. Fortunately, this LCD is quite rugged, and a few errant knocks are unlikely to shatter the protective cover over the LCD, and scratches won't easily mar its surface. However, if you want to be on the safe side, there are several protective products you can purchase to keep your LCD safe—and, in some cases, make it a little easier to view. Here's a quick overview of your options.

- **Plastic overlays.** The simplest solution (although not always the cheapest) is to apply a plastic overlay sheet or "skin" cut to fit your LCD. These adhere either by static electricity or through a light adhesive coating that's even less clingy than stick-it notes. You can cut down overlays made for PDAs (although these can be pricey at up to $19.95 for a set of several sheets), or purchase overlays sold specifically for digital cameras. Vendors such as Zagg (www.zagg.com) offer overlays of this type. These products will do a good job of shielding your Alpha's LCD screen from scratches and minor impacts, but will not offer much protection from a good whack.
- **Acrylic/glass/polycarbonate shields.** Sony offers a clip-on polycarbonate LCD shield for the A390, the PCK-LH3AM, which costs about $12. The equivalent model for the A290 is the PCK-LH2AM. A company in China called GGS makes a very popular glass screen protector for various Alpha models. (See Figure 9.2.)

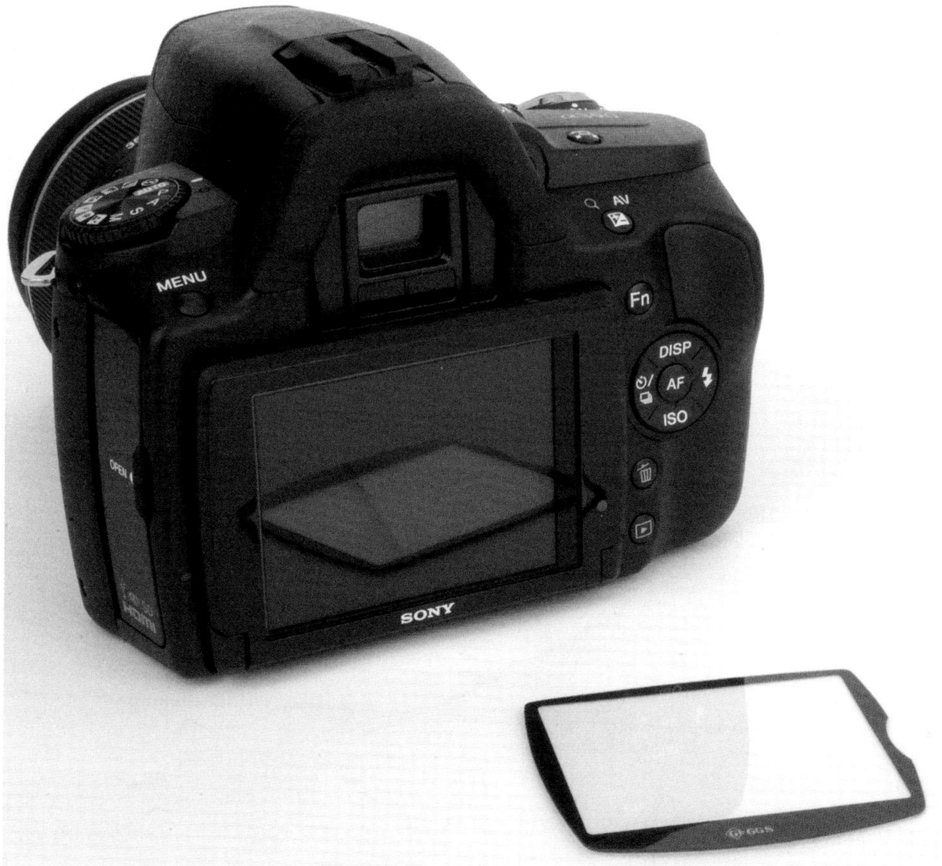

Figure 9.2
Tough glass screen shields can protect your LCD from scratches.

Unfortunately, it seems to be available only through eBay, so I can't give you a specific URL to visit. There are a number of different sellers offering these shields for $5 to $12, plus shipping, and I've ordered from several of them with good luck. The protectors attach using strips of sticky adhesive that hold the panel flush and tight, but which allow the protector to be pried off and the adhesive removed easily if you want to remove or replace the shield. They don't attenuate your view of the LCD and are non-reflective enough for use under a variety of lighting conditions.

- **Hoods.** Various hood-type devices are available for the Alpha series, including a fold-up hood offered by Sony itself. My objection to these hoods is that you must close them to use the optical viewfinder, and then open them if you want to review your image. They are best suited for protecting/shielding the LCD when using the Live View feature, as you can then leave the hood unfolded all the time while shooting.

All Your Eggs in One Basket?

The debate about whether it's better to use one large memory card or several smaller ones has been going on since even before there were memory cards. I can remember when computer users wondered whether it was smarter to install a pair of 200MB (not *gigabyte*) hard drives in their computer, or if they should go for one of those new-fangled 500MB models. By the same token, a few years ago the user groups were full of proponents who insisted that you ought to use 128MB memory card cards rather than the huge 512MB versions. Today, most of the arguments involve 4GB cards versus 8GB cards, and I expect that as prices for 16 and 32GB memory cards continue to drop, they'll find their way into the debate as well. I just bought two high-speed 32GB cards for *less* than I paid for a 4GB Secure Digital or Memory Stick card only 18 months ago.

Why all the fuss? Are 8GB memory cards more likely to fail than 4GB cards? Are you risking all your photos if you trust your images to a larger card? Isn't it better to use several smaller cards, so that if one fails you lose only half as many photos? Or, isn't it wiser to put all your photos onto one larger card, because the more cards you use, the better your odds of misplacing or damaging one and losing at least some pictures?

In the end, the "eggs in one basket" argument boils down to statistics, and how you happen to use your Alpha. The rationales can go both ways. If you have multiple smaller cards, you do increase your chances of something happening to one of them, so, arguably, you might be boosting the odds of losing some pictures. If all your images are important, the fact that you've lost 100 rather than 200 pictures isn't very comforting.

Also, consider that the eggs/basket scenario assumes that the cards that are lost or damaged are always full. It's actually likely that your 8GB card might suffer a mishap when it's less than half full. Indeed, it's *more* likely that a large card won't be completely filled before it's offloaded to a computer. I often use only one quarter to one half of the capacity of my larger cards in a single session. I'm thankful that the extra room is there when I need it, but I don't always use it. So the reality is that you might not lose any more shots with a single 8GB card than with multiple 4GB cards. A bad card—of whatever size—might contain, say 3GB of images, so the size of the card won't really matter in such cases.

If you shoot photojournalist-type pictures, you probably change memory cards when they're less than completely full in order to avoid the need to do so at a crucial moment. (When I shoot sports, my cards rarely reach 80 to 90 percent of capacity before I change them.) Using multiple smaller cards means you have to change them that more often, which can be a real pain when you're taking a lot of photos. As an example, if you use 1GB memory cards with an Alpha A390 and shoot RAW & JPEG FINE, you may get only a few dozen pictures on the card. That's almost exactly the capacity of a 36-exposure roll of film (remember those?). In my book, I prefer keeping all my eggs in one basket, and then making very sure that nothing happens to that basket.

There is really only one good reason to justify limiting yourself to smaller memory cards when larger ones can be purchased at the same cost per-gigabyte. One of them is when every single picture is precious to you and the loss of any of them would be a disaster. If you're a wedding photographer, for example, and unlikely to be able to restage the nuptials if a memory card goes bad, you'll probably want to shoot no more pictures than you can afford to lose on a single card, and have an assistant ready to copy each card removed from the camera onto a backup hard drive or DVD onsite.

To be even safer, you'd want to alternate cameras or have a second photographer at least partially duplicating your coverage so your shots are distributed over several memory cards simultaneously. Or, you might consider *interleaving* your shots. Say you don't shoot weddings, but you do go on vacation from time to time. Take 50 or so pictures on one card, or whatever number of images might fill about 25 percent of its capacity. Then, replace it with a different card and shoot about 25 percent of that card's available space. Repeat these steps with diligence (you'd have to be determined to go through this inconvenience), and, if you use four or more memory cards you'll find your pictures from each location scattered among the different memory cards. If you lose or damage one, you'll still have *some* pictures from all the various stops on your trip on the other cards. That's more work than I like to do (I usually tote around a netbook and portable hard disk and copy the files to the drive as I go), but it's an option. (See Figure 9.3.)

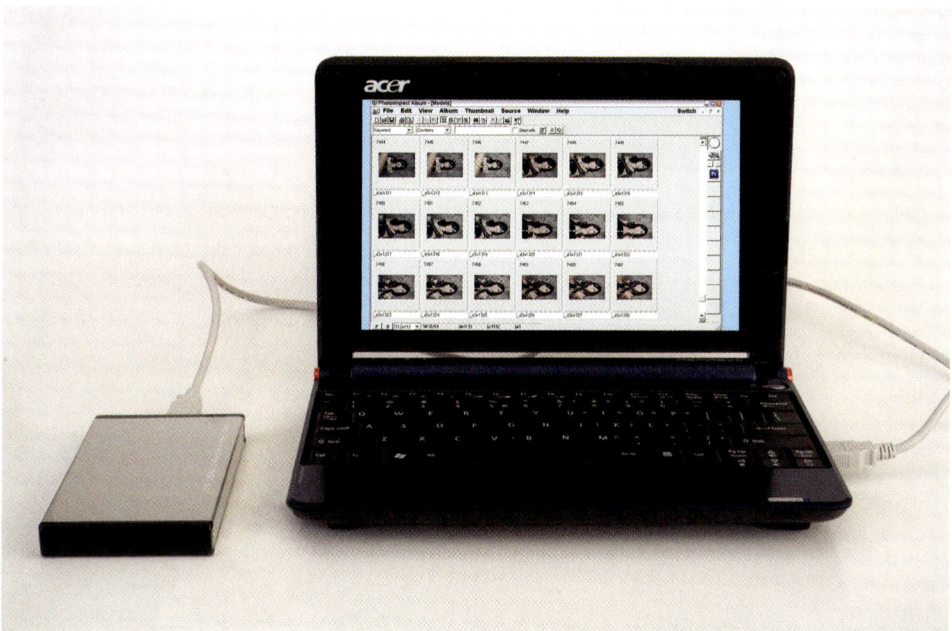

Figure 9.3
A netbook and a portable hard drive make a good backup option when you travel.

What Can Go Wrong?

There are lots of things that can go wrong with your memory card, but the ones that aren't caused by human stupidity are statistically very rare. Yes, a memory card's internal bit bin or controller can suddenly fail due to a manufacturing error or some inexplicable event caused by old age. However, if your memory card works for the first week or two that you own it, it should work forever. There's really not a lot that can wear out.

The typical memory card is rated for a Mean Time Between Failures of 1,000,000 hours of use. That's constant use 24/7 for more than 100 years! According to the manufacturers, they are good for 10,000 insertions in your camera, and should be able to retain their data (and that's without an external power source) for something on the order of 11 years. Of course, with the millions of memory cards in use, there are bound to be a few lemons here or there.

Given the reliability of solid-state memory, compared to magnetic memory, though, it's more likely that your memory card problems will stem from something that you do. Secure Digital or Memory Stick memory cards are small and easy to misplace if you're not careful. For that reason, it's a good idea to keep them in their original cases or a "card safe" offered by Gepe (www.gepecardsafe.com), Pelican (www.pelican.com), and others. Always placing your memory card in a case can provide protection from the second-most common mishap that befalls memory cards: the common household laundry. If you slip a memory card in a pocket rather than a case or your camera bag often enough, sooner or later it's going to end up in the washing machine and probably the clothes dryer, too. There are plenty of reports of relieved digital camera owners who've laundered their memory cards and found they still worked fine, but it's not uncommon for such mistreatment to do some damage.

Memory cards can also be stomped on, accidentally bent, dropped into the ocean, chewed by pets, and otherwise rendered unusable in myriad ways. It's also remotely possible to force a card into your Alpha's memory card slot incorrectly if you're diligent enough, doing little damage to the card itself, but possibly damaging the camera internally, eliminating its ability to read or write to any memory card. This almost never happens, but don't discount the ingenuity of a determined fumble-fingers.

Or, if the card is formatted in your computer with a memory card reader, your Alpha may fail to recognize it. Occasionally, I've found that a memory card used in one camera would fail if used in a different camera (until I reformatted it in Windows, and then again in the camera). Every once in awhile, a card goes completely bad and—seemingly—can't be salvaged.

Another way to lose images is to do commonplace things with your memory card at an inopportune time. If you remove the card from the Alpha while the camera is writing images to the card, you'll lose any photos in the buffer and may damage the file structure of the card, making it difficult or impossible to retrieve the other pictures you've taken. The same thing can happen if you remove the memory card from your computer's card reader while the computer is writing to the card (say, to erase files you've already moved to your computer). You can avoid this by *not* using your computer to erase files on a memory card but, instead, always reformatting the card in your Alpha before you use it again.

What Can You Do?

Pay attention: If you're having problems, the *first* thing you should do is *stop* using that memory card. Don't take any more pictures. Don't do anything with the card until you've figured out what's wrong. Your second line of defense (your first line is to be sufficiently careful with your cards that you avoid problems in the first place) is to *do no harm* that hasn't already been done. Read the rest of this section and then, if necessary, decide on a course of action (such as using a data recovery service or software described later) before you risk damaging the data on your card further.

Now that you've calmed down, the first thing to check is whether you've actually inserted a card in the camera. The Alpha cameras will actually "take" pictures with no memory card inserted, although a warning is displayed on the LCD (as a flashing NO CARD message in the lower-right corner) and in the viewfinder as a flashing 0 indicator (showing you can take zero shots before the buffer becomes full!). In Live View mode, the LCD shows a helpful No Card warning. It's hard to take photos without a memory card installed, but it is possible.

Things get more exciting when the card itself is put in jeopardy. If you lose a card, there's not a lot you can do other than take a picture of a similar card and print up some "Have You Seen This Lost Flash Memory?" flyers to post on utility poles all around town.

If all you care about is reusing the card, and have resigned yourself to losing the pictures, try reformatting the card in your camera. You may find that reformatting removes the corrupted data and restores your card to health. Sometimes I've had success reformatting a card in my computer using a memory card reader (this is normally a no-no because your operating system doesn't understand the needs of your Alpha), and *then* reformatting again in the camera.

If your memory card is not behaving properly, and you *do* want to recover your images, things get a little more complicated. If your pictures are very valuable, either to you or to others (for example, a wedding), you can always turn to professional data recovery firms. Be prepared to pay hundreds of dollars to get your pictures back, but these pros often do an amazing job. You wouldn't want them working on your memory card on behalf of the police if you'd tried to erase some incriminating pictures. There are many firms of this type, and I've never used them myself, so I can't offer a recommendation. Use a Google search to turn up a ton of them.

THE ULTIMATE IRONY

I recently purchased an 8GB Kingston memory card that was furnished with some nifty OnTrack data recovery software. The first thing I did was format the card to make sure it was okay. Then I hunted around for the free software, only to discover it was preloaded onto the memory card. I was supposed to copy the software to my computer before using the memory card for the first time.

Fortunately, I had the OnTrack software that would reverse my dumb move, so I could retrieve the software. No, wait. I *didn't* have the software I needed to recover the software I erased. I'd reformatted it to oblivion. Chalk this one up as either the ultimate irony or Stupid Author Trick #523.

A more reasonable approach is to try special data recovery software you can install on your computer and use to attempt to resurrect your "lost" images yourself. They may not actually be gone completely. Perhaps your memory card's "table of contents" is jumbled, or only a few pictures are damaged in such a way that your camera and computer can't read some or any of the pictures on the card. Some of the available software was written specifically to reconstruct lost pictures, while other utilities are more general-purpose applications that can be used with any media, including floppy disks and hard disk drives. They have names like OnTrack, Photo Rescue 2, Digital Image Recovery, MediaRecover, Image Recall, and the aptly named Recover My Photos. You'll find a comprehensive list and links, as well as some picture-recovery tips at www.ultimateslr.com/memory-card-recovery.php. I like Rescue Pro (Figure 9.4), which came free with one of my SanDisk cards.

DIMINISHING RETURNS

Usually, once you've recovered any images on a memory card, reformatted it, and returned it to service, it will function reliably for the rest of its useful life. However, if you find a particular card going bad more than once, you'll almost certainly want to stop using it forever. See if you can get it replaced by the manufacturer, if you can, but, in the case of memory card failures, the third time is never the charm.

Cleaning Your Sensor

Yes, your Alpha A390/A290 does have an anti-static coating on the cover that protects the sensor. And it does have an automatic sensor dust removal system that activates every time you turn on the camera. But, even with those high tech aids, you'll still get some stubborn dust on your sensor. There's no avoiding it. No matter how careful you are,

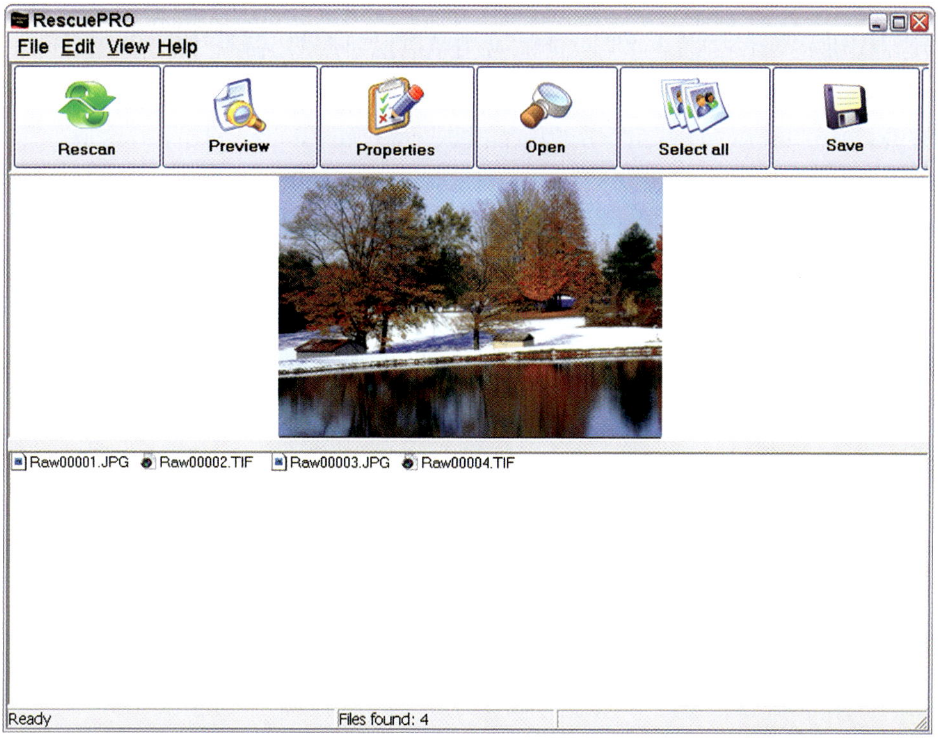

Figure 9.4 Rescue Pro is available from SanDisk.

some dust is going to settle on your camera and on the mounts of your lenses, eventually making its way inside your camera to settle in the mirror chamber. As you take photos, the mirror flipping up and down causes the dust to become airborne and eventually make its way past the shutter curtain to come to rest on the anti-aliasing filter atop your sensor. There, dust and particles can show up in every single picture you take at a small enough aperture to bring the foreign matter into sharp focus. No matter how careful you are and how cleanly you work, eventually you will get some of this dust on your camera's sensor. But even the cleanest-working photographers using Sony cameras are far from immune.

Dust the FAQs, Ma'am

Here are some of the most frequently asked questions about sensor dust issues.

Q. I see tiny specks in my viewfinder. Do I have dust on my sensor?

A. If you see sharp, well-defined specks, they are clinging to the underside of your focus screen and not on your sensor. They have absolutely no effect on your photographs, and are merely annoying or distracting.

Q. I can see dust on my mirror. How can I remove it?

A. Like focus-screen dust, any artifacts that have settled on your mirror won't affect your photos. You can often remove dust on the mirror or focus screen with a bulb air blower, which will loosen it and whisk it away. Stubborn dust on the focus screen can sometimes be gently flicked away with a soft brush designed for cleaning lenses. I don't recommend brushing the mirror or touching it in any way. The mirror is a special front-surface-silvered optical device (unlike conventional mirrors, which are silvered on the back side of a piece of glass or plastic) and can be easily scratched. If you can't blow mirror dust off, it's best to just forget about it. You can't see it in the viewfinder, anyway.

Q. I see a bright spot in the same place in all of my photos. Is that sensor dust?

A. You've probably got either a "hot" pixel or one that is permanently "stuck" due to a defect in the sensor. A hot pixel is one that shows up as a bright spot only during long exposures as the sensor warms. A pixel stuck in the "on" position always appears in the image. Both show up as bright red, green, or blue pixels, usually surrounded by a small cluster of other improperly illuminated pixels, caused by the camera's interpolating the hot or stuck pixel into its surroundings, as shown in Figure 9.5. A stuck pixel can also be permanently dark. Either kind is likely to show up when they contrast with plain, evenly colored areas of your image.

Finding one or two hot or stuck pixels in your sensor is unfortunately fairly common. They can be "removed" by telling the Alpha to ignore them through a simple process called *pixel mapping*, described in the sidebar that follows.

Bad pixels can also show up on your camera's color LCD panel, but, unless they are abundant, the wisest course is to just ignore them. The Alpha A390 cameras can remove bad pixels that show up during Live View using the Pixel Mapping

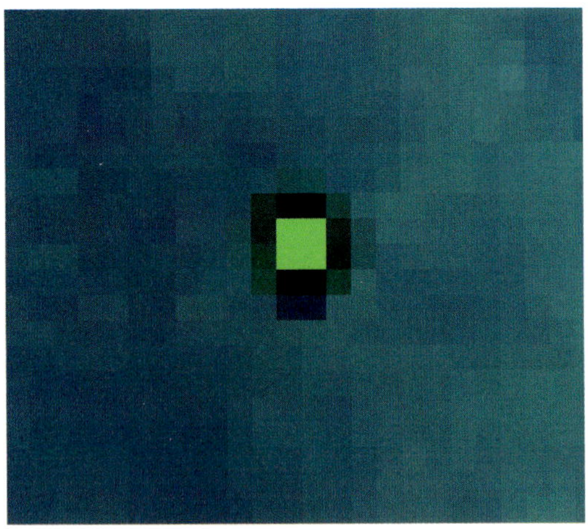

Figure 9.5
A stuck pixel is surrounded by improperly interpolated pixels created by the Alpha's demosaicing algorithm.

option found in the Setup 3 menu, as described in Chapter 3 and the sidebar that follows. (Remember that the A290 does not have Live view, and Pixel Mapping is not available.)

Q. I see an irregular out-of-focus blob in the same place in my photos. Is that sensor dust?

A. Yes. Sensor contaminants can take the form of tiny spots, larger blobs, or even curvy lines if they are caused by minuscule fibers that have settled on the sensor. They'll appear out of focus because they aren't actually on the sensor surface but, rather, a fraction of a millimeter above it on the filter that covers the sensor. The smaller the f/stop used, the more in-focus the dust becomes. At large apertures, it may not be visible at all.

Q. I never see any dust on my sensor. What's all the fuss about?

A. Those who never have dust problems with their Sony Alpha fall into one of four categories: those for whom the camera's automatic dust removal features are working well; those who seldom change their lenses and have clean working habits that minimize the amount of dust that invades their cameras in the first place; those who simply don't notice the dust (often because they don't shoot many macro photos or other pictures using the small f/stops that make dust evident in their images); and those who are very, very lucky.

PIXEL MAPPING

To induce your Alpha to find and "map out" bad pixels that show in the LCD during Live View, just follow these steps:

1. Change to Live View mode.
2. Place the lens cap on the front of your lens, so that Live View "sees" a totally black image.
3. Press the MENU button, and navigate to Setup 3 menu and choose Pixel Mapping (available only when the A390 is in Live View mode).
4. Select OK on the screen that pops up.
5. The Alpha will examine the scene. Do not turn off the camera while pixel mapping is underway. The camera detects bright pixels that should not appear in the black image, and stores their location so that those pixels will not be used in the future.
6. When pixel mapping is completed, press the center controller button, and then the MENU button, to exit. Bad pixels that show during Live View will be nullified.

Identifying and Dealing with Stubborn Dust

Sensor dust that isn't automatically removed by the Alpha's anti-dust features is less of a problem than it might be because it shows up only under certain circumstances. Indeed, you might have dust on your sensor right now and not be aware of it. The dust doesn't actually settle on the sensor itself, but, rather, on a protective filter a very tiny distance above the sensor, subjecting it to the phenomenon of *depth-of-focus*. Depth-of-focus is the distance the focal plane can be moved and still render an object in sharp focus. At f/2.8 to f/5.6 or even smaller, sensor dust, particularly if small, is likely to be outside the range of depth-of-focus and blur into an unnoticeable dot.

However, if you're shooting at f/16 to f/22 or smaller, those dust motes suddenly pop into focus. Forget about trying to spot them by peering directly at your sensor with the shutter open and the lens removed. The period at the end of this sentence, about .33mm in diameter, could block a group of pixels measuring 40 × 40 pixels (160 pixels in all!). Dust spots that are even smaller than that can easily show up in your images if you're shooting large, empty areas that are light colored. Dust motes are most likely to show up in the sky, as in Figure 9.6, or in white backgrounds of your seamless product shots and are less likely to be a problem in images that contain lots of dark areas and detail.

To see if you have dust on your sensor, take a few test shots of a plain, blank surface (such as a piece of paper or a cloudless sky) at small f/stops, such as f/22, and a few wide open. Open Photoshop, copy several shots into a single document in separate layers, then flip back and forth between layers to see if any spots you see are present in all layers. You may have to boost contrast and sharpness to make the dust easier to spot.

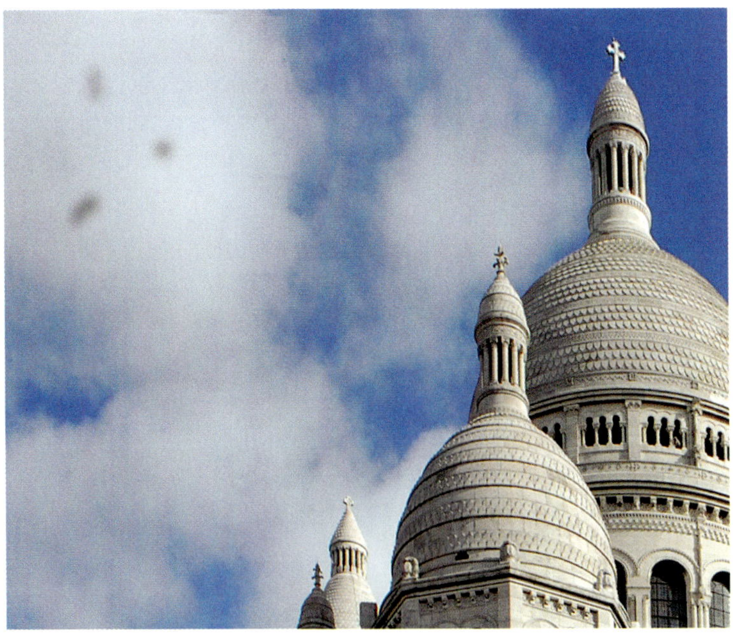

Figure 9.6
Only the dust spots in the sky are apparent in this shot.

Avoiding Dust

Of course, the easiest way to protect your sensor from dust is to prevent it from settling on the sensor in the first place. Here are my stock tips for eliminating the problem before it begins.

- **Clean environment.** Avoid working in dusty areas if you can do so. Hah! Serious photographers will take this one with a grain of salt, because it usually makes sense to go where the pictures are. Only a few of us are so paranoid about sensor dust (considering that it is so easily removed) that we'll avoid moderately grimy locations just to protect something that is, when you get down to it, just a tool. If you find a great picture opportunity at a raging fire, during a sandstorm, or while surrounded by dust clouds, you might hesitate to take the picture, but, with a little caution (don't remove your lens in these situations, and clean the camera afterwards!) you can still shoot. However, it still makes sense to store your camera in a clean environment. One place cameras and lenses pick up a lot of dust is inside a camera bag. Clean your bag from time to time, and you can avoid problems.
- **Clean lenses.** There are a few paranoid types that avoid swapping lenses in order to minimize the chance of dust getting inside their cameras. It makes more sense just to use a blower or brush to dust off the rear lens mount of the replacement lens first, so you won't be introducing dust into your camera simply by attaching a new, dusty lens. Do this before you remove the lens from your camera, and then avoid stirring up dust before making the exchange.
- **Work fast.** Minimize the time your camera is lens-less and exposed to dust. That means having your replacement lens ready and dusted off, and a place to set down the old lens as soon as it is removed, so you can quickly attach the new lens.
- **Let gravity help you.** Face the camera downward when the lens is detached so any dust in the mirror box will tend to fall away from the sensor. Turn your back to any breezes, indoor forced air vents, fans, or other sources of dust to minimize infiltration.
- **Protect the lens you just removed.** Once you've attached the new lens, quickly put the end cap on the one you just removed to reduce the dust that might fall on it.
- **Clean out the vestibule.** From time to time, remove the lens while in a relatively dust-free environment and use a blower bulb like the one shown in Figure 9.7 (*not* compressed air or a vacuum hose) to clean out the mirror box area. A blower bulb is generally safer than a can of compressed air, or a strong positive/negative airflow, which can tend to drive dust further into nooks and crannies.

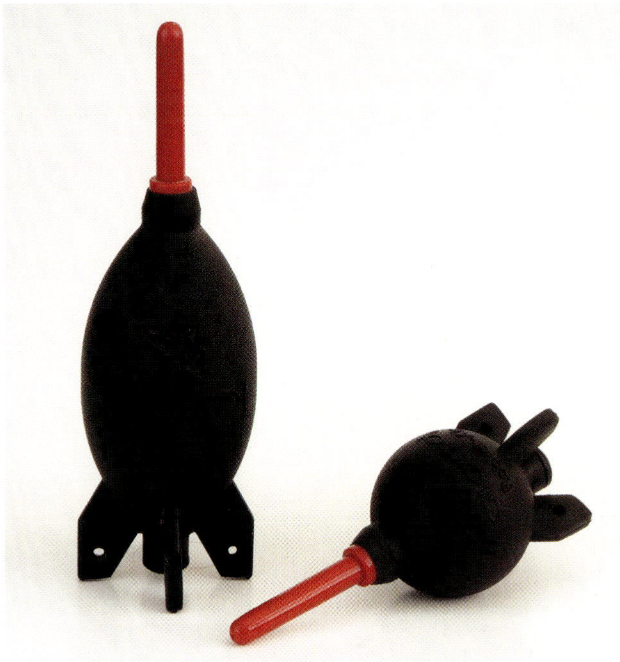

Figure 9.7
Use a robust air bulb like the Giottos Rocket for cleaning your sensor.

- **Be prepared.** If you're embarking on an important shooting session, it's a good idea to clean your sensor *now*, rather than come home with hundreds or thousands of images with dust spots caused by flecks that were sitting on your sensor before you even started. Before I left on my recent trip to Spain, I put both cameras I was taking through a rigid cleaning regimen, figuring they could remain dust-free for a measly 10 days. I even left my bulky blower bulb at home. It was a big mistake, but my intentions were good. I now have a smaller version of the Giottos Rocket Blower, and *that* goes with me everywhere.
- **Clone out existing spots in your image editor.** Photoshop and other editors have a clone tool or healing brush you can use to copy pixels from surrounding areas over the dust spot or dead pixel. This process can be tedious, especially if you have lots of dust spots and/or lots of images to be corrected. The advantage is that this sort of manual fix-it probably will do the least damage to the rest of your photo. Only the cloned pixels will be affected. Photoshop CS5's Healing Brush used in Content Aware mode is especially adept at removing artifacts of this type.
- **Use filtration in your image editor.** A semi-smart filter like Photoshop's Dust & Scratches filter can remove dust and other artifacts by selectively blurring areas that the plug-in decides represent dust spots. This method can work well if you have many dust spots, because you won't need to patch them manually. However, any automated method like this has the possibility of blurring areas of your image that you didn't intend to soften.

Sensor Cleaning

Those new to the concept of sensor dust actually hesitate before deciding to clean their camera themselves. Isn't it a better idea to pack up your Alpha and send it to a Sony service center so their crack technical staff can do the job for you? Or, at the very least, shouldn't you let the friendly folks at your local camera store do it?

If you choose to let someone else clean your sensor, they will be using methods that are more or less identical to the techniques you would use yourself. None of these techniques are difficult, and the only difference between their cleaning and your cleaning is that they might have done it dozens or hundreds of times. If you're careful, you can do just as good a job.

Of course vendors like Sony won't tell you this, but it's not because they don't trust you. It's not that difficult for a real goofball to mess up his camera by hurrying or taking a shortcut. Perhaps the person uses the "Bulb" method of holding the shutter open and a finger slips, allowing the shutter curtain to close on top of a sensor cleaning brush. Or, someone tries to clean the sensor using masking tape, and ends up with goo all over its surface. If Sony recommended *any* method that's mildly risky, someone would do it wrong, and then the company would face lawsuits from those who'd contend they did it exactly in the way the vendor suggested, so the ruined camera is not their fault.

You can see that vendors like Sony tend to be conservative in their recommendations, and, in doing so, make it seem as if sensor cleaning is more daunting and dangerous than it really is. Some vendors recommend only dust-off cleaning, through the use of reasonably gentle blasts of air, while condemning more serious scrubbing with swabs and cleaning fluids. However, these cleaning kits for the exact types of cleaning they recommended against are for sale in Japan only, where, apparently, your average photographer is more dexterous than those of us in the rest of the world. These kits are similar to those used by official repair staff to clean your sensor if you decide to send your camera in for a dust-up.

As I noted, sensors can be affected by dust particles that are much smaller than you might be able to spot visually on the surface of your lens. The filters that cover sensors tend to be fairly hard compared to optical glass. Cleaning the 23.6mm × 15.8mm sensor in your Sony Alpha within the tight confines of the mirror box can call for a steady hand and careful touch. If your sensor's filter becomes scratched through inept cleaning, you can't simply remove it yourself and replace it with a new one.

There are four basic kinds of cleaning processes that can be used to remove dusty and sticky stuff that settles on your dSLR's sensor. All of these must be performed with the shutter locked open. I'll describe these methods and provide instructions for locking the shutter later in this section.

- **Air cleaning.** This process involves squirting blasts of air inside your camera with the shutter locked open. This works well for dust that's not clinging stubbornly to your sensor.
- **Brushing.** A soft, very fine brush is passed across the surface of the sensor's filter, dislodging mildly persistent dust particles and sweeping them off the imager.
- **Liquid cleaning.** A soft swab dipped in a cleaning solution such as ethanol is used to wipe the sensor filter, removing more obstinate particles.
- **Tape cleaning.** There are some who get good results by applying a special form of tape to the surface of their sensor. When the tape is peeled off, all the dust goes with it. Supposedly. I'd be remiss if I didn't point out right now that this form of cleaning is somewhat controversial; the other three methods are much more widely accepted. Now that Sony has equipped the front-sensor filter with a special anti-dust coating, I wouldn't chance damaging that coating by using any kind of adhesive tape.

Placing the Shutter in the Locked and Fully Upright Position for Landing

Make sure you're using a fully charged battery.

1. Press the MENU button.
2. Choose Setup 3 menu and select Cleaning Mode and press the center controller button.
3. The screen that pops up says After cleaning turn camera off. Continue? Choose OK and press the center controller button.
4. You'll hear the mirror flip up. (See Figure 9.8.)
5. Remove the lens and use one of the methods described below to remove dust and grime from your sensor. Be careful not to accidentally switch the power off or open the memory card or battery compartment doors as you work. If that happens, the shutter may be damaged if it closes on your cleaning tool.
6. When you're finished, turn off the power, replace your lens, and switch your camera back on.

Air Cleaning

Your first attempts at cleaning your sensor should always involve gentle blasts of air. Many times, you'll be able to dislodge dust spots, which will fall off the sensor and, with luck, out of the mirror box. Attempt one of the other methods only when you've already tried air cleaning and it didn't remove all the dust.

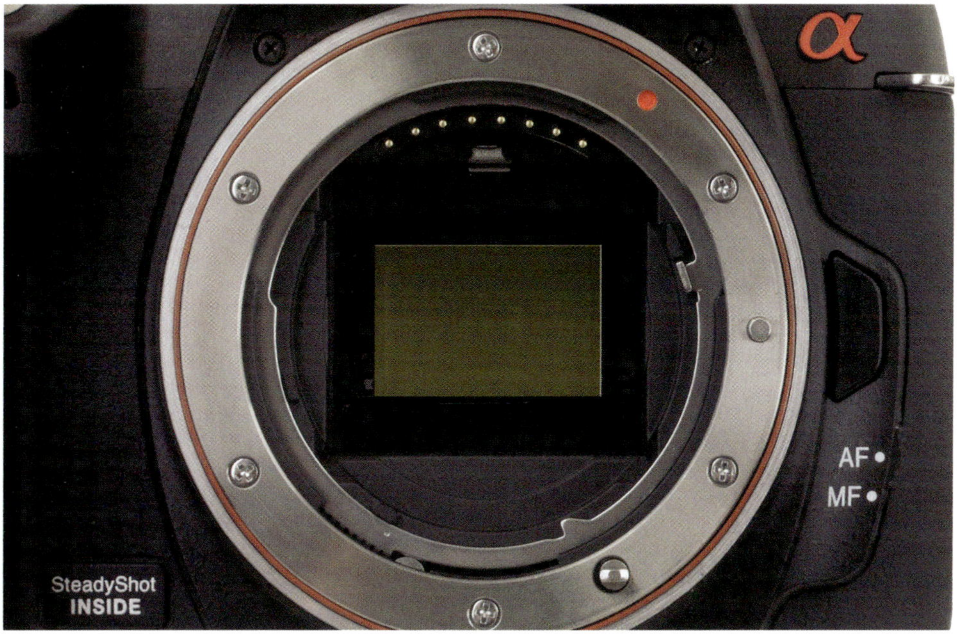

Figure 9.8
With the mirror flipped up, the sensor is exposed and available for manual cleaning.

Here are some tips for air cleaning:

- **Use a clean, powerful air bulb.** Your best bet is bulb cleaners designed for the job, like the Giottos Rockets shown earlier in Figure 9.7. Smaller bulbs, like those air bulbs with a brush attached sometimes sold for lens cleaning or weak nasal aspirators may not provide sufficient air or a strong enough blast to do much good.
- **Hold the Sony Alpha upside down.** Then look up into the mirror box as you squirt your air blasts, increasing the odds that gravity will help pull the expelled dust downward, away from the sensor. You may have to use some imagination in positioning yourself. (And don't let dust fall into your eye!) (See Figure 9.9.)
- **Never use air canisters.** The propellant inside these cans can permanently coat your sensor if you tilt the can while spraying. It's not worth taking a chance.
- **Avoid air compressors.** Super-strong blasts of air are likely to force dust under the sensor filter.

Brush Cleaning

If your dust is a little more stubborn and can't be dislodged by air alone, you may want to try a brush, charged with static electricity, which can pick off dust spots by electrical attraction. One good, but expensive, option is the Sensor Brush sold at www.visible-dust.com. A cheaper version can be purchased at www.copperhillimages.com. You need a 16mm version, like the one shown in Figure 9.10, which can be stroked across the long dimension of your Alpha's sensor.

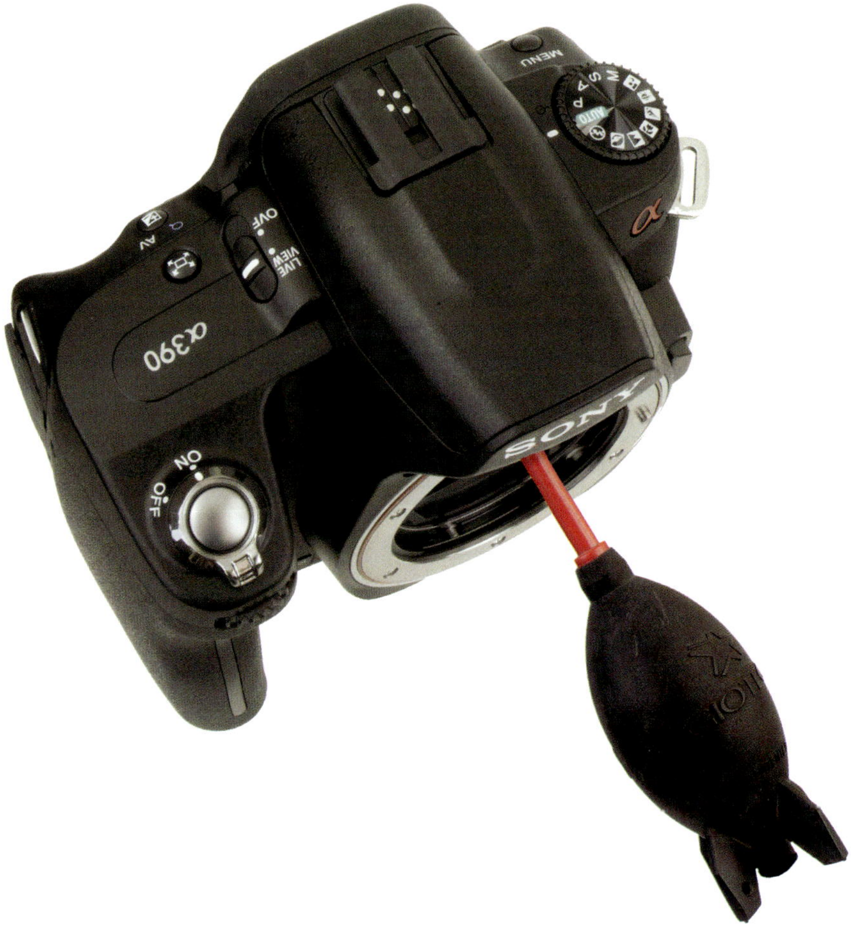

Figure 9.9
Hold the camera facing lens mount downward to allow dust to fall out.

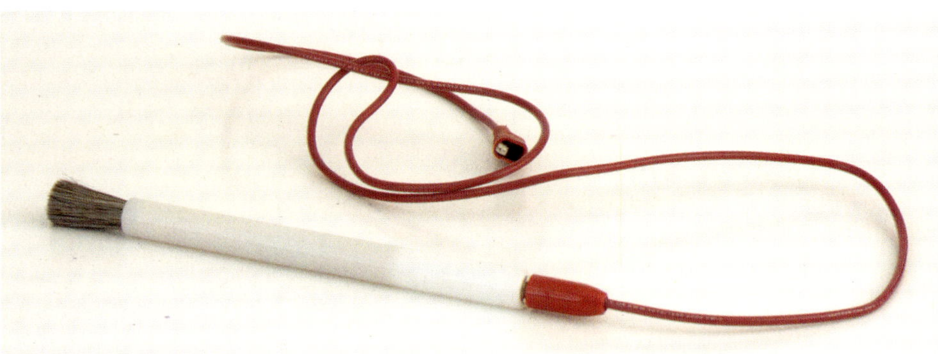

Figure 9.10
A proper brush is required for dusting off your sensor. The long cord shown is attached to a grounded object to reduce static electricity.

Ordinary artist's brushes are much too coarse and stiff and have fibers that are tangled or can come loose and settle on your sensor. A good sensor brush's fibers are resilient and described as "thinner than a human hair." Moreover, the brush has a wooden handle that reduces the risk of static sparks. Check out my *Digital SLR Pro Secrets* book if you want to make a sensor brush (or sensor swabs) yourself.

Brush cleaning is done with a dry brush by gently swiping the surface of the sensor filter with the tip. The dust particles are attracted to the brush particles and cling to them. You should clean the brush with compressed air before and after each use, and store it in an appropriate air-tight container between applications to keep it clean and dust-free. Although these special brushes are expensive, one should last you a long time.

Liquid Cleaning

Unfortunately, you'll often encounter really stubborn dust spots that can't be removed with a blast of air or flick of a brush. These spots may be combined with some grease or a liquid that causes them to stick to the sensor filter's surface. In such cases, liquid cleaning with a swab may be necessary. During my first clumsy attempts to clean my own sensor, I accidentally got my blower bulb tip too close to the sensor, and some sort of deposit from the tip of the bulb ended up on the sensor. I panicked until I discovered that liquid cleaning did a good job of removing whatever it was that took up residence on my sensor.

You can make your own swabs out of pieces of plastic (some use fast food restaurant knives, with the tip cut at an angle to the proper size) covered with a soft cloth or Pec-Pad, as shown in Figures 9.11 and 9.12. However, if you've got the bucks to spend, you

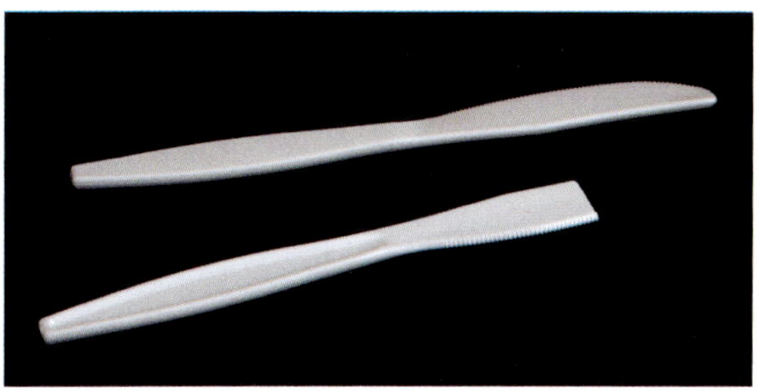

Figure 9.11 You can make your own sensor swab from a plastic knife that's been truncated.

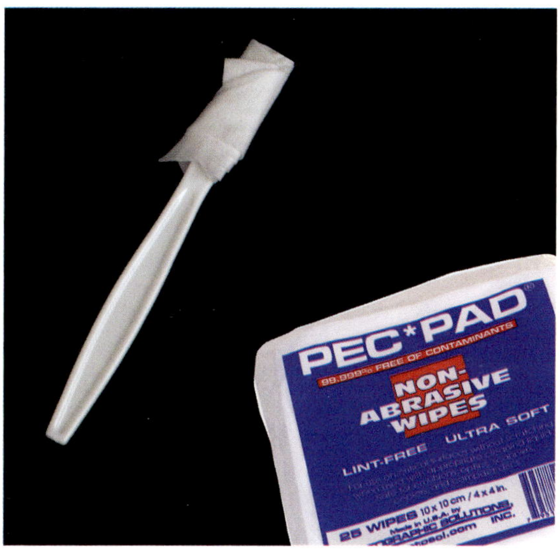

Figure 9.12 Carefully wrap a Pec-Pad around the swab.

can't go wrong with good quality commercial sensor cleaning swabs, such as those sold by Photographic Solutions, Inc. (www.photosol.com/swabproduct.htm).

You want a sturdy swab that won't bend or break so you can apply gentle pressure to the swab as you wipe the sensor surface. Use the swab with methanol (as pure as you can get it, particularly medical grade; other ingredients can leave a residue), or the Eclipse solution also sold by Photographic Solutions. Eclipse is actually quite a bit purer than even medical-grade methanol. A couple drops of solution should be enough, unless you have a spot that's extremely difficult to remove. In that case, you may need to use extra solution on the swab to help "soak" the dirt off.

Once you overcome your nervousness at touching your Alpha's sensor, the process is easy. You'll wipe continuously with the swab in one direction, then flip it over and wipe in the other direction. You need to completely wipe the entire surface; otherwise, you may end up depositing the dust you collect at the far end of your stroke. Wipe; don't rub.

If you want a close-up look at your sensor to make sure the dust has been removed, you can pay $50-$100 for a special sensor "microscope" with an illuminator. (See Figure 9.13.) Or, you can do like I do and work with a plain old Carson MiniBrite PO-25

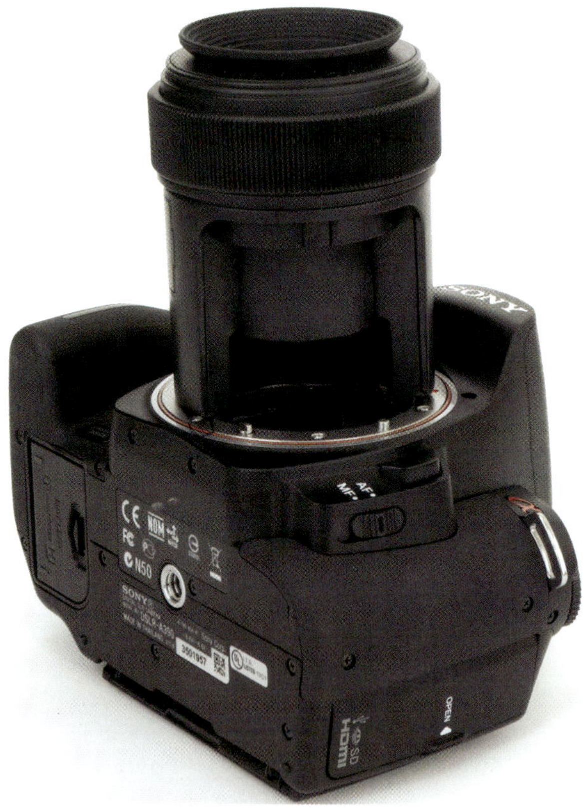

Figure 9.13 The SensorKlear sensor scope allows you to clean your sensor while viewing a magnified image.

illuminated 3X magnifier, as seen in Figure 9.14. (Older packaging and ads may call this a 2X magnifier, but it's actually a 3X unit.) It has a built-in LED and, held a few inches from the lens mount with the lens removed from your Alpha, provides a sharp, close-up view of the sensor, with enough contrast to reveal any dust that remains. If you want to buy one, you'll find a link at www.dslrguides.com/carson.

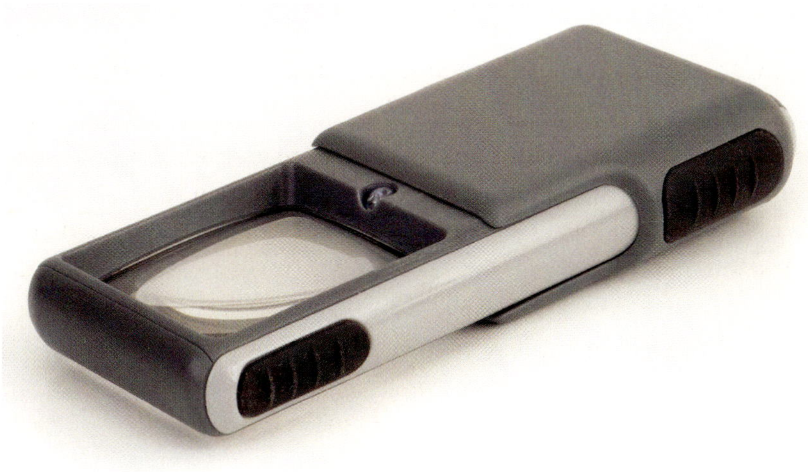

Figure 9.14
The Carson Mini-Brite is an inexpensive illuminated magnifier you can use to examine your sensor.

Tape Cleaning

There are people who absolutely swear by the tape method of sensor cleaning. The concept seems totally wacky, and I have never tried it personally, so I can't say with certainty that it either does or does not work. In the interest of completeness, I'm including it here. I can't give you a recommendation, so if you have problems, please don't blame me. The Sony Alpha A390/A290 is still too new to have generated any reports of users accidentally damaging the anti-dust coating on the sensor filter using this method.

Tape cleaning works by applying a layer of Scotch Brand Magic Tape to the sensor. This is a minimally sticky tape that some of the tape cleaning proponents claim contains no adhesive. I did check this out with 3M, and can say that Magic Tape certainly *does* contain an adhesive. The question is whether the adhesive comes off when you peel back the tape, taking any dust spots on your sensor with it. The folks who love this method claim there is no residue. There have been reports from those who don't like the method that residue is left behind. This is all anecdotal evidence, so you're pretty much on your own in making the decision whether to try out the tape cleaning method.

Glossary

Here are some terms you might encounter while reading this book or working with your Sony Alpha.

additive primary colors The red, green, and blue hues that are used alone or in combinations to create all other colors that you capture with a digital camera, view on a computer monitor, or work with in an image-editing program, such as Photoshop. *See also* CMYK color model.

Adobe RGB One of two color space choices offered by the Sony Alpha. Adobe RGB is an expanded color space useful for commercial and professional printing, and it can reproduce a larger number of colors. Sony recommends against using this color space if your images will be displayed primarily on your computer screen or output by your personal printer. *See also* sRGB.

ambient lighting Diffuse, non-directional lighting that doesn't appear to come from a specific source but, rather, bounces off walls, ceilings, and other objects in the scene when a picture is taken.

analog/digital converter The electronics built into a camera that convert the analog information captured by the Alpha's sensor into digital bits that can be stored as an image bitmap.

angle of view The area of a scene that a lens can capture, determined by the focal length of the lens. Lenses with a shorter focal length have a wider angle of view than lenses with a longer focal length.

anti-alias A process that smoothes the look of rough edges in images (called *jaggies* or *staircasing*) by adding partially transparent pixels along the boundaries of diagonal lines that are merged into a smoother line by our eyes. *See also* jaggies.

Aperture priority A camera setting that allows you to specify the lens opening or f/stop that you want to use, with the camera selecting the required shutter speed automatically based on its light-meter reading. This setting is represented by the abbreviation A on the Alpha's mode dial. *See also* Shutter priority.

artifact A type of noise in an image, or an unintentional image component produced in error by a digital camera during processing, usually caused by the JPEG compression process in digital cameras.

aspect ratio The proportions of an image as printed, displayed on a monitor, or captured by a digital camera. The Sony Alpha cameras offer both the traditional 3:2 aspect ratio used by most other digital SLRs, and also the 16:9 ("HDTV") aspect ratio.

autofocus A camera setting that allows the Sony Alpha to choose the correct focus distance for you, based on the contrast of an image (the image will be at maximum contrast when in sharp focus). The camera can be set for *Single-shot (Single Autofocus)*, in which the lens is not focused until the shutter release is partially depressed; *Continuous Autofocus,* in which the lens refocuses constantly as you frame and reframe the image; and *Automatic Autofocus*, which allows the camera to switch back and forth between Single-shot and Continuous Autofocus, based on subject movement.

backlighting A lighting effect produced when the main light source is located behind the subject. Backlighting can be used to create a silhouette effect, or to illuminate translucent objects. *See also* front lighting and sidelighting.

barrel distortion A lens defect that causes straight lines at the top or side edges of an image to bow outward into a barrel shape. *See also* pincushion distortion.

blooming An image distortion caused when a photosite in an image sensor has absorbed all the photons it can handle so that additional photons reaching that pixel overflow to affect surrounding pixels, producing unwanted brightness and overexposure around the edges of objects.

blur To soften an image or part of an image by throwing it out of focus, or by allowing it to become soft due to subject or camera motion. Blur can also be applied in an image-editing program.

bokeh A term derived from the Japanese word for blur, which describes the aesthetic qualities of the out-of-focus parts of an image. Some lenses produce "good" bokeh and others offer "bad" bokeh. Some lenses produce uniformly illuminated out-of-focus discs. Others produce a disc that has a bright edge and a dark center, creating a "doughnut" effect, which is the worst from a bokeh standpoint. Lenses that generate a bright center that fades to a darker edge are favored, because their bokeh allows the circle of confusion to blend more smoothly with the surroundings. The bokeh characteristics of a lens are most important when you're using selective focus (say, when shooting a portrait) to deemphasize the background, or when shallow depth-of-field is a given because you're working with a macro lens, with a long telephoto, or with a wide-open aperture. *See also* circle of confusion.

bounce lighting Light bounced off a reflector, including ceiling and walls, to provide a soft, natural-looking light.

bracketing Taking a series of photographs of the same subject at different settings, including exposure and white balance, to help ensure that one setting will be the correct one.

buffer The digital camera's internal memory where an image is stored immediately after it is taken until it can be written to the camera's non-volatile (semi-permanent) memory or a memory card.

burst mode The digital camera's equivalent of the film camera's motor drive, used to take multiple shots within a short period of time, at a rate of 2.5 frames per second, each stored in a memory buffer temporarily before writing them to the media.

calibration A process used to correct for the differences in the output of a printer or monitor when compared to the original image. Once you've calibrated your scanner, monitor, and/or your image editor, the images you see on the screen more closely represent what you'll get from your printer, even though calibration is never perfect.

Camera Raw A plug-in included with Photoshop and Photoshop Elements that can manipulate the unprocessed images captured by digital cameras, such as the Sony Alpha's ARW files. The latest versions of this module can also work with JPEG and TIFF images.

camera shake Movement of the camera, aggravated by slower shutter speeds, that produces a blurred image, unless countered by the Alpha's SteadyShot feature.

CCD *See* charge-coupled device (CCD).

Center weighted meter A light-measuring device that emphasizes the area in the middle of the frame when calculating the correct exposure for an image. *See also* Multi segment and Spot meter.

charge-coupled device (CCD) A type of solid-state sensor that captures the image used in scanners and digital cameras.

chromatic aberration An image defect, often seen as green or purple fringing around the edges of an object, caused by a lens failing to focus all colors of a light source at the same point. *See also* fringing.

circle of confusion A term applied to the fuzzy discs produced when a point of light is out of focus. The circle of confusion is not a fixed size. The viewing distance and amount of enlargement of the image determine whether we see a particular spot on the image as a point or as a disc. *See also* bokeh.

close-up lens A lens add-on that allows you to take pictures at a distance that is less than the closest-focusing distance of the lens alone.

CMYK color model A way of defining all possible colors in percentages of cyan, magenta, yellow, and frequently, black. (K represents black, to differentiate it from blue in the RGB color model.) Black is added to improve rendition of shadow detail. CMYK is commonly used for printing (both on press and with your inkjet or laser color printer).

color correction Changing the relative amounts of color in an image to produce a desired effect, typically a more accurate representation of those colors. Color correction can fix faulty color balance in the original image, or compensate for the deficiencies of the inks used to reproduce the image.

compression Reducing the size of a file by encoding using fewer bits of information to represent the original. Some compression schemes, such as JPEG, operate by discarding some image information, while others, such as RAW, preserve all the detail in the original, discarding only redundant data.

continuous autofocus An automatic focusing setting in which the camera constantly refocuses the image as you frame the picture. This setting is often the best choice for moving subjects.

contrast The range between the lightest and darkest tones in an image. A high-contrast image is one in which the shades fall at the extremes of the range between white and black. In a low-contrast image, the tones are closer together.

dedicated flash An electronic flash unit designed to work with the automatic exposure features of a specific camera.

depth-of-field A distance range in a photograph in which all included portions of an image are at least acceptably sharp.

diaphragm An adjustable component, similar to the iris in the human eye, that can open and close to provide specific-sized lens openings, or f/stops, and thus control the amount of light reaching the sensor or film.

diffuse lighting Soft, low-contrast lighting.

digital processing chip A solid-state device found in digital cameras (such as the Sony Alpha's BIONZ module) that's in charge of applying the image algorithms to the raw picture data prior to storage on the memory card.

diopter A value used to represent the magnification power of a lens, calculated as the reciprocal of a lens's focal length (in meters). Diopters are most often used to represent the optical correction used in a viewfinder to adjust for limitations of the photographer's eyesight, and to describe the magnification of a close-up lens attachment.

equivalent focal length A digital camera's focal length translated into the corresponding values for a 35mm film camera. This value can be calculated for lenses used with the Sony Alpha by multiplying by 1.5.

evaluative metering A system of exposure calculation that looks at many different segments of an image to determine the brightest and darkest portions. The Sony Alpha uses this system when you select the Multi segment metering mode.

exchangeable image file format (Exif) Developed to standardize the exchange of image data between hardware devices and software. A variation on JPEG, Exif is used by most digital cameras, and includes information such as the date and time a photo was taken, the camera settings, resolution, amount of compression, and other data.

Exif *See* exchangeable image file format (Exif).

exposure The amount of light allowed to reach the film or sensor, determined by the intensity of the light, the amount admitted by the iris of the lens, the length of time determined by the shutter speed, and the ISO sensitivity setting.

exposure values (EV) EV settings are a way of adding or decreasing exposure without the need to reference f/stops or shutter speeds. For example, if you tell your camera to add +1EV, it will provide twice as much exposure, either by using a larger f/stop, slower shutter speed, or both.

fill lighting In photography, lighting used to illuminate shadows. Reflectors or additional incandescent lighting or electronic flash can be used to brighten shadows. One common technique outdoors is to use the camera's flash as a fill.

filter In photography, a device that fits over the lens, changing the light in some way. In image editing, a feature that changes the pixels in an image to produce blurring, sharpening, and other special effects. Photoshop includes several interesting filter effects, including Lens Blur and Photo Filters.

flash sync The timing mechanism that ensures that an internal or external electronic flash fires at the correct time during the exposure cycle. A digital SLR's flash sync speed is the highest shutter speed that can be used with flash, ordinarily 1/160th of a second with the Sony Alpha. *See also* front-curtain sync (first-curtain sync) and rear-curtain sync (second-curtain sync).

focal length The distance between the film and the optical center of the lens when the lens is focused on infinity, usually measured in millimeters.

focal plane A line, perpendicular to the optical access, that passes through the focal point forming a plane of sharp focus when the lens is set at infinity. A focal plane indicator (a line drawn through a circle) is engraved on the top surface of the Sony Alpha to the right of the mode dial.

focus tracking The ability of the automatic focus feature of a camera to change focus as the distance between the subject and the camera changes. One type of focus tracking is *predictive*, in which the mechanism anticipates the motion of the object being focused on, and adjusts the focus to suit.

format To erase a memory card and prepare it to accept files.

fringing A chromatic aberration that produces fringes of color around the edges of subjects, caused by a lens's inability to focus the various wavelengths of light onto the same spot. Purple fringing is especially troublesome with backlit images.

front-curtain sync (first-curtain sync) The default kind of electronic flash synchronization technique, originally associated with focal plane shutters, which consists of a traveling set of curtains, including a *front curtain*, which opens to reveal the film or sensor, and a *rear curtain*, which follows at a distance determined by shutter speed to conceal the film or sensor at the conclusion of the exposure. For a flash picture to be taken, the entire sensor must be exposed at one time to the brief flash exposure, so the image is exposed after the front curtain has reached the other side of the focal plane, but before the rear curtain begins to move. Front-curtain sync causes the flash to fire at the beginning of this period when the shutter is completely open, in the instant that the first curtain of the focal plane shutter finishes its movement across the film or sensor plane. With slow shutter speeds, this feature can create a blur effect from the ambient light, showing as patterns that follow a moving subject with the subject shown sharply frozen at the beginning of the blur trail. *See also* rear-curtain sync (second-curtain sync).

front lighting Illumination that comes from the direction of the camera. *See also* backlighting and sidelighting.

f/stop The relative size of the lens aperture, which helps determine both exposure and depth-of-field. The larger the f/stop number, the smaller the f/stop itself.

graduated filter A lens attachment with variable density or color from one edge to another. A graduated neutral-density filter, for example, can be oriented so the neutral density portion is concentrated at the top of the lens's view with the less dense or clear portion at the bottom, thus reducing the amount of light from a very bright sky while not interfering with the exposure of the landscape in the foreground. Graduated filters can also be split into several color sections to provide a color gradient between portions of the image.

gray card A piece of cardboard or other material with a standardized 18-percent reflectance. Gray cards can be used as a reference for determining correct exposure or for setting white balance.

high contrast A wide range of density in a print, negative, or other image.

highlights The brightest parts of an image containing detail.

histogram A kind of chart showing the relationship of tones in an image using a series of 256 vertical bars, one for each brightness level. A histogram chart, such as the one the Sony Alpha can display during picture review, or, with the A390 model, in real time when using Live View mode, typically looks like a curve with one or more slopes and peaks, depending on how many highlight, midtone, and shadow tones are present in the image. The Alpha can also display separate histograms for brightness, as well as the red, green, and blue channels of an image.

hot shoe A mount on top of a camera used to hold an electronic flash, while providing an electrical connection between the flash and the camera. Sony cameras use a proprietary, non-standard hot shoe.

hyperfocal distance A point of focus where everything from half that distance to infinity appears to be acceptably sharp. For example, if your lens has a hyperfocal distance of four feet, everything from two feet to infinity would be sharp. The hyperfocal distance varies by the lens and the aperture in use. If you know you'll be making a grab shot without warning, sometimes it is useful to turn off your camera's automatic focus, and set the lens to infinity, or, better yet, the hyperfocal distance. Then, you can snap off a quick picture without having to wait for the lag that occurs with most digital cameras as their autofocus locks in.

image rotation A feature that senses whether a picture was taken in horizontal or vertical orientation. That information is embedded in the picture file so that the camera and compatible software applications can automatically display the image in the correct orientation.

image stabilization A technology that compensates for camera shake, which, in Sony's SteadyShot implementation, is achieved by adjusting the position of the camera sensor. Some other vendors, such as Nikon and Canon, move the lens elements in response to movements of the camera (which means that the feature is available only with lenses designed to provide it).

incident light Light falling on a surface.

International Organization for Standardization (ISO) A governing body that provides standards used to represent film speed, or the equivalent sensitivity of a digital camera's sensor. Digital camera sensitivity is expressed in ISO settings.

interpolation A technique digital cameras, scanners, and image editors use to create new pixels required whenever you resize or change the resolution of an image based on the values of surrounding pixels. Devices such as scanners and digital cameras can also use interpolation to create pixels in addition to those actually captured, thereby increasing the apparent resolution or color information in an image.

ISO *See* International Organization for Standardization (ISO).

jaggies Staircasing effect of lines that are not perfectly horizontal or vertical, caused by pixels that are too large to represent the line accurately. *See also* anti-alias.

JPEG A file "lossy" format (short for Joint Photographic Experts Group) that supports 24-bit color and reduces file sizes by selectively discarding image data. Digital cameras generally use JPEG compression to pack more images onto memory cards. You can select how much compression is used (and, therefore, how much information is thrown away) by selecting from among the Standard, Fine, Super Fine, or other quality settings offered by your camera. *See also* RAW.

Kelvin (K) A unit of measure based on the absolute temperature scale in which absolute zero is zero; it's used to describe the color of continuous-spectrum light sources and applied when setting white balance. For example, daylight has a color temperature of about 5,500K, and a tungsten lamp has a temperature of about 3,400K.

lag time The interval between when the shutter is pressed and when the picture is actually taken. During that span, the camera may be automatically focusing and calculating exposure. With digital SLRs like the Sony Alpha, lag time is generally very short; with non-dSLRs, the elapsed time easily can be one second or more.

latitude The range of camera exposures that produces acceptable images with a particular digital sensor or film.

lens flare A feature of conventional photography that is both a bane and a creative outlet. It is an effect produced by the reflection of light internally among elements of an optical lens. Bright light sources within or just outside the field of view cause lens flare. Flare can be reduced by the use of coatings on the lens elements or with the use of lens hoods. Photographers sometimes use the effect as a creative technique, and Photoshop includes a filter that lets you add lens flare at your whim.

lighting ratio The proportional relationship between the amount of light falling on the subject from the main light and other lights, expressed in a ratio, such as 3:1.

Live View The ability of some Sony cameras, including the Alpha A390 model, to provide a real-time preview image, as seen by the sensor, on the rear-panel color LCD, achieved by flipping a mirror in the pentaprism that diverts light from the optical viewfinder to a secondary sensor used only for Live View display.

lossless compression An image-compression scheme, such as TIFF, that preserves all image detail. When the image is decompressed, it is identical to the original version.

lossy compression An image-compression scheme, such as JPEG, that creates smaller files by discarding image information, which can affect image quality.

macro lens A lens that provides continuous focusing from infinity to extreme close-ups, often to a reproduction ratio of 1:2 (half life-size) or 1:1 (life-size).

maximum burst The number of frames that can be exposed at the current settings until the buffer fills.

midtones Parts of an image with tones of an intermediate value, usually in the 25 to 75 percent brightness range. Many image-editing features allow you to manipulate midtones independently from the highlights and shadows.

mirror lock-up The ability of the Alpha to retract its mirror to allow access to the sensor for cleaning.

Multi segment The Sony metering system that measures multiple areas of the image and calculates exposure based on an intelligent evaluation of what type of scene is being photographed. *See also* Spot meter and Center weighted meter.

neutral color A color in which red, green, and blue are present in equal amounts, producing a gray.

neutral-density filter A gray camera filter that reduces the amount of light entering the camera without affecting the colors.

noise In an image, pixels with randomly distributed color values. Visual noise in digital photographs tends to be the product of low light conditions and long exposures, particularly when you've set your camera to a higher ISO rating than normal.

noise reduction A technology used to cut down on the amount of random information in a digital picture, usually caused by long exposures and/or increased sensitivity ratings.

normal lens A lens that makes the image in a photograph appear in a perspective that is like that of the original scene, typically with a field of view of roughly 45 degrees.

overexposure A condition in which too much light reaches the film or sensor, producing a dense negative or a very bright/light print, slide, or digital image.

pincushion distortion A type of lens distortion in which lines at the top and side edges of an image are bent inward, producing an effect that looks like a pincushion. *See also* barrel distortion.

polarizing filter A filter that forces light, which normally vibrates in all directions, to vibrate only in a single plane, reducing or removing the specular reflections from the surface of objects.

Program mode The exposure mode where the Alpha makes all the settings for you, but allows some fine-tuning of shutter speed, aperture, and other settings.

RAW An image file format, such as the ARW format in the Sony Alpha, that includes all the unprocessed information captured by the camera after conversion to digital form. RAW files are very large compared to JPEG files and must be processed by a special program such as Sony Image Data Converter SR, or Adobe's Camera Raw filter after being downloaded from the camera.

rear-curtain sync (second-curtain sync) An optional kind of electronic flash synchronization technique, originally associated with focal plane shutters, which consists of a traveling set of curtains, including a *front (first) curtain* (which opens to reveal the film or sensor) and a *rear (second) curtain* (which follows at a distance determined by shutter speed to conceal the film or sensor at the conclusion of the exposure). For a flash picture to be taken, the entire sensor must be exposed at one time to the brief flash exposure, so the image is exposed after the front curtain has reached the other side of the focal plane, but before the rear curtain begins to move. Rear-curtain sync causes the flash to fire at the end of the exposure, an instant before the second or rear curtain of the focal plane shutter begins to move. With slow shutter speeds, this feature can create a blur effect from the ambient light, showing as patterns that follow a moving subject with the subject shown sharply frozen at the end of the blur trail. If you were shooting a photo of The Flash, the superhero would appear sharp, with a ghostly trail behind him. *See also* front-curtain sync (first-curtain sync).

red-eye An effect from flash photography that appears to make a person's eyes glow red, or an animal's yellow or green. It's caused by light bouncing from the retina of the eye and is most pronounced in dim illumination (when the irises are wide open) and when the electronic flash is close to the lens and, therefore, prone to reflect directly back. Image editors can fix red-eye through cloning other pixels over the offending red or orange ones.

RGB color A color model that represents the three colors—red, green, and blue—used by devices such as scanners or monitors to reproduce color. Photoshop works in RGB mode by default, and even displays CMYK images by converting them to RGB.

saturation The purity of color; the amount by which a pure color is diluted with white or gray.

selective focus Choosing a lens opening that produces a shallow depth-of-field. Usually this is used to isolate a subject in portraits, close-ups, and other types of images, by causing most other elements in the scene to be blurred.

self-timer A mechanism that delays the opening of the shutter for some seconds after the release has been operated.

sensitivity A measure of the degree of response of a film or sensor to light, measured using the ISO setting.

shadow The darkest part of an image, represented on a digital image by pixels with low numeric values.

sharpening Increasing the apparent sharpness of an image by boosting the contrast between adjacent pixels that form an edge.

shutter In a conventional film camera, the shutter is a mechanism consisting of blades, a curtain, a plate, or some other movable cover that controls the time during which light reaches the film. Digital cameras may use actual mechanical shutters for the slower shutter speeds (less than 1/160th second) and an electronic shutter for higher speeds.

Shutter priority An exposure mode, represented by the letter S on the Alpha's mode dial, in which you set the shutter speed and the camera determines the appropriate f/stop. *See also* Aperture priority.

sidelighting Applying illumination from the left or right sides of the camera. *See also* backlighting and front lighting.

slave unit An accessory flash unit that supplements the main flash, usually triggered electronically when the slave senses the light output by the main unit, or through radio waves. Slave units can also be triggered by the pre-flash normally used to measure exposure, so you may need to set your main flash to Manual to avoid this.

slow sync An electronic flash synchronizing method that uses a slow shutter speed so that ambient light is recorded by the camera in addition to the electronic flash illumination. This allows the background to receive more exposure for a more realistic effect.

specular highlight Bright spots in an image caused by reflection of light sources.

Spot meter An exposure system that concentrates on a small area in the center of the viewfinder. *See also* Center weighted meter and Multi segment.

sRGB One of two color space choices available with the Sony Alpha. The sRGB setting is recommended for images that will be output locally on the user's own printer, as this color space matches that of the typical inkjet printer and a properly calibrated monitor fairly closely. *See also* Adobe RGB.

subtractive primary colors Cyan, magenta, and yellow, which are the printing inks that theoretically absorb all color and produce black. In practice, however, they generate a muddy brown, so black is added to preserve detail (especially in shadows). The combination of the three colors and black is referred to as CMYK. (K represents black, to differentiate it from blue in the RGB model.)

time exposure A picture taken by leaving the shutter open for a long period, usually more than one second. The camera is generally locked down with a tripod to prevent blur during the long exposure. For exposures longer than 30 seconds, you need to use the Bulb setting.

through-the-lens (TTL) A system of providing viewing and exposure calculation through the actual lens taking the picture.

tungsten light Light from ordinary room lamps and ceiling fixtures, as opposed to fluorescent illumination.

underexposure A condition in which too little light reaches the film or sensor, producing a thin negative, a dark slide, a muddy-looking print, or a dark digital image.

unsharp masking The process for increasing the contrast between adjacent pixels in an image, increasing sharpness, especially around edges.

vignetting Dark corners of an image, often produced by using a lens hood that is too small for the field of view, a lens that does not completely fill the image frame, or generated artificially using image-editing techniques.

white balance The adjustment of a digital camera to the color temperature of the light source. Interior illumination is relatively red; outdoor light is relatively blue. Digital cameras like the Alpha set correct white balance automatically or let you do it through menus. Image editors can often do some color correction of images that were exposed using the wrong white balance setting, especially when working with RAW files that contain the information originally captured by the camera before white balance was applied.

Index

A

B

D

E

F

G

H

I

M

N

O

P

Q

R

V

W

Z